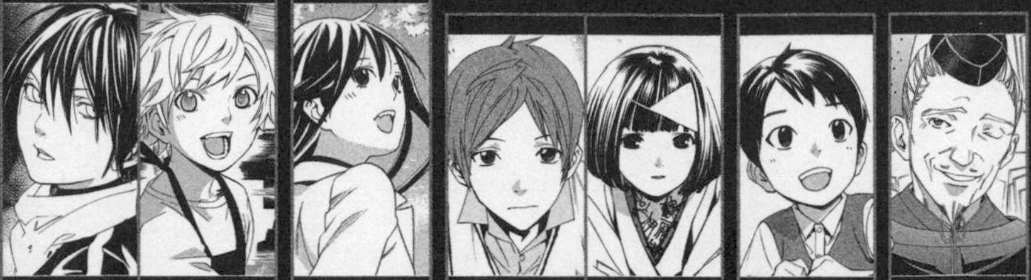

YATO
A minor deity who always wears a sweatsuit.

YUKINÉ
Yato's shinki who turns into swords.

HIYORI IKI
A high school student who has become half ayakashi.

KÔTO FUJISAKI
Yato's "father."

STRAY
A shinki who serves an unspecified number of deities.

EBISU
A business-god in the making, one of the Seven Gods of Fortune.

TENJIN
The god of learning, Sugawara no Michizane.

characters

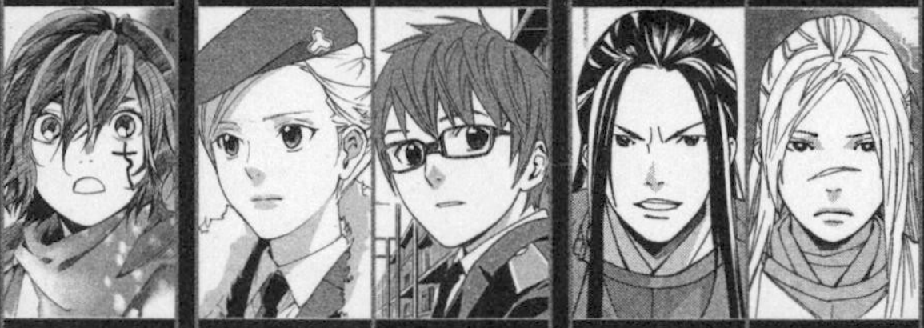

NANA
A powerful shinki who once rebelled against the Heavens.

BISHAMONTEN
A powerful warrior god, one of the Seven Gods of Fortune.

KAZUMA
A navigational shinki who serves as guide to Bishamon.

TAKEMIKAZUCHI
A warrior god who longs for the chaos of war.

KIUN
Takemikazuchi's shinki who has earned the title of Thunder Blade.

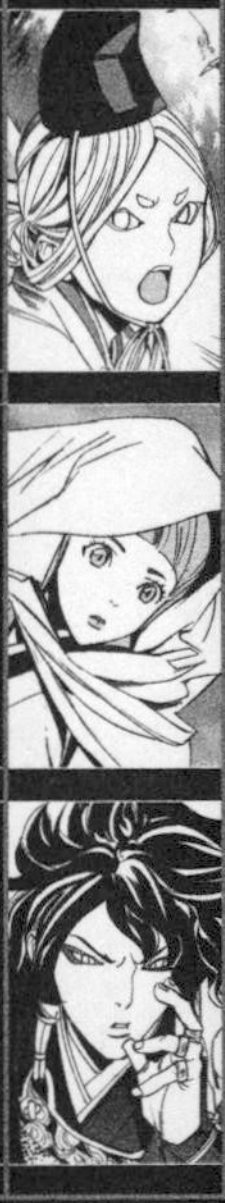

SHINATSUHIKO

SAKUYA-BIMÉ

KAGUTSUCHI

CHAPTER 64: DEAR ONE

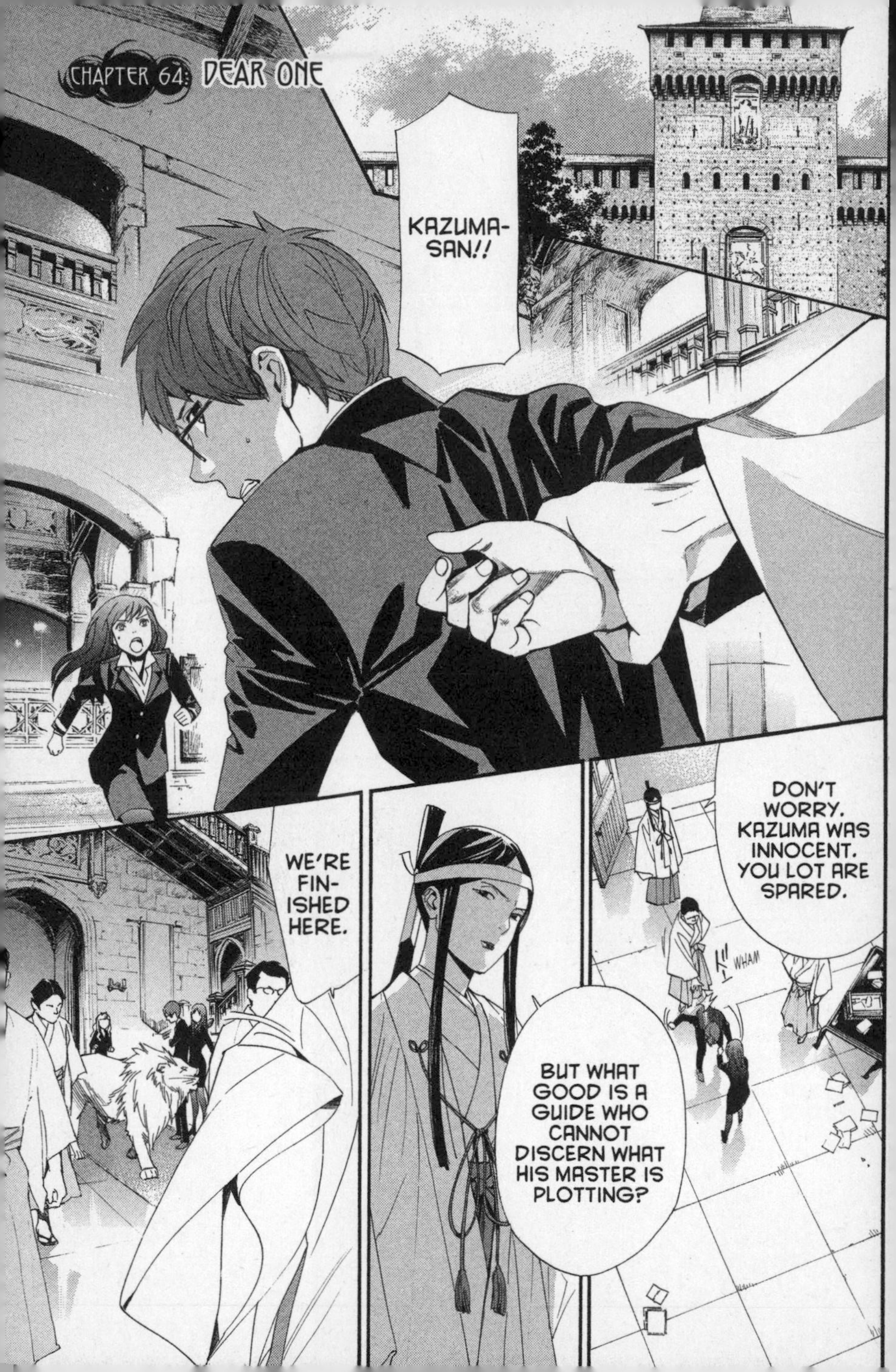
KAZUMA-SAN!!
DON'T WORRY. KAZUMA WAS INNOCENT. YOU LOT ARE SPARED.
WHAM
BUT WHAT GOOD IS A GUIDE WHO CANNOT DISCERN WHAT HIS MASTER IS PLOTTING?
WE'RE FIN-ISHED HERE.

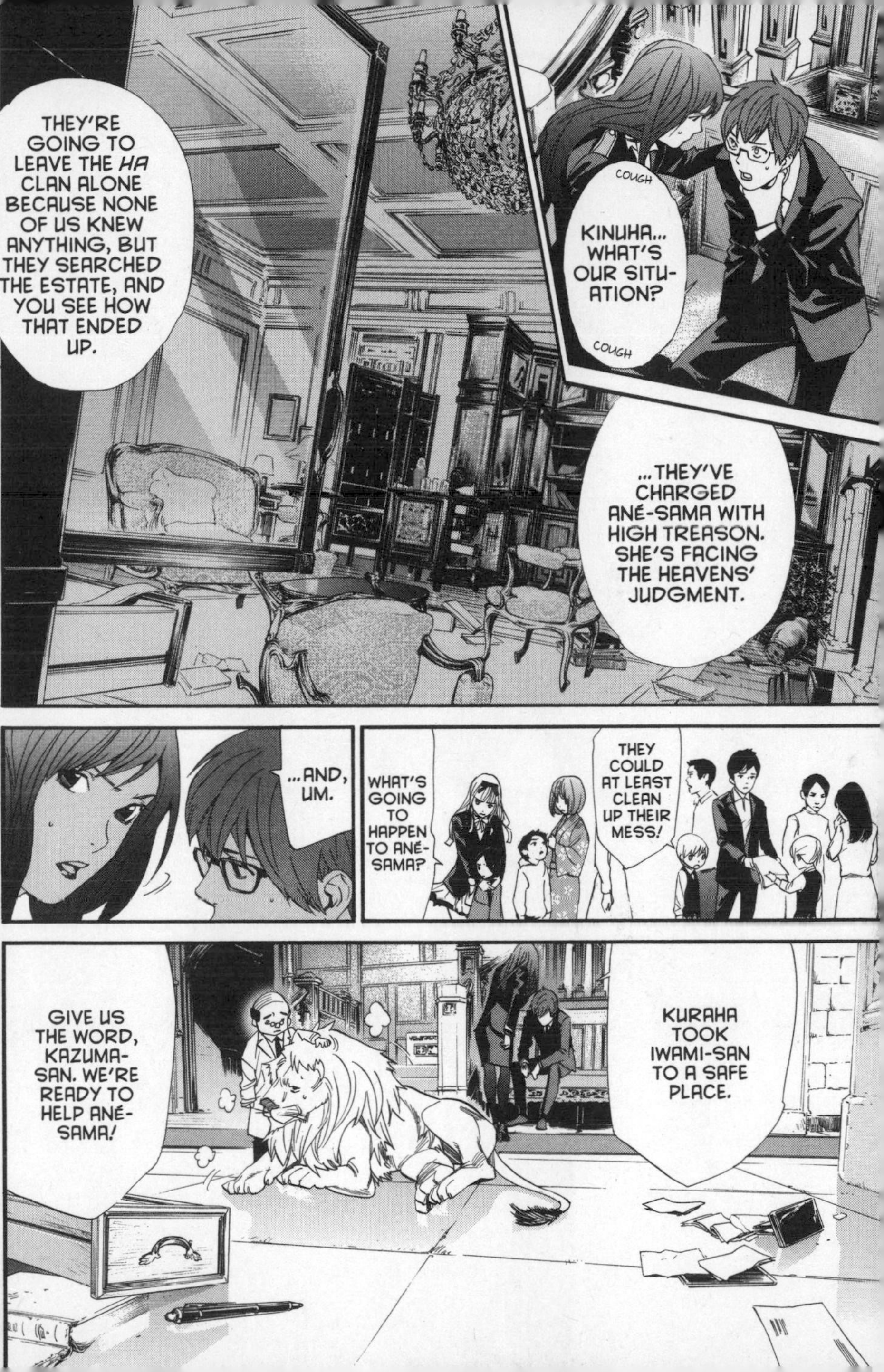
COUGH
KINUHA... WHAT'S OUR SITUATION?
COUGH
...THEY'VE CHARGED ANÉ-SAMA WITH HIGH TREASON. SHE'S FACING THE HEAVENS' JUDGMENT.
THEY'RE GOING TO LEAVE THE *HA* CLAN ALONE BECAUSE NONE OF US KNEW ANYTHING, BUT THEY SEARCHED THE ESTATE, AND YOU SEE HOW THAT ENDED UP.
THEY COULD AT LEAST CLEAN UP THEIR MESS!
WHAT'S GOING TO HAPPEN TO ANÉ-SAMA?
...AND, UM.
KURAHA TOOK IWAMI-SAN TO A SAFE PLACE.
GIVE US THE WORD, KAZUMA-SAN. WE'RE READY TO HELP ANÉ-SAMA!

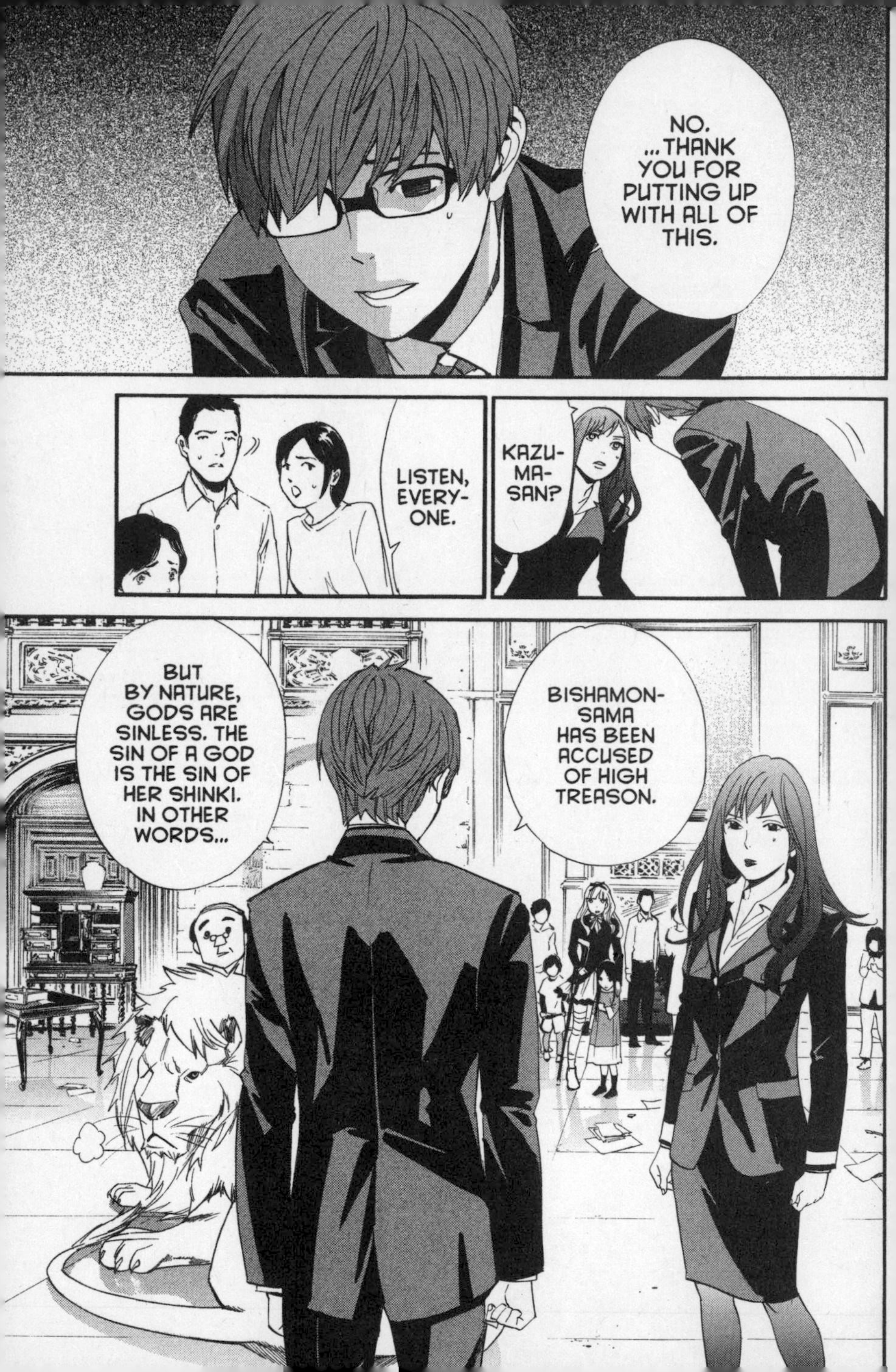
NO. ...THANK YOU FOR PUTTING UP WITH ALL OF THIS.
KAZU-MA-SAN?
LISTEN, EVERY-ONE.
BISHAMON-SAMA HAS BEEN ACCUSED OF HIGH TREASON.
BUT BY NATURE, GODS ARE SINLESS. THE SIN OF A GOD IS THE SIN OF HER SHINKI. IN OTHER WORDS...

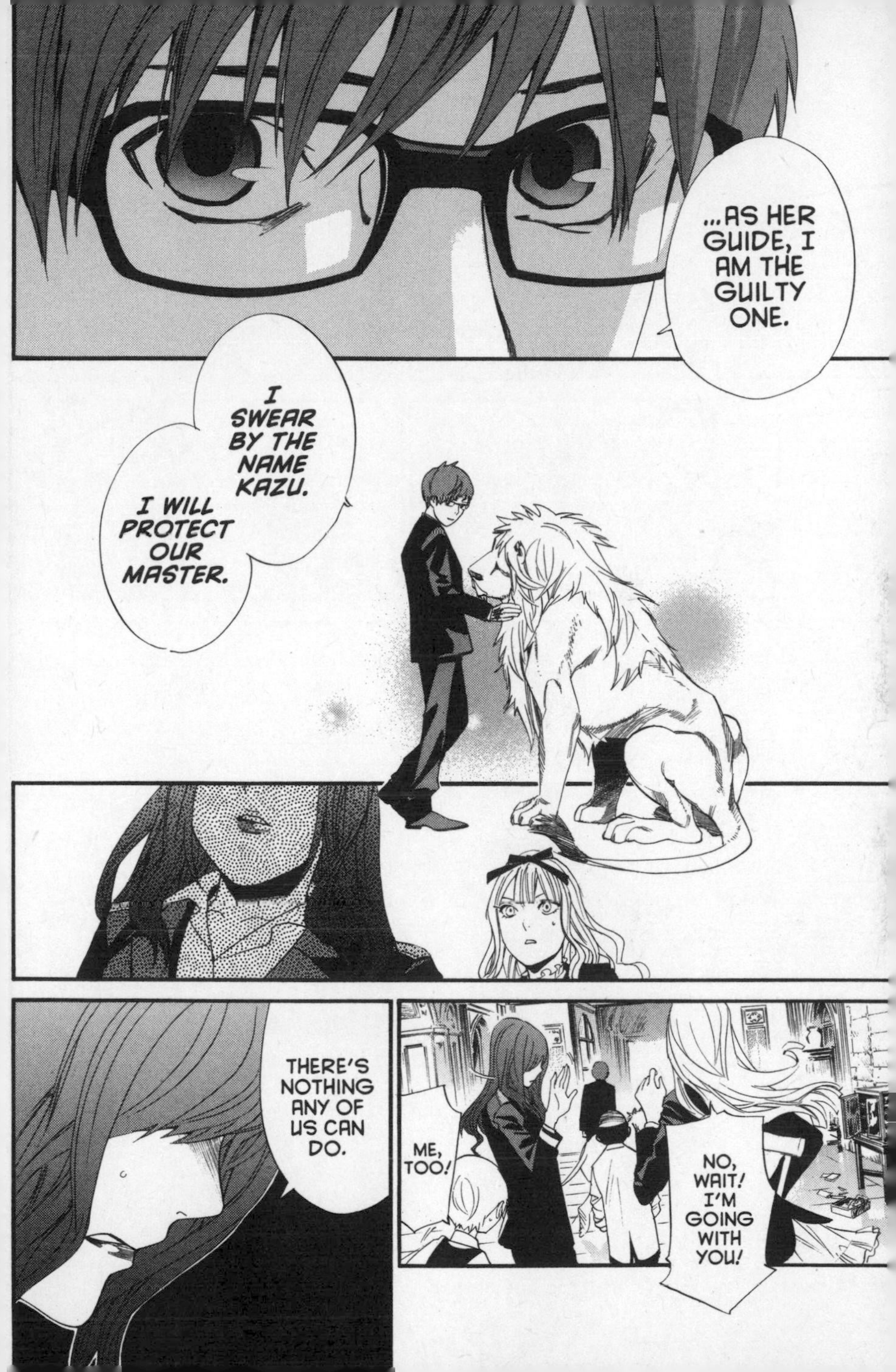
...AS HER GUIDE, I AM THE GUILTY ONE.
I SWEAR BY THE NAME KAZU.
I WILL PROTECT OUR MASTER.
NO, WAIT! I'M GOING WITH YOU!
ME, TOO!
THERE'S NOTHING ANY OF US CAN DO.

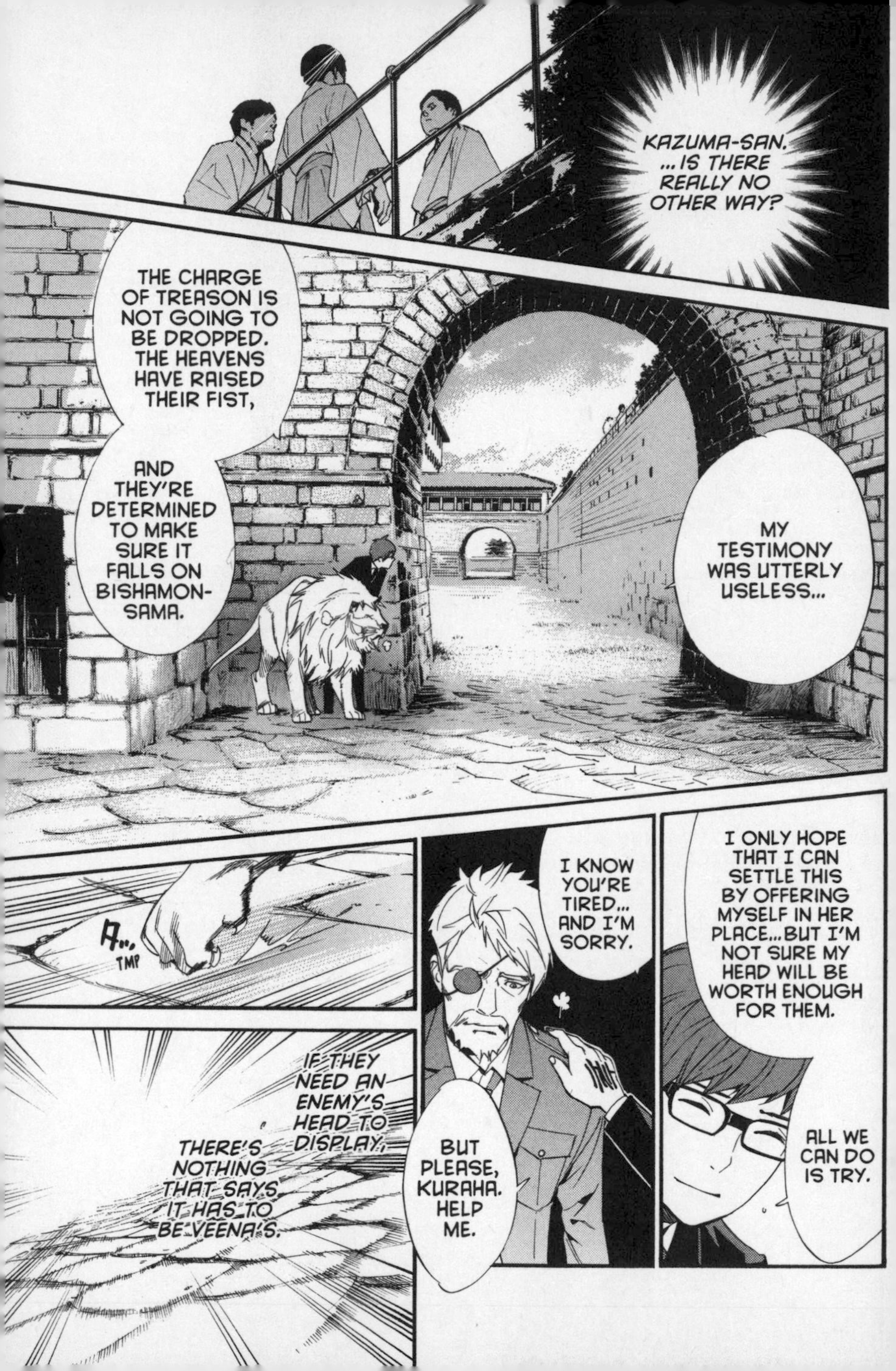
KAZUMA-SAN. ...IS THERE REALLY NO OTHER WAY?
MY TESTIMONY WAS UTTERLY USELESS...
THE CHARGE OF TREASON IS NOT GOING TO BE DROPPED. THE HEAVENS HAVE RAISED THEIR FIST,
AND THEY'RE DETERMINED TO MAKE SURE IT FALLS ON BISHAMON-SAMA.
I ONLY HOPE THAT I CAN SETTLE THIS BY OFFERING MYSELF IN HER PLACE...BUT I'M NOT SURE MY HEAD WILL BE WORTH ENOUGH FOR THEM.
I KNOW YOU'RE TIRED... AND I'M SORRY.
ALL WE CAN DO IS TRY.
BUT PLEASE, KURAHA. HELP ME.
TMP
IF THEY NEED AN ENEMY'S HEAD TO DISPLAY,
THERE'S NOTHING THAT SAYS IT HAS TO BE VEENA'S.

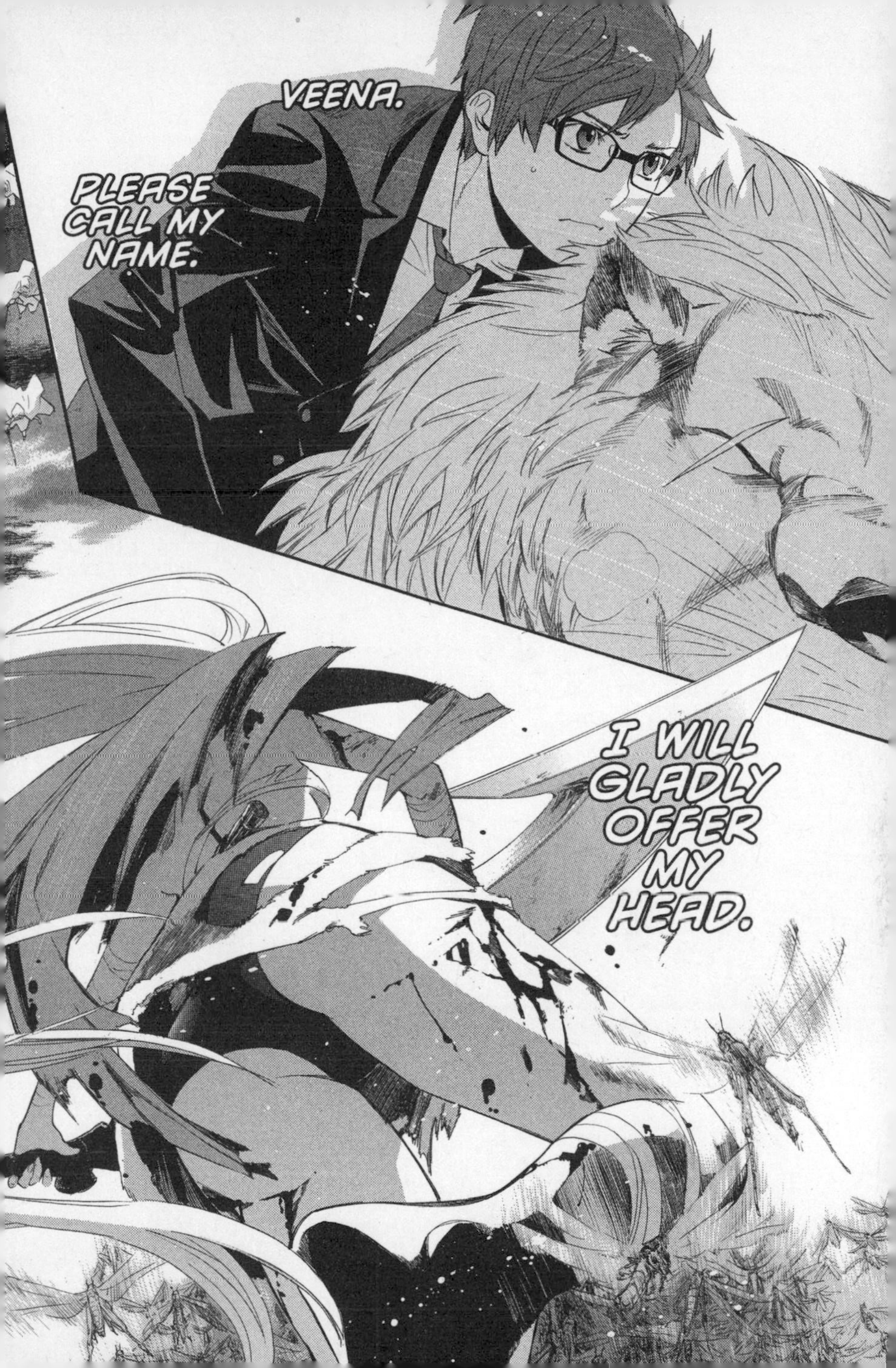
VEENA.
PLEASE CALL MY NAME.
I WILL GLADLY OFFER MY HEAD.

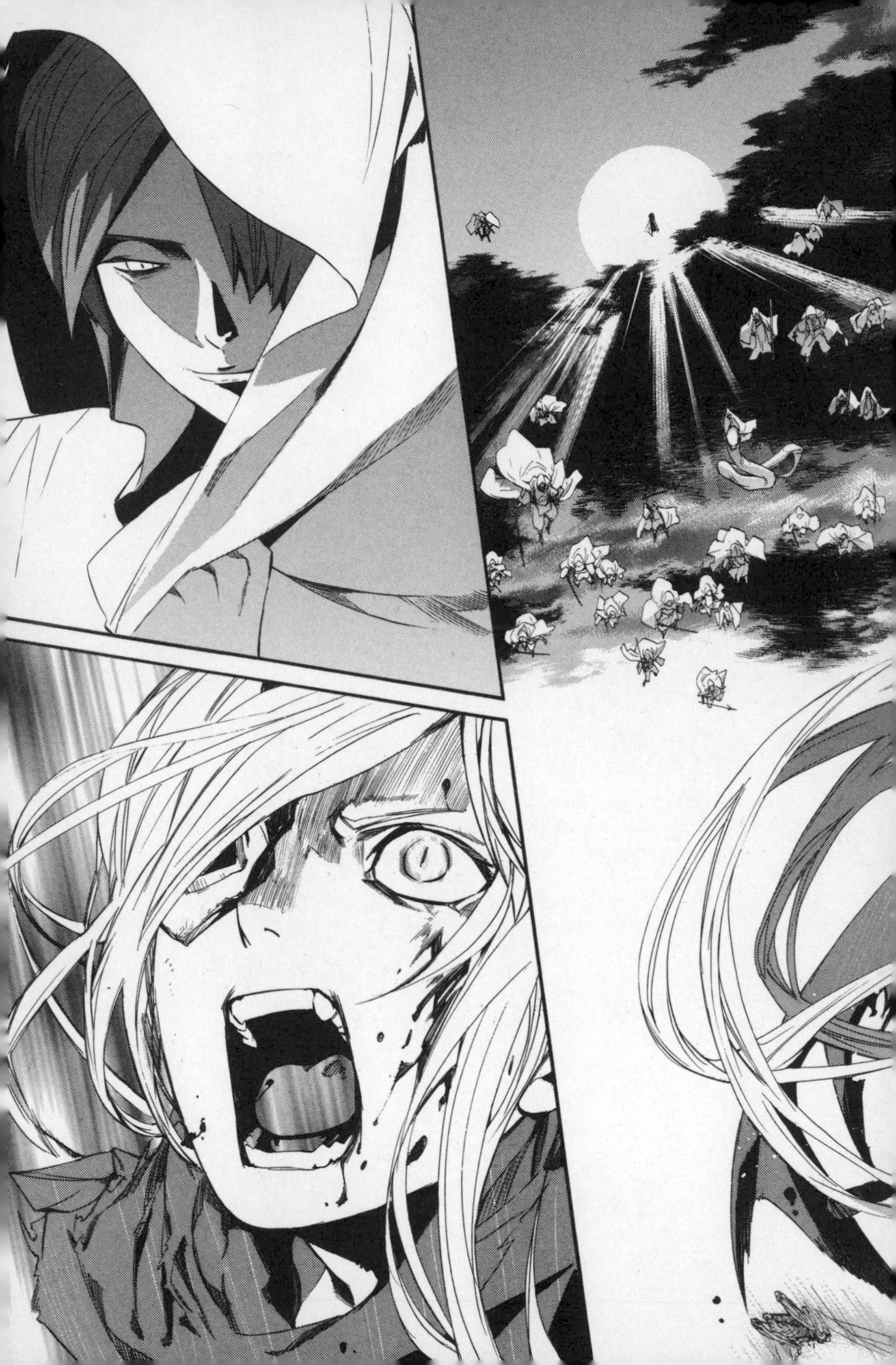

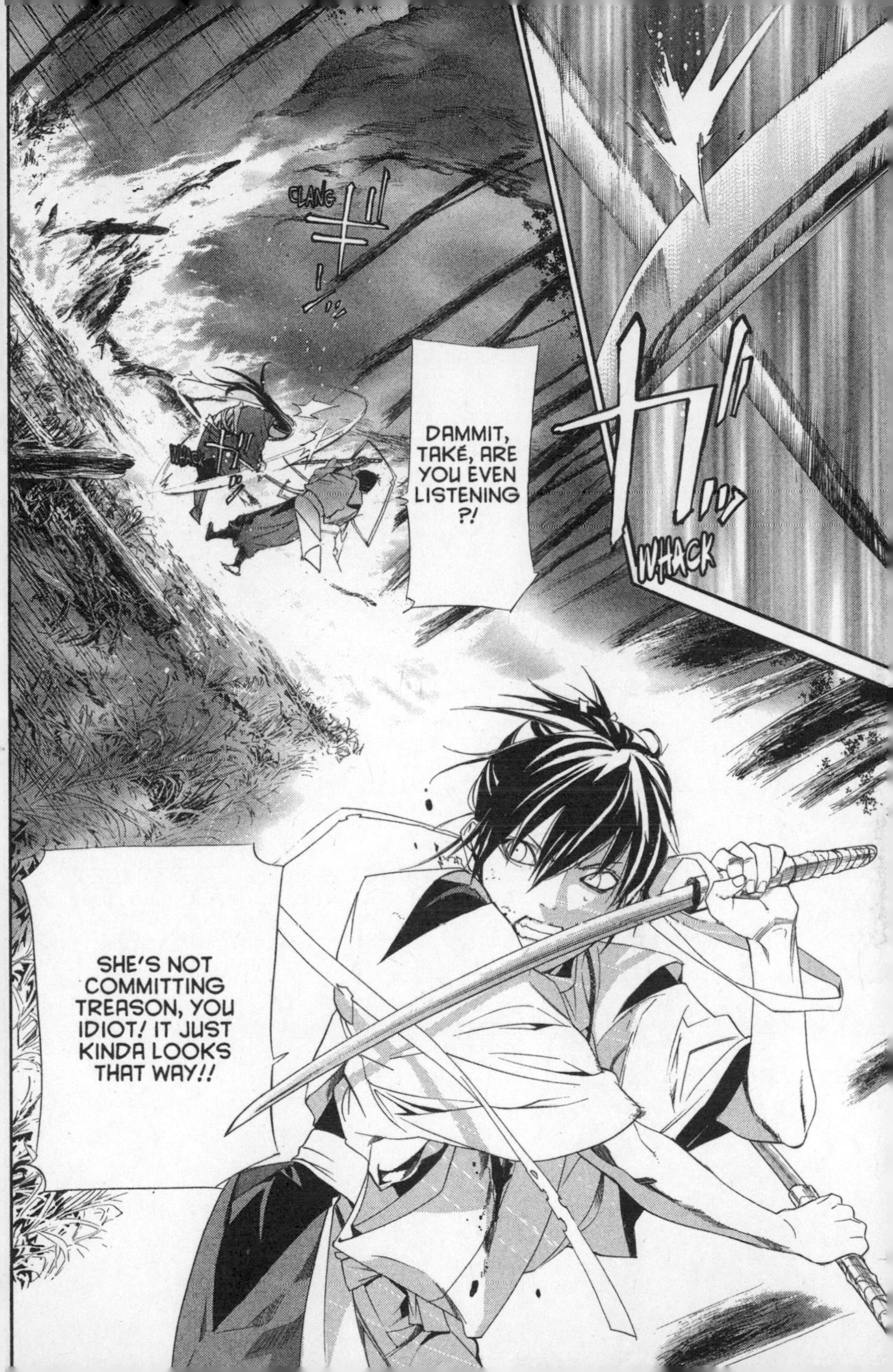
WHACK
DAMMIT, TAKÉ, ARE YOU EVEN LISTENING ?!
CLANG
WHACK
SHE'S NOT COMMITTING TREASON, YOU IDIOT! IT JUST KINDA LOOKS THAT WAY!!

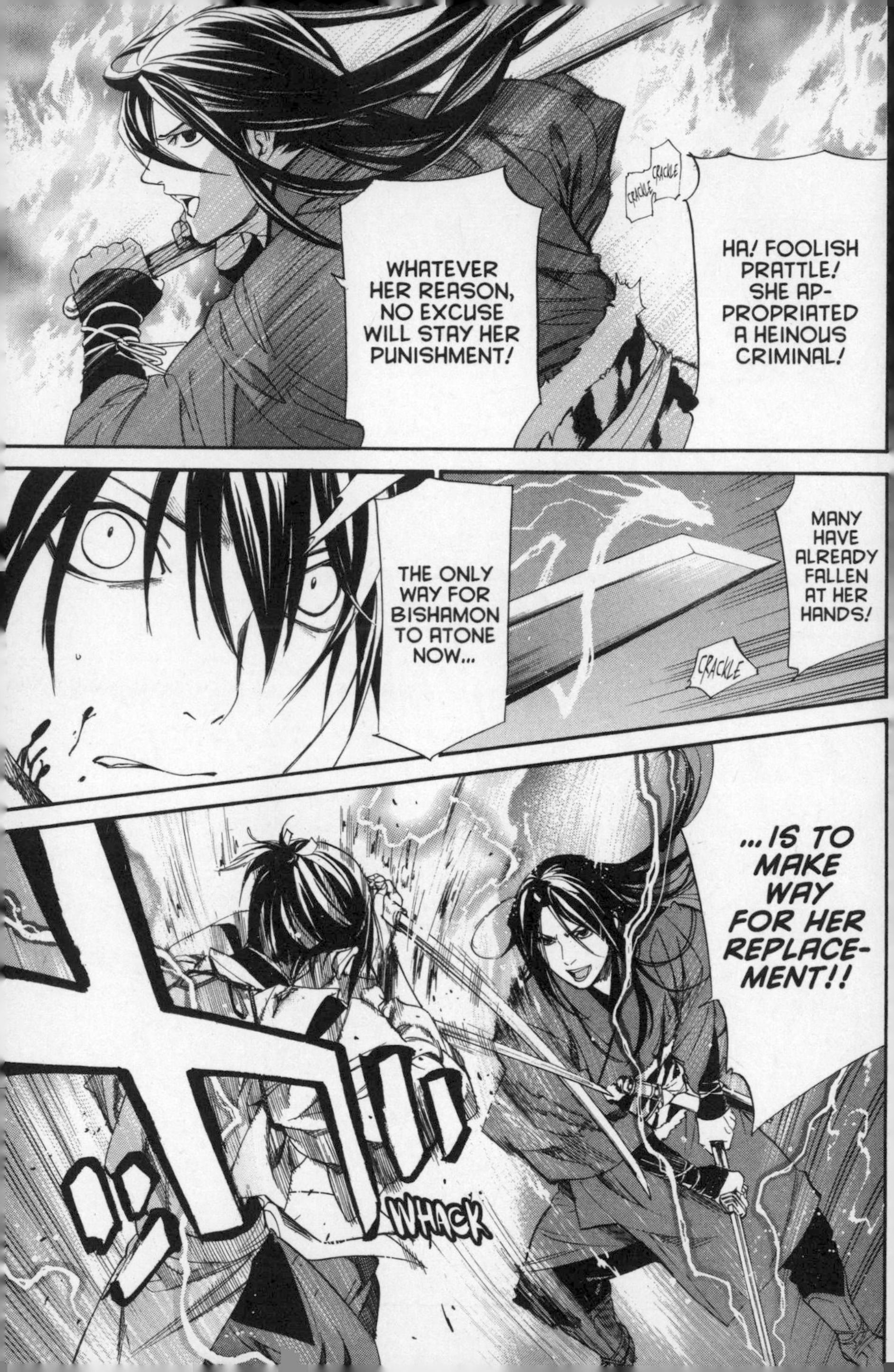
CRACKLE
CRACKLE
HA! FOOLISH PRATTLE! SHE AP-PROPRIATED A HEINOUS CRIMINAL!
WHATEVER HER REASON, NO EXCUSE WILL STAY HER PUNISHMENT!
MANY HAVE ALREADY FALLEN AT HER HANDS!
CRACKLE
THE ONLY WAY FOR BISHAMON TO ATONE NOW...
...IS TO MAKE WAY FOR HER REPLACE-MENT!!
WHACK

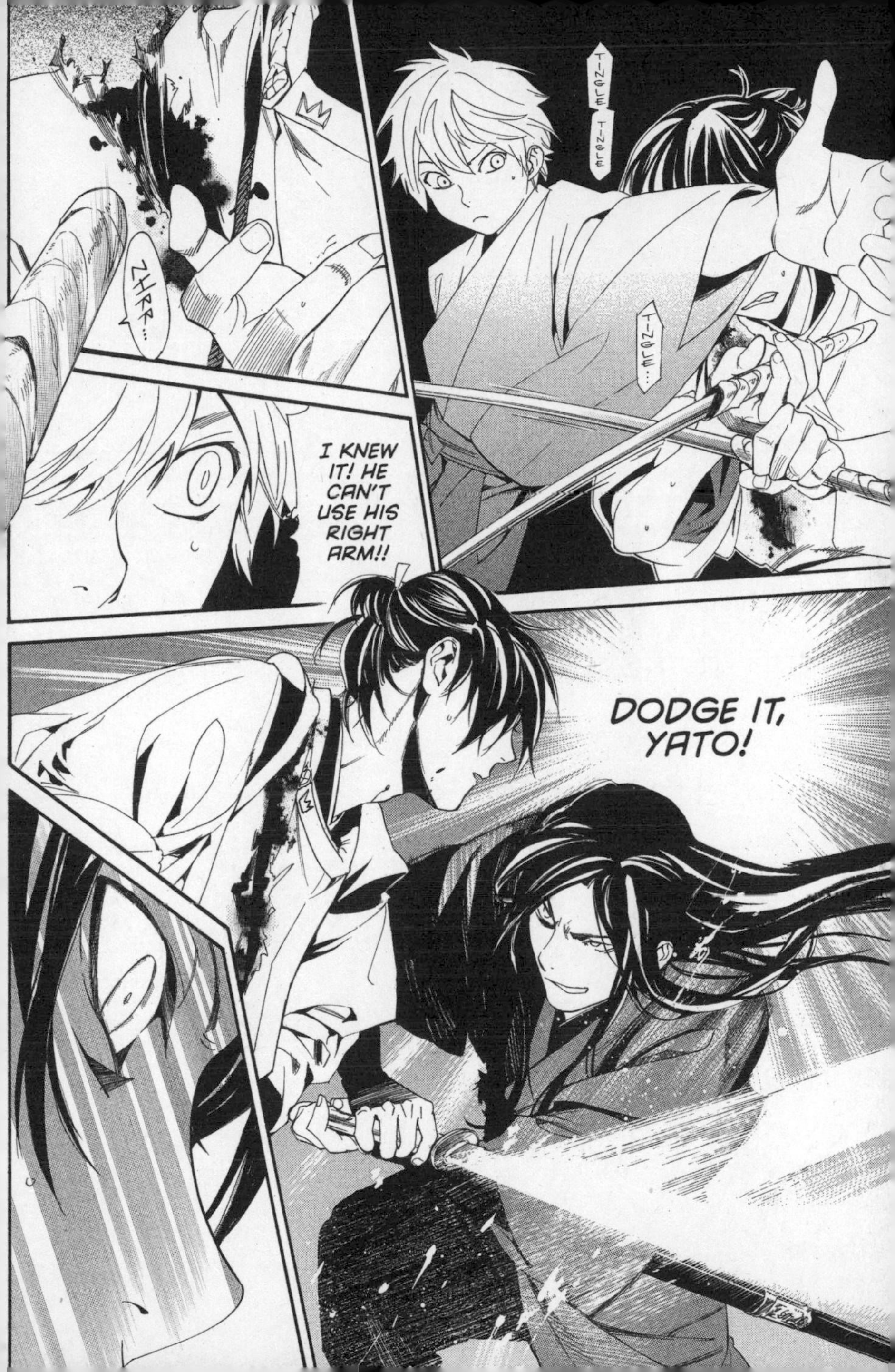
TINGLE TINGLE
TINGLE...
ZHRR...
I KNEW IT! HE CAN'T USE HIS RIGHT ARM!!
DODGE IT, YATO!

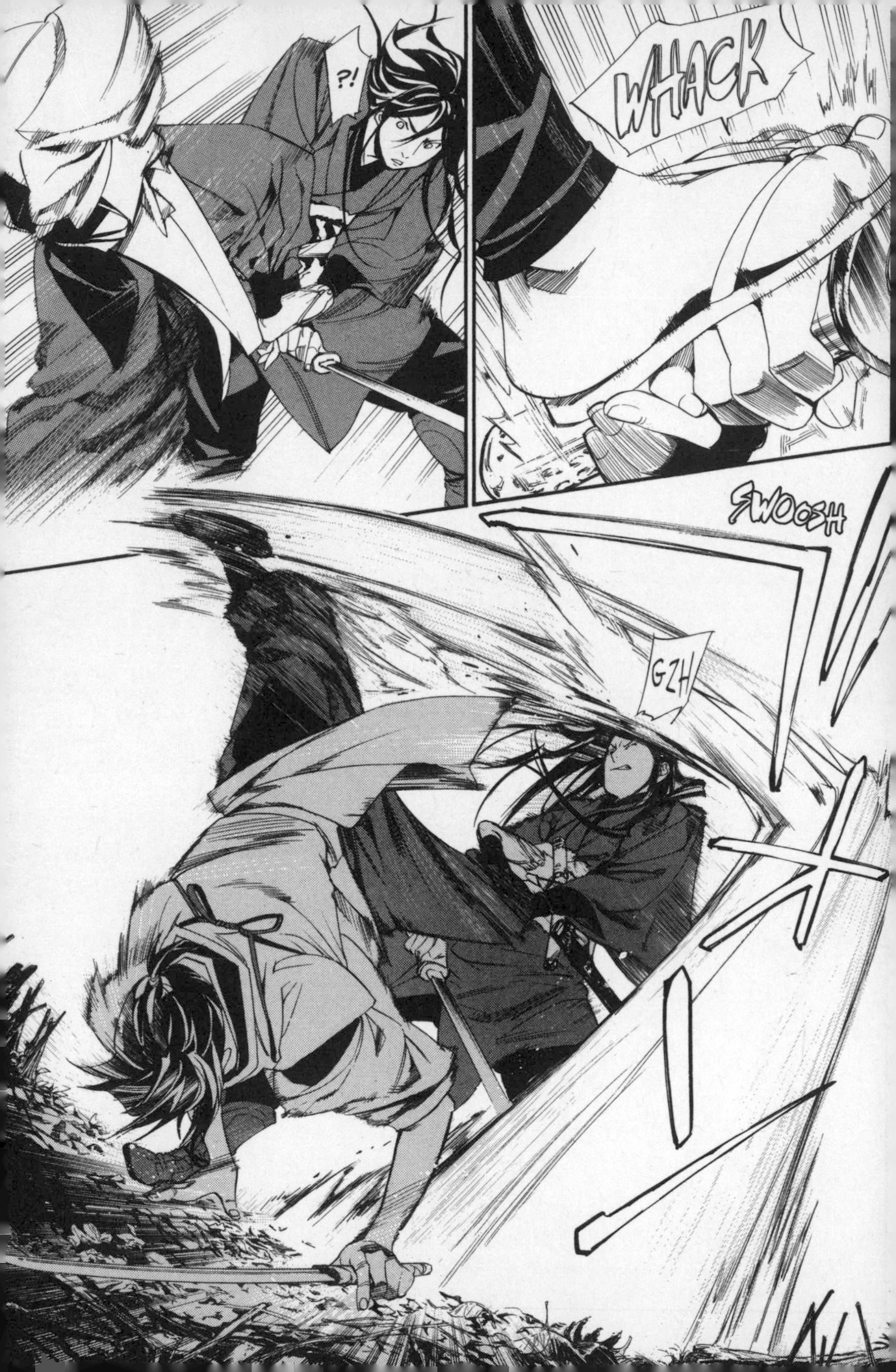
WHACK
?!
SWOOSH
GZH

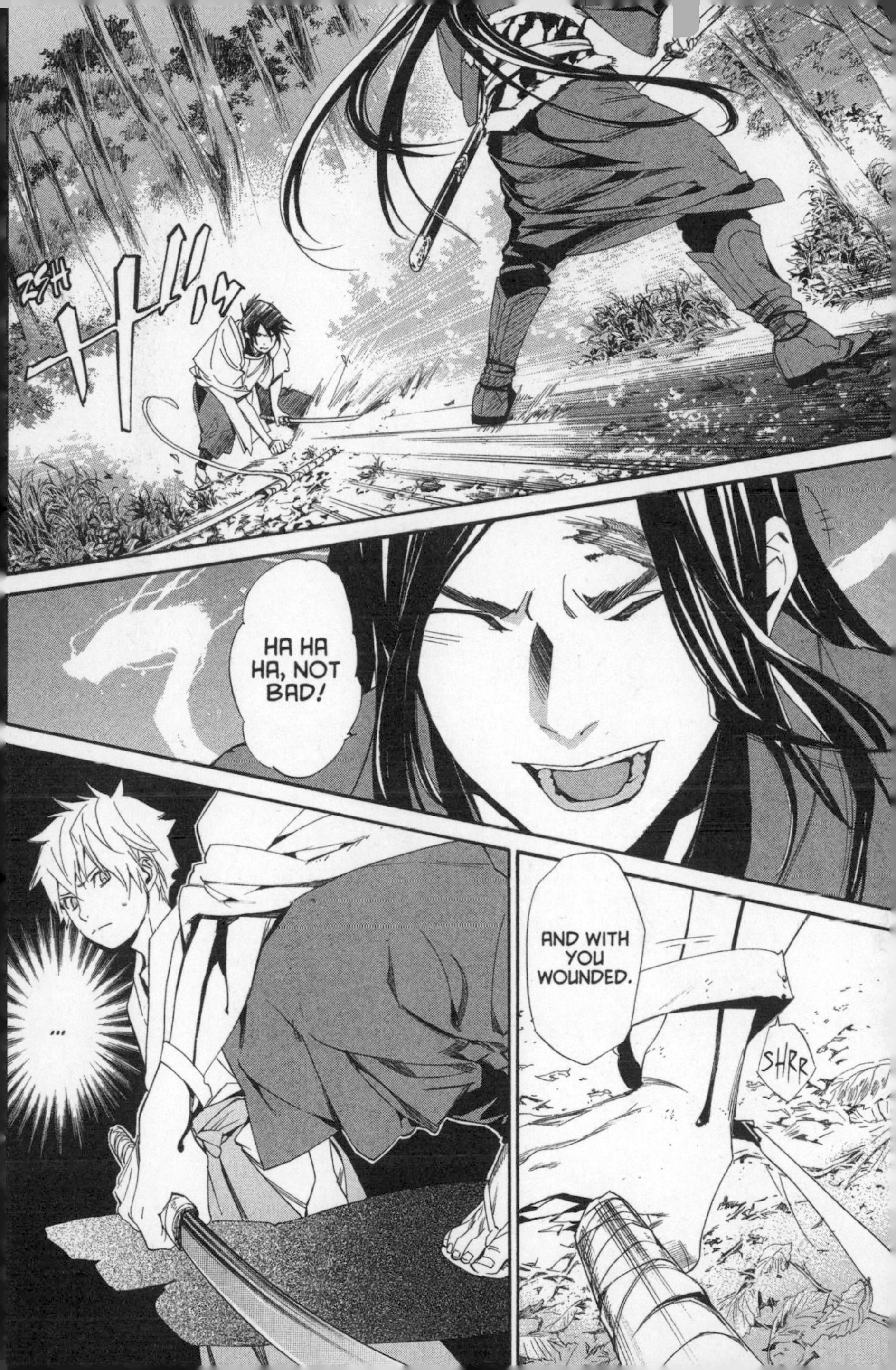
ZSH
HA HA HA, NOT BAD!
AND WITH YOU WOUNDED.
SHRR
...

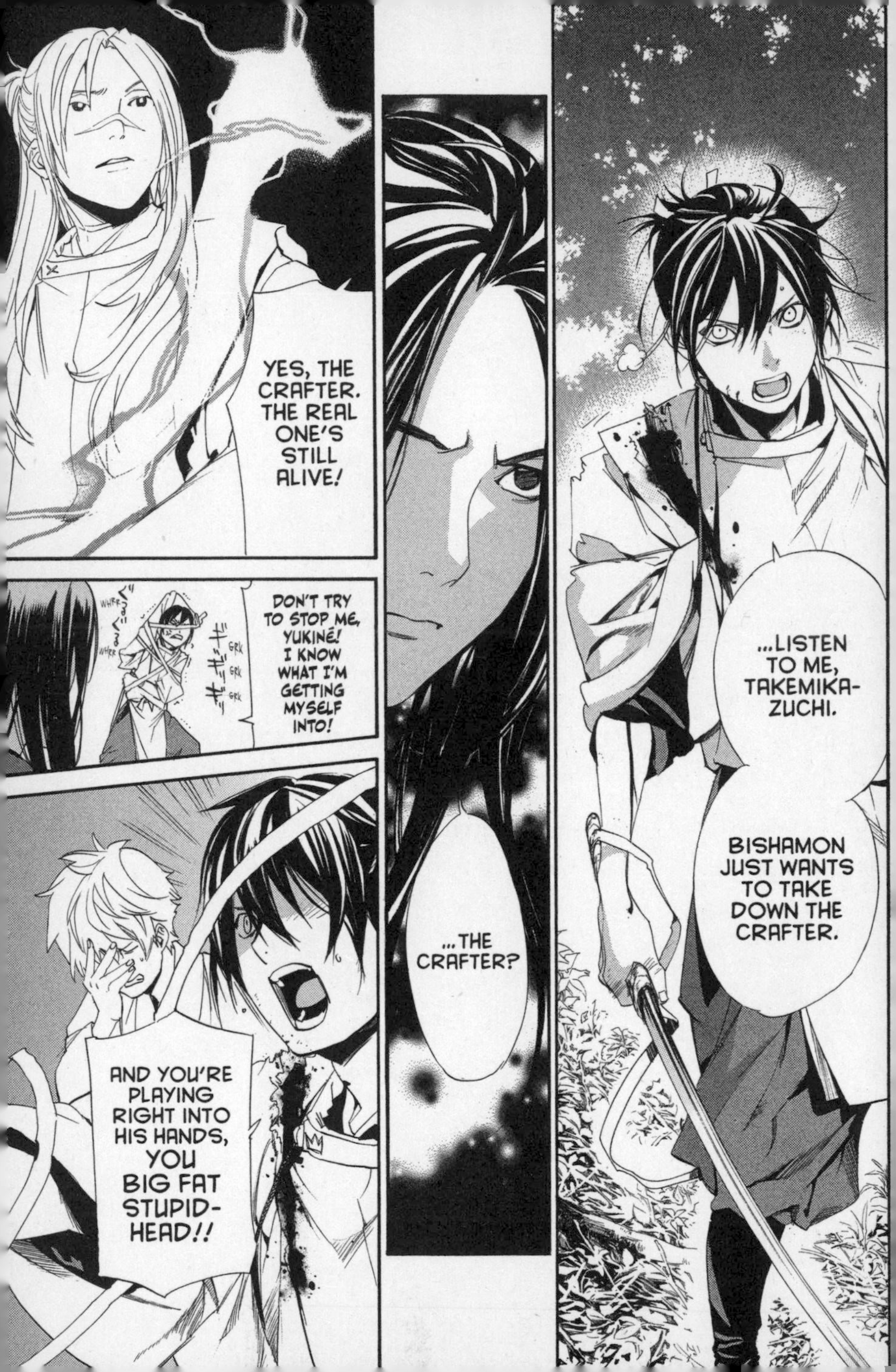
...LISTEN TO ME, TAKEMIKA-ZUCHI.
BISHAMON JUST WANTS TO TAKE DOWN THE CRAFTER.
...THE CRAFTER?
YES, THE CRAFTER. THE REAL ONE'S STILL ALIVE!
DON'T TRY TO STOP ME, YUKINE! I KNOW WHAT I'M GETTING MYSELF INTO!
WHRR
WHRR
GRK
GRK
GRK
AND YOU'RE PLAYING RIGHT INTO HIS HANDS, YOU BIG FAT STUPID-HEAD!!

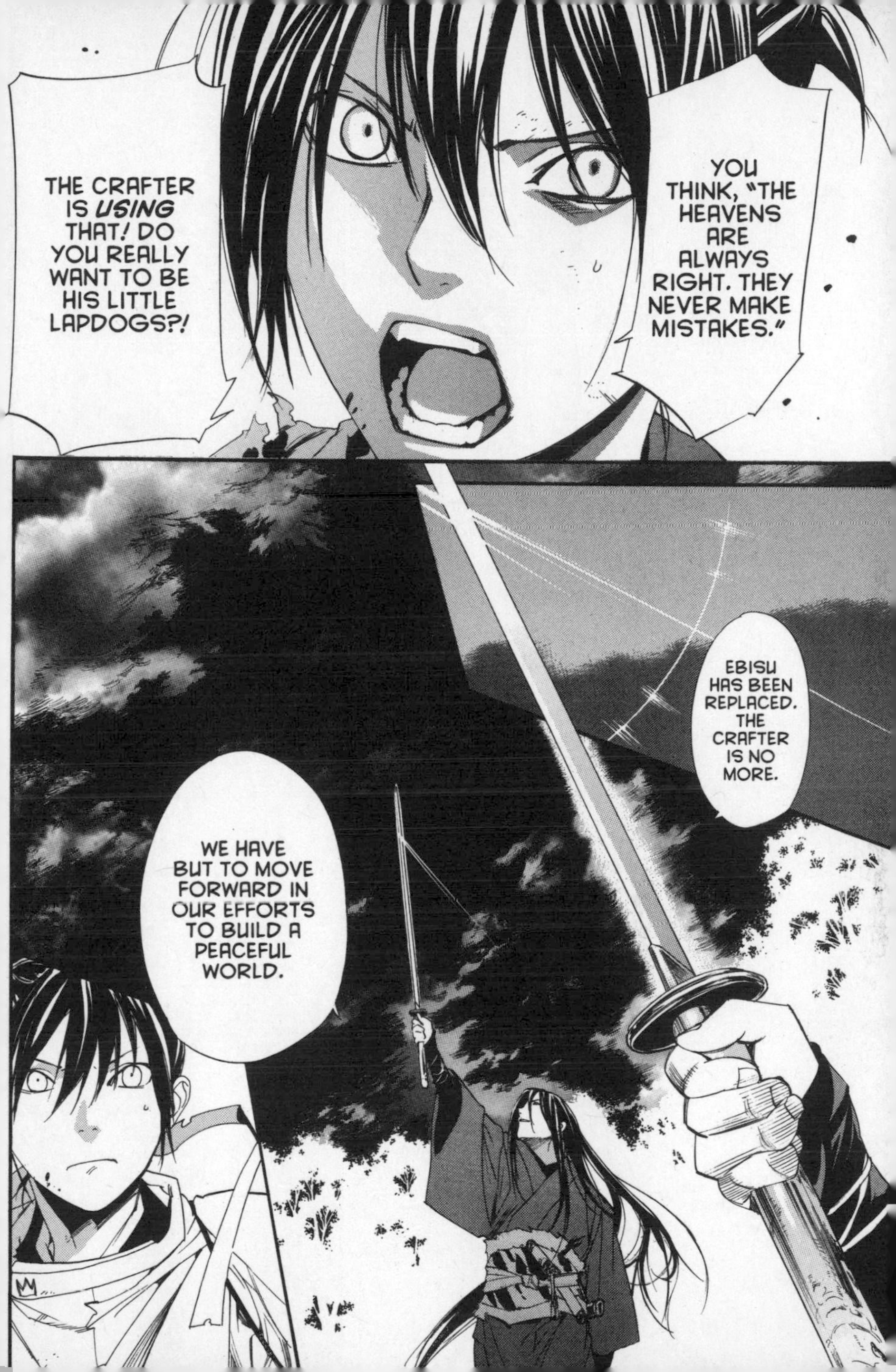
YOU THINK, "THE HEAVENS ARE ALWAYS RIGHT. THEY NEVER MAKE MISTAKES."
THE CRAFTER IS *USING* THAT! DO YOU REALLY WANT TO BE HIS LITTLE LAPDOGS?!
EBISU HAS BEEN REPLACED. THE CRAFTER IS NO MORE.
WE HAVE BUT TO MOVE FORWARD IN OUR EFFORTS TO BUILD A PEACEFUL WORLD.

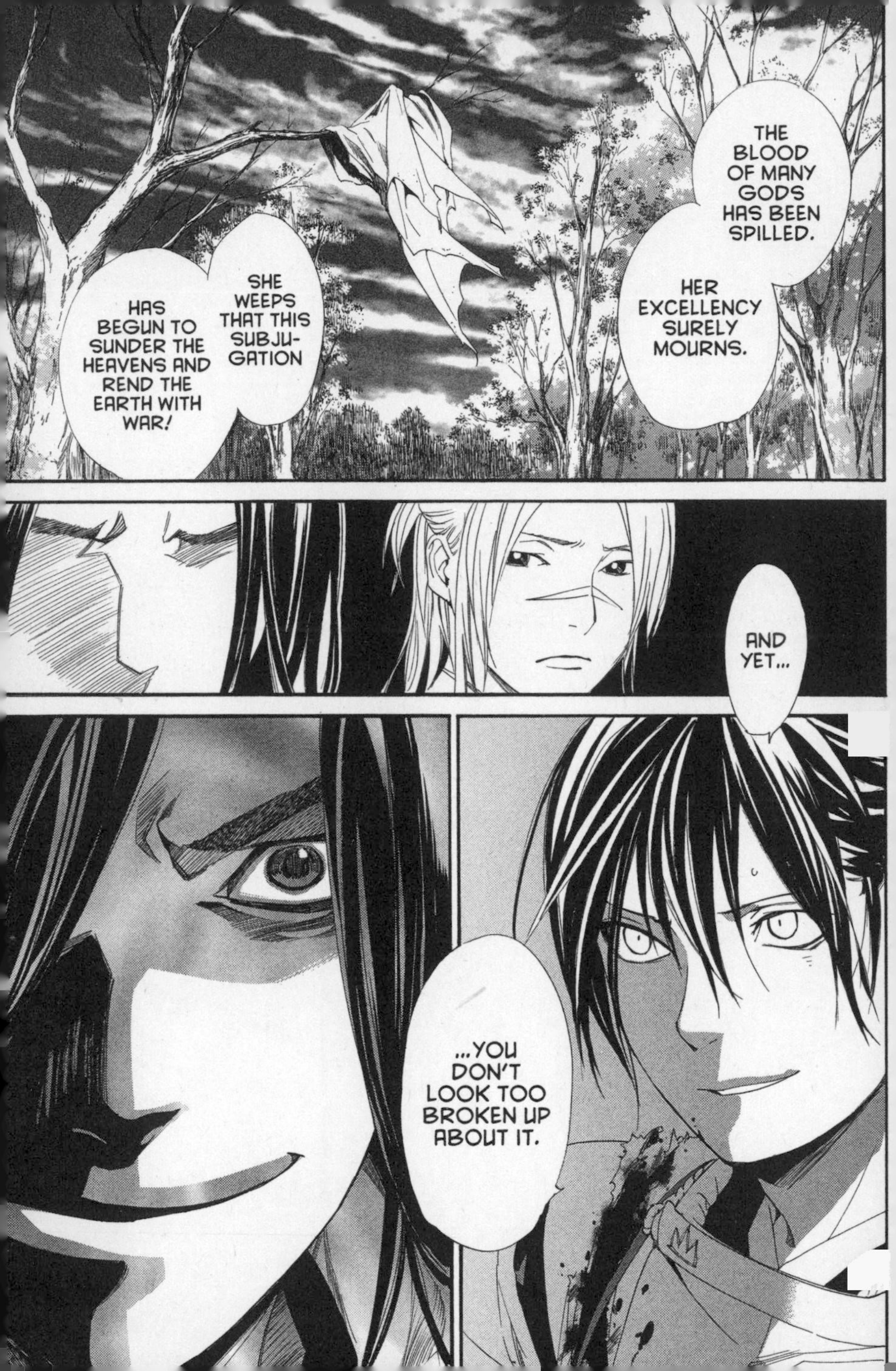
THE BLOOD OF MANY GODS HAS BEEN SPILLED.
HER EXCELLENCY SURELY MOURNS.
SHE WEEPS THAT THIS SUBJU-GATION
HAS BEGUN TO SUNDER THE HEAVENS AND REND THE EARTH WITH WAR!
AND YET...
...YOU DON'T LOOK TOO BROKEN UP ABOUT IT.

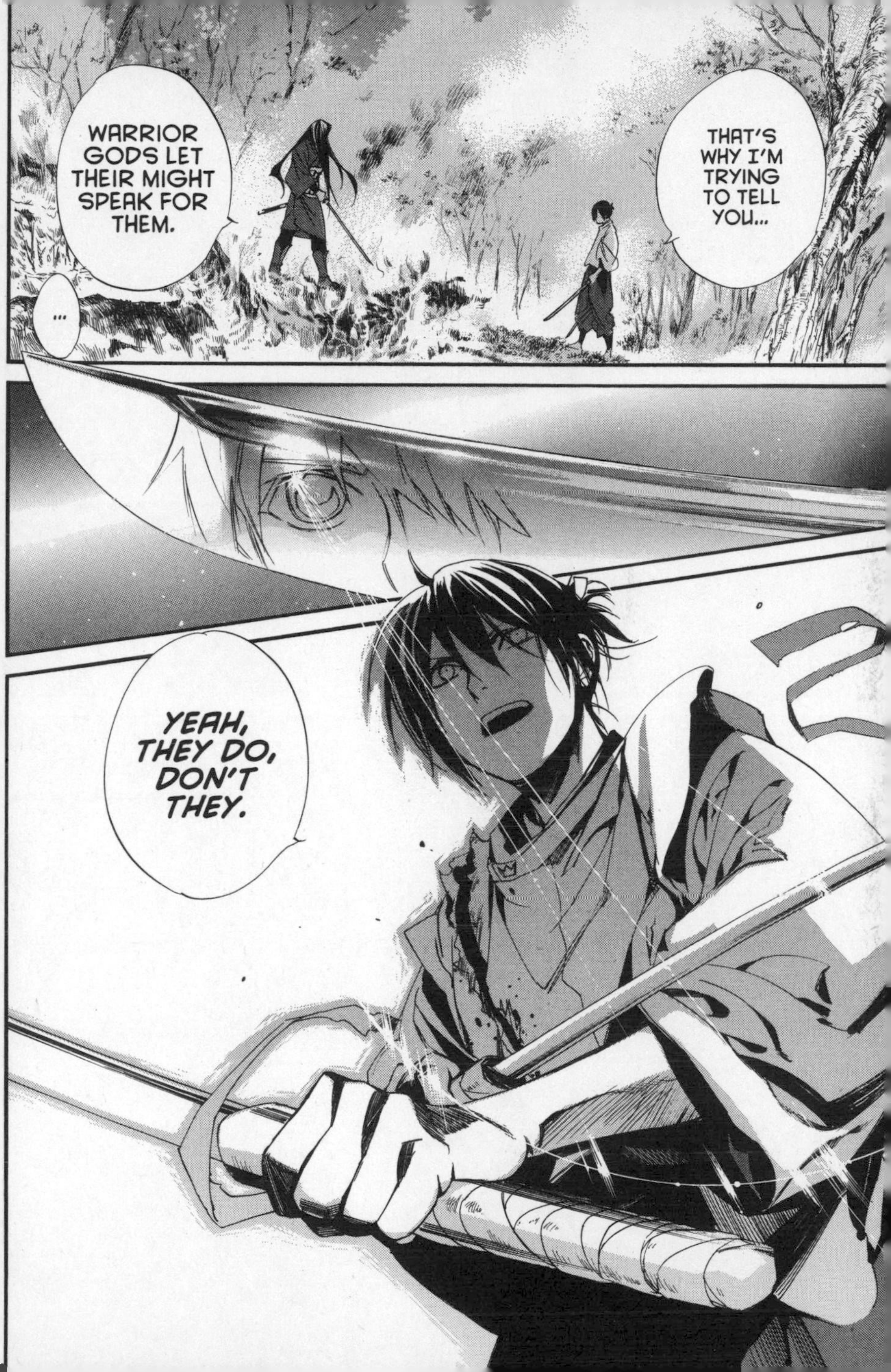
THAT'S WHY I'M TRYING TO TELL YOU...
WARRIOR GODS LET THEIR MIGHT SPEAK FOR THEM.
...
YEAH, THEY DO, DON'T THEY.

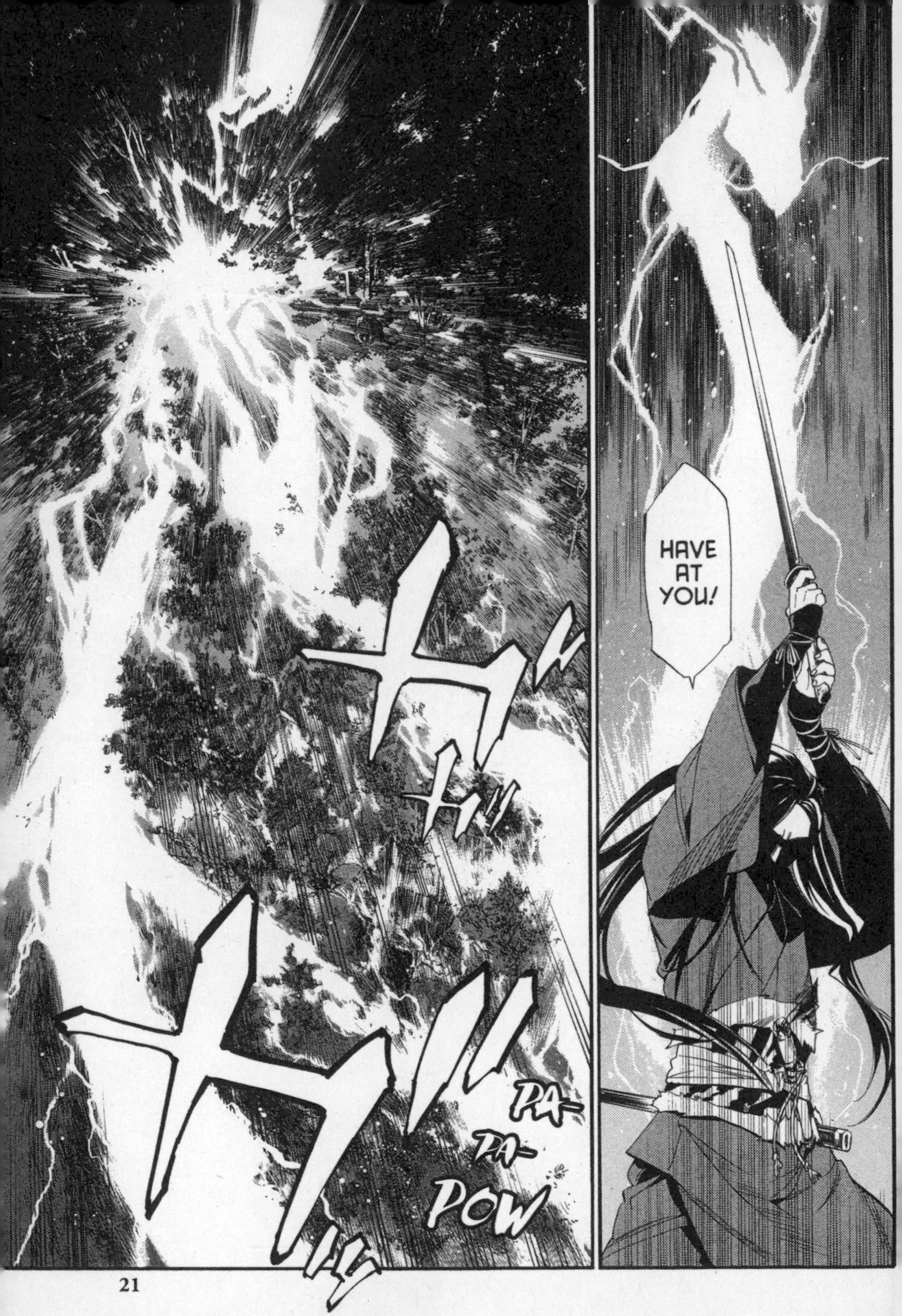
HAVE AT YOU!
PA-PA-POW

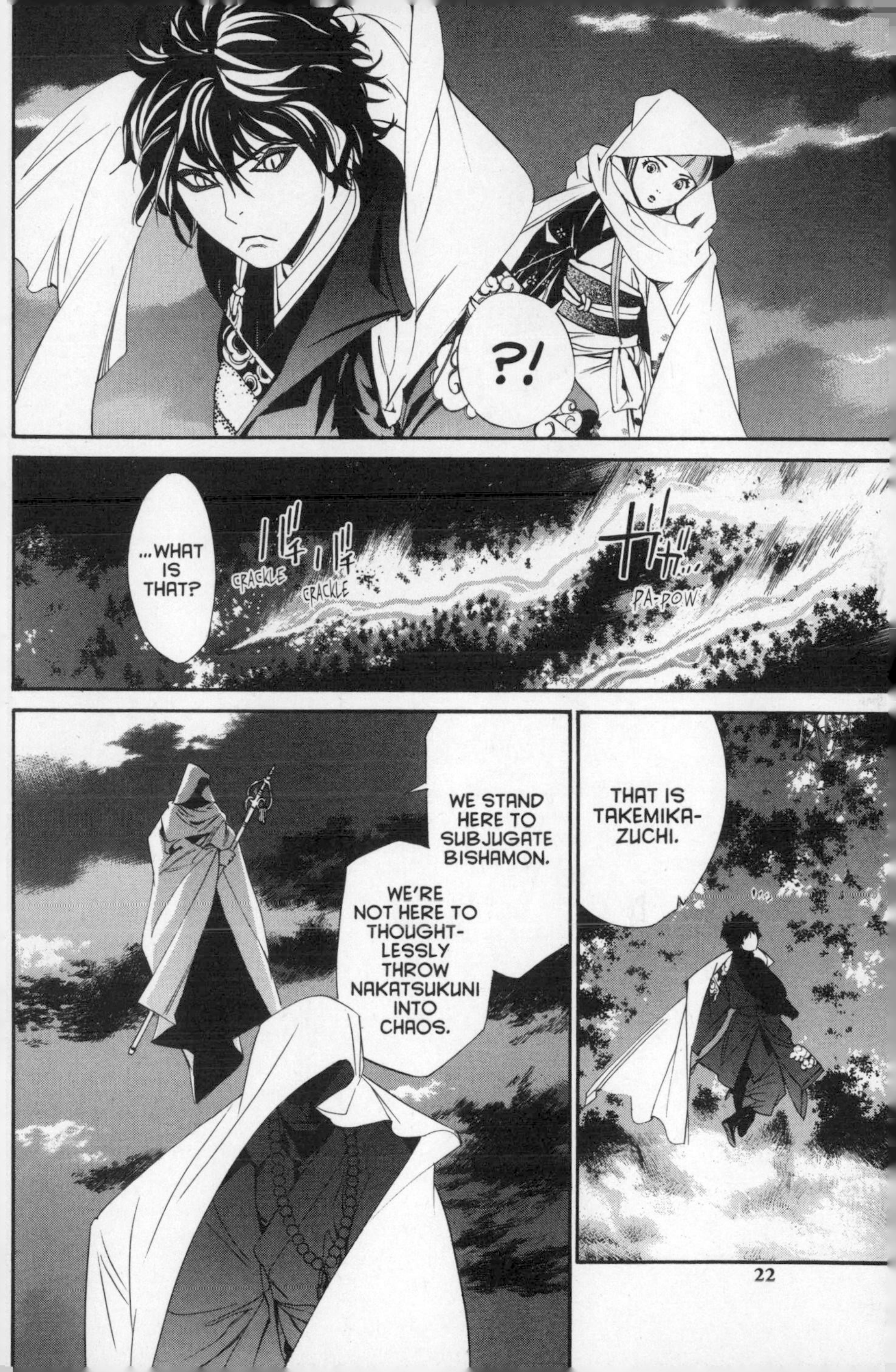
?!
PA-POW
CRACKLE
CRACKLE
...WHAT IS THAT?
THAT IS TAKEMIKA-ZUCHI.
WE STAND HERE TO SUBJUGATE BISHAMON.
WE'RE NOT HERE TO THOUGHT-LESSLY THROW NAKATSUKUNI INTO CHAOS.

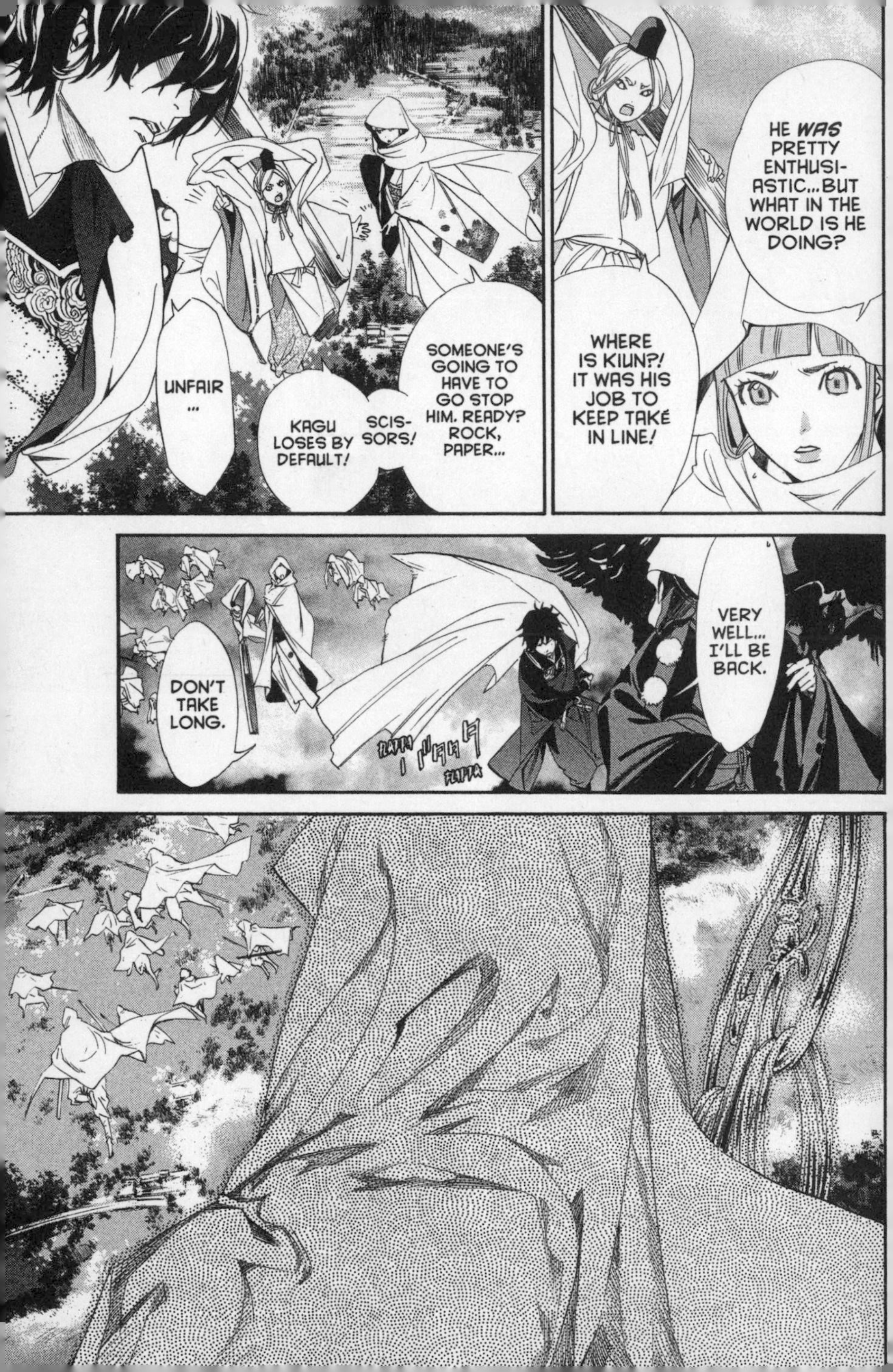
HE *WAS* PRETTY ENTHUSI-ASTIC...BUT WHAT IN THE WORLD IS HE DOING?
WHERE IS KIUN?! IT WAS HIS JOB TO KEEP TAKÉ IN LINE!
SOMEONE'S GOING TO HAVE TO GO STOP HIM. READY? ROCK, PAPER...
SCIS-SORS!
KAGU LOSES BY DEFAULT!
UNFAIR ...
VERY WELL... I'LL BE BACK.
DON'T TAKE LONG.

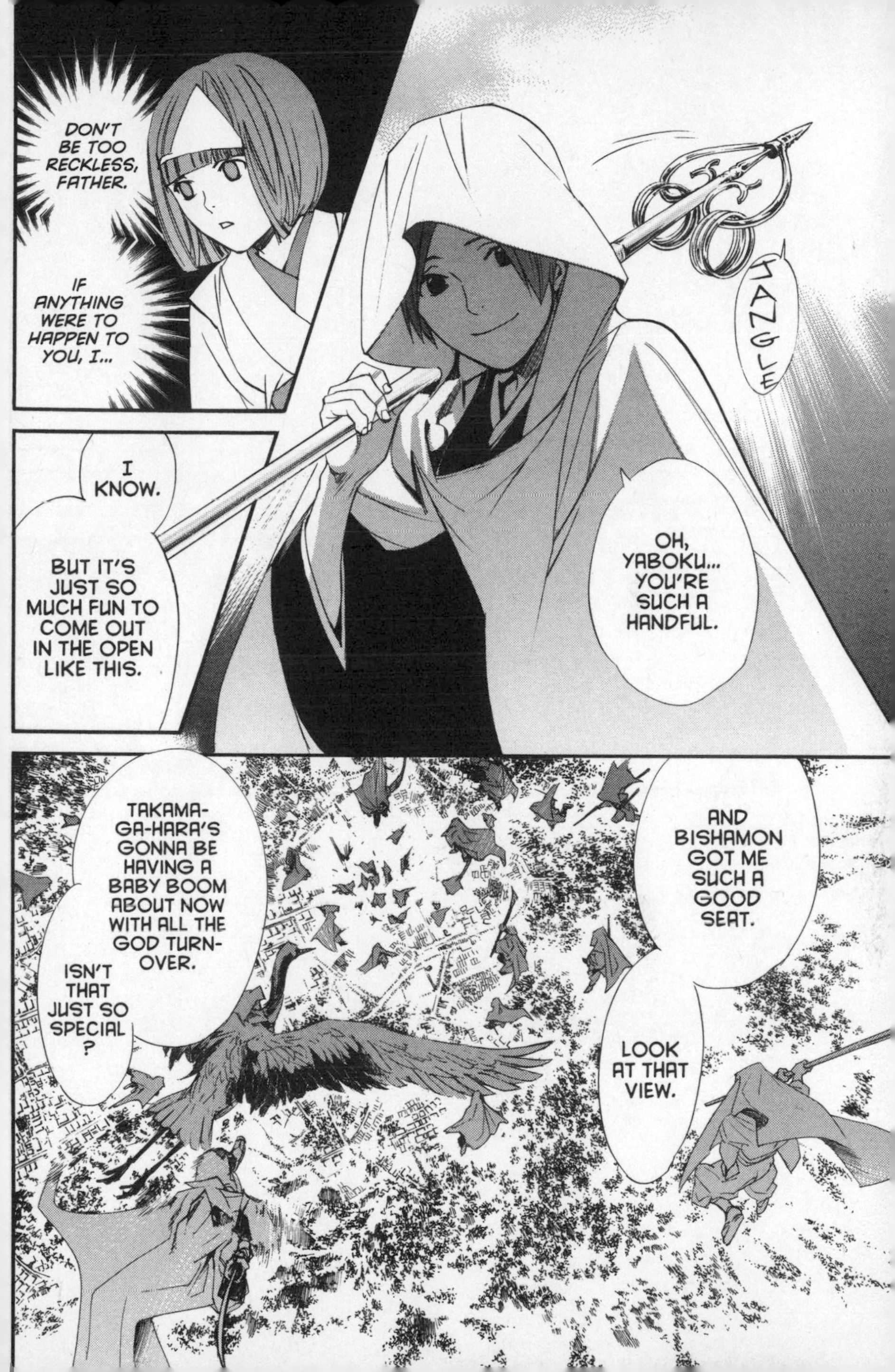
JANGLE
OH, YABOKU... YOU'RE SUCH A HANDFUL.
DON'T BE TOO RECKLESS, FATHER.
IF ANYTHING WERE TO HAPPEN TO YOU, I...
I KNOW.
BUT IT'S JUST SO MUCH FUN TO COME OUT IN THE OPEN LIKE THIS.
AND BISHAMON GOT ME SUCH A GOOD SEAT.
LOOK AT THAT VIEW.
TAKAMA-GA-HARA'S GONNA BE HAVING A BABY BOOM ABOUT NOW WITH ALL THE GOD TURN-OVER.
ISN'T THAT JUST SO SPECIAL?

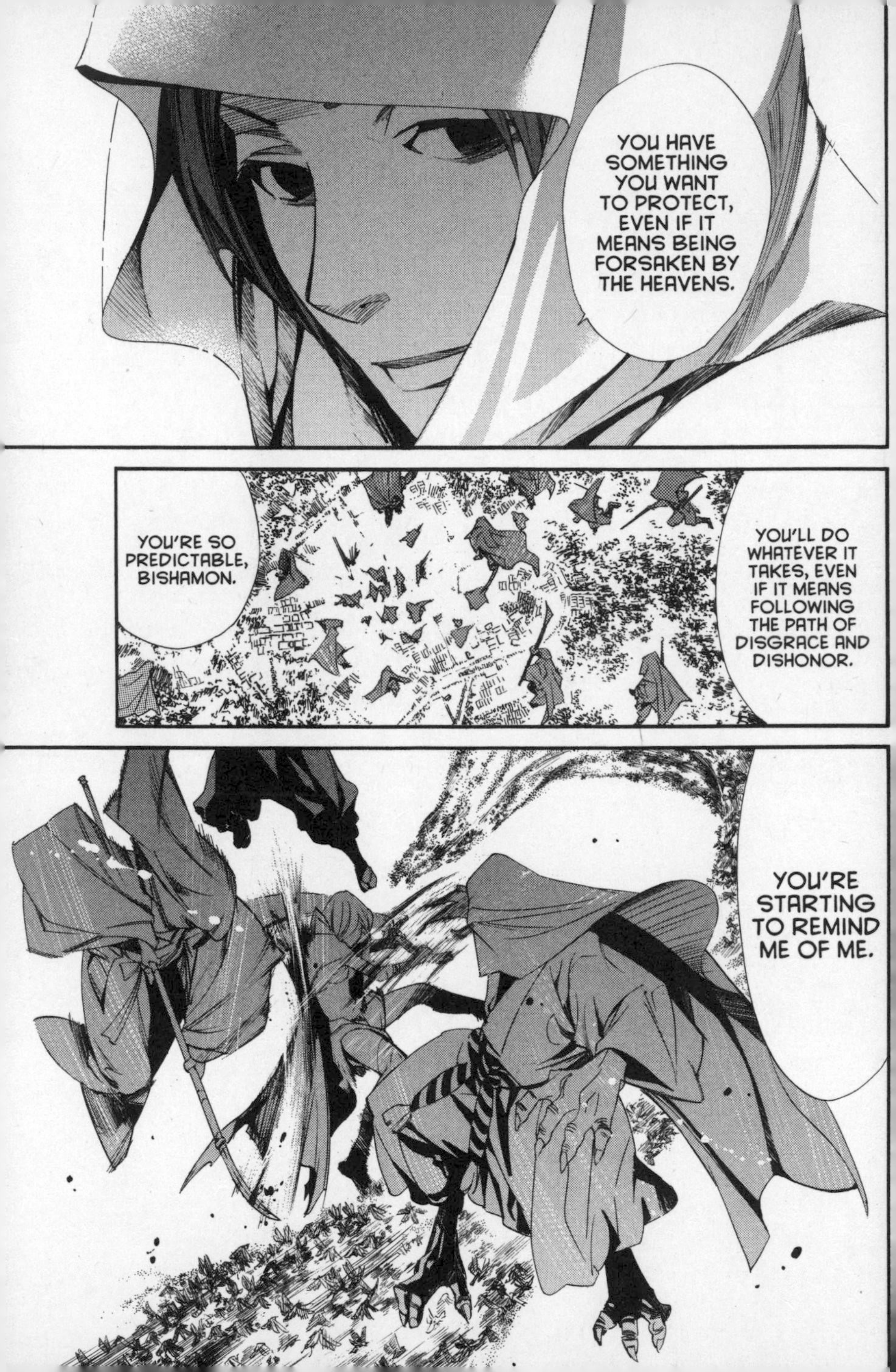
YOU HAVE SOMETHING YOU WANT TO PROTECT, EVEN IF IT MEANS BEING FORSAKEN BY THE HEAVENS.
YOU'LL DO WHATEVER IT TAKES, EVEN IF IT MEANS FOLLOWING THE PATH OF DISGRACE AND DISHONOR.
YOU'RE SO PREDICTABLE, BISHAMON.
YOU'RE STARTING TO REMIND ME OF ME.

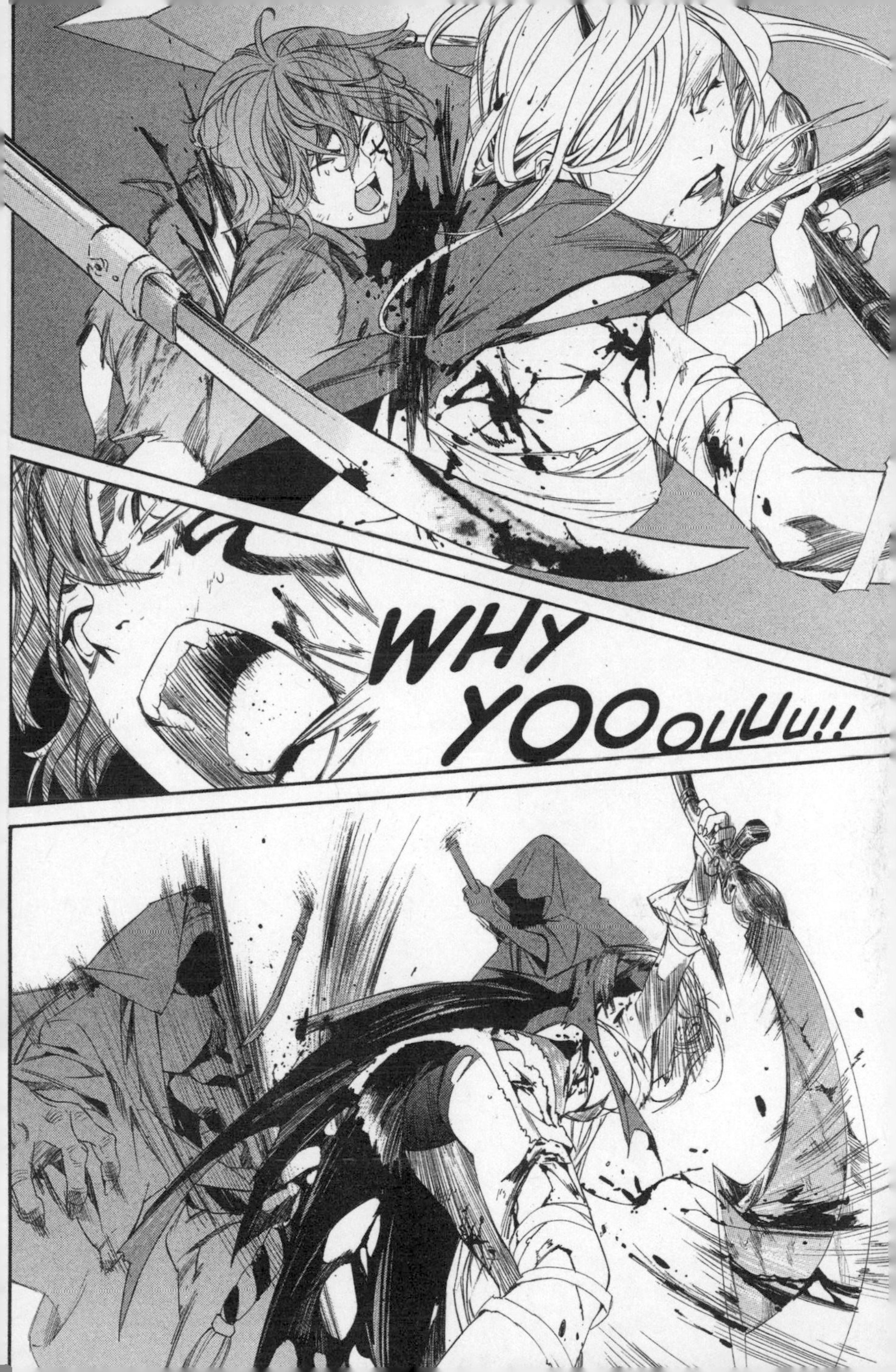
WHY YOOouUu!!

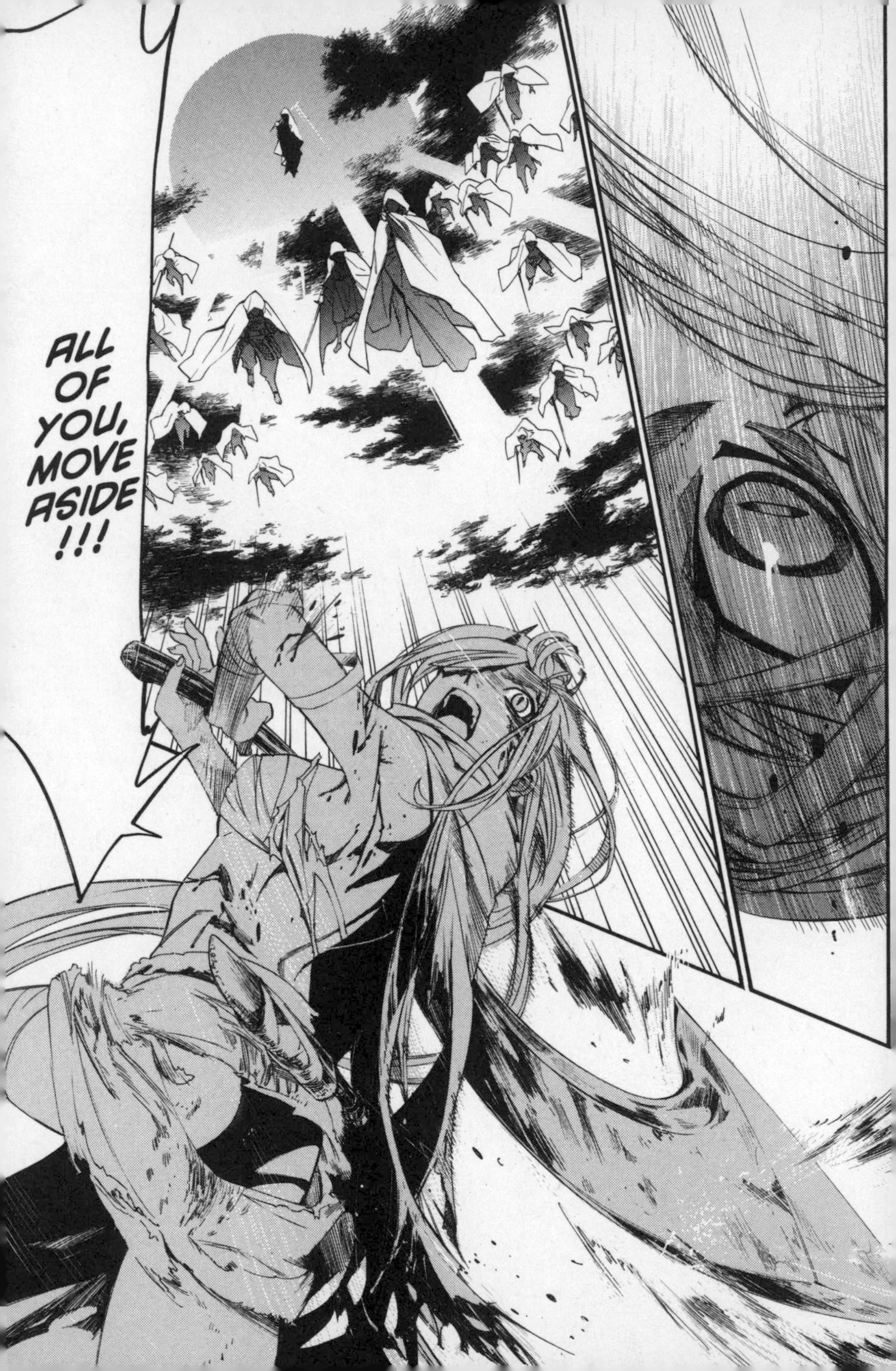
ALL OF YOU, MOVE ASIDE!!!

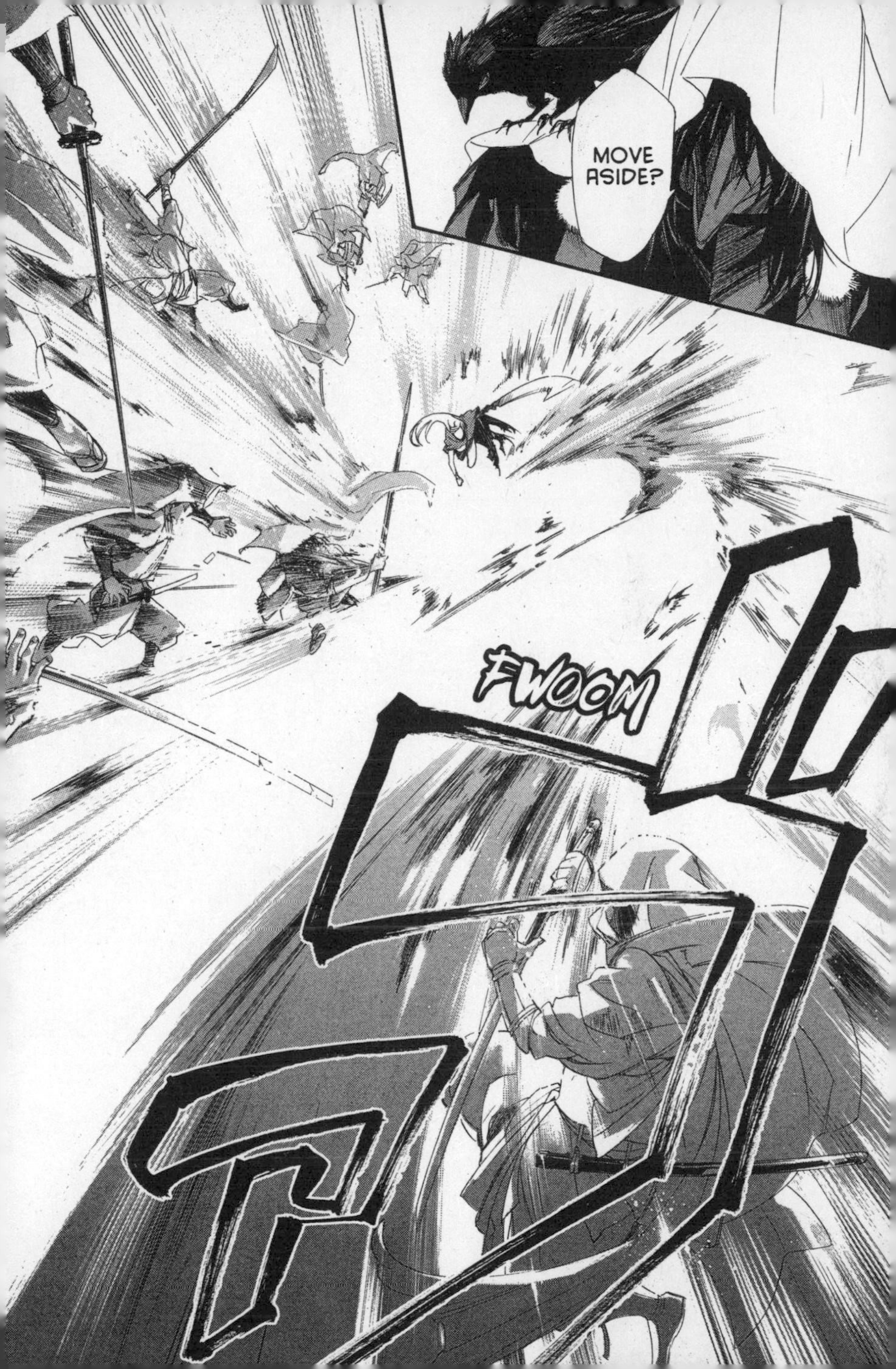
MOVE ASIDE?
FWOOM

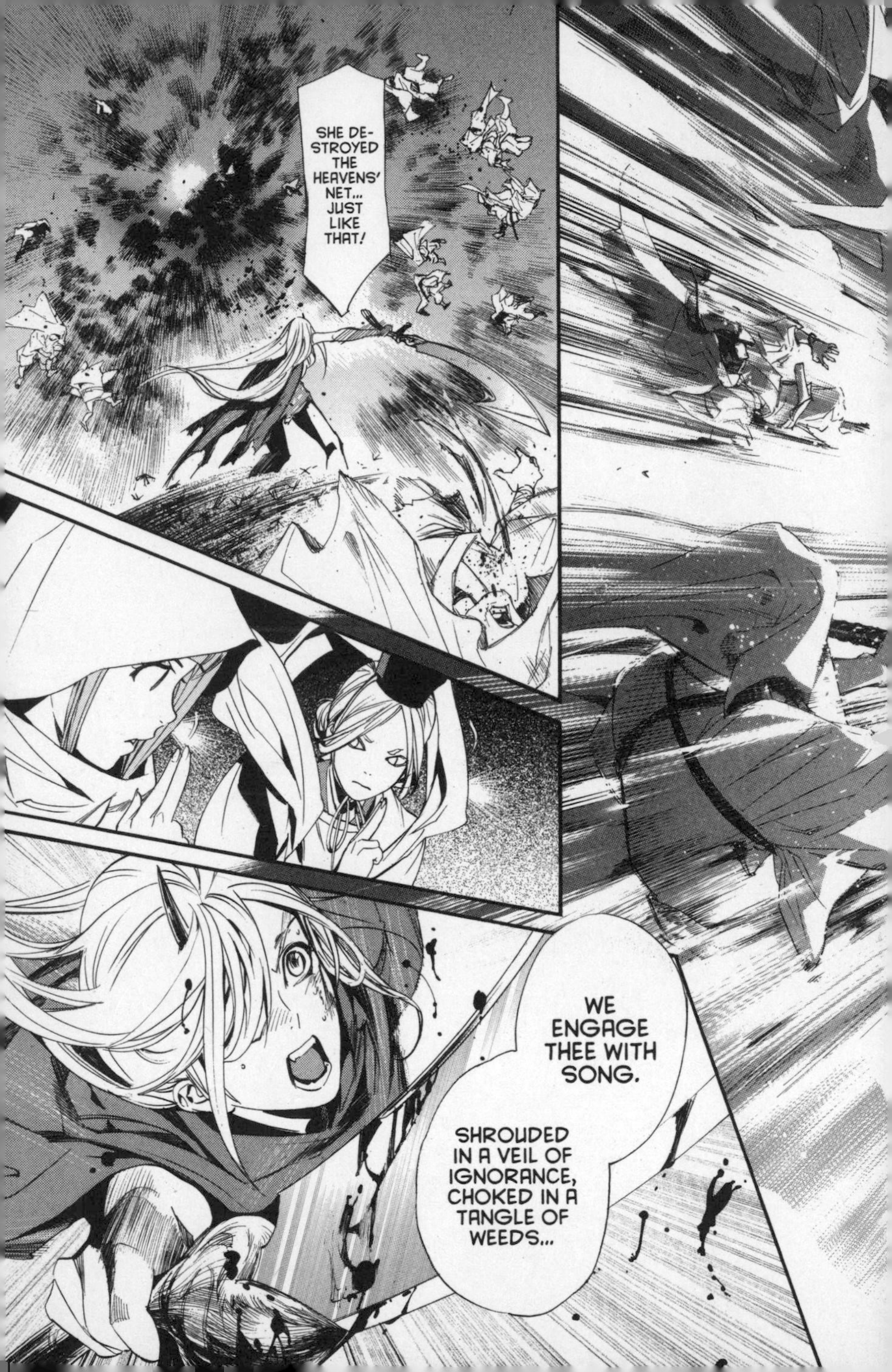
SHE DE-STROYED THE HEAVENS' NET... JUST LIKE THAT!
WE ENGAGE THEE WITH SONG.
SHROUDED IN A VEIL OF IGNORANCE, CHOKED IN A TANGLE OF WEEDS...

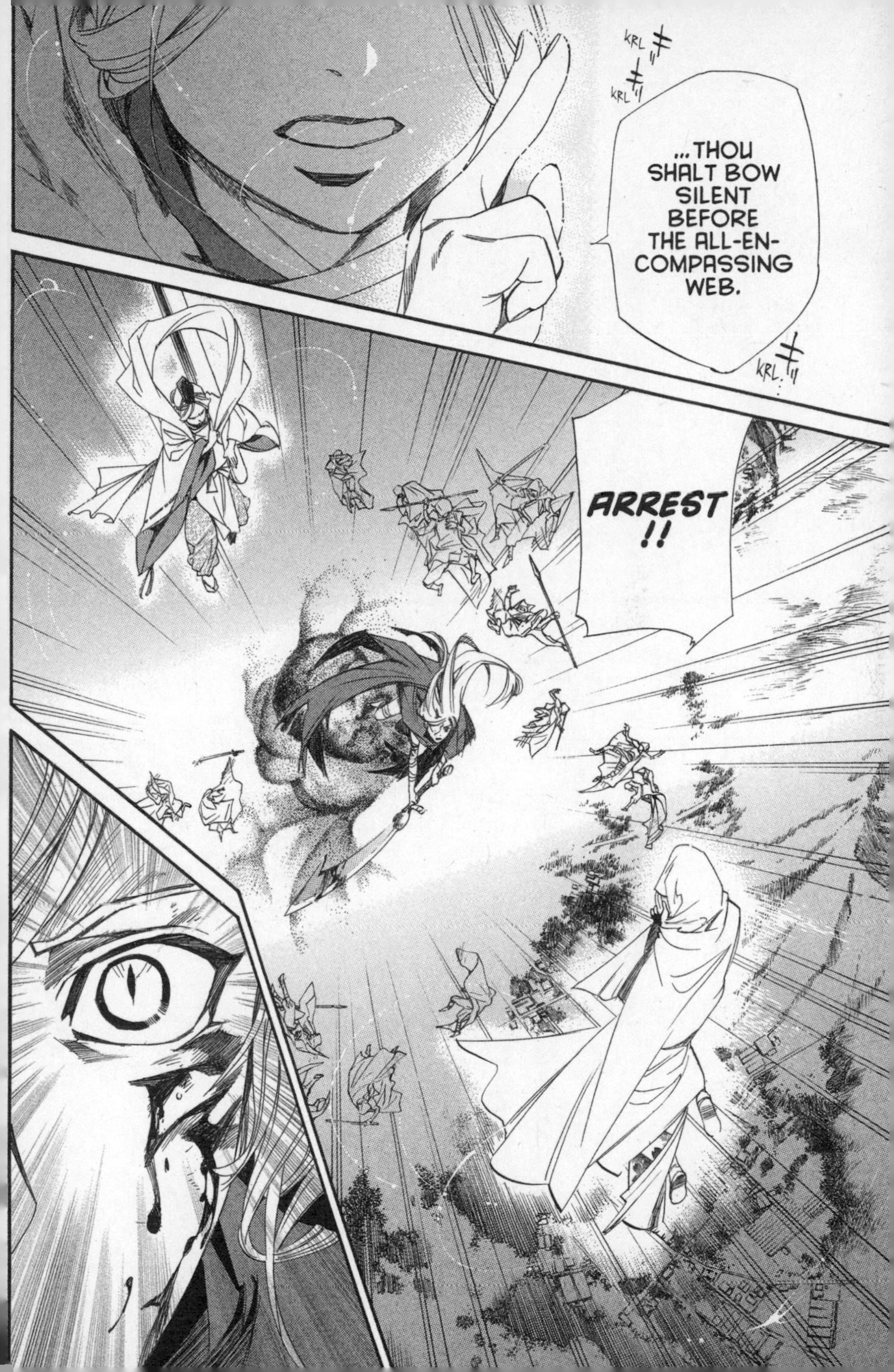
KRL
KRL
...THOU SHALT BOW SILENT BEFORE THE ALL-EN-COMPASSING WEB.
KRL
ARREST !!

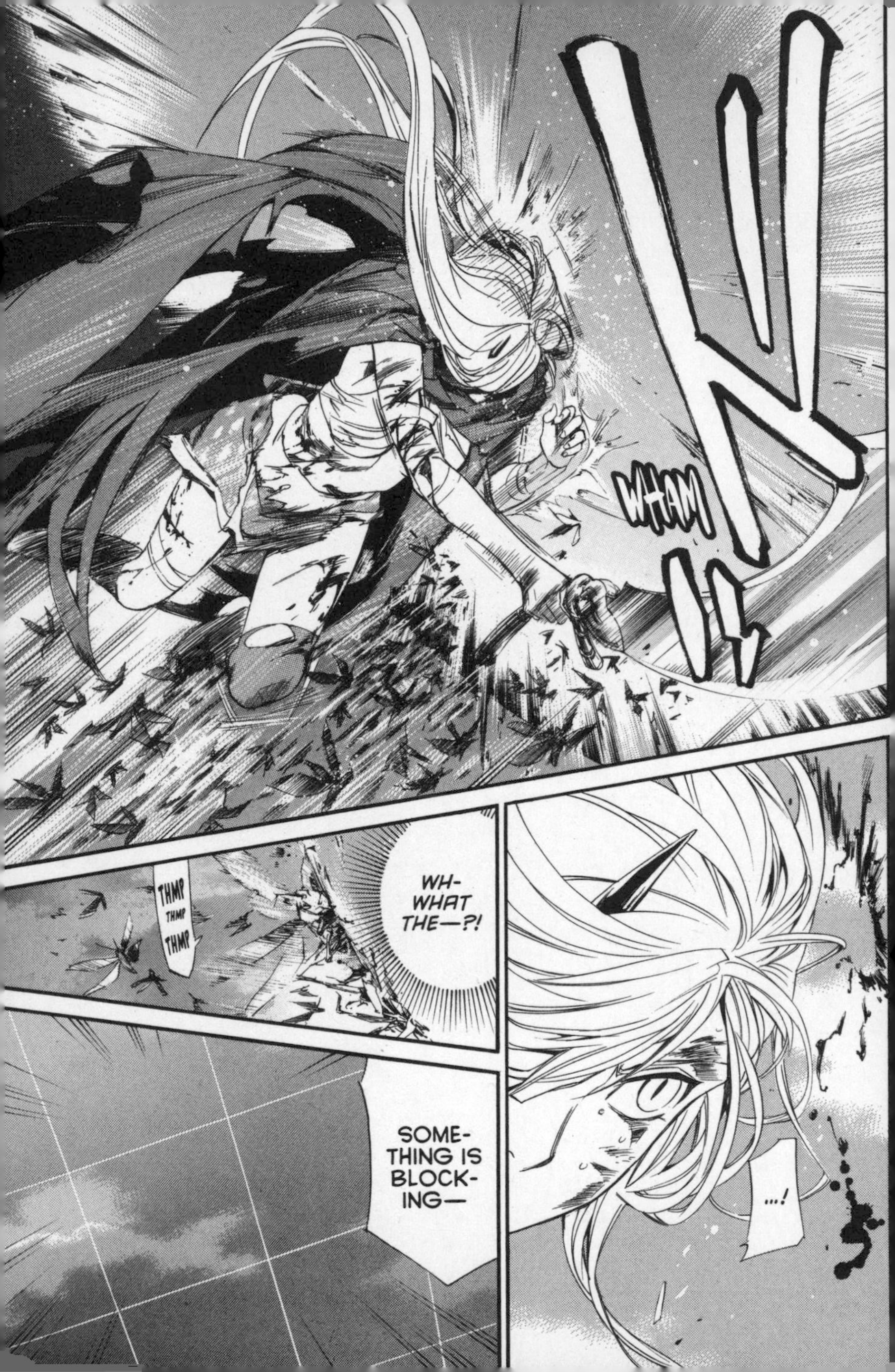
WHAM
...!
WH- WHAT THE—?!
THMP THMP THMP
SOME- THING IS BLOCK- ING—

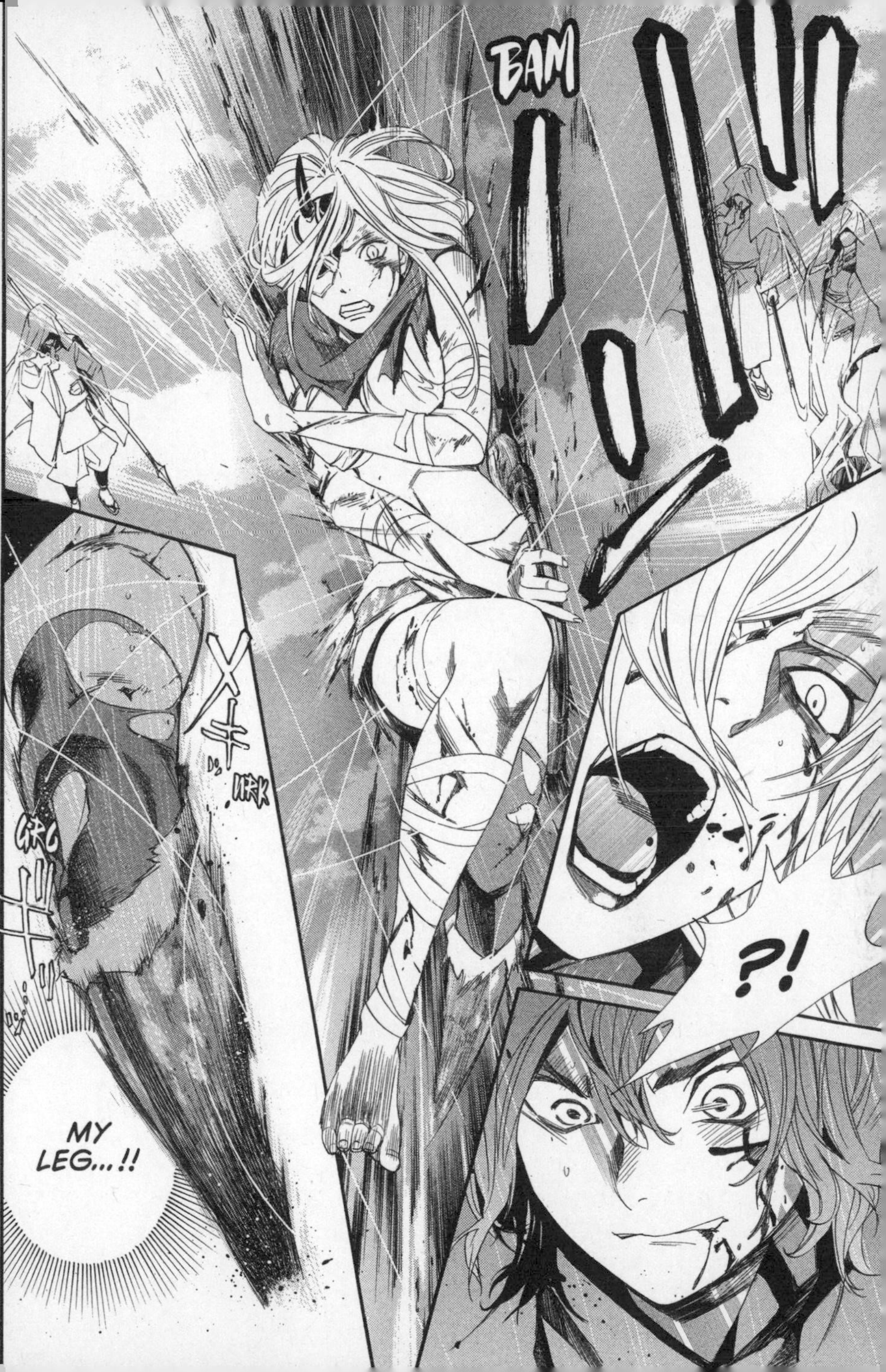
BAM
?!
NRK
GRG
MY LEG...!!

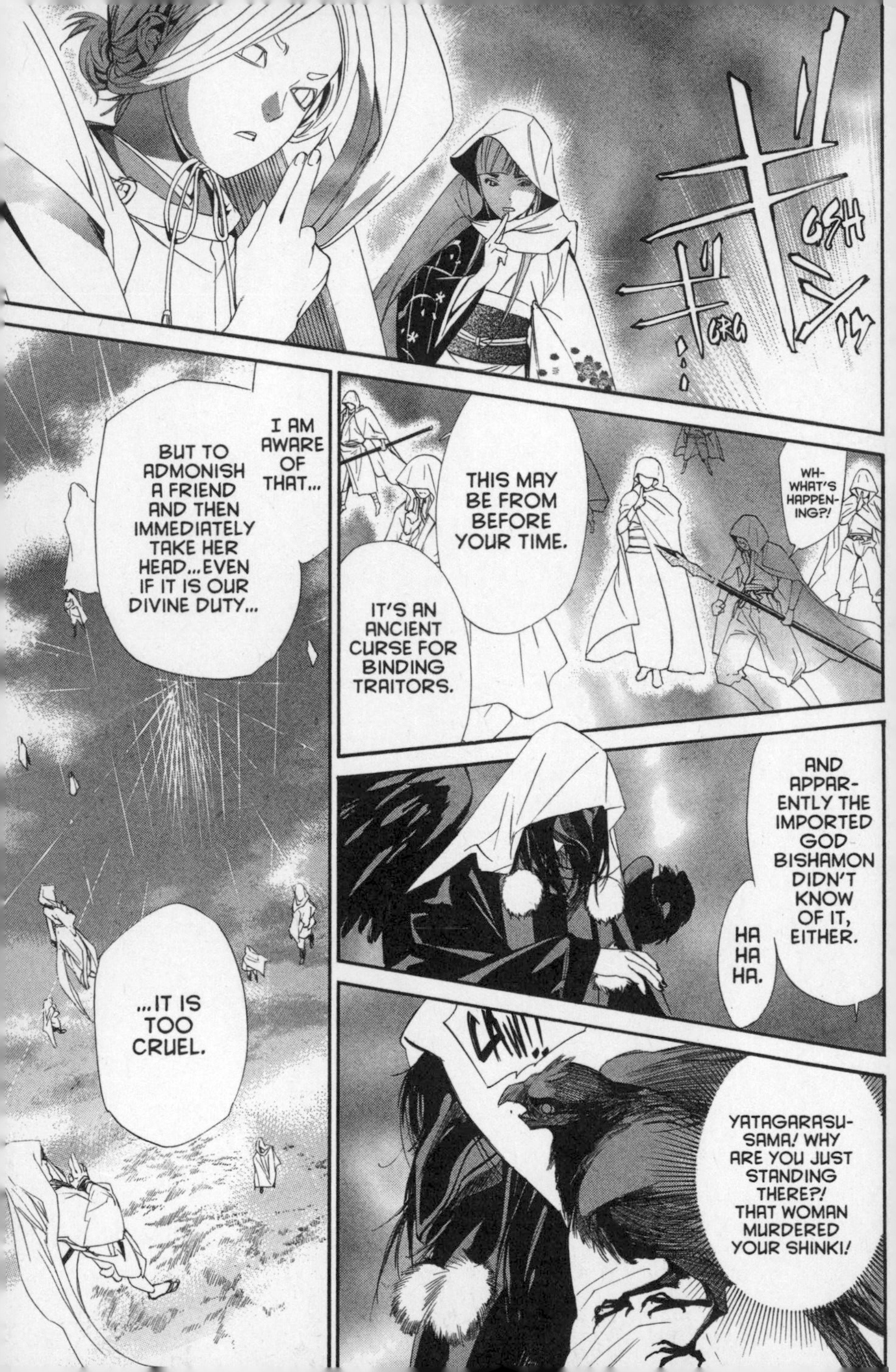
GSH
CRG
WH-WHAT'S HAPPENING?!
THIS MAY BE FROM BEFORE YOUR TIME.
IT'S AN ANCIENT CURSE FOR BINDING TRAITORS.
AND APPARENTLY THE IMPORTED GOD BISHAMON DIDN'T KNOW OF IT, EITHER.
HA HA HA.
CAW!!
YATAGARASU-SAMA! WHY ARE YOU JUST STANDING THERE?! THAT WOMAN MURDERED YOUR SHINKI!
I AM AWARE OF THAT...
BUT TO ADMONISH A FRIEND AND THEN IMMEDIATELY TAKE HER HEAD...EVEN IF IT IS OUR DIVINE DUTY...
...IT IS TOO CRUEL.

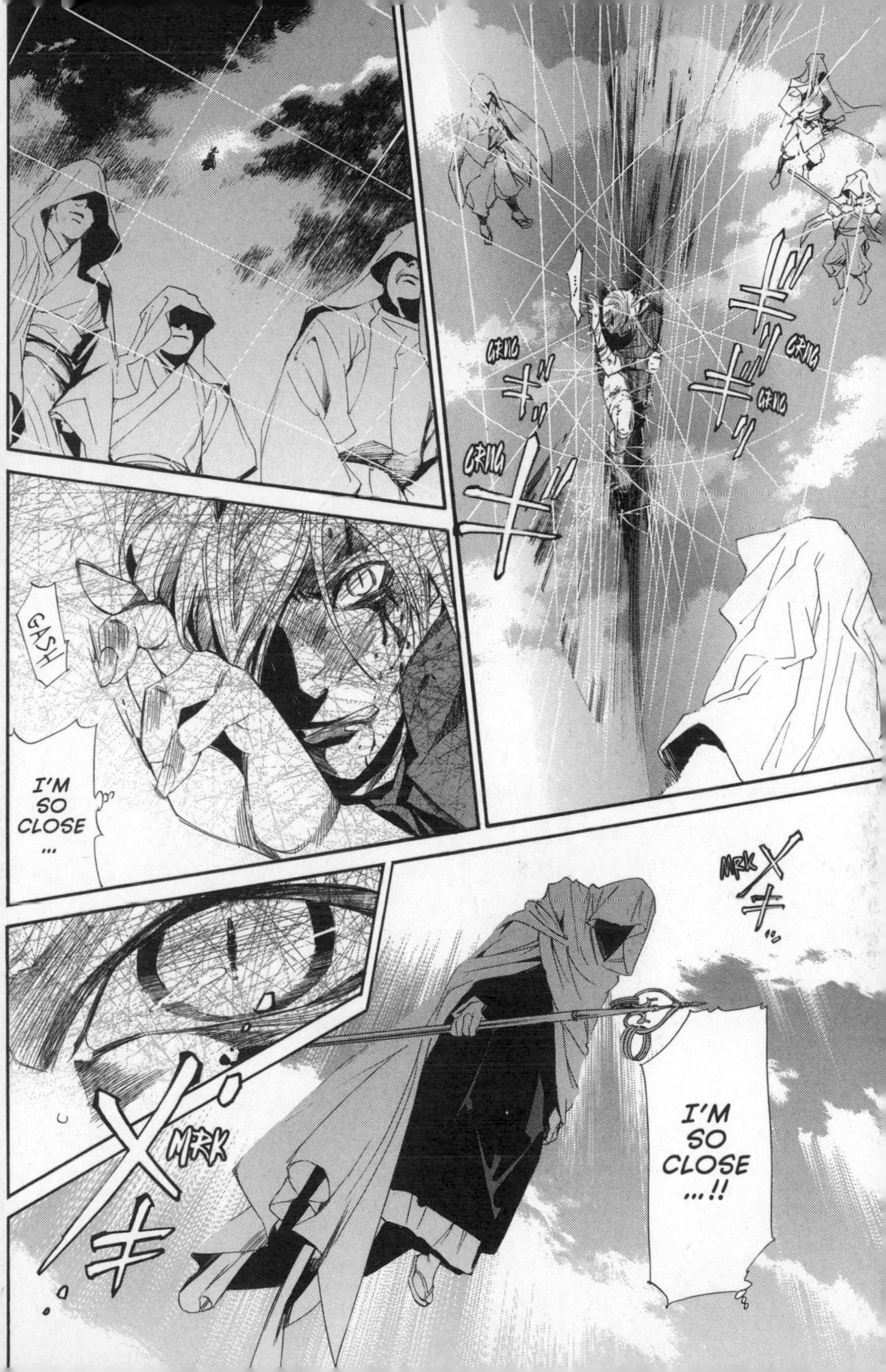

...
CRIIG
CRIIG
CRIIG
CRIIG
GASH
I'M SO CLOSE ...
MRK
I'M SO CLOSE ...!!
MRK

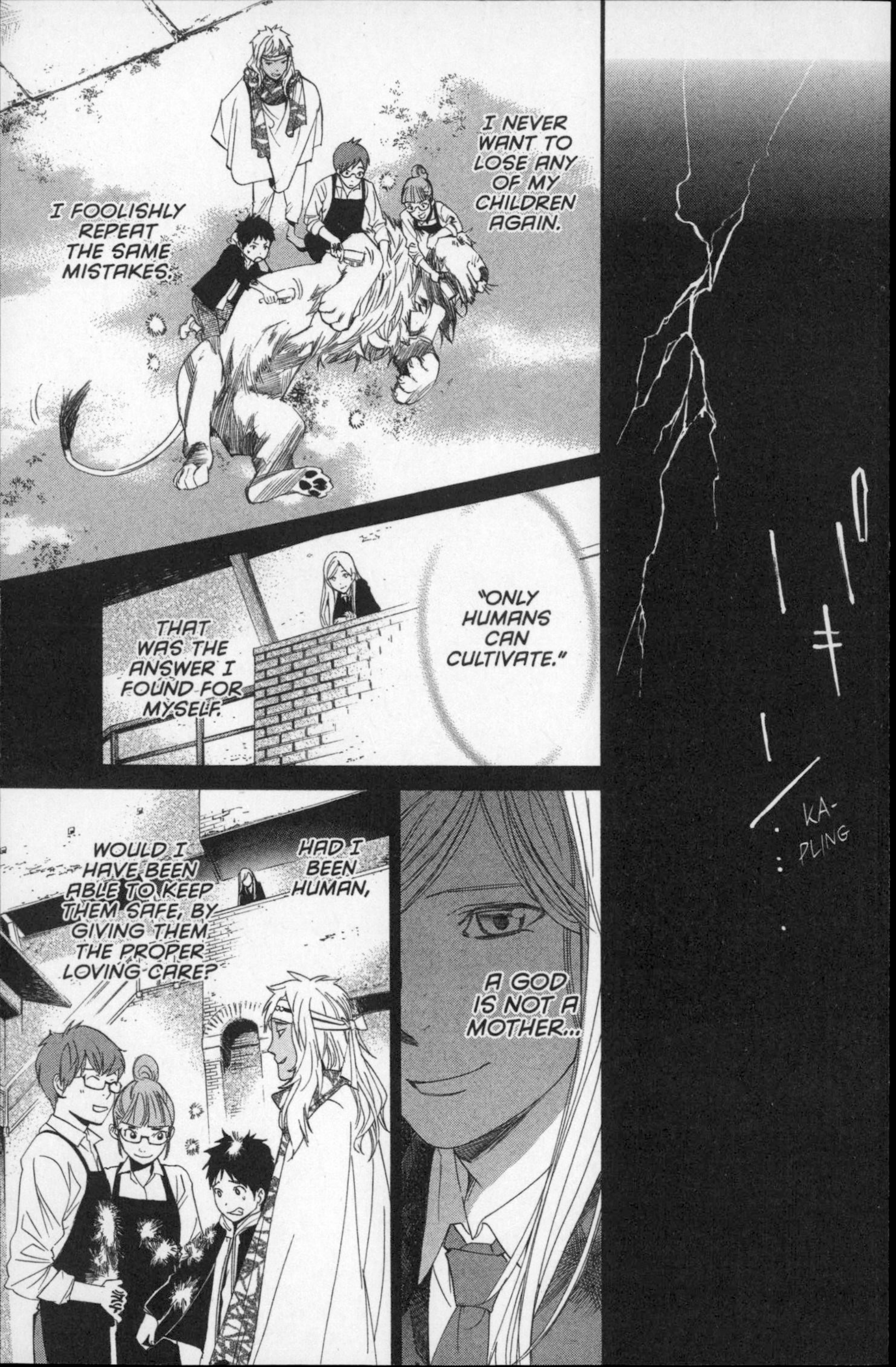
パキーン
KA-PLING
I NEVER WANT TO LOSE ANY OF MY CHILDREN AGAIN.
I FOOLISHLY REPEAT THE SAME MISTAKES.
"ONLY HUMANS CAN CULTIVATE."
THAT WAS THE ANSWER I FOUND FOR MYSELF.
A GOD IS NOT A MOTHER...
HAD I BEEN HUMAN,
WOULD I HAVE BEEN ABLE TO KEEP THEM SAFE, BY GIVING THEM THE PROPER LOVING CARE?

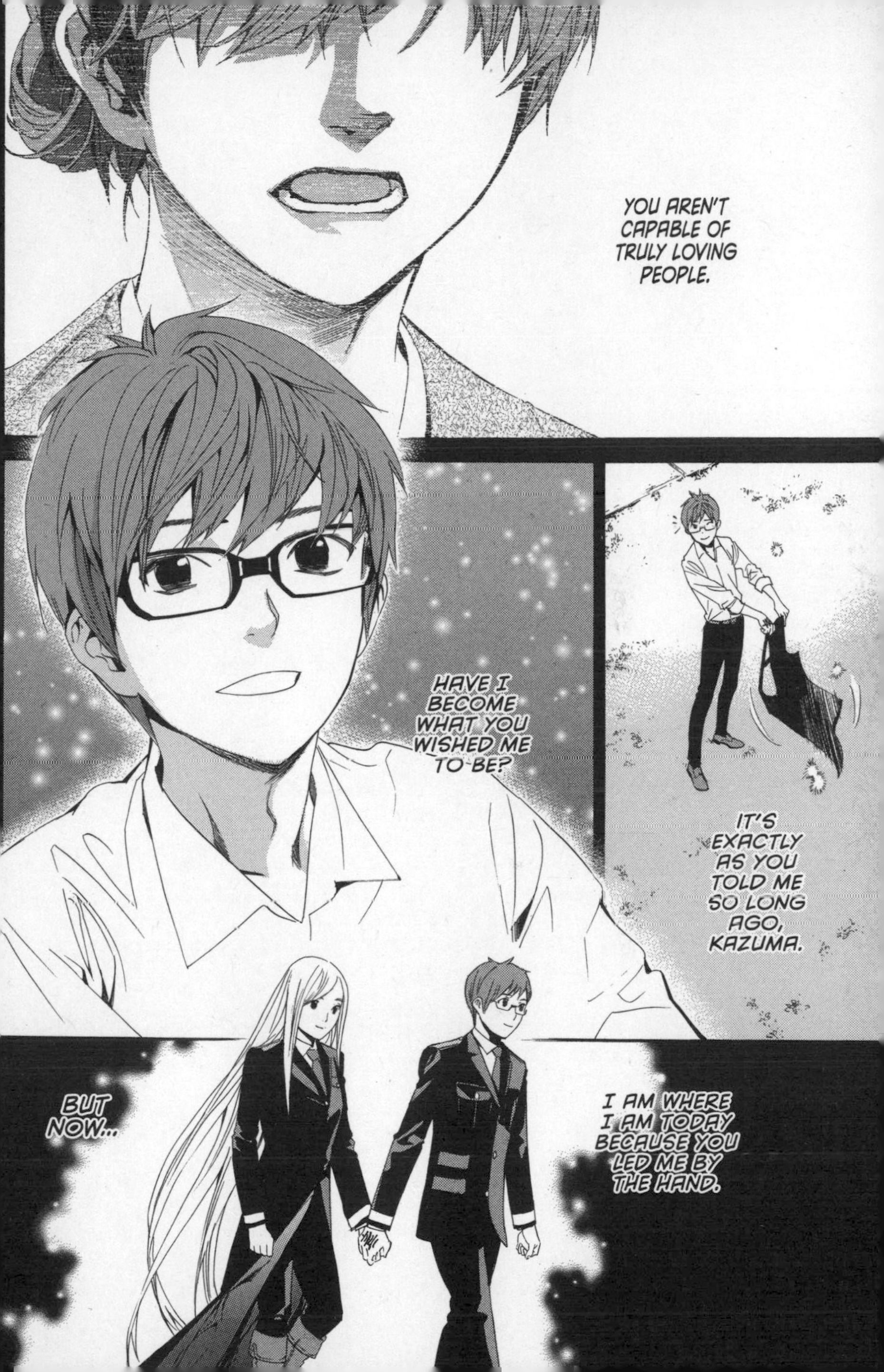
YOU AREN'T CAPABLE OF TRULY LOVING PEOPLE.
IT'S EXACTLY AS YOU TOLD ME SO LONG AGO, KAZUMA.
HAVE I BECOME WHAT YOU WISHED ME TO BE?
I AM WHERE I AM TODAY BECAUSE YOU LED ME BY THE HAND.
BUT NOW...

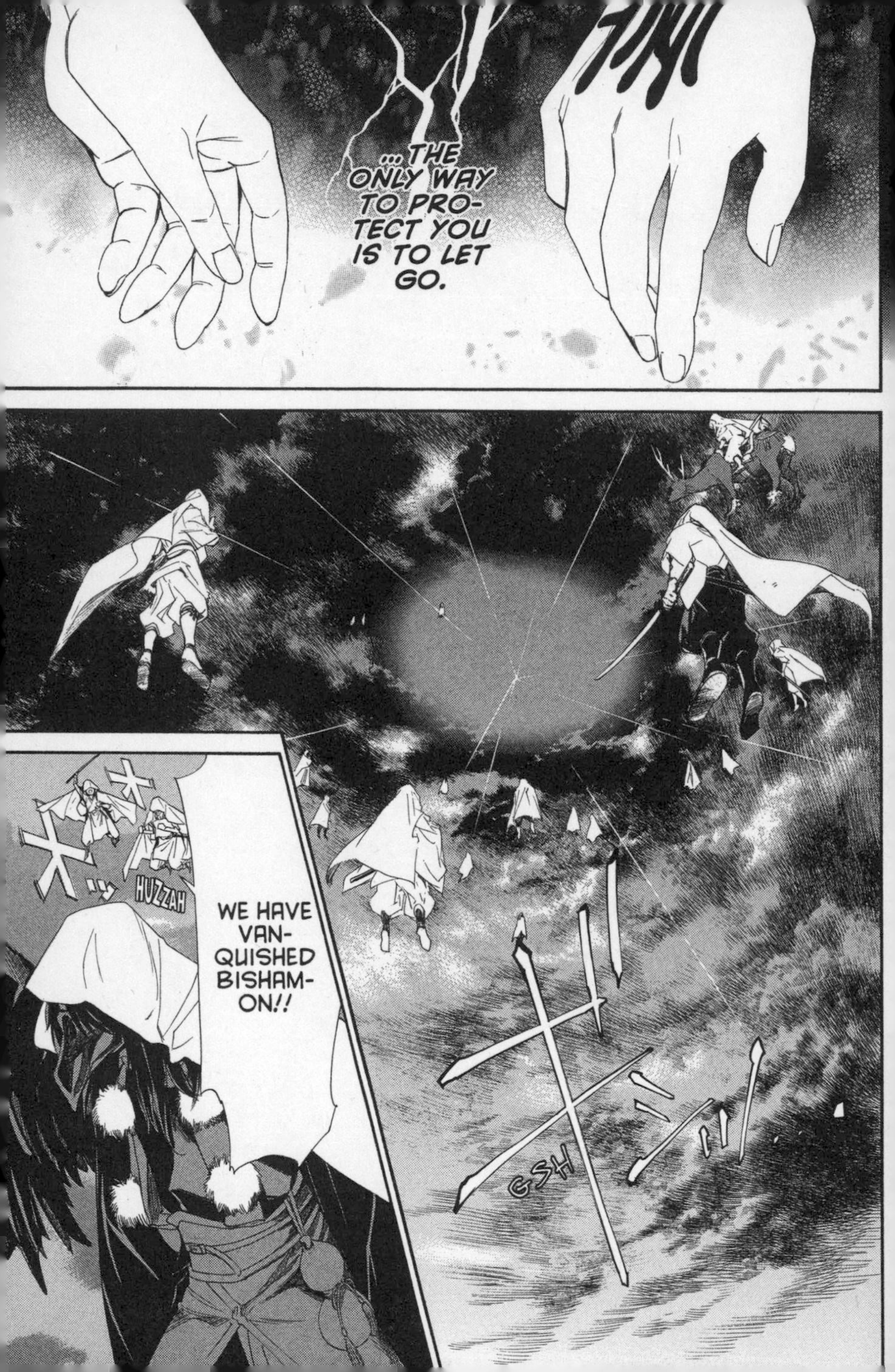
...THE ONLY WAY TO PROTECT YOU IS TO LET GO.
GSH
WE HAVE VAN-QUISHED BISHAM-ON!!
HUZZAH

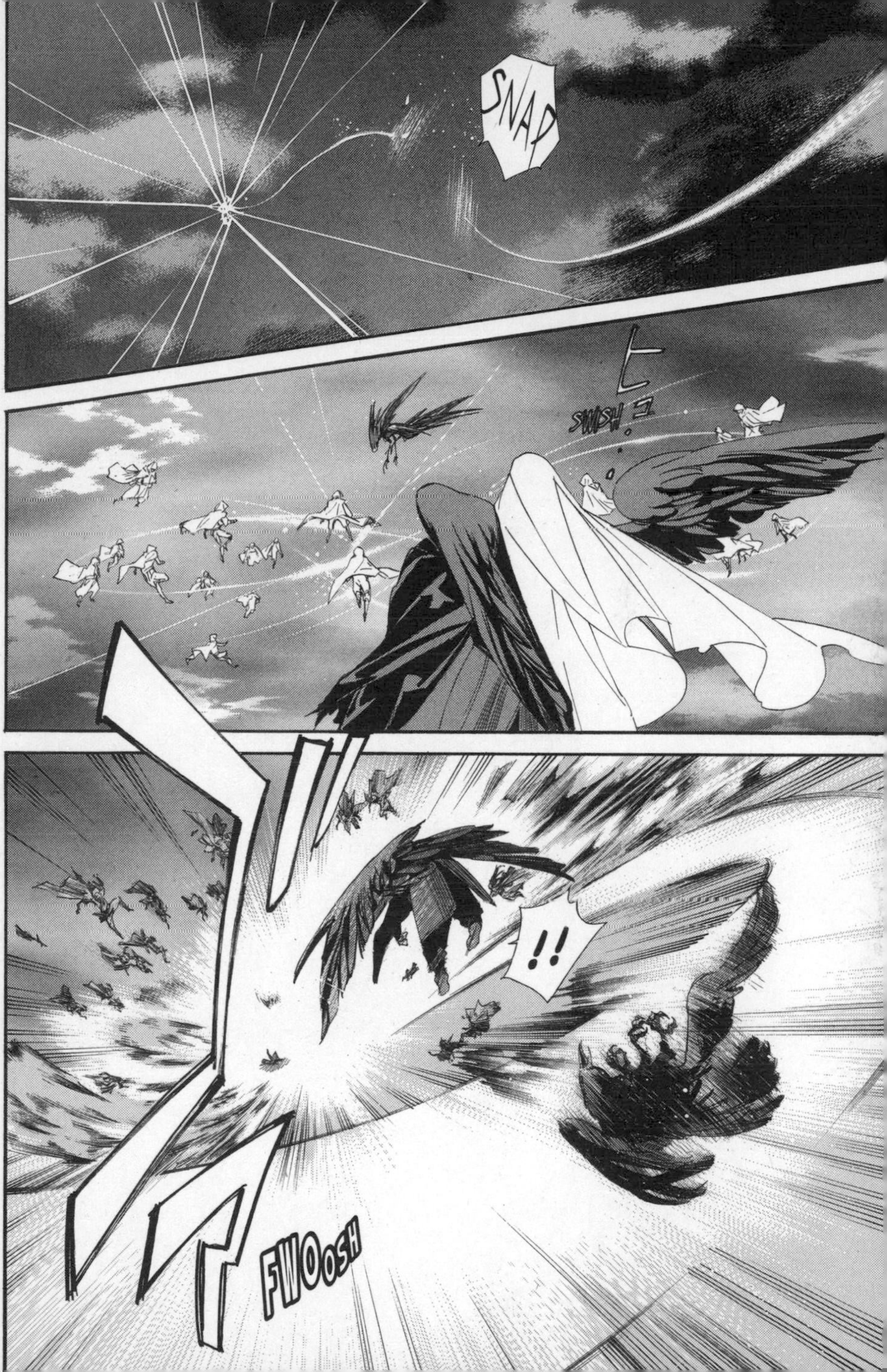
SNAP
SWISH
!!
FWOosh

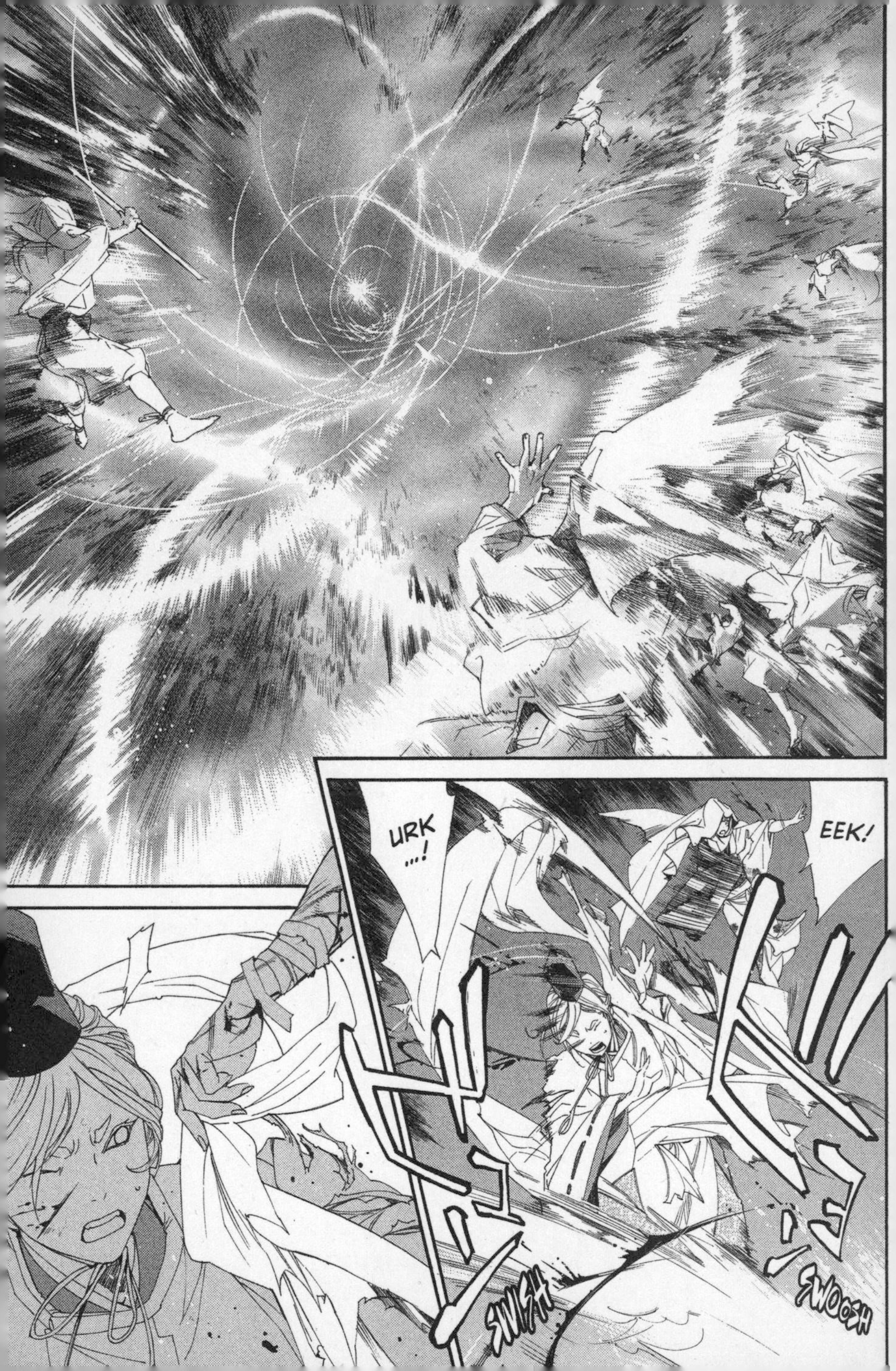
EEK!
URK ...!
SWOOSH
SWISH

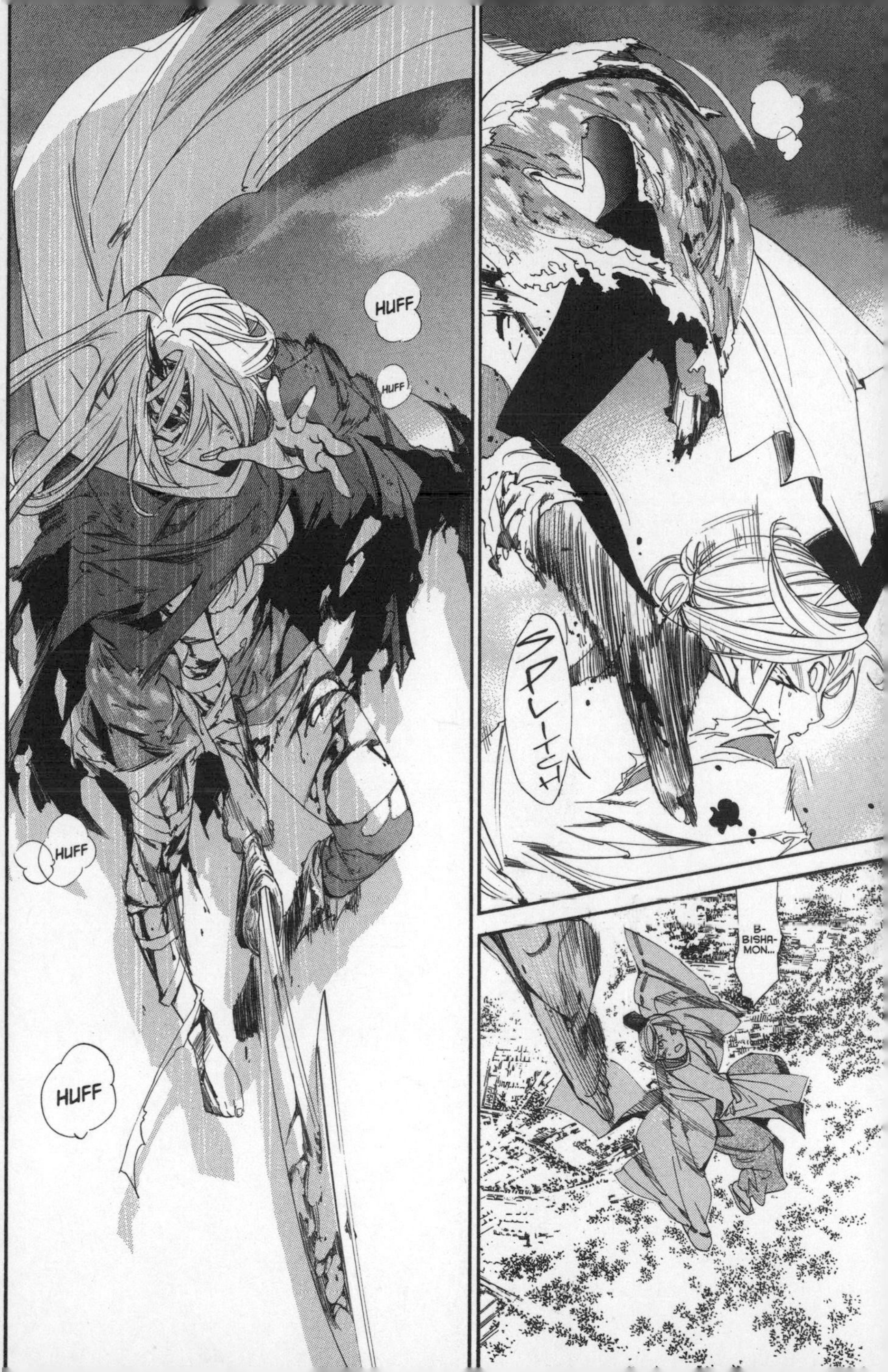
SPLITCH
B-BISHAMON...
HUFF
HUFF
HUFF
HUFF

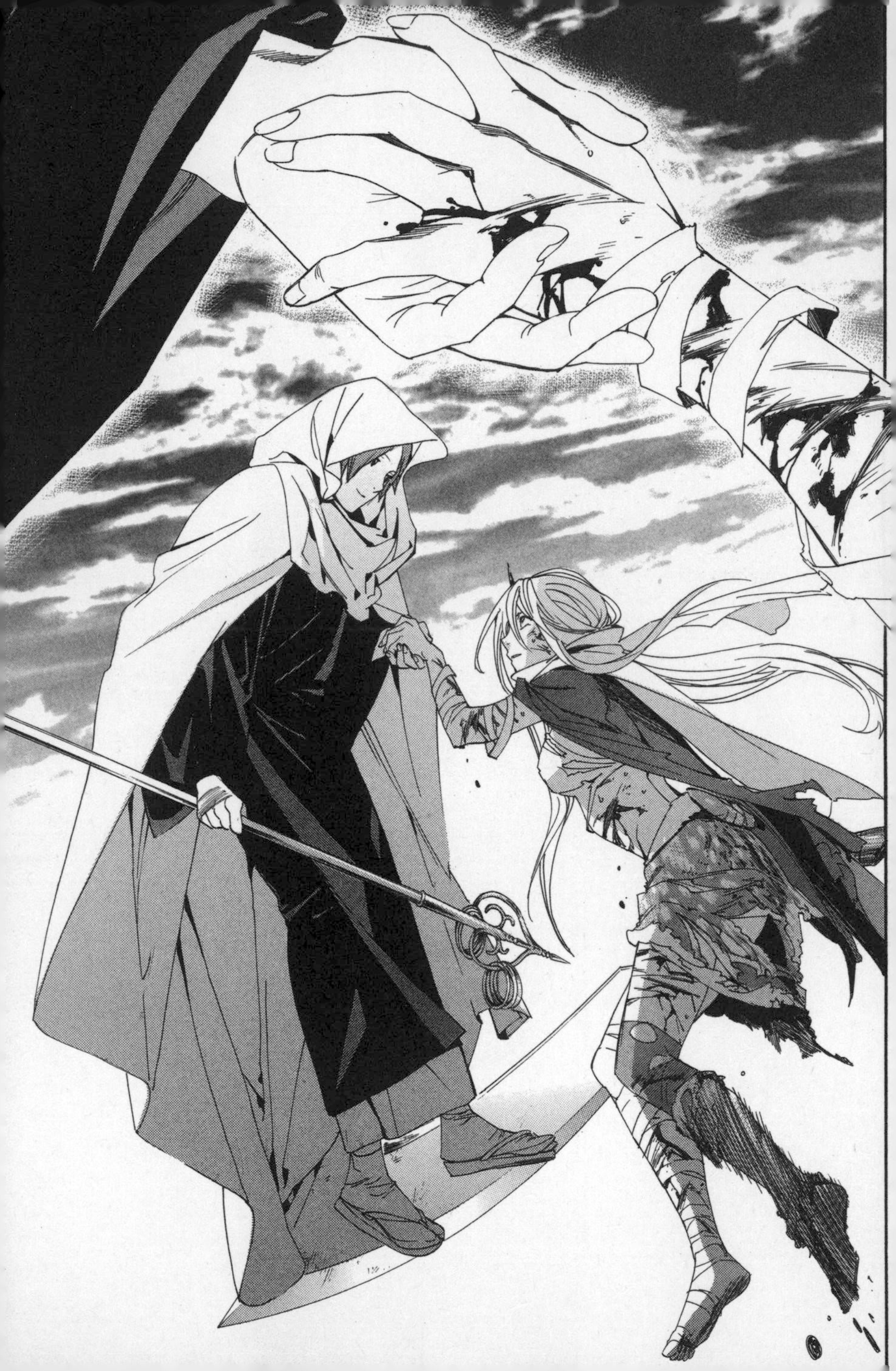

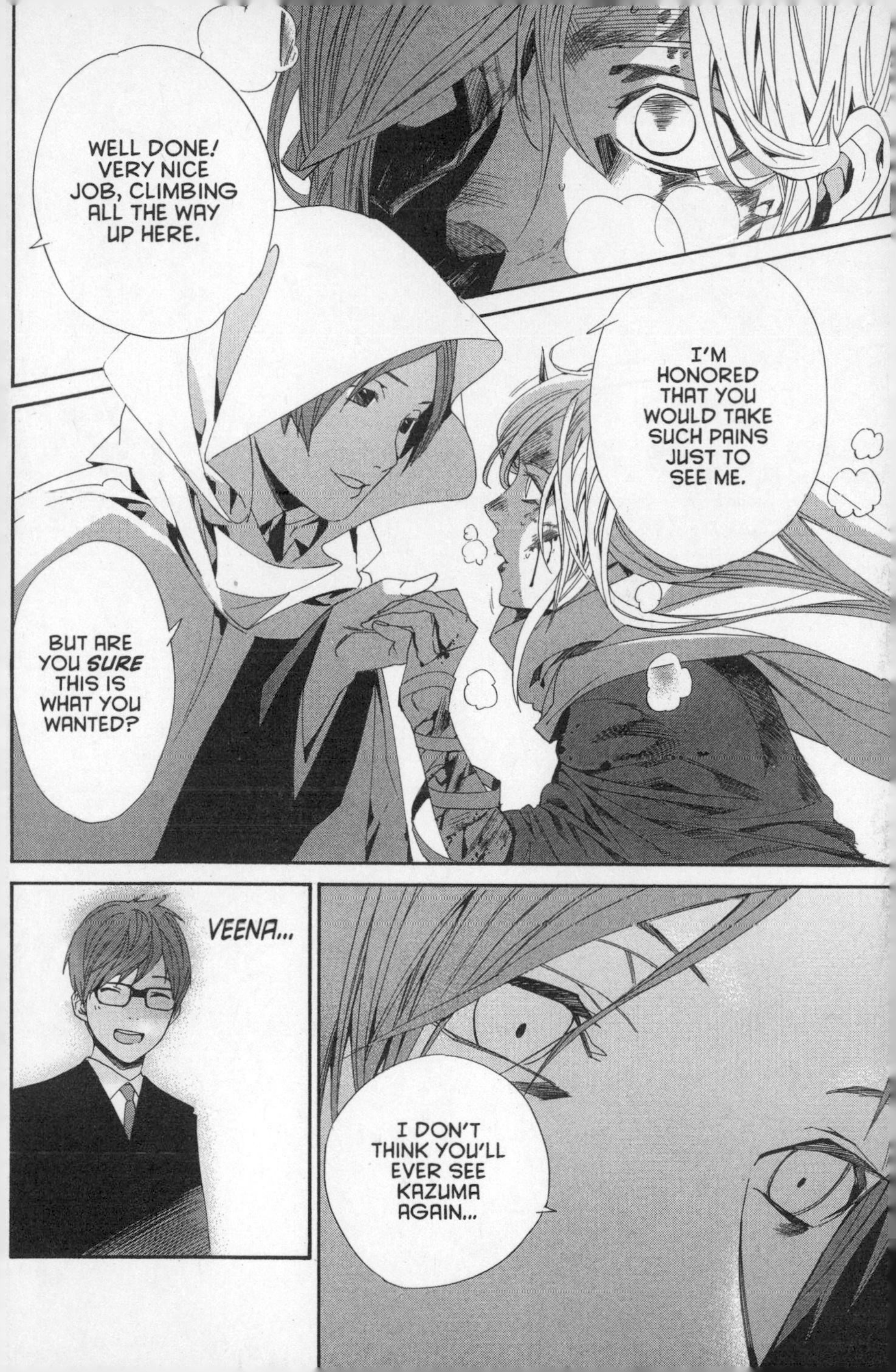
WELL DONE! VERY NICE JOB, CLIMBING ALL THE WAY UP HERE.
I'M HONORED THAT YOU WOULD TAKE SUCH PAINS JUST TO SEE ME.
BUT ARE YOU *SURE* THIS IS WHAT YOU WANTED?
I DON'T THINK YOU'LL EVER SEE KAZUMA AGAIN...
VEENA...

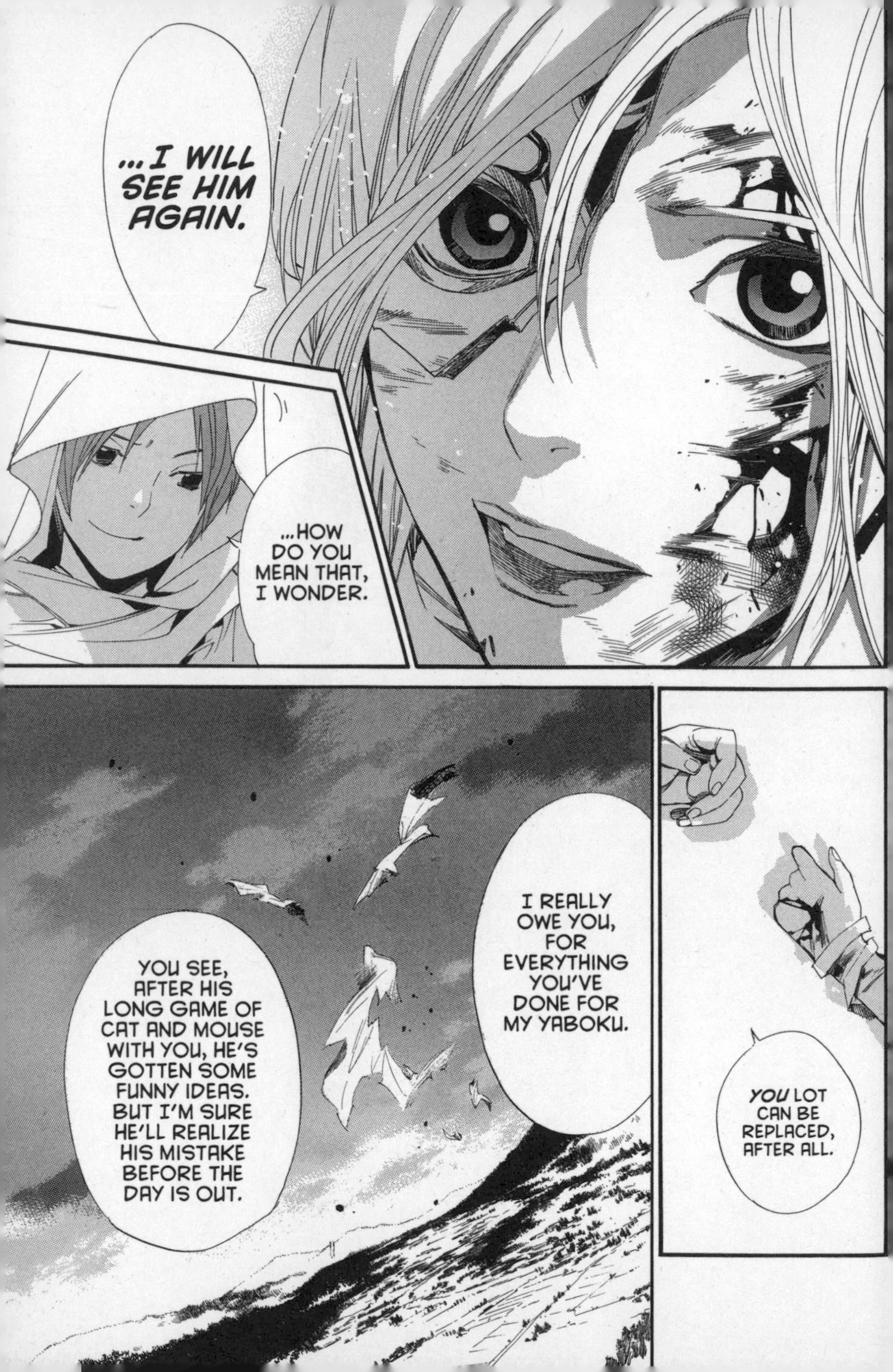
...I WILL SEE HIM AGAIN.
...HOW DO YOU MEAN THAT, I WONDER.
YOU LOT CAN BE REPLACED, AFTER ALL.
I REALLY OWE YOU, FOR EVERYTHING YOU'VE DONE FOR MY YABOKU.
YOU SEE, AFTER HIS LONG GAME OF CAT AND MOUSE WITH YOU, HE'S GOTTEN SOME FUNNY IDEAS. BUT I'M SURE HE'LL REALIZE HIS MISTAKE BEFORE THE DAY IS OUT.

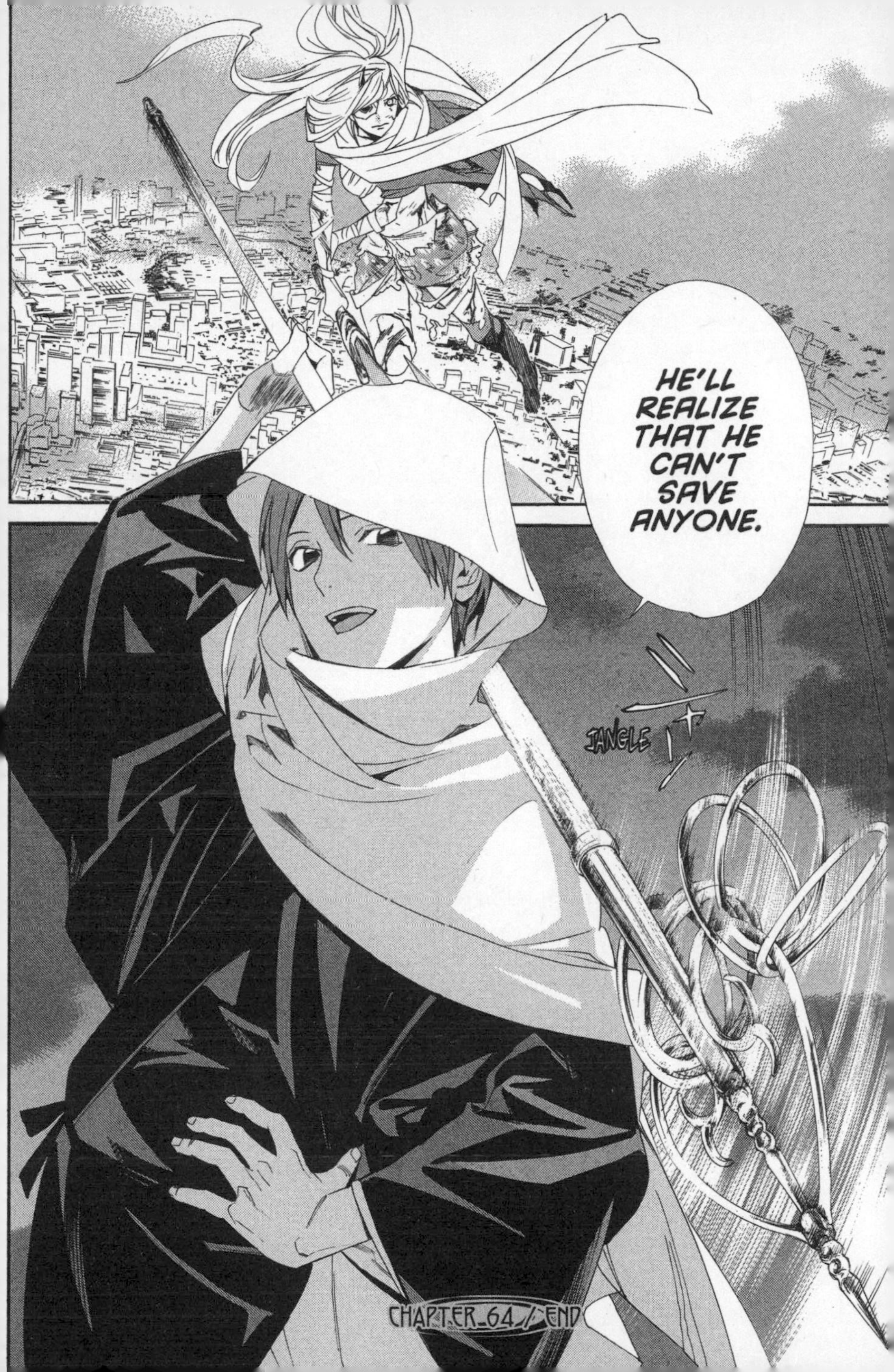
HE'LL REALIZE THAT HE CAN'T SAVE ANYONE.
JANGLE
CHAPTER 64 / END

野

兽

神

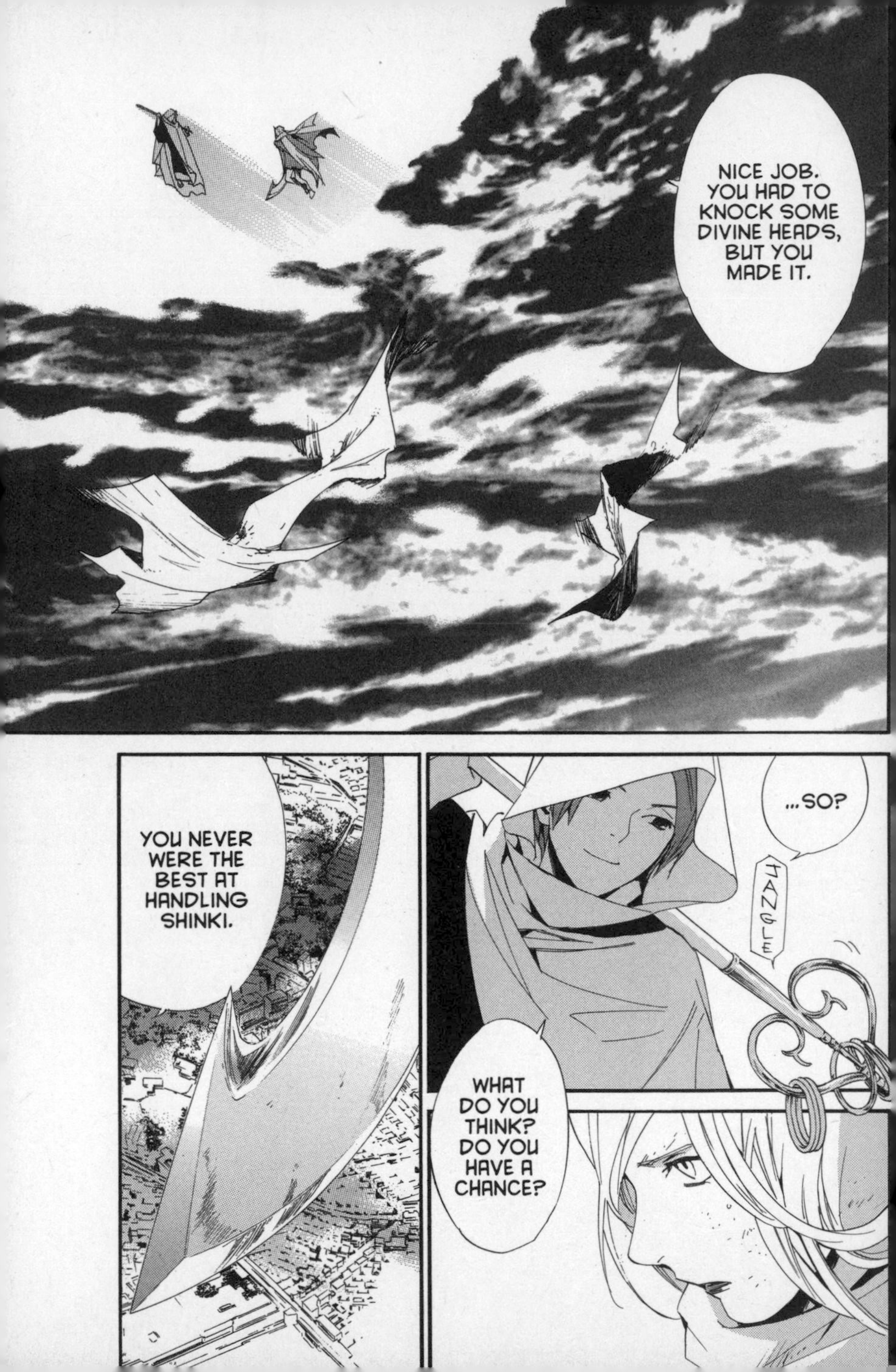
NICE JOB. YOU HAD TO KNOCK SOME DIVINE HEADS, BUT YOU MADE IT.
...SO?
JANGLE
WHAT DO YOU THINK? DO YOU HAVE A CHANCE?
YOU NEVER WERE THE BEST AT HANDLING SHINKI.

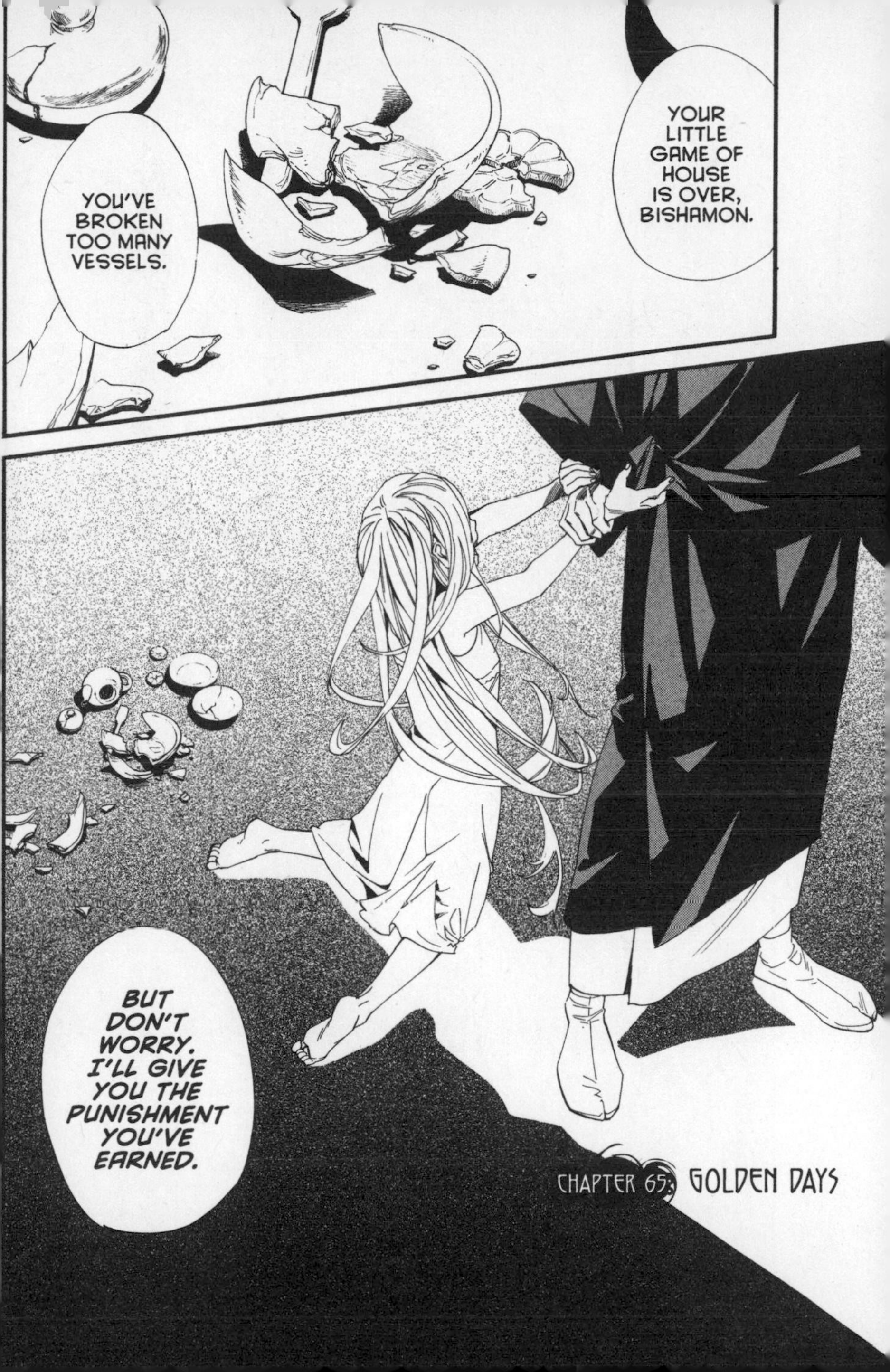
YOUR LITTLE GAME OF HOUSE IS OVER, BISHAMON.
YOU'VE BROKEN TOO MANY VESSELS.
BUT DON'T WORRY. I'LL GIVE YOU THE PUNISHMENT YOU'VE EARNED.
CHAPTER 65: GOLDEN DAYS

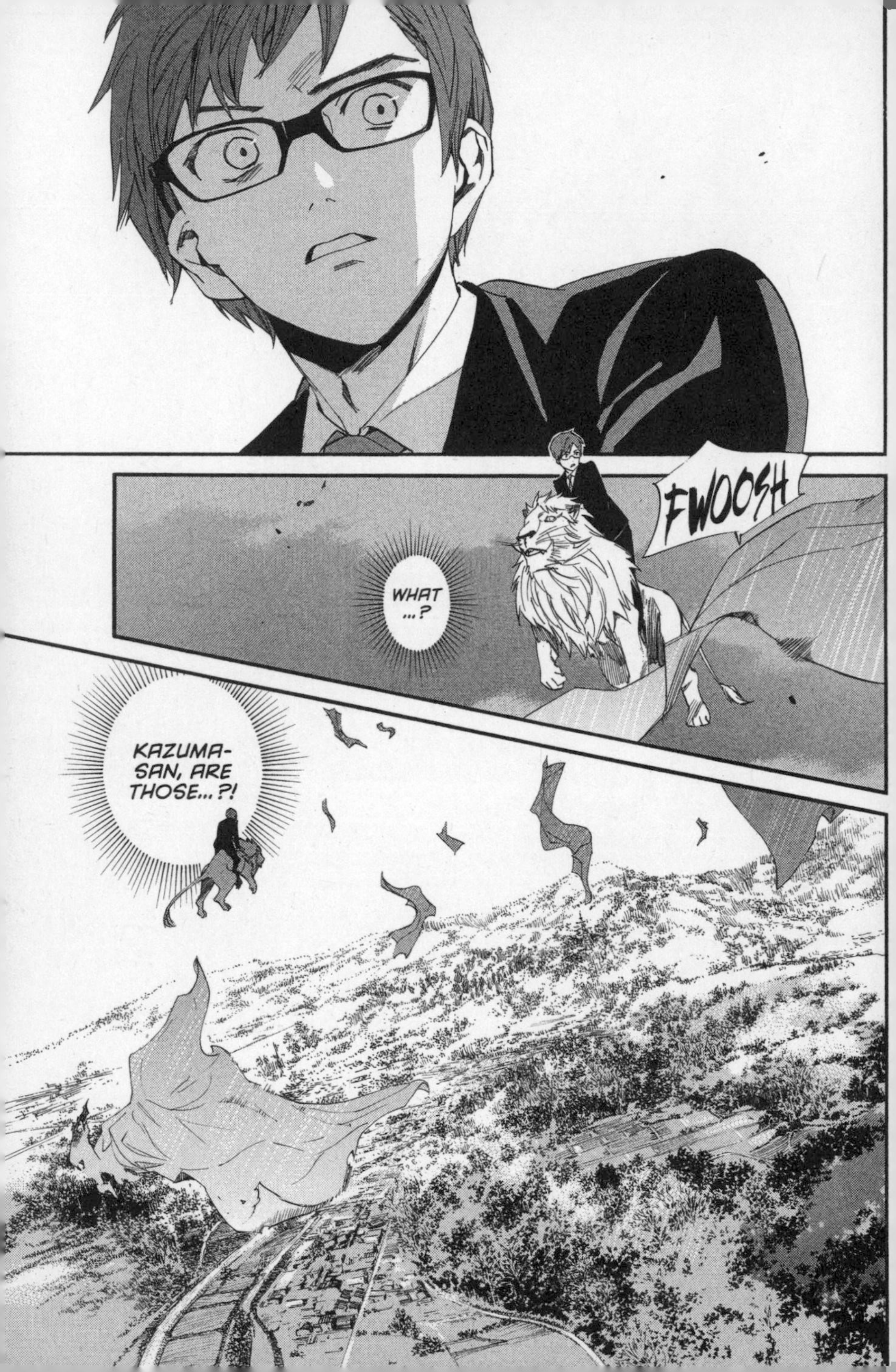
FWOOSH
WHAT ...?
KAZUMA-SAN, ARE THOSE...?!

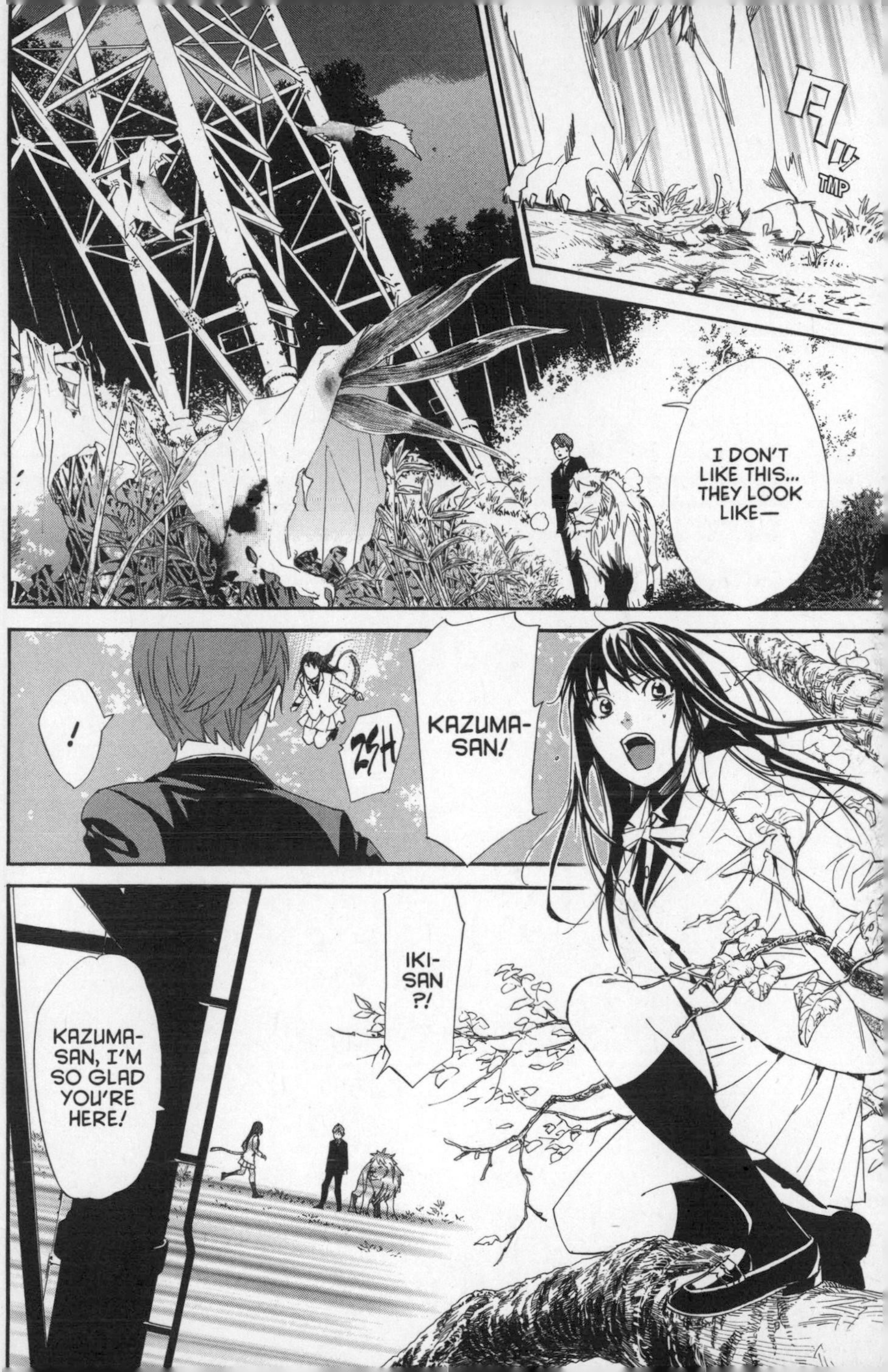
TMP
I DON'T LIKE THIS... THEY LOOK LIKE—
KAZUMA-SAN!
ZSH
!
IKI-SAN?!
KAZUMA-SAN, I'M SO GLAD YOU'RE HERE!

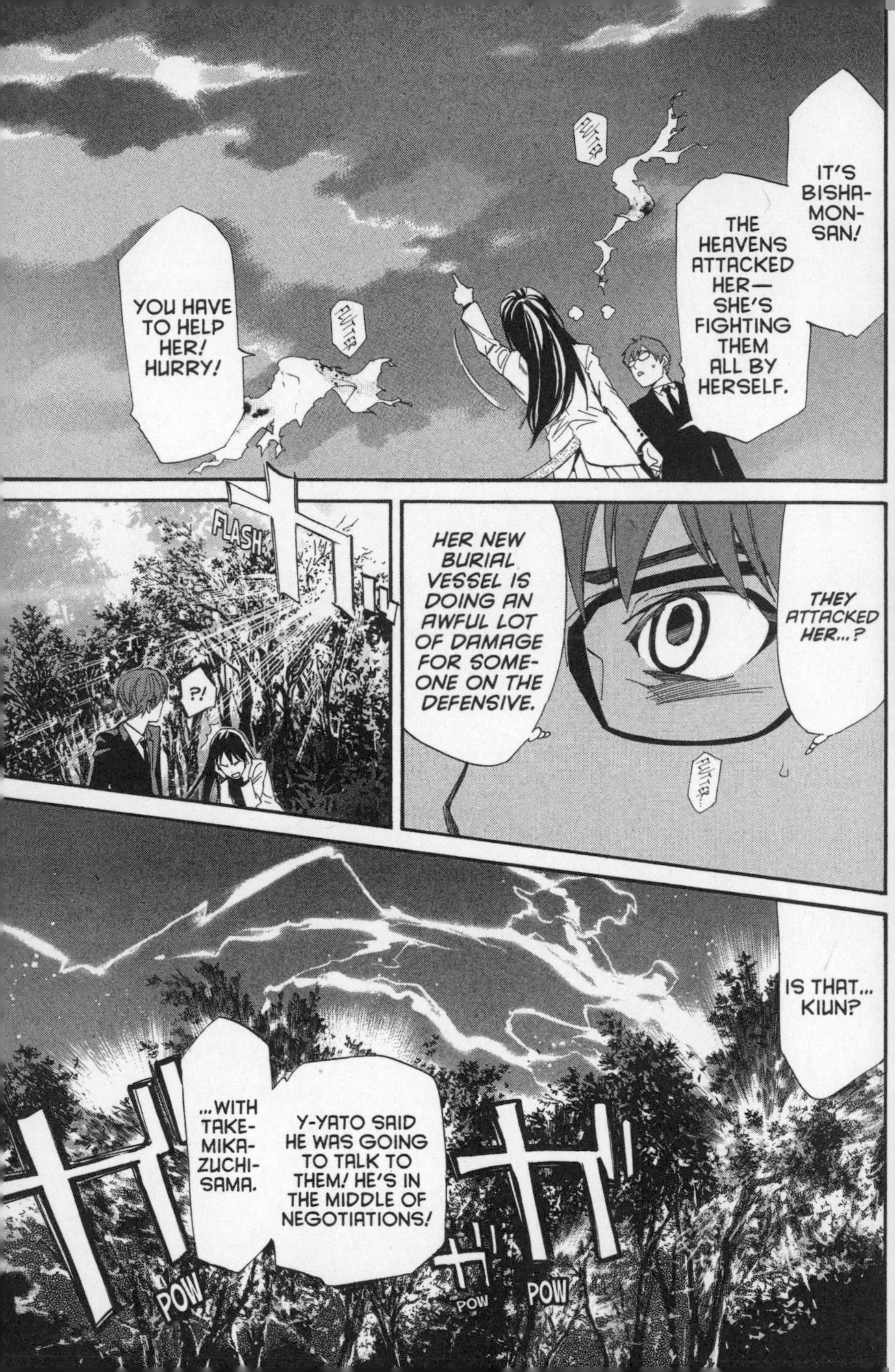
IT'S BISHA-MON-SAN!
THE HEAVENS ATTACKED HER— SHE'S FIGHTING THEM ALL BY HERSELF.
FLUTTER
FLUTTER
YOU HAVE TO HELP HER! HURRY!
THEY ATTACKED HER...?
HER NEW BURIAL VESSEL IS DOING AN AWFUL LOT OF DAMAGE FOR SOME-ONE ON THE DEFENSIVE.
FLUTTER...
FLASH
?!
IS THAT... KIUN?
Y-YATO SAID HE WAS GOING TO TALK TO THEM! HE'S IN THE MIDDLE OF NEGOTIATIONS!
...WITH TAKE-MIKA-ZUCHI-SAMA.
POW
POW
POW

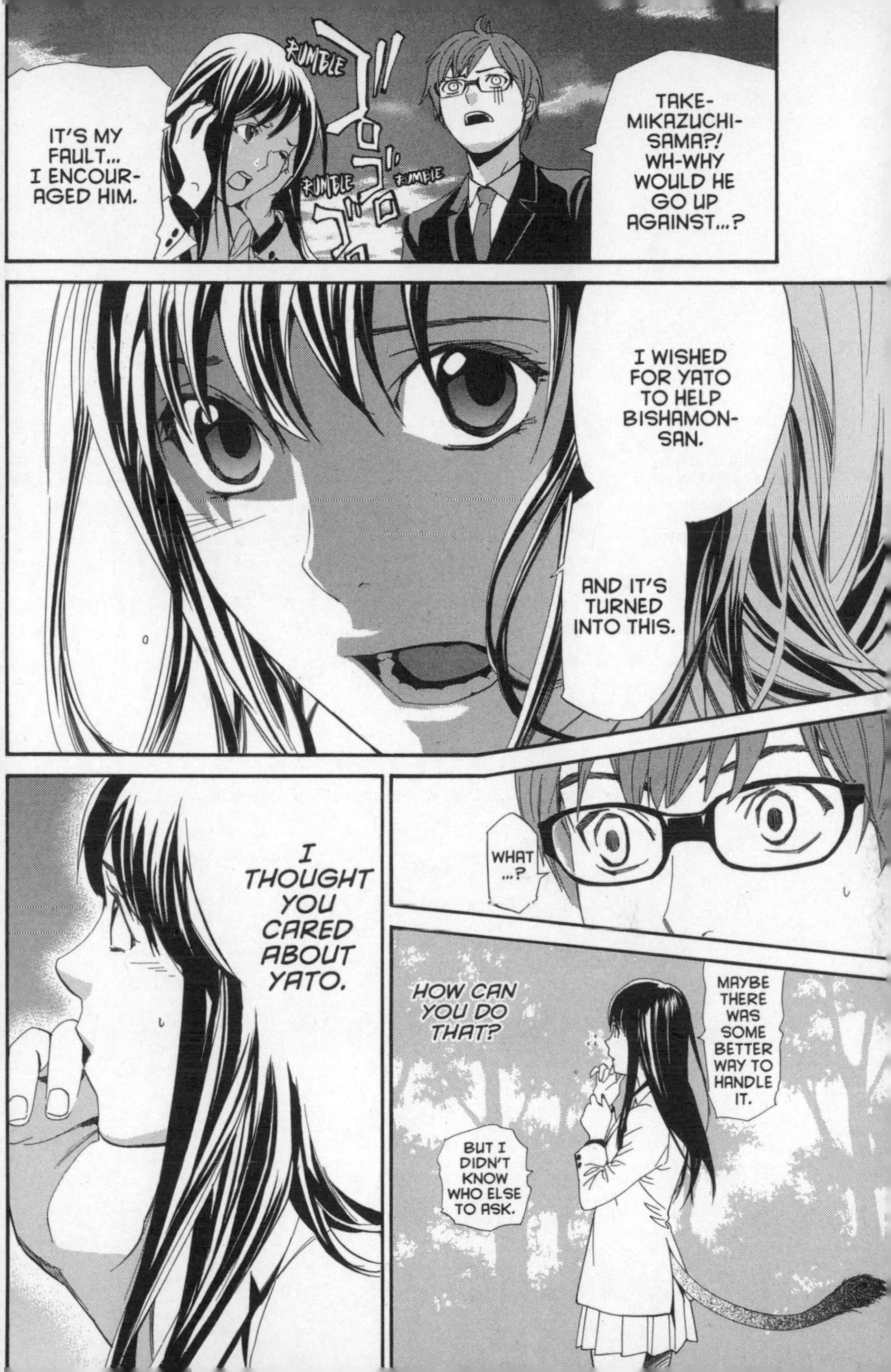
TAKE-MIKAZUCHI-SAMA?! WH-WHY WOULD HE GO UP AGAINST...?
RUMBLE
RUMBLE
RUMBLE
IT'S MY FAULT... I ENCOURAGED HIM.
I WISHED FOR YATO TO HELP BISHAMON-SAN.
AND IT'S TURNED INTO THIS.
WHAT ...?
MAYBE THERE WAS SOME BETTER WAY TO HANDLE IT.
HOW CAN YOU DO THAT?
BUT I DIDN'T KNOW WHO ELSE TO ASK.
I THOUGHT YOU CARED ABOUT YATO.

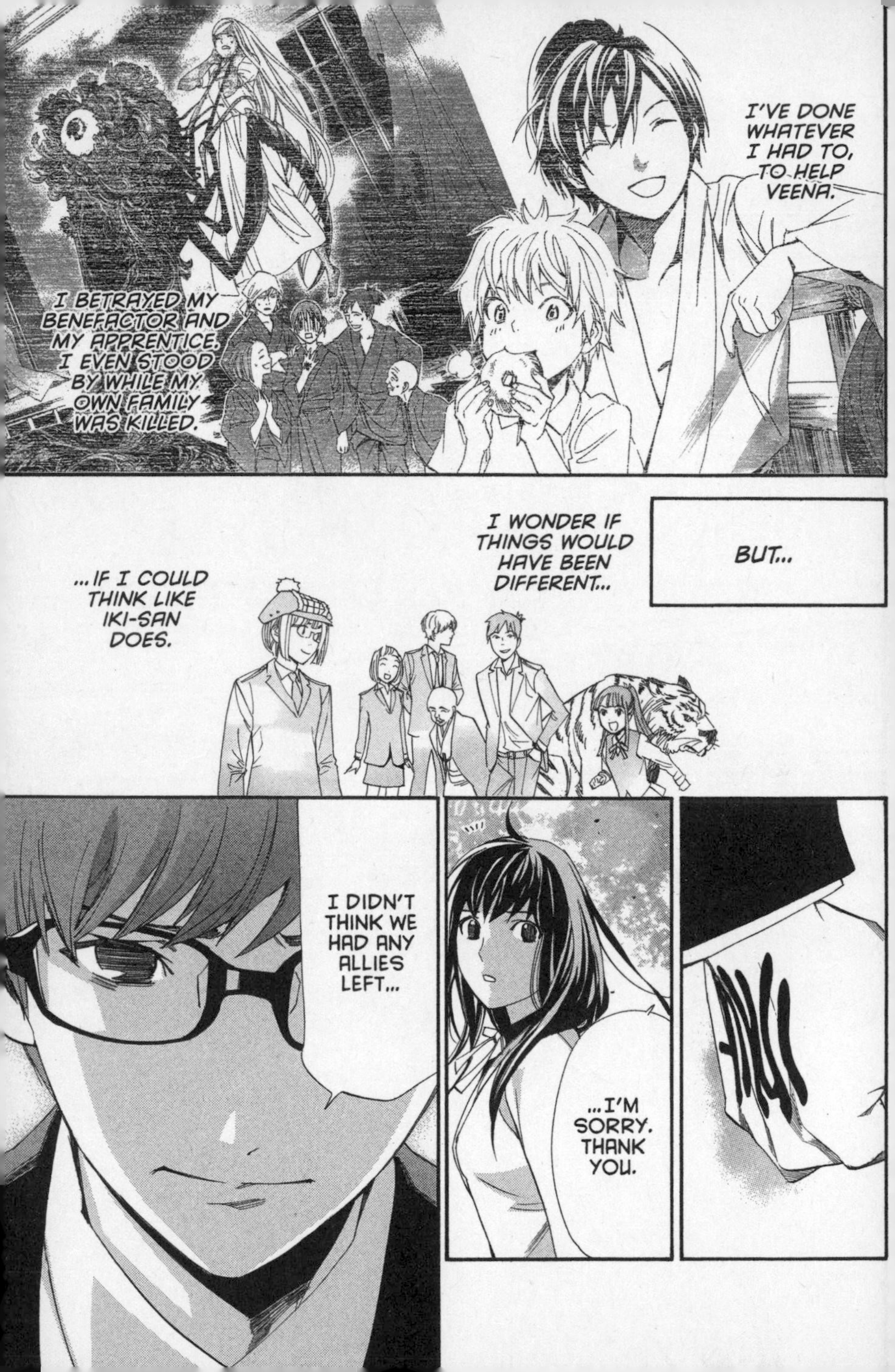
I'VE DONE WHATEVER I HAD TO, TO HELP VEENA.
I BETRAYED MY BENEFACTOR AND MY APPRENTICE. I EVEN STOOD BY WHILE MY OWN FAMILY WAS KILLED.
BUT...
I WONDER IF THINGS WOULD HAVE BEEN DIFFERENT...
...IF I COULD THINK LIKE IKI-SAN DOES.
...I'M SORRY. THANK YOU.
I DIDN'T THINK WE HAD ANY ALLIES LEFT...

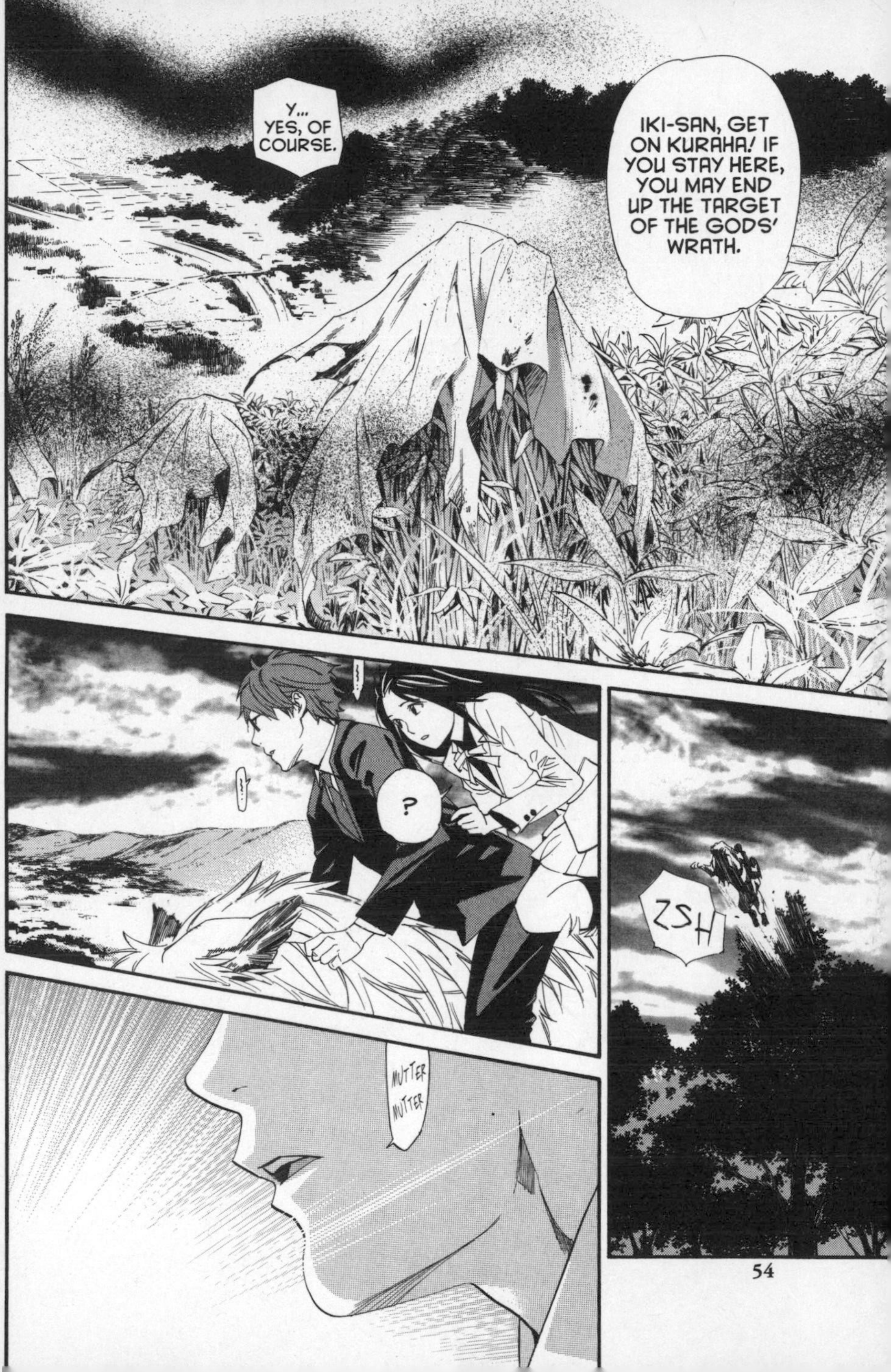
IKI-SAN, GET ON KURAHA! IF YOU STAY HERE, YOU MAY END UP THE TARGET OF THE GODS' WRATH.
Y... YES, OF COURSE.
ZSH
...
...
?
MUTTER MUTTER

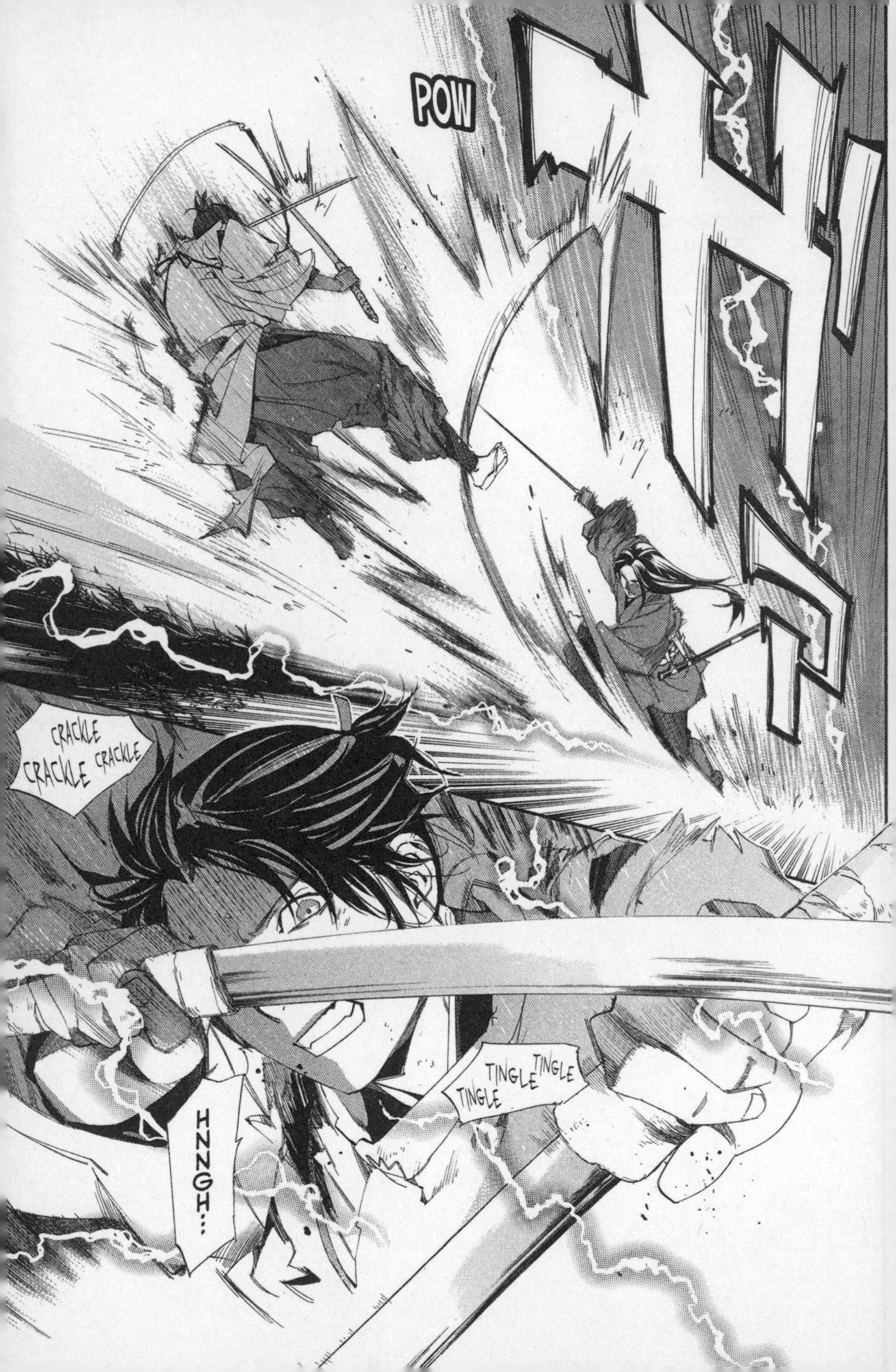
POW
CRACKLE CRACKLE CRACKLE
TINGLE TINGLE TINGLE
HNNGH...

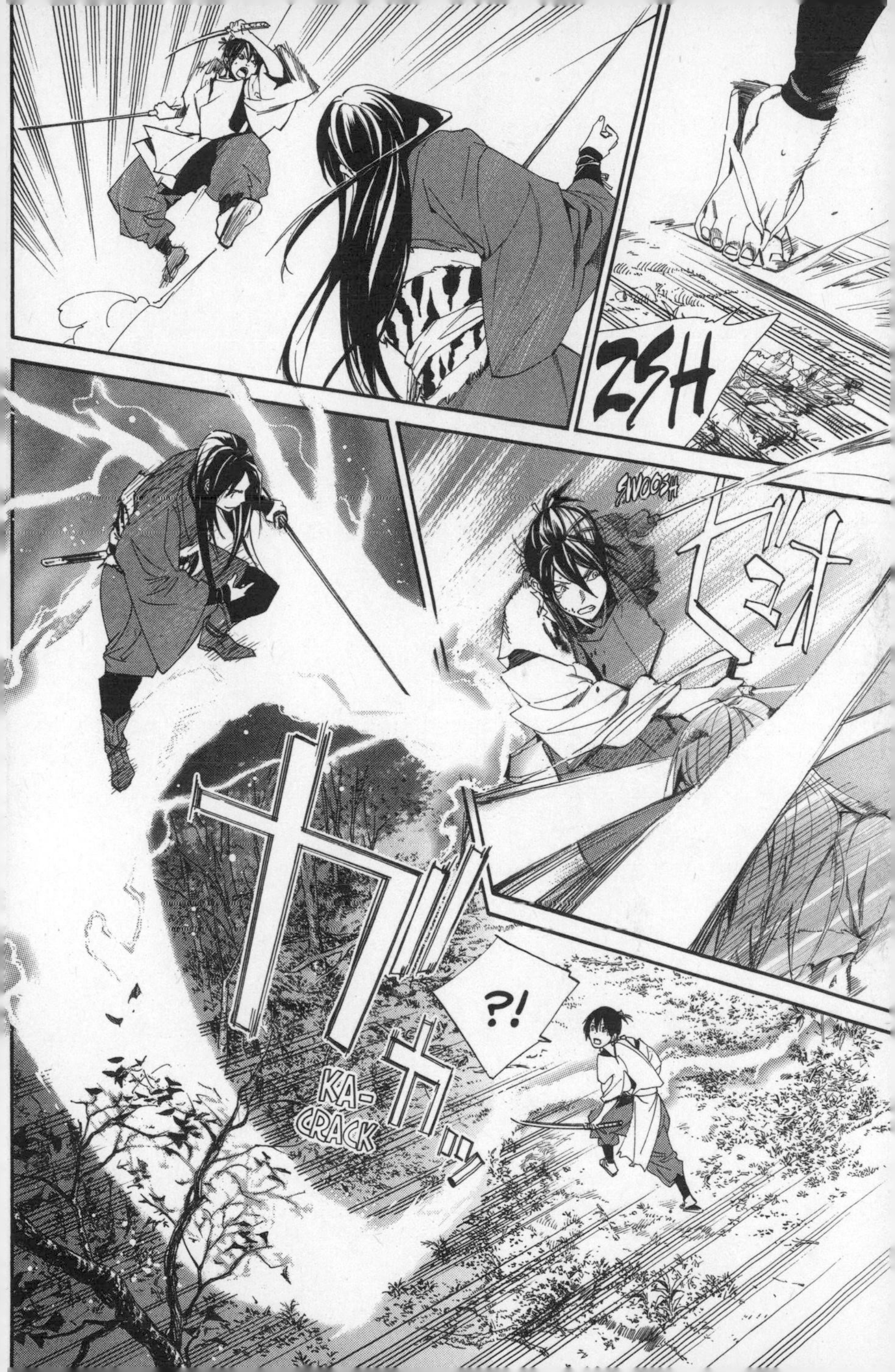
ZSH
SWOOSH
?!
KA-
CRACK

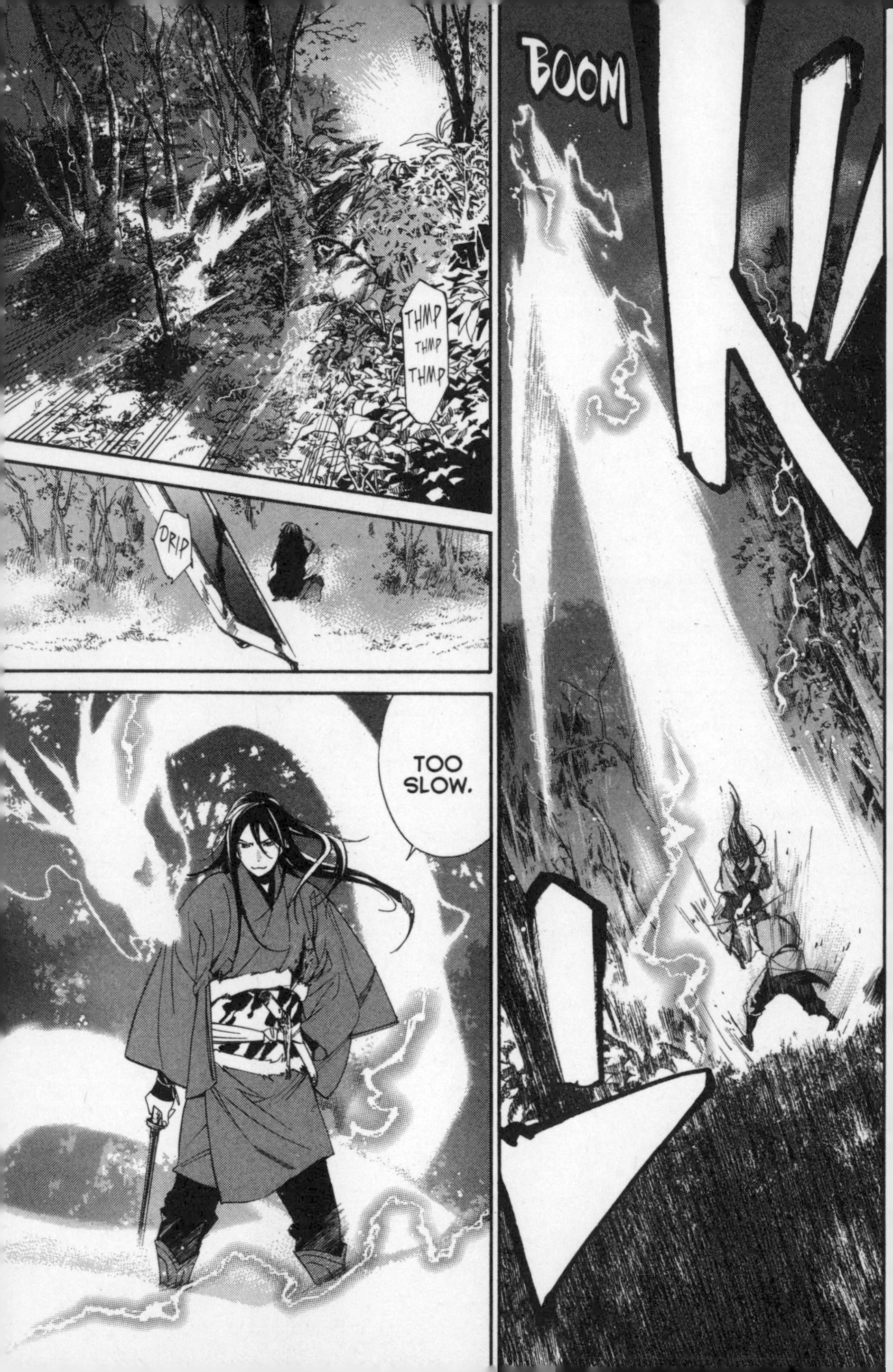
BOOM
THMP THMP THMP
DRIP
TOO SLOW.

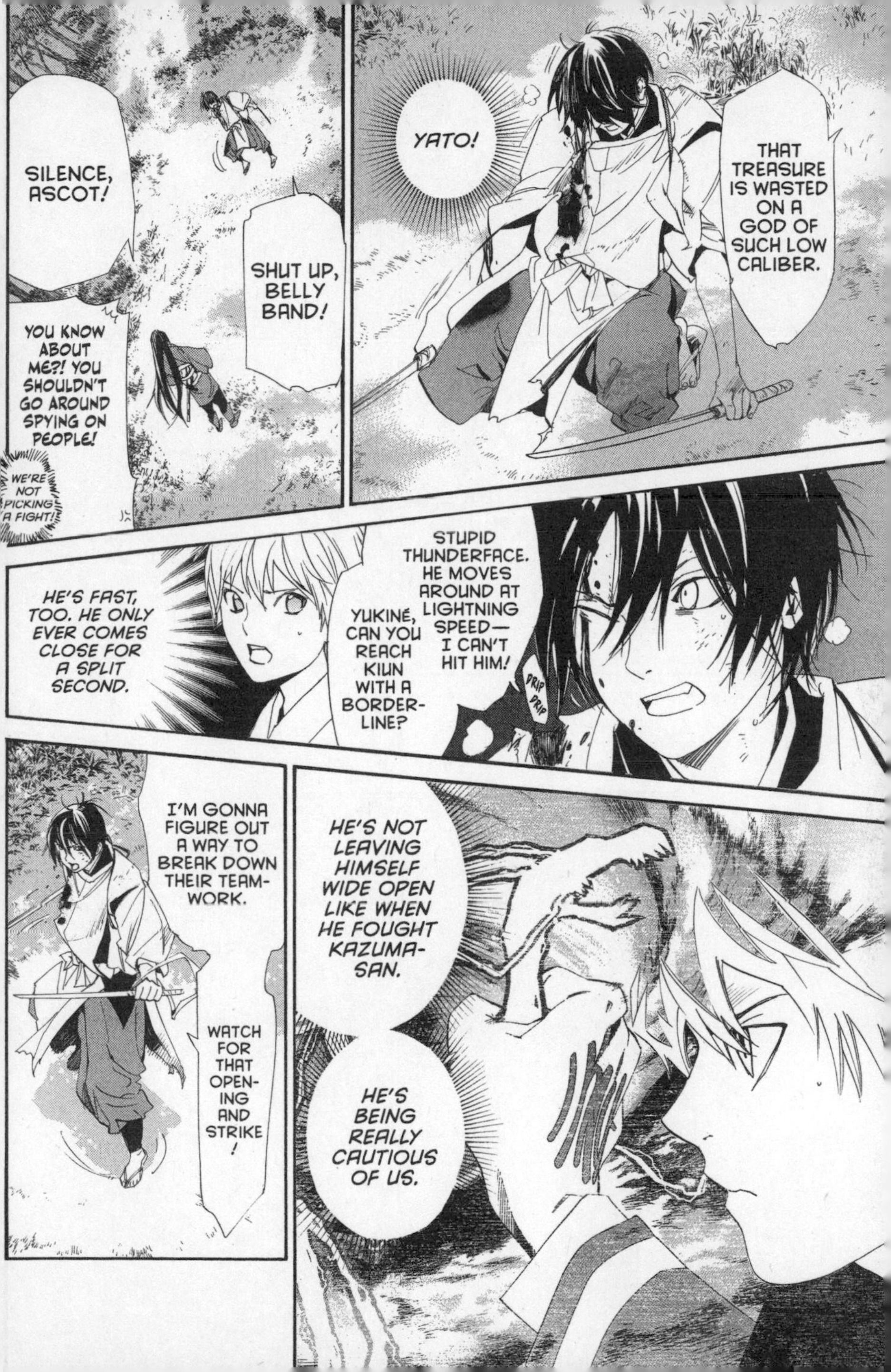
THAT TREASURE IS WASTED ON A GOD OF SUCH LOW CALIBER.
YATO!
SHUT UP, BELLY BAND!
SILENCE, ASCOT!
YOU KNOW ABOUT ME?! YOU SHOULDN'T GO AROUND SPYING ON PEOPLE!
WE'RE NOT PICKING A FIGHT!
STUPID THUNDERFACE. HE MOVES AROUND AT LIGHTNING SPEED—I CAN'T HIT HIM!
DRIP DRIP
YUKINÉ, CAN YOU REACH KIUN WITH A BORDERLINE?
HE'S FAST, TOO. HE ONLY EVER COMES CLOSE FOR A SPLIT SECOND.
HE'S NOT LEAVING HIMSELF WIDE OPEN LIKE WHEN HE FOUGHT KAZUMA-SAN.
HE'S BEING REALLY CAUTIOUS OF US.
I'M GONNA FIGURE OUT A WAY TO BREAK DOWN THEIR TEAM-WORK.
WATCH FOR THAT OPENING AND STRIKE!

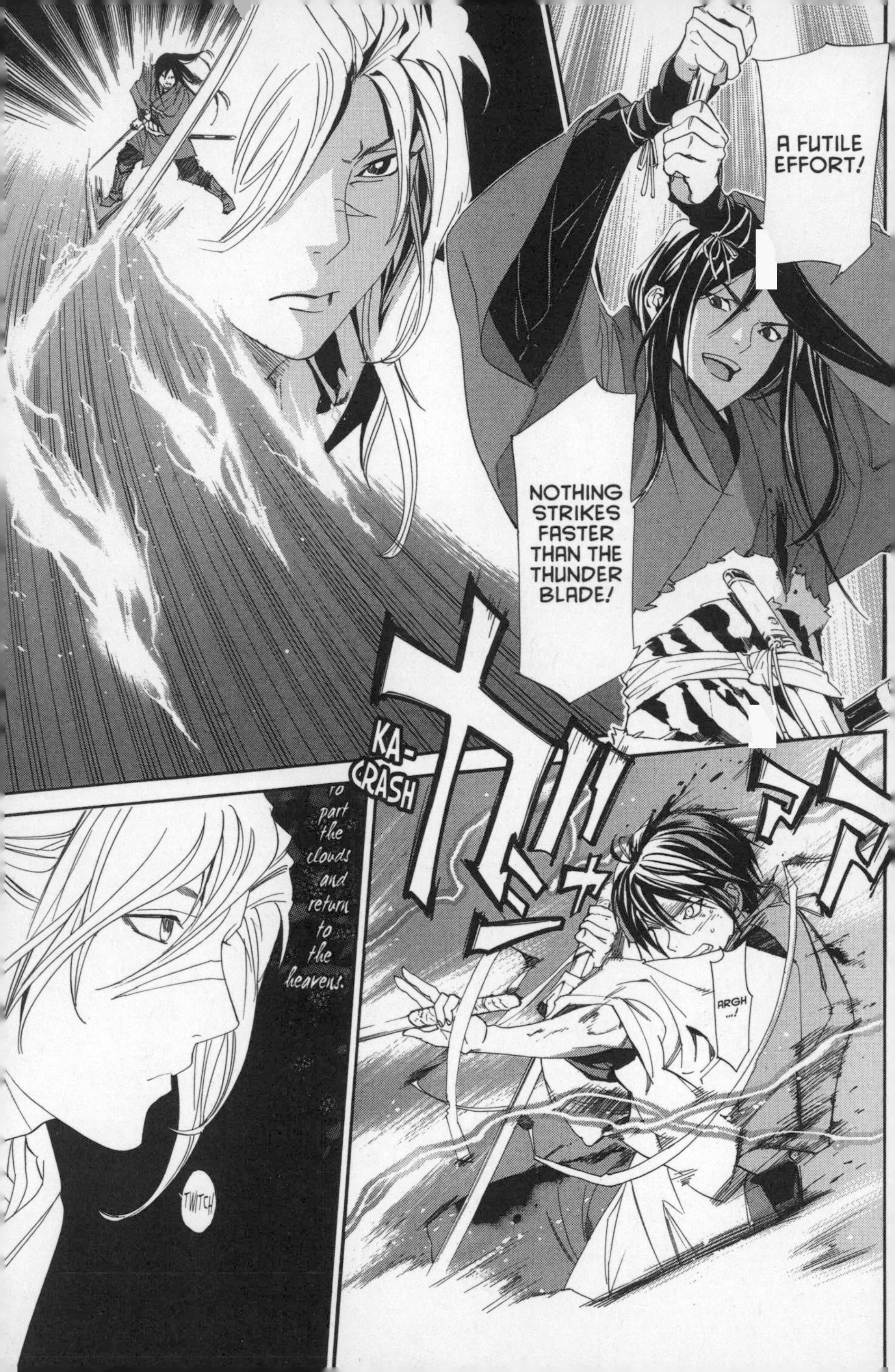
A FUTILE EFFORT!
NOTHING STRIKES FASTER THAN THE THUNDER BLADE!
KA-CRASH
ARGH ...!
to part the clouds and return to the heavens.
TWITCH

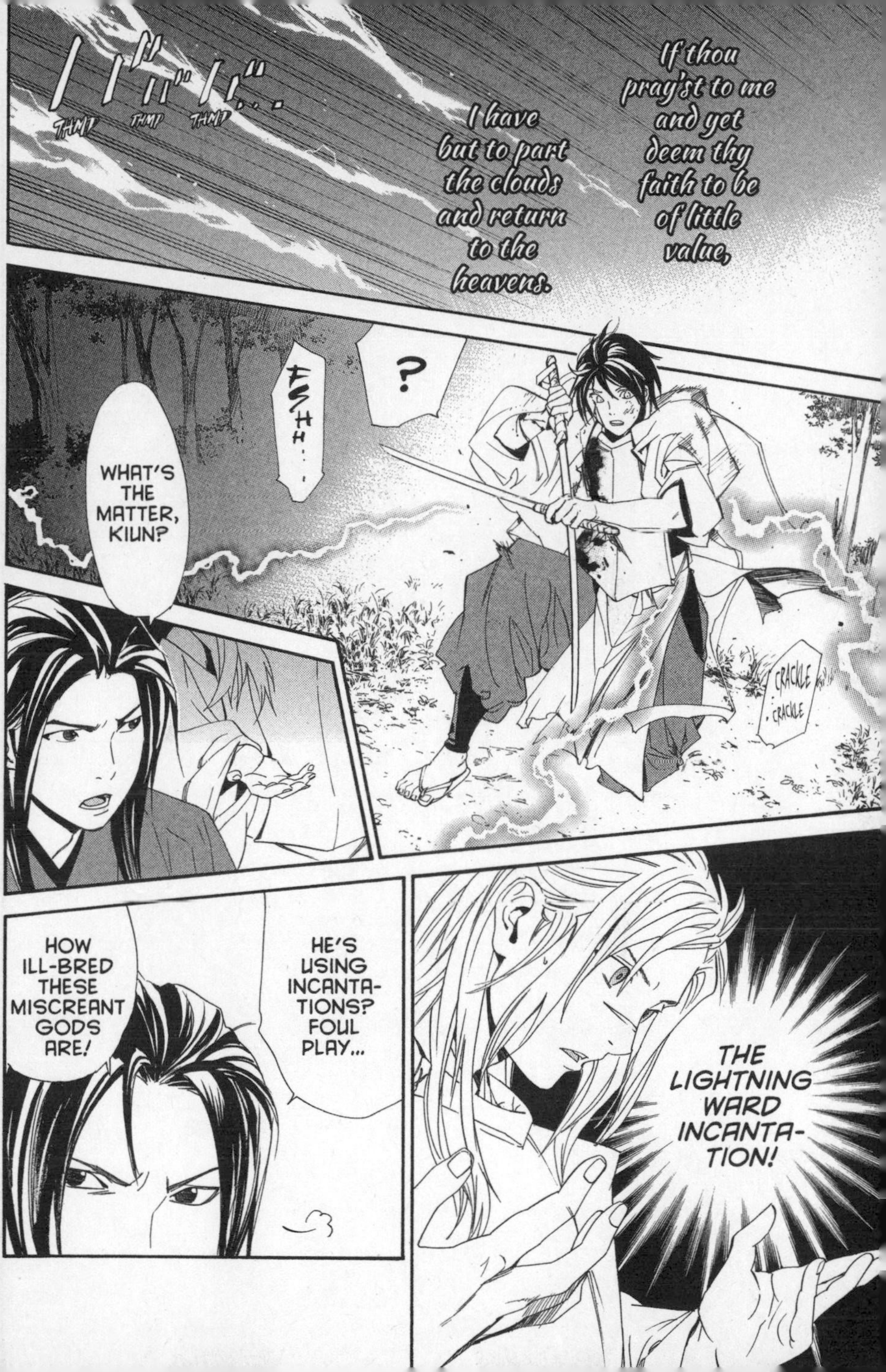
THMP THMP THMP
If thou pray'st to me and yet deem thy faith to be of little value,
I have but to part the clouds and return to the heavens.
?
FSHH...
CRACKLE CRACKLE
WHAT'S THE MATTER, KIUN?
THE LIGHTNING WARD INCANTATION!
HE'S USING INCANTATIONS? FOUL PLAY...
HOW ILL-BRED THESE MISCREANT GODS ARE!

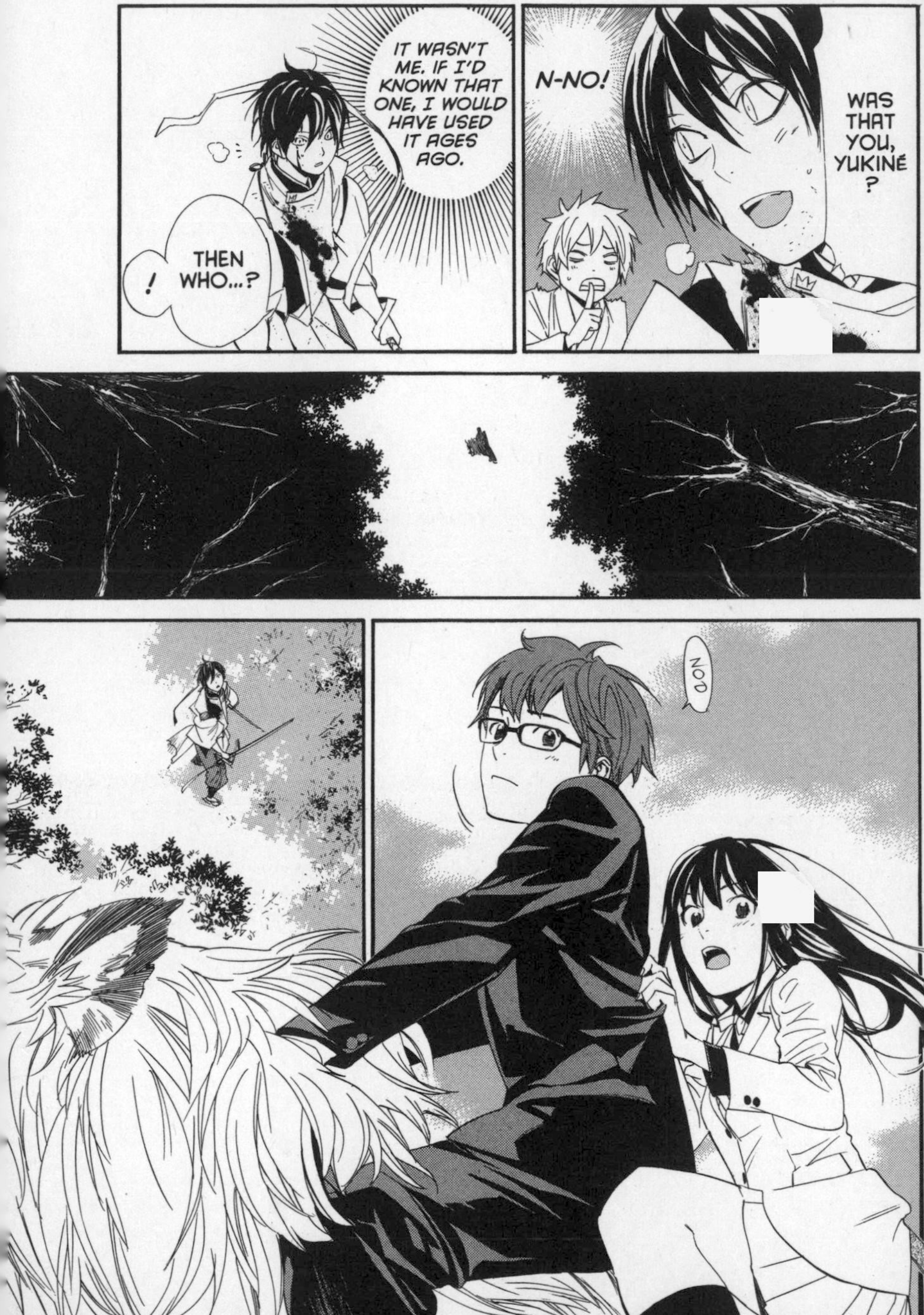
WAS THAT YOU, YUKINÉ?
N-NO!
IT WASN'T ME. IF I'D KNOWN THAT ONE, I WOULD HAVE USED IT AGES AGO.
THEN WHO...?
!

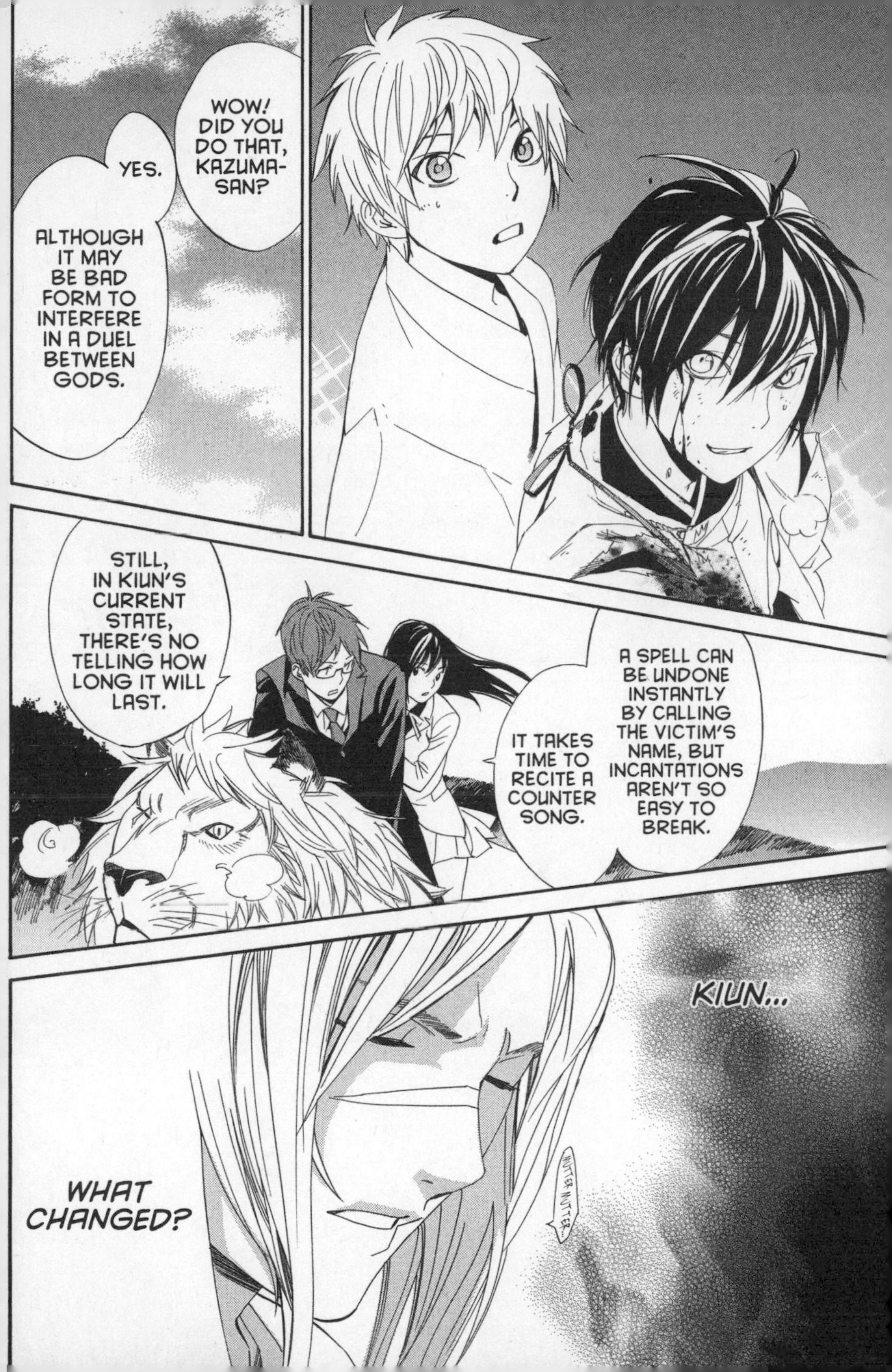
WOW! DID YOU DO THAT, KAZUMA-SAN?
YES.
ALTHOUGH IT MAY BE BAD FORM TO INTERFERE IN A DUEL BETWEEN GODS.
STILL, IN KIUN'S CURRENT STATE, THERE'S NO TELLING HOW LONG IT WILL LAST.
A SPELL CAN BE UNDONE INSTANTLY BY CALLING THE VICTIM'S NAME, BUT INCANTATIONS AREN'T SO EASY TO BREAK.
IT TAKES TIME TO RECITE A COUNTER SONG.
KIUN...
MUTTER MUTTER...
WHAT CHANGED?

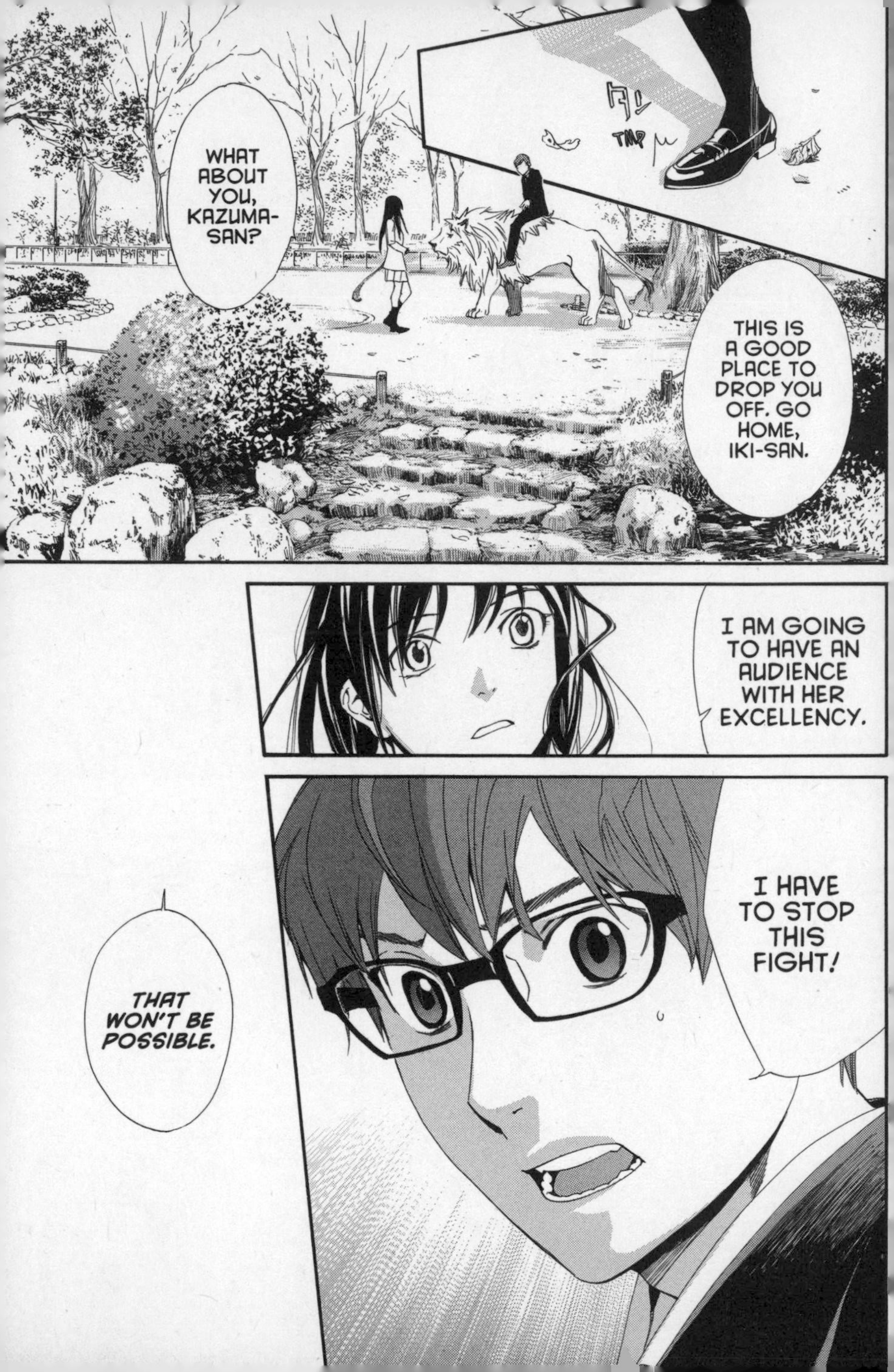
TMP
THIS IS A GOOD PLACE TO DROP YOU OFF. GO HOME, IKI-SAN.
WHAT ABOUT YOU, KAZUMA-SAN?
I AM GOING TO HAVE AN AUDIENCE WITH HER EXCELLENCY.
I HAVE TO STOP THIS FIGHT!
THAT WON'T BE POSSIBLE.

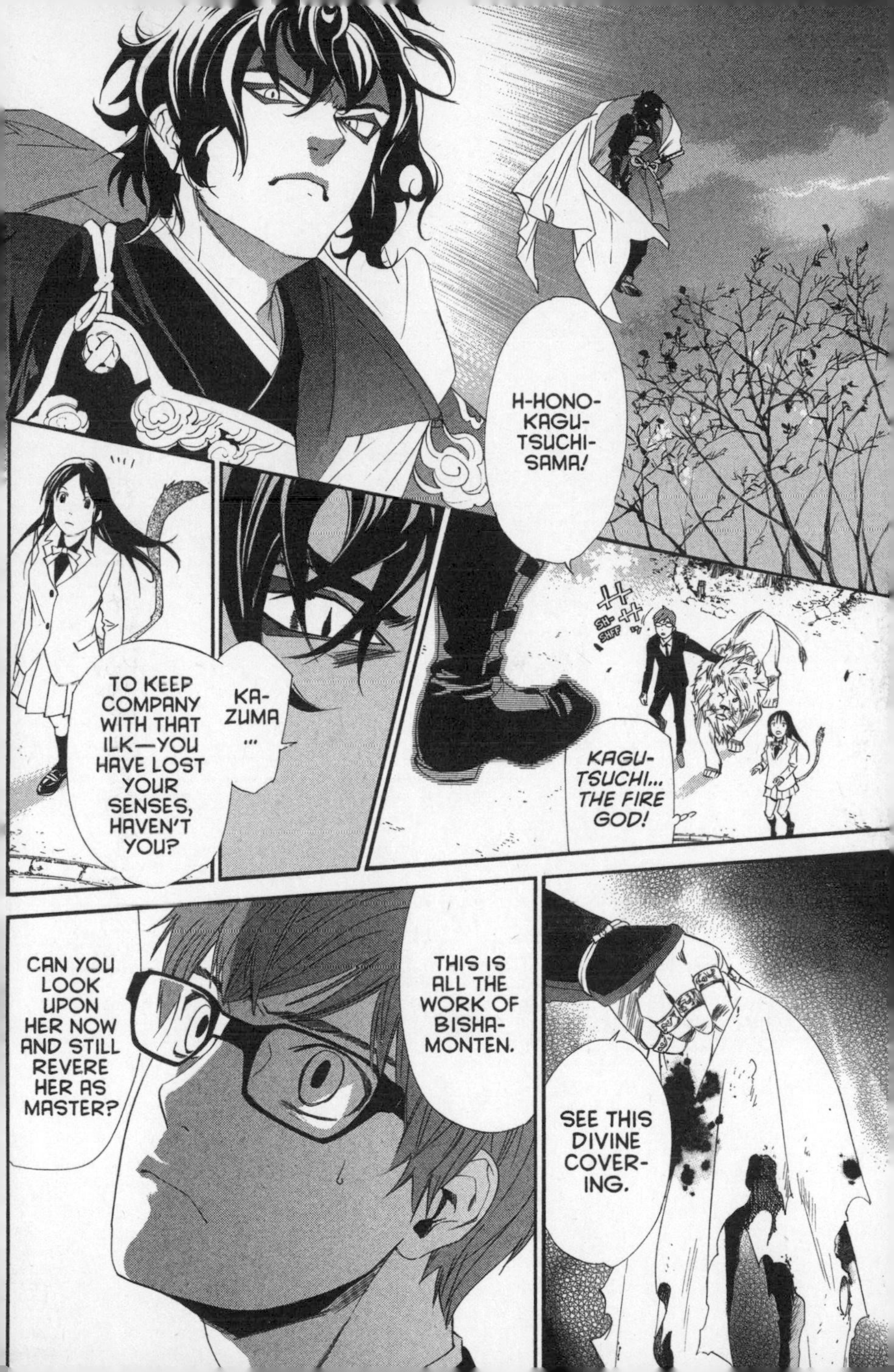
H-HONO-KAGU-TSUCHI-SAMA!
SH-SHFF
KAGU-TSUCHI... THE FIRE GOD!
KA-ZUMA...
TO KEEP COMPANY WITH THAT ILK—YOU HAVE LOST YOUR SENSES, HAVEN'T YOU?
SEE THIS DIVINE COVERING.
THIS IS ALL THE WORK OF BISHAMONTEN.
CAN YOU LOOK UPON HER NOW AND STILL REVERE HER AS MASTER?

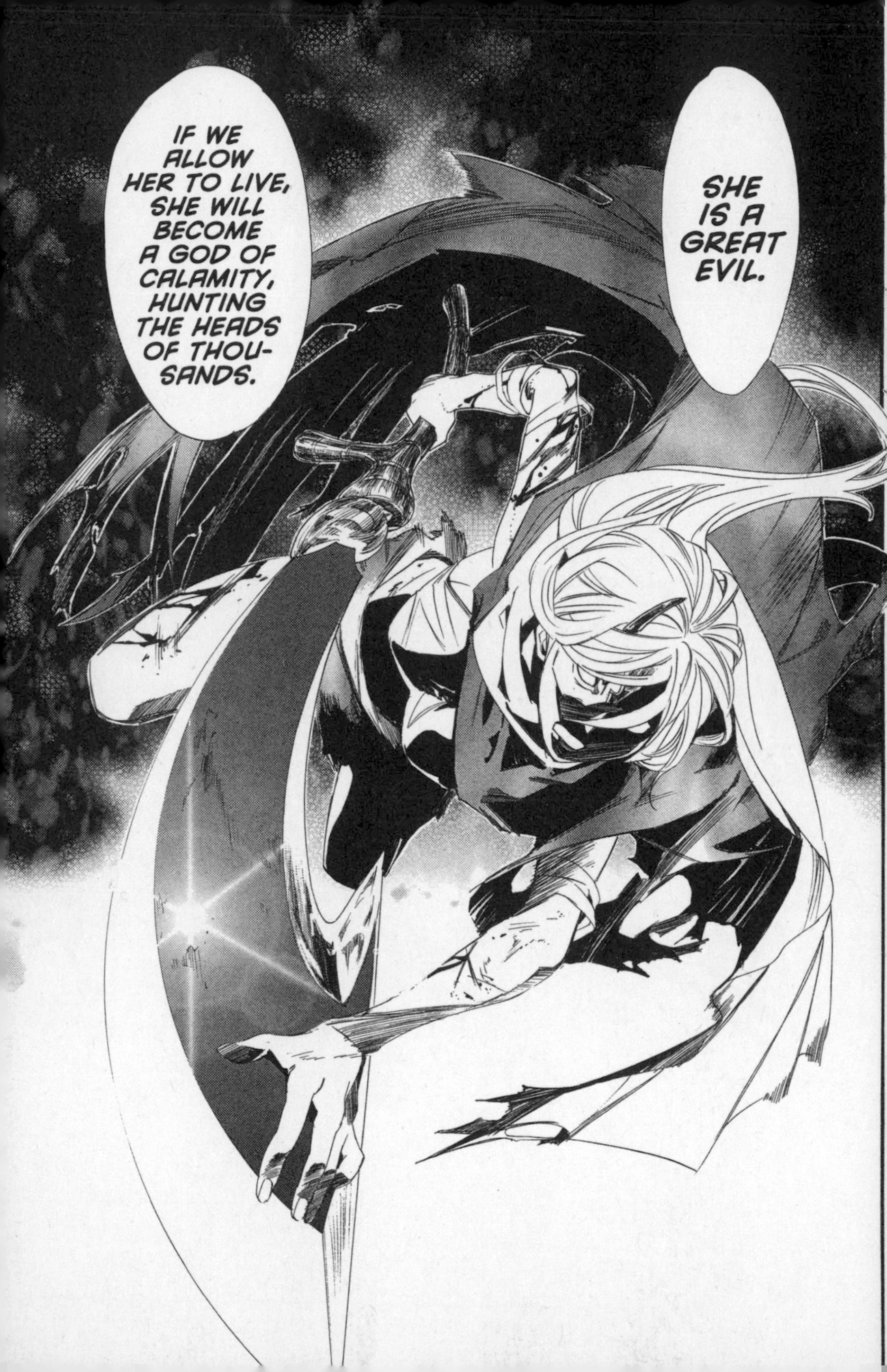
SHE IS A GREAT EVIL.
IF WE ALLOW HER TO LIVE, SHE WILL BECOME A GOD OF CALAMITY, HUNTING THE HEADS OF THOU-SANDS.

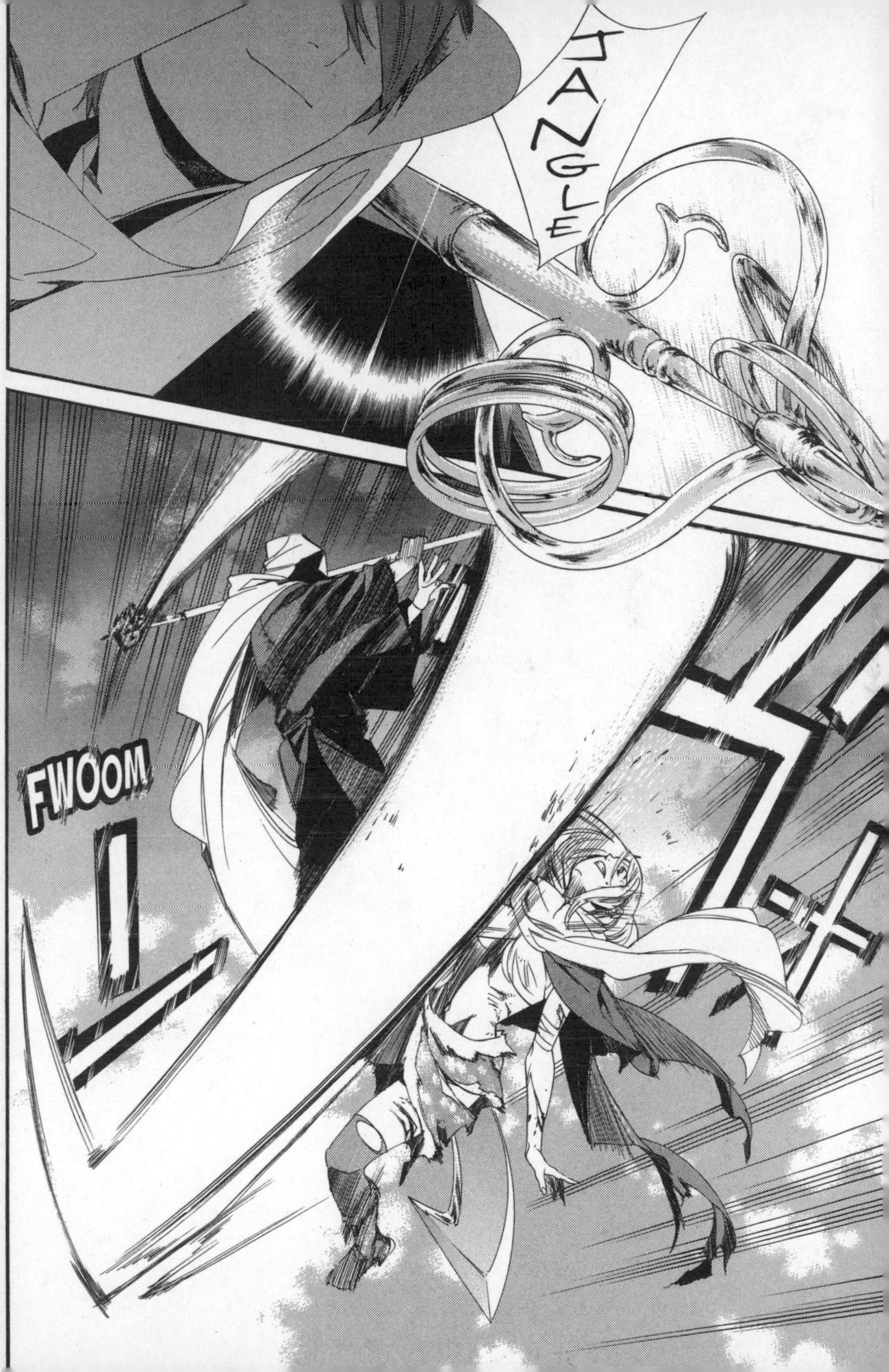
JANGLE
FWOOM

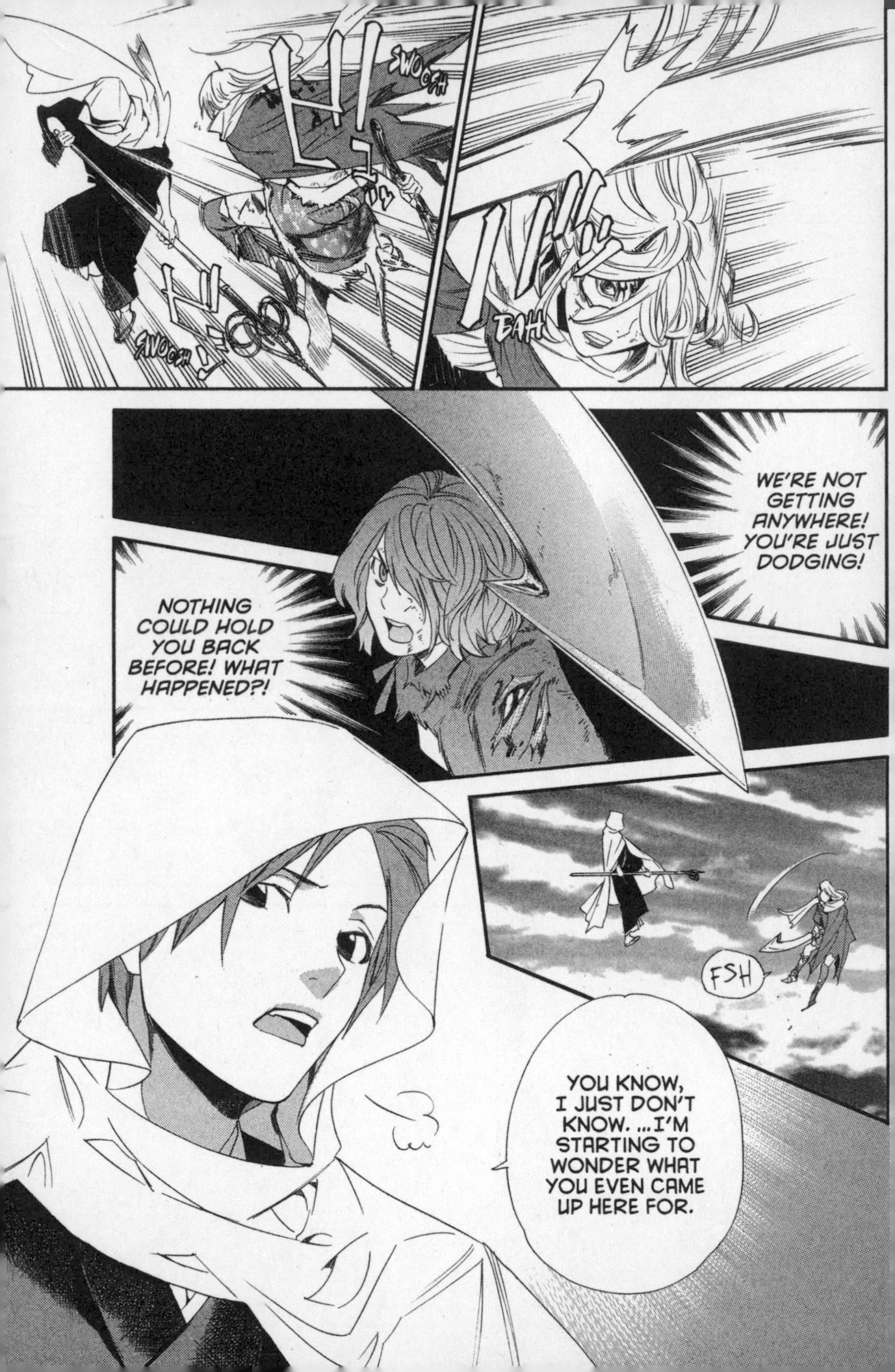

BAH
SWOOSH
SWOOSH
WE'RE NOT GETTING ANYWHERE! YOU'RE JUST DODGING!
NOTHING COULD HOLD YOU BACK BEFORE! WHAT HAPPENED?!
FSH
YOU KNOW, I JUST DON'T KNOW. ...I'M STARTING TO WONDER WHAT YOU EVEN CAME UP HERE FOR.

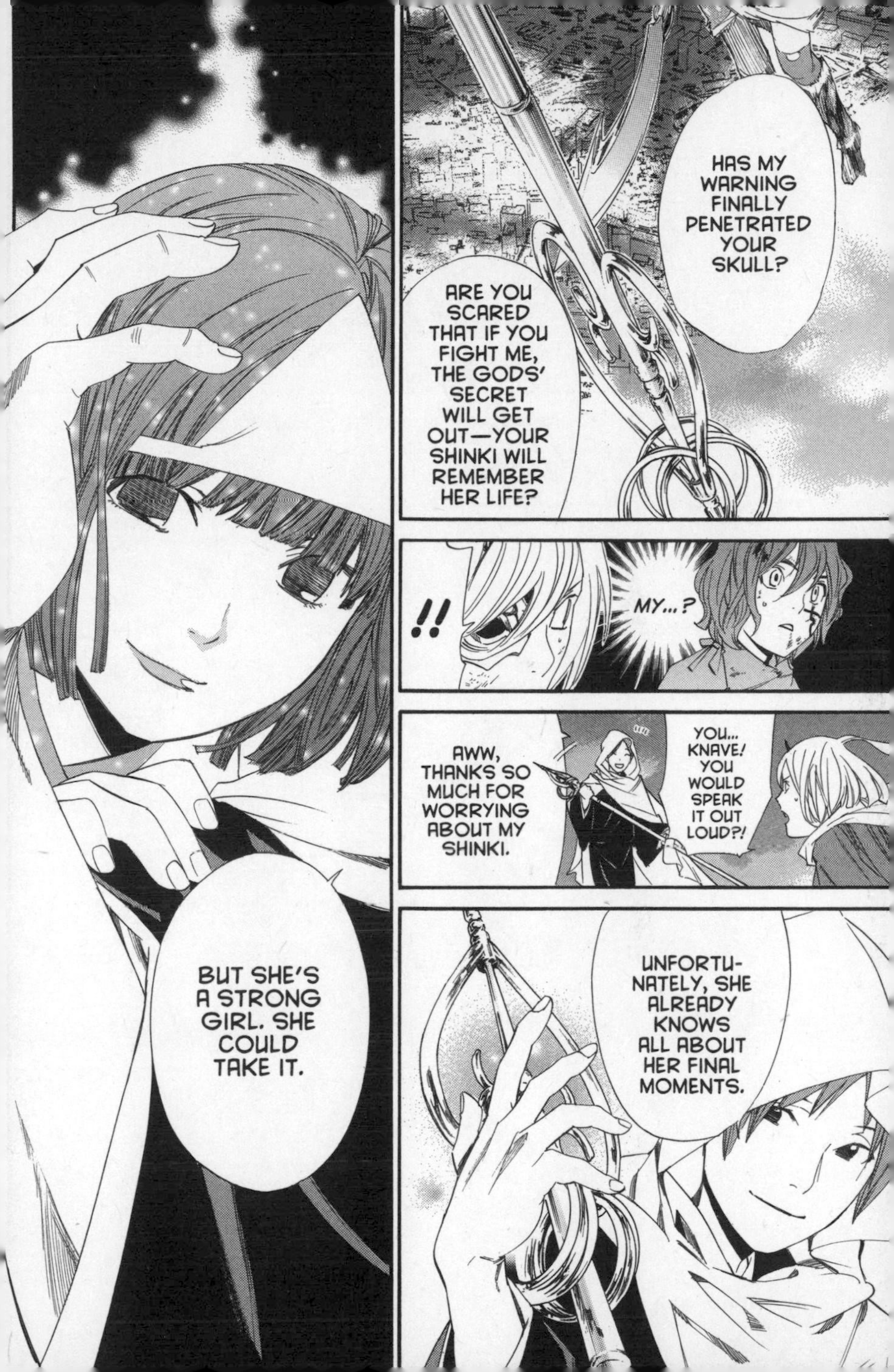
HAS MY WARNING FINALLY PENETRATED YOUR SKULL?
ARE YOU SCARED THAT IF YOU FIGHT ME, THE GODS' SECRET WILL GET OUT—YOUR SHINKI WILL REMEMBER HER LIFE?
MY...?
!!
YOU... KNAVE! YOU WOULD SPEAK IT OUT LOUD?!
AWW, THANKS SO MUCH FOR WORRYING ABOUT MY SHINKI.
UNFORTU-NATELY, SHE ALREADY KNOWS ALL ABOUT HER FINAL MOMENTS.
BUT SHE'S A STRONG GIRL. SHE COULD TAKE IT.

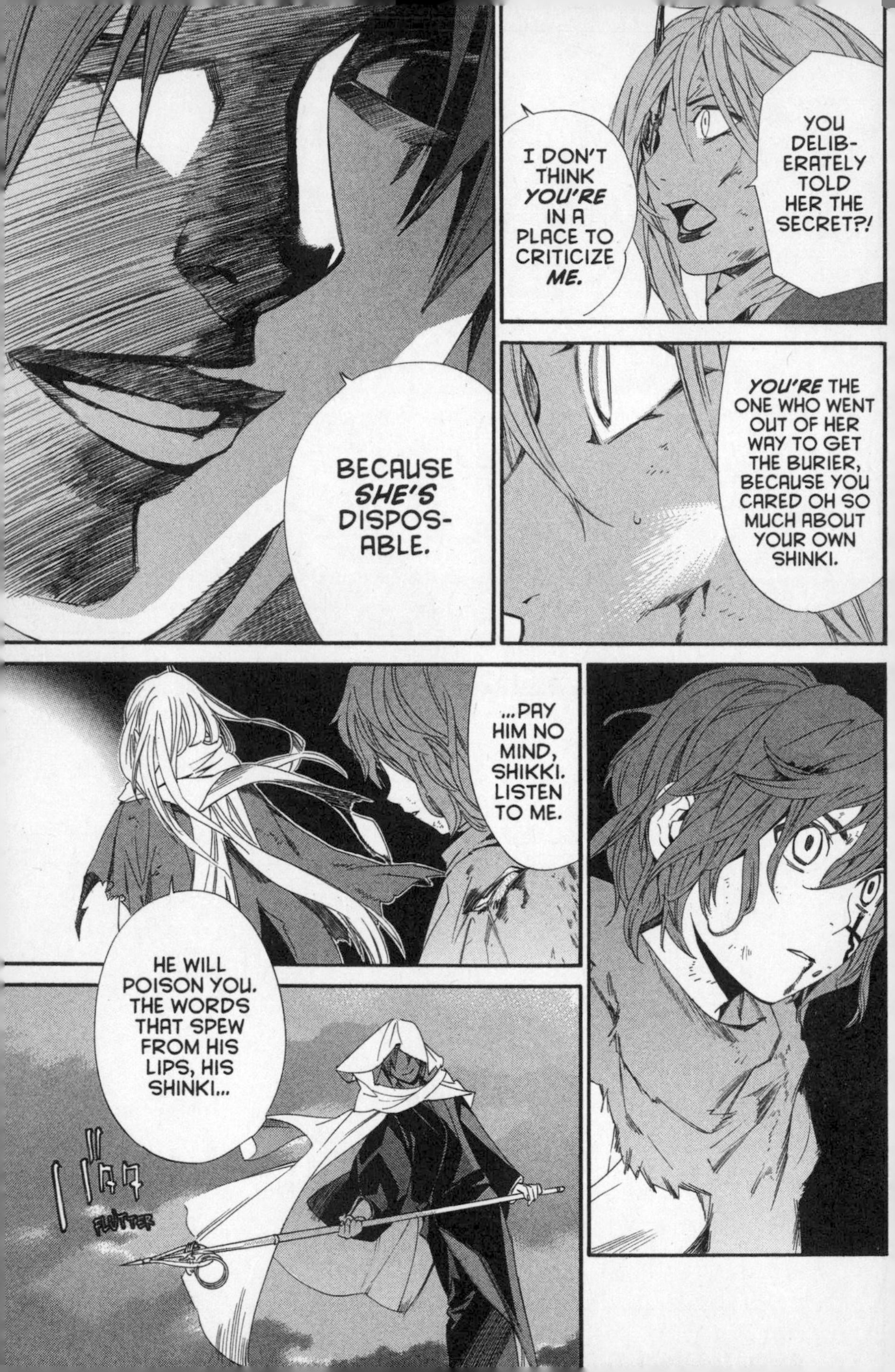
YOU DELIB-ERATELY TOLD HER THE SECRET?!
I DON'T THINK *YOU'RE* IN A PLACE TO CRITICIZE *ME.*
YOU'RE THE ONE WHO WENT OUT OF HER WAY TO GET THE BURIER, BECAUSE YOU CARED OH SO MUCH ABOUT YOUR OWN SHINKI.
BECAUSE *SHE'S* DISPOS-ABLE.
...PAY HIM NO MIND, SHIKKI. LISTEN TO ME.
HE WILL POISON YOU. THE WORDS THAT SPEW FROM HIS LIPS, HIS SHINKI...
FLUTTER

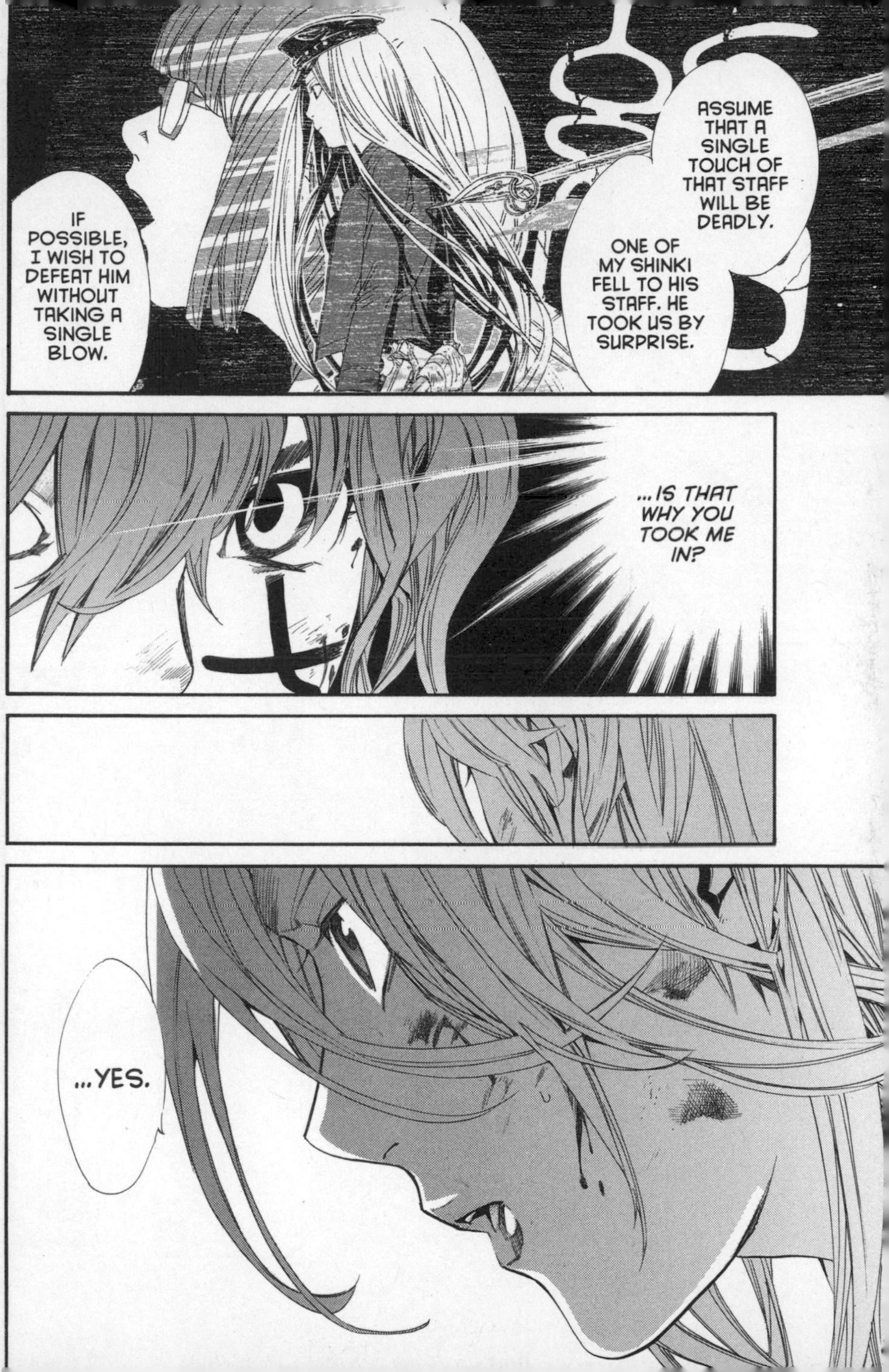
ASSUME THAT A SINGLE TOUCH OF THAT STAFF WILL BE DEADLY.
ONE OF MY SHINKI FELL TO HIS STAFF. HE TOOK US BY SURPRISE.
IF POSSIBLE, I WISH TO DEFEAT HIM WITHOUT TAKING A SINGLE BLOW.
...IS THAT WHY YOU TOOK ME IN?
...YES.

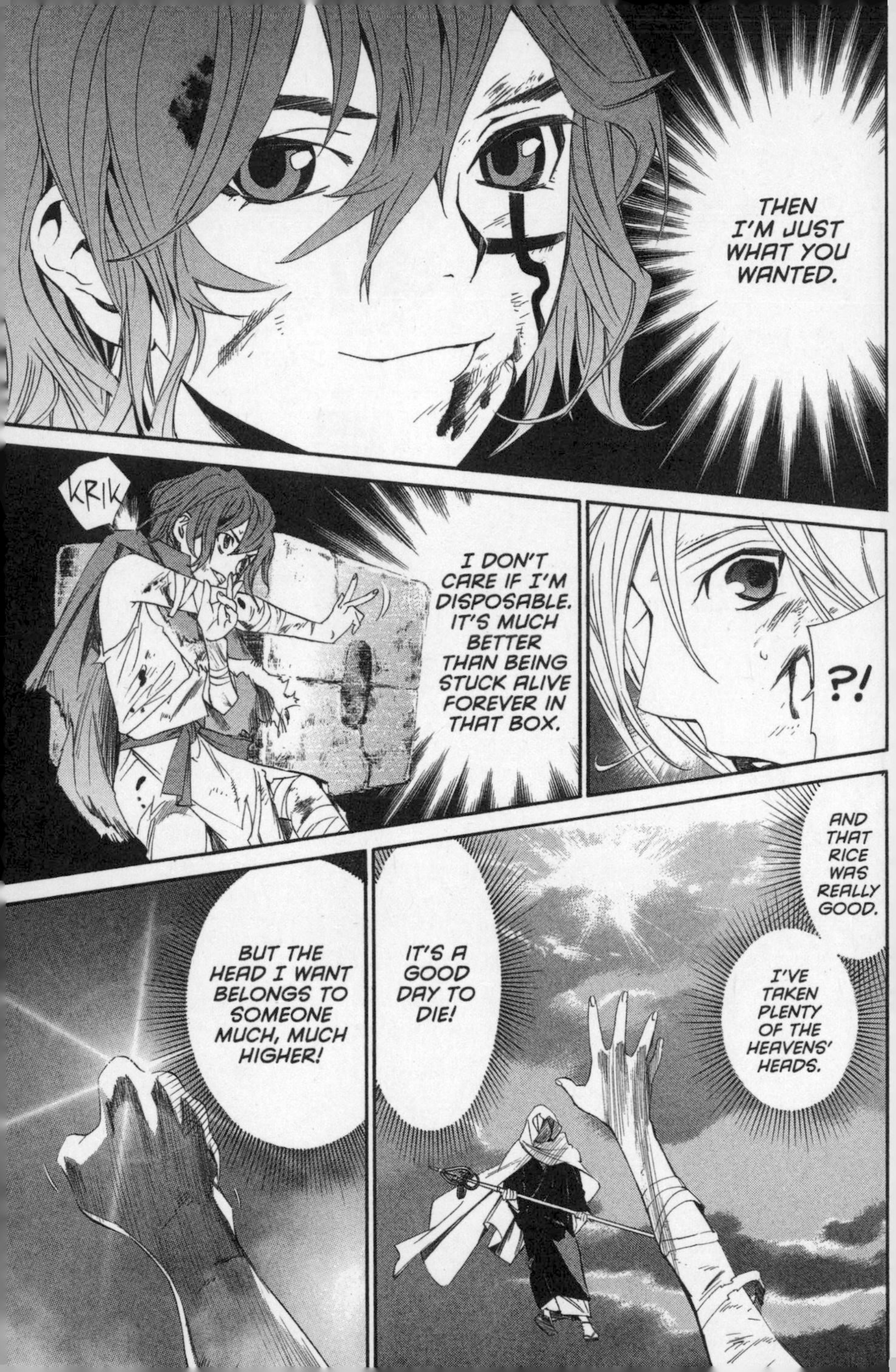
THEN I'M JUST WHAT YOU WANTED.
?!
I DON'T CARE IF I'M DISPOSABLE. IT'S MUCH BETTER THAN BEING STUCK ALIVE FOREVER IN THAT BOX.
KRIK
AND THAT RICE WAS REALLY GOOD.
I'VE TAKEN PLENTY OF THE HEAVENS' HEADS.
IT'S A GOOD DAY TO DIE!
BUT THE HEAD I WANT BELONGS TO SOMEONE MUCH, MUCH HIGHER!

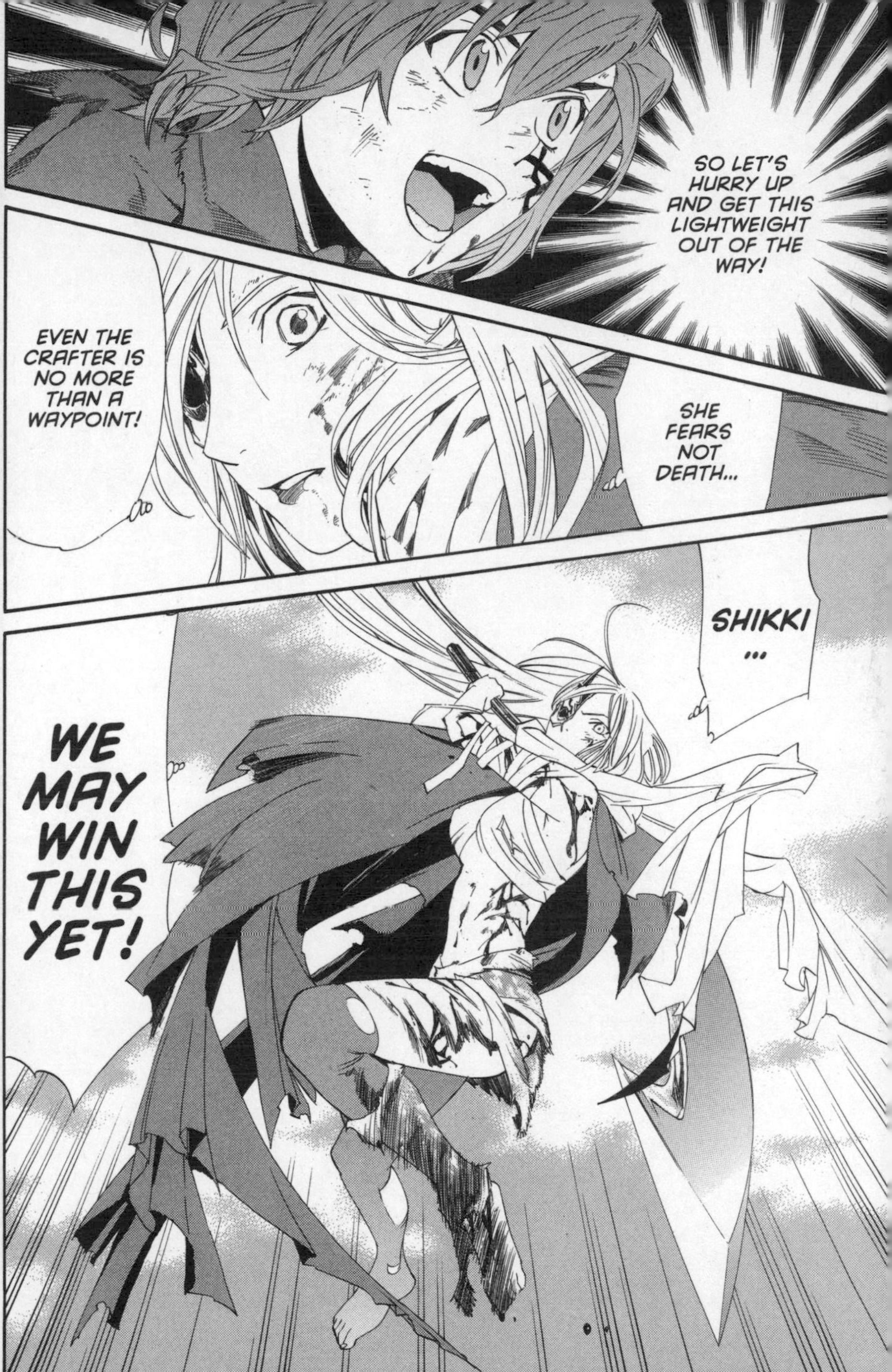
SO LET'S HURRY UP AND GET THIS LIGHTWEIGHT OUT OF THE WAY!
SHE FEARS NOT DEATH...
EVEN THE CRAFTER IS NO MORE THAN A WAYPOINT!
SHIKKI ...
WE MAY WIN THIS YET!

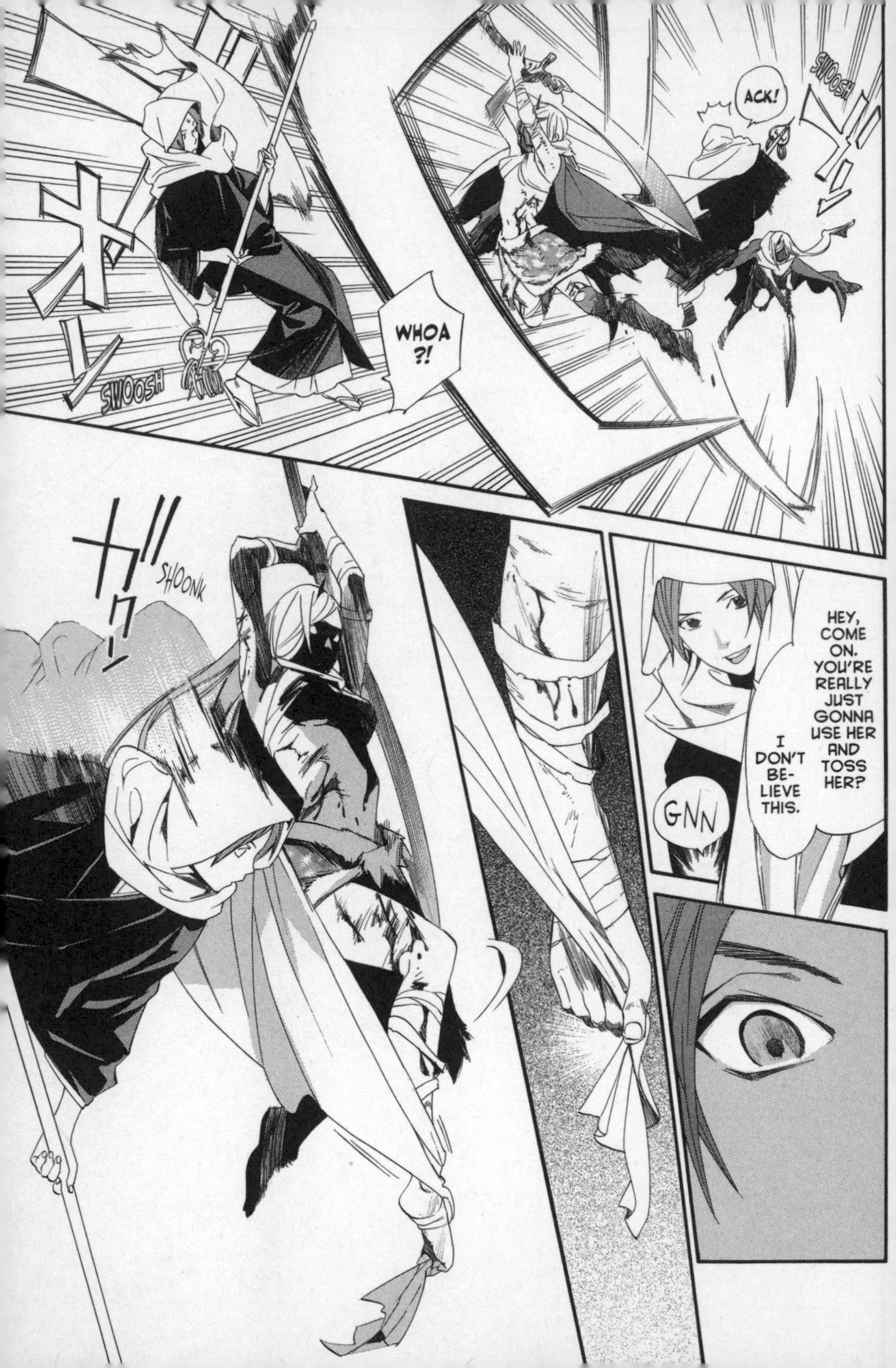
SWOOSH
ACK!
WHOA ?!
SWOOSH
SHOONK
HEY, COME ON. YOU'RE REALLY JUST GONNA USE HER AND TOSS HER?
I DON'T BE-LIEVE THIS.
GNN

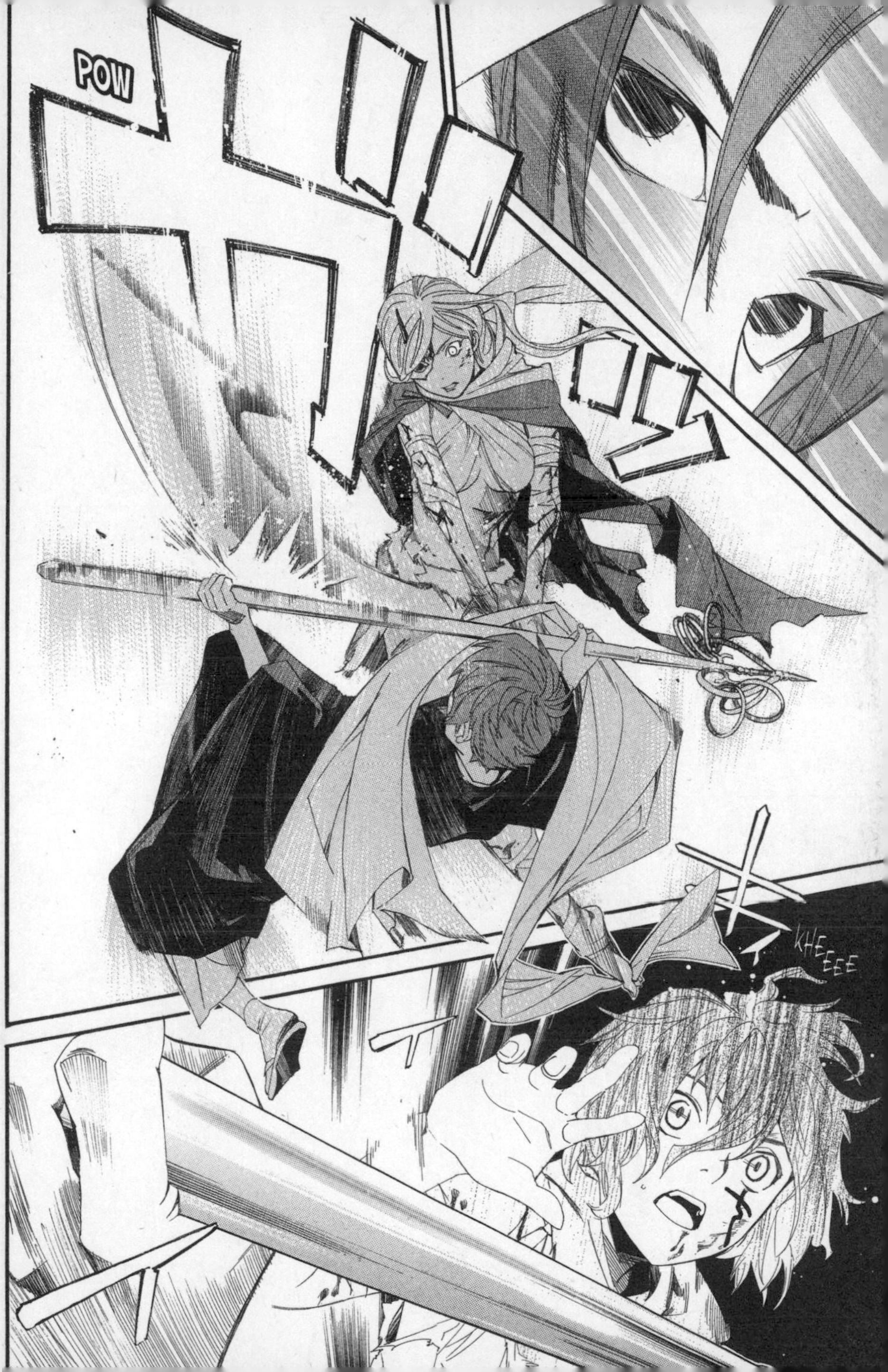
POW
KHEEEE

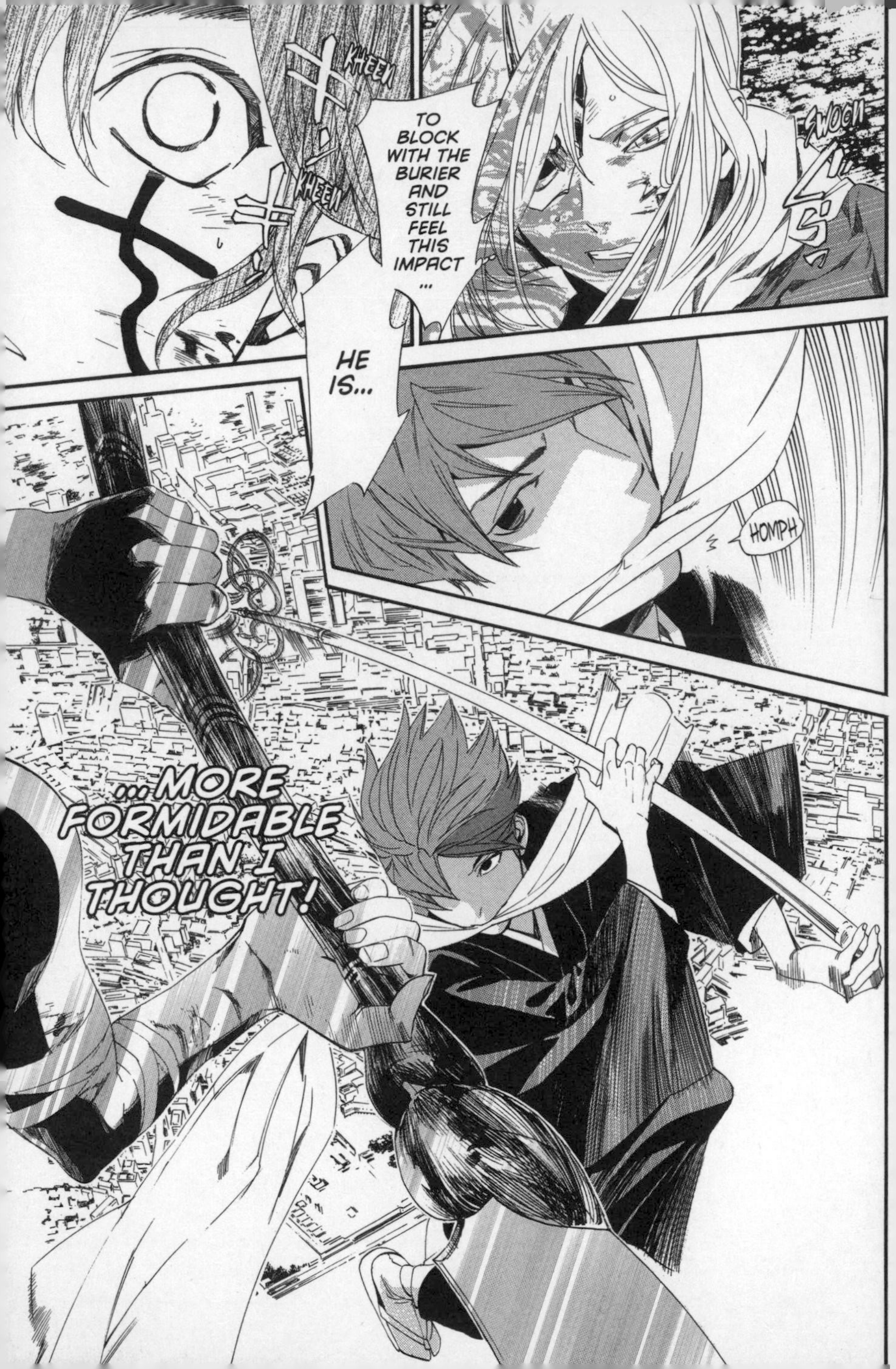
SWOON
TO BLOCK WITH THE BURIER AND STILL FEEL THIS IMPACT ...
KHEEN
KHEEN
HE IS...
HOMPH
...MORE FORMIDABLE THAN I THOUGHT!

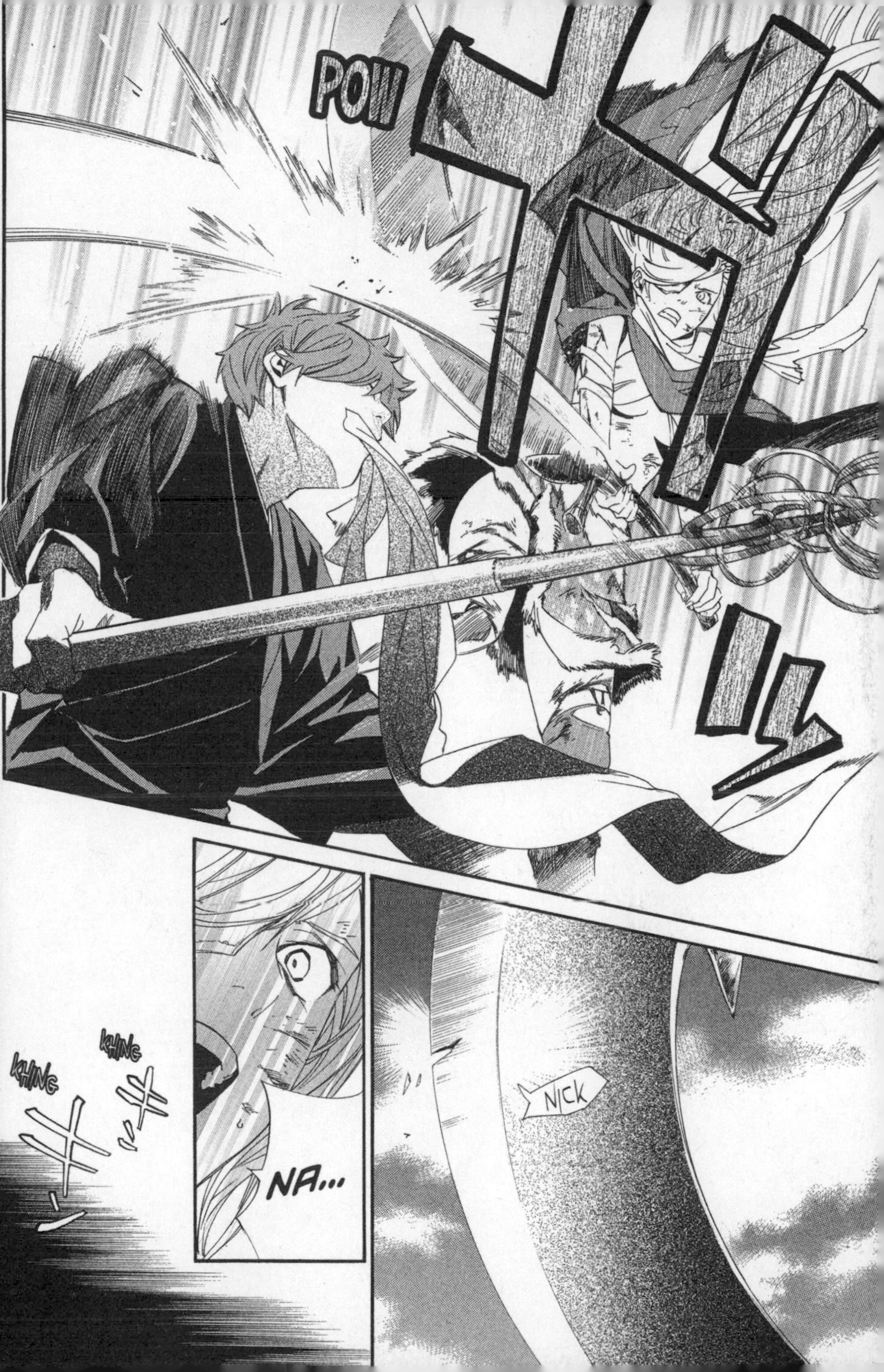
POW
NICK
NA...
KHING
KHING

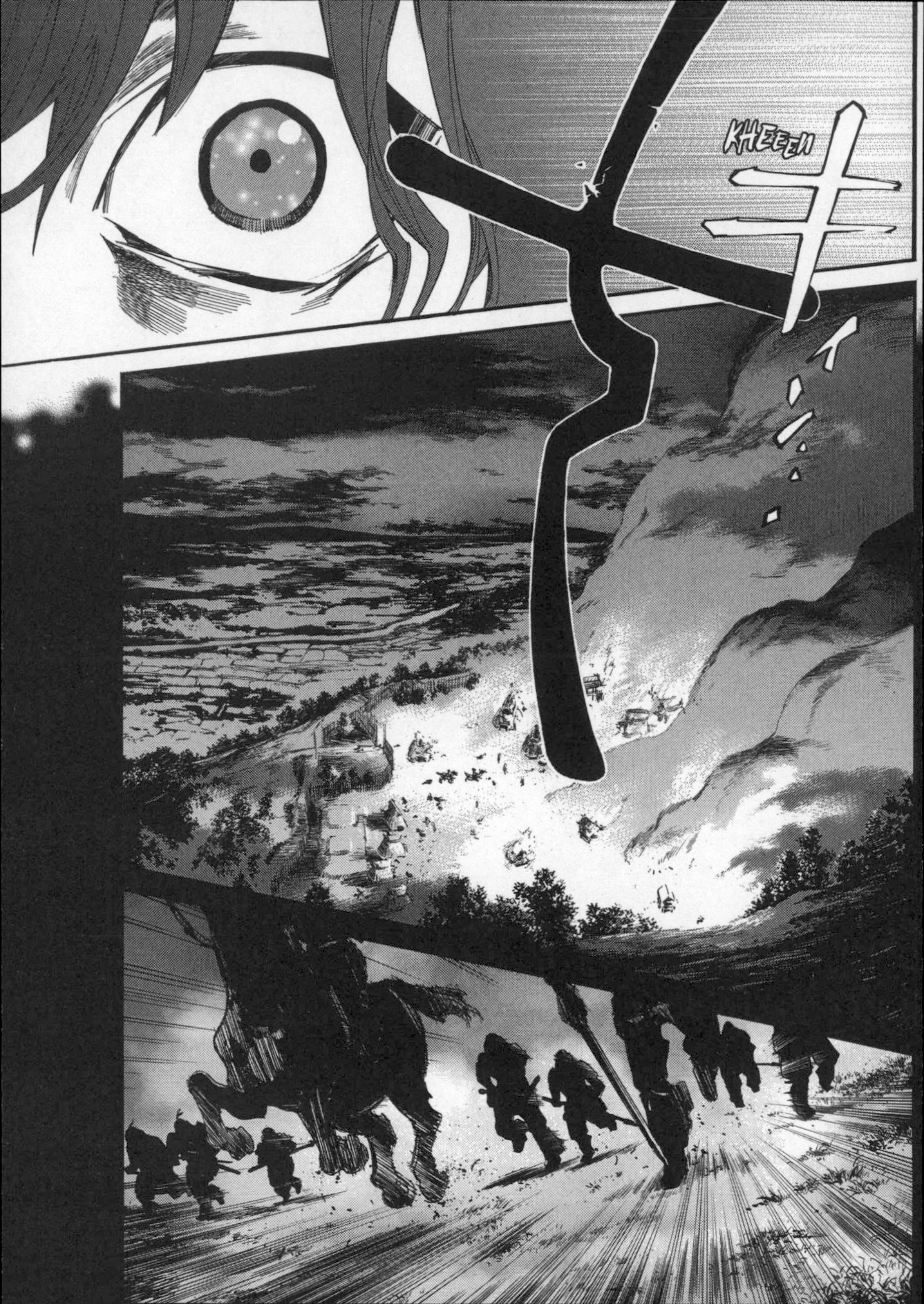

KHEEEN

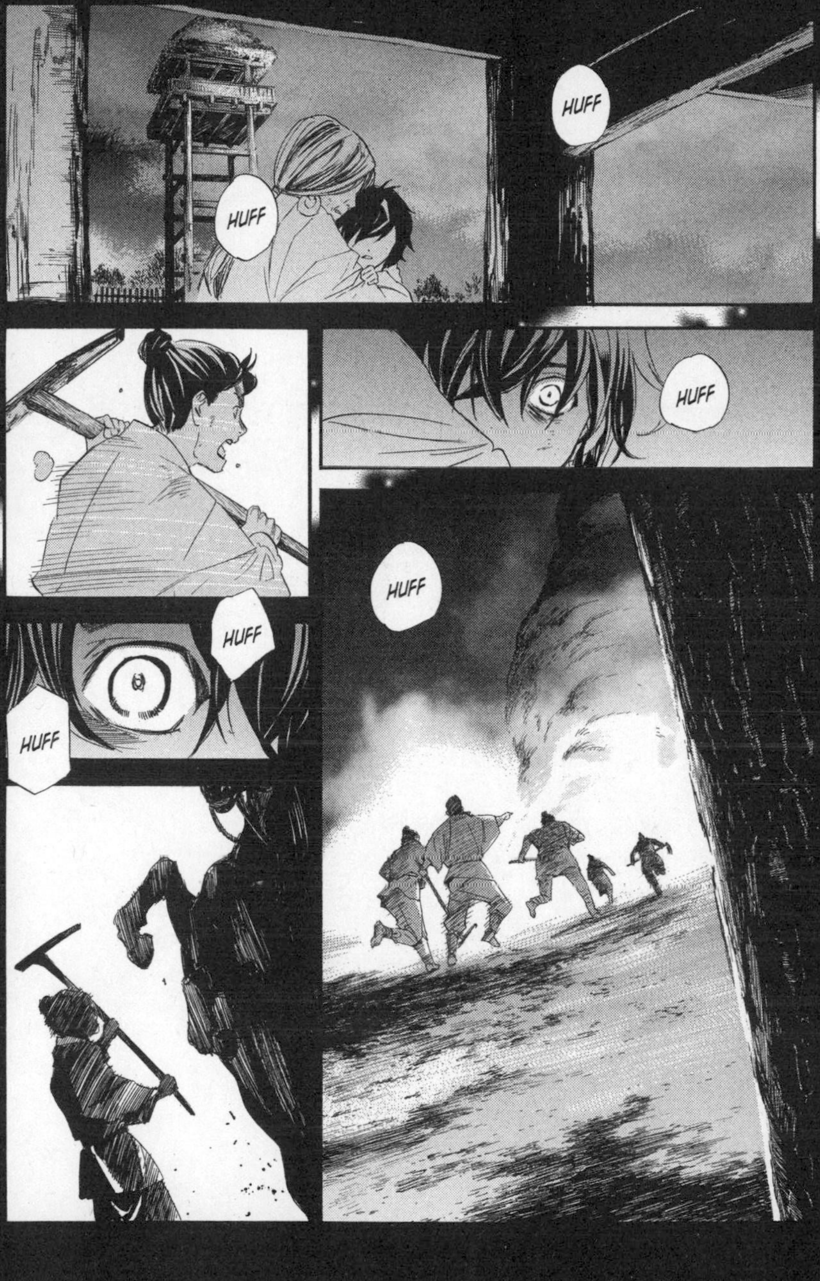
HUFF
HUFF
HUFF
HUFF
HUFF
HUFF

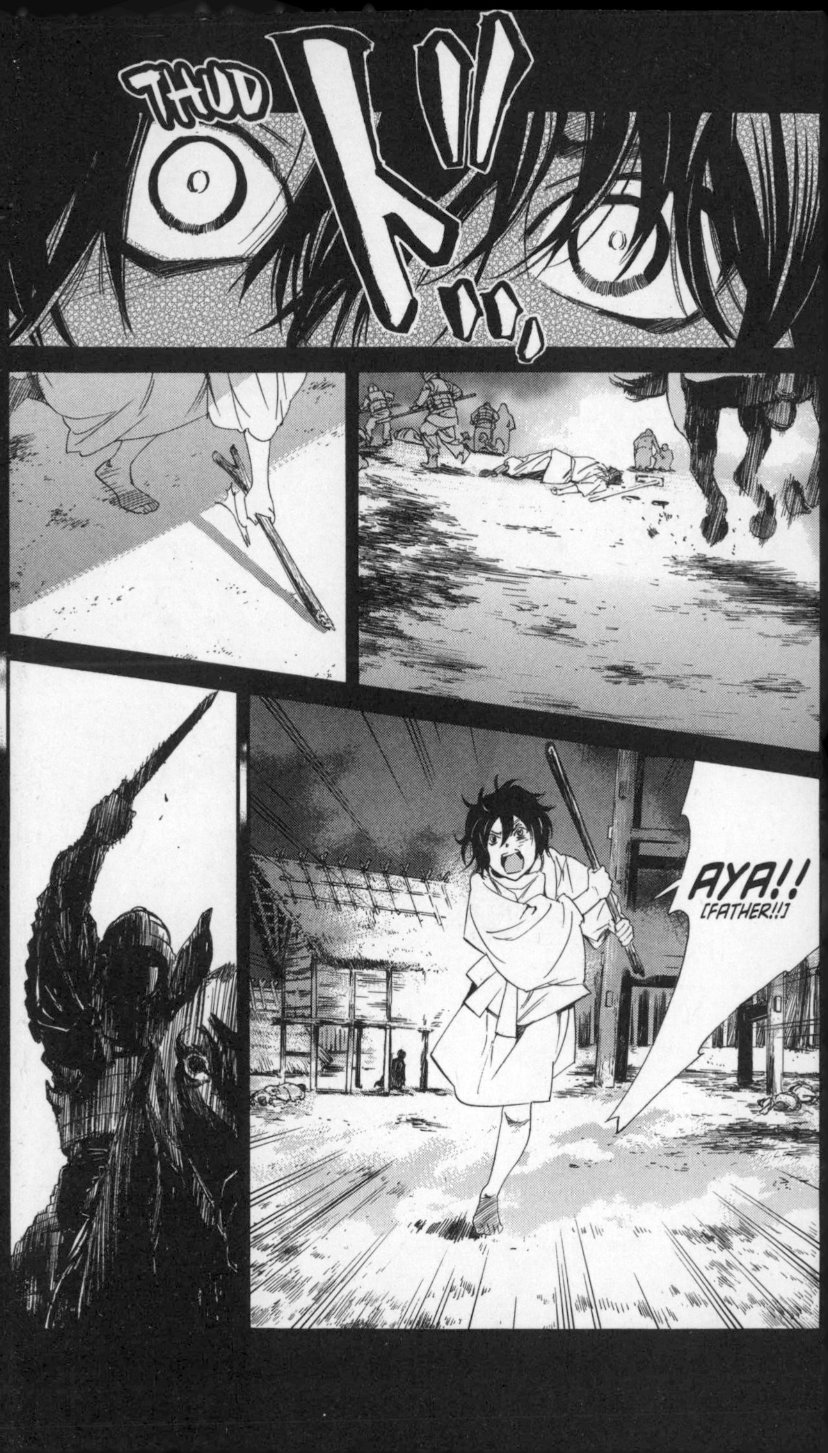
THUD
AYA!!
[FATHER!!]

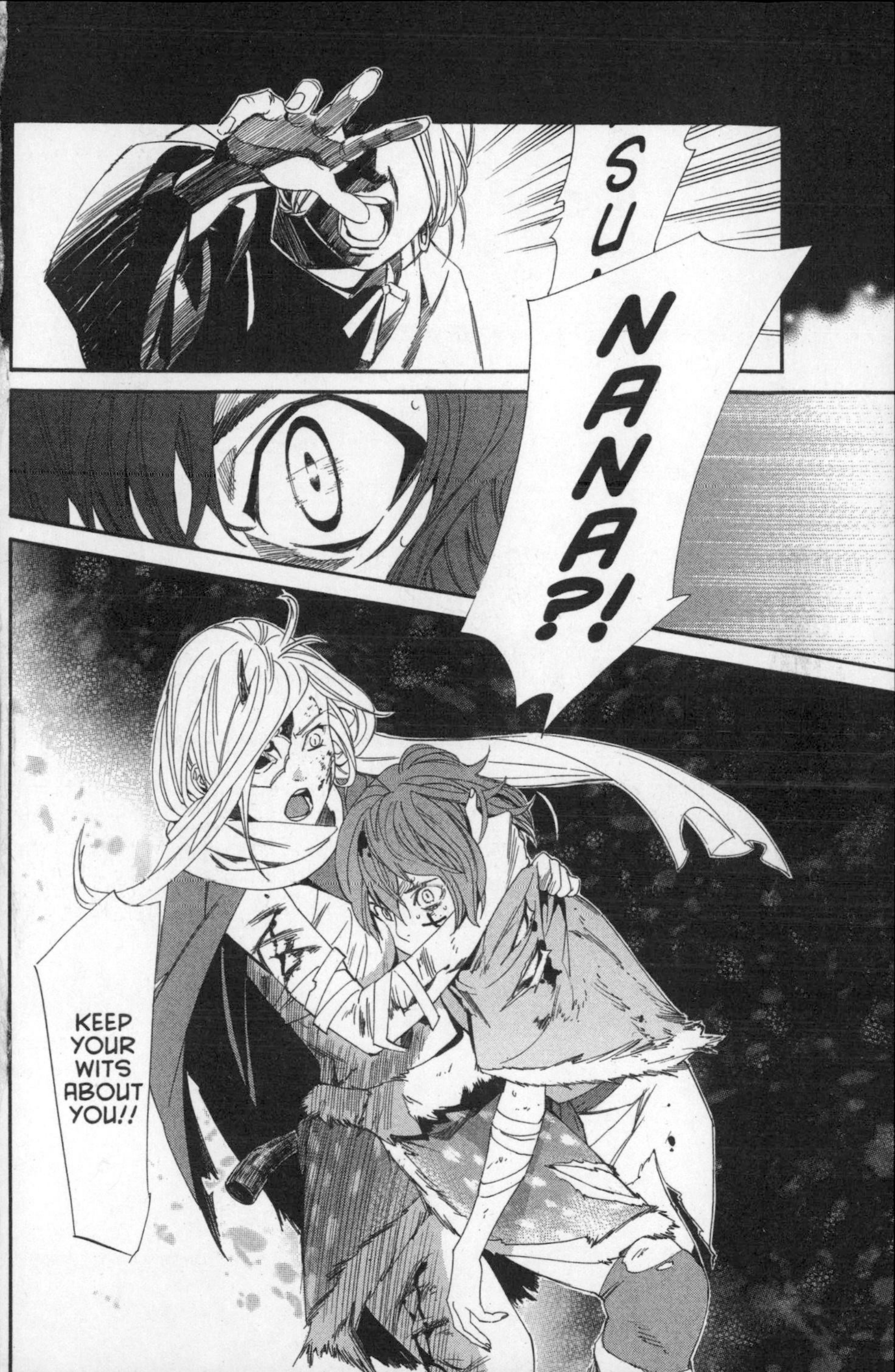
SU-
NANA?!
KEEP YOUR WITS ABOUT YOU!!

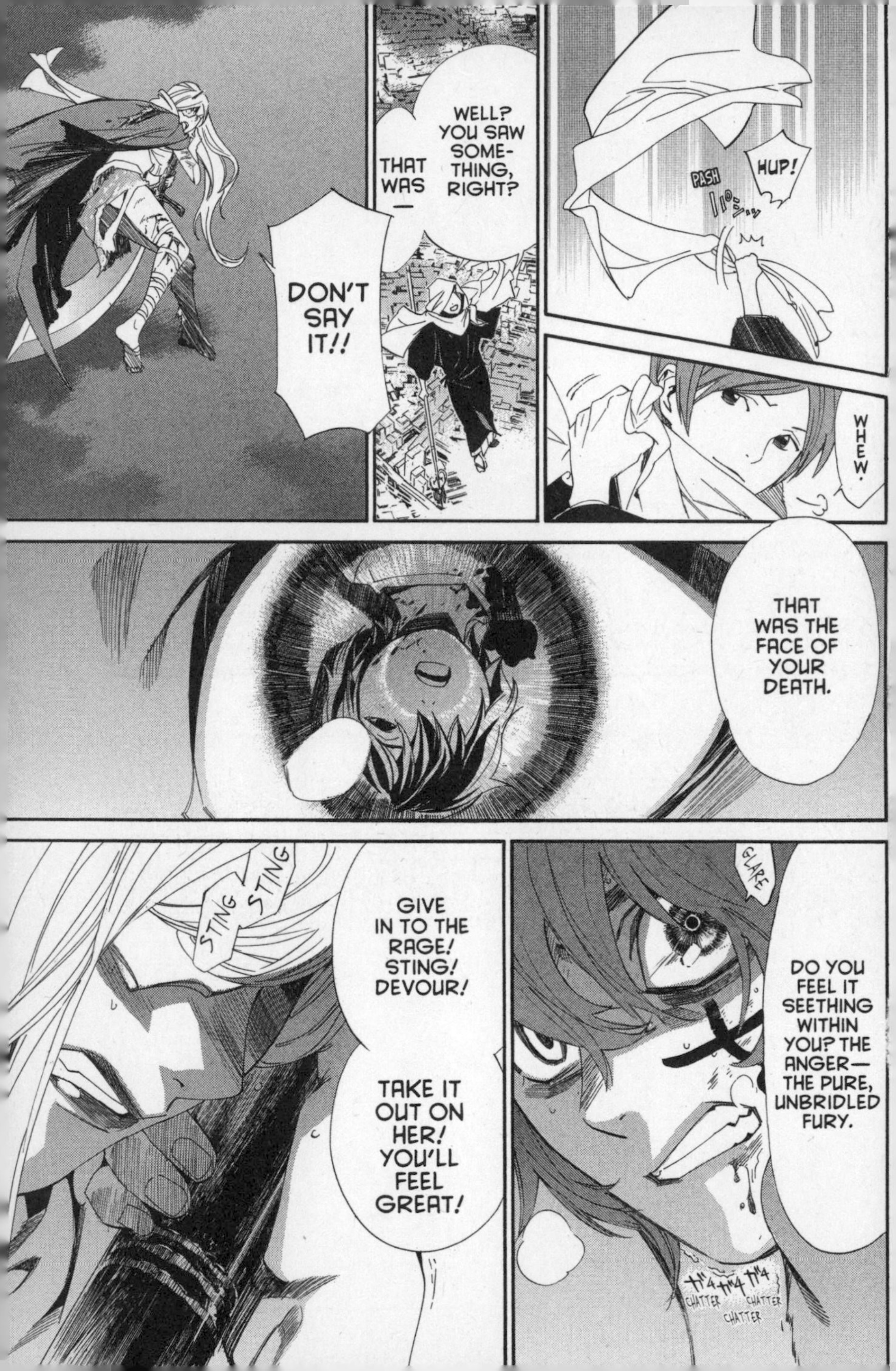
HUP!
PASH
WHEW.
WELL? YOU SAW SOME-THING, RIGHT?
THAT WAS—
DON'T SAY IT!!
THAT WAS THE FACE OF YOUR DEATH.
GLARE
DO YOU FEEL IT SEETHING WITHIN YOU? THE ANGER— THE PURE, UNBRIDLED FURY.
CHATTER CHATTER CHATTER
STING STING
GIVE IN TO THE RAGE! STING! DEVOUR!
TAKE IT OUT ON HER! YOU'LL FEEL GREAT!

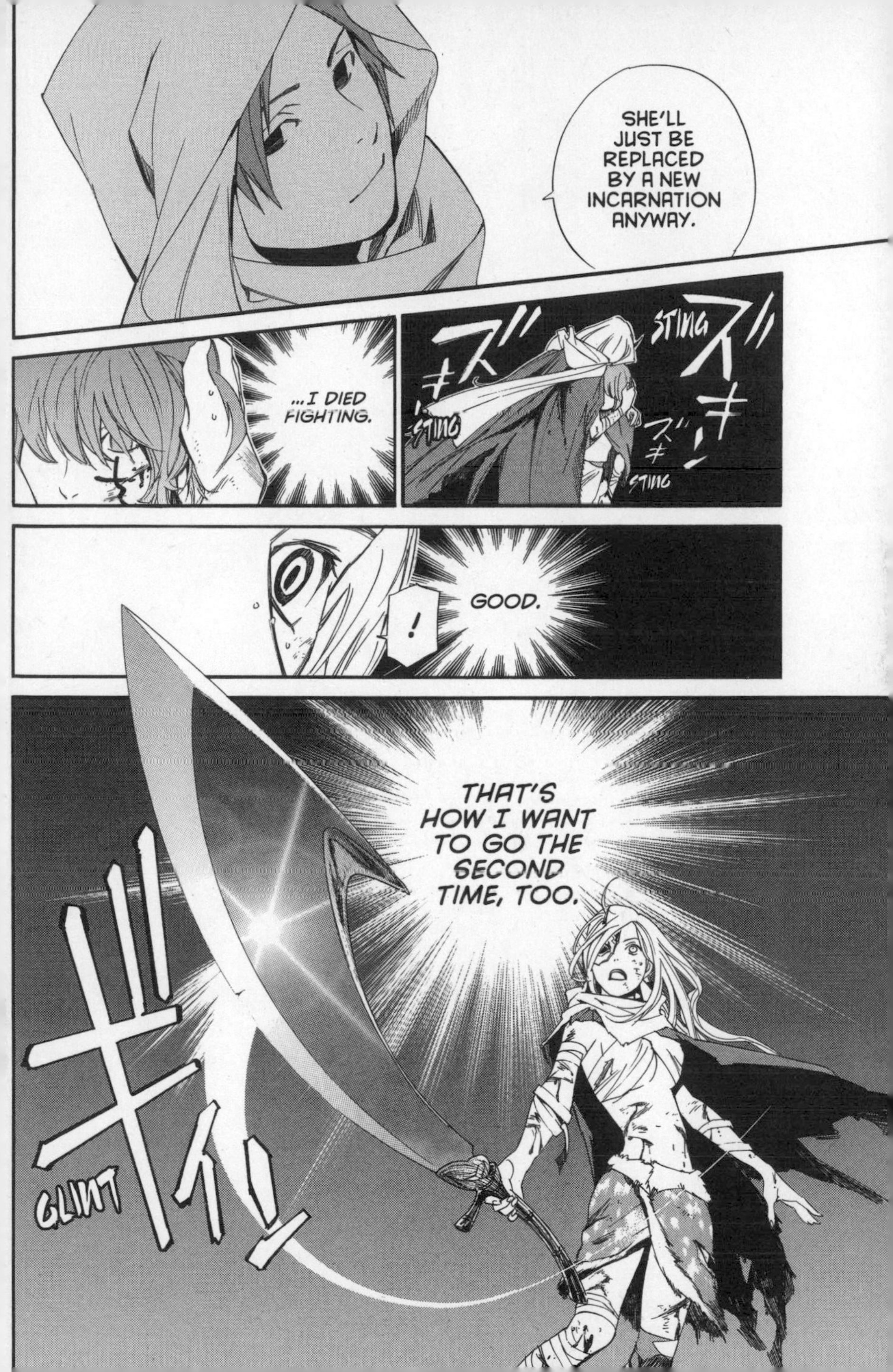
SHE'LL JUST BE REPLACED BY A NEW INCARNATION ANYWAY.
STING
STING
STING
...I DIED FIGHTING.
GOOD.
!
THAT'S HOW I WANT TO GO THE SECOND TIME, TOO.
GLINT

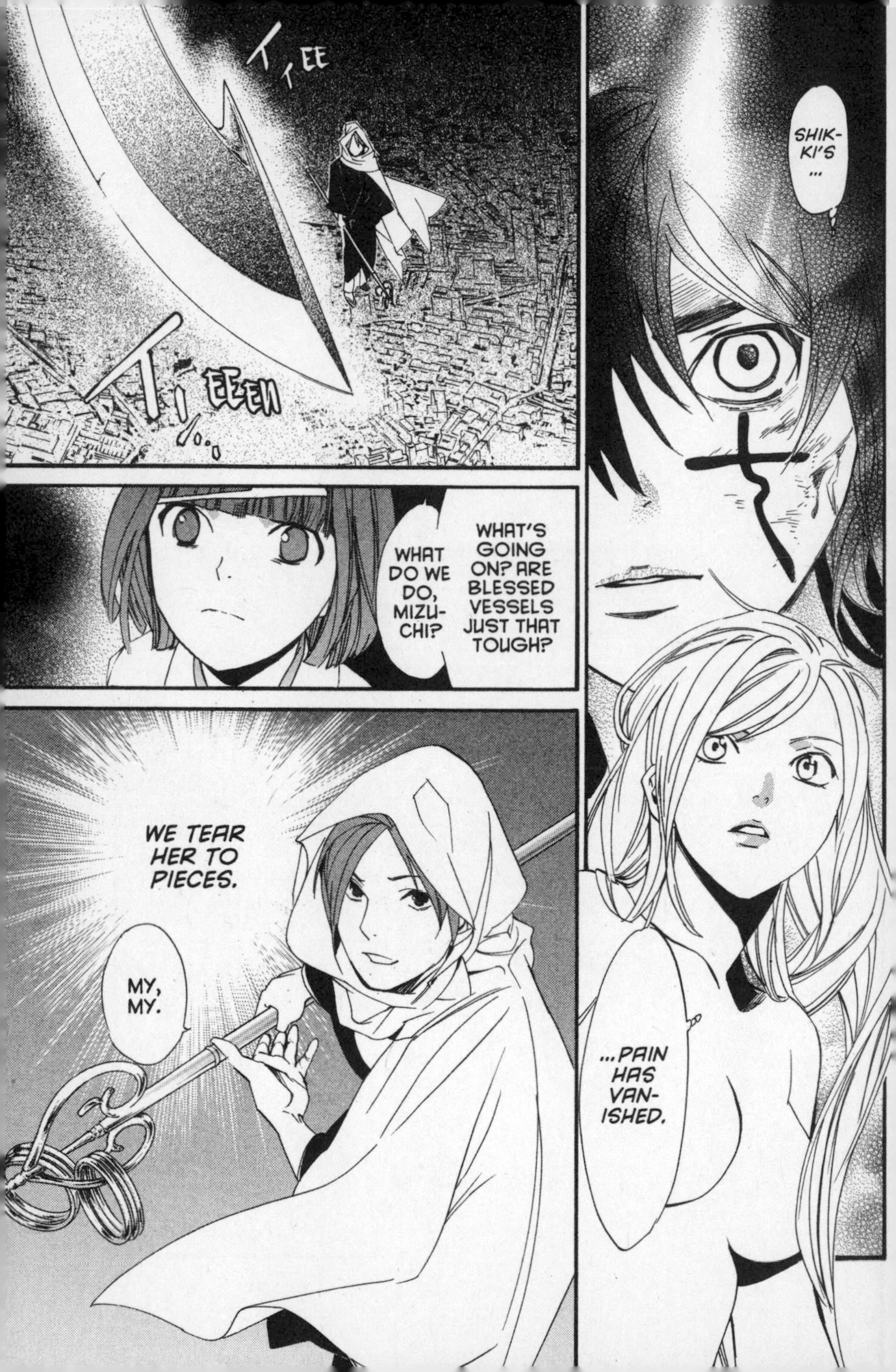
SHIK-KI'S ...
...PAIN HAS VAN-ISHED.
WHAT'S GOING ON? ARE BLESSED VESSELS JUST THAT TOUGH?
WHAT DO WE DO, MIZU-CHI?
WE TEAR HER TO PIECES.
MY, MY.

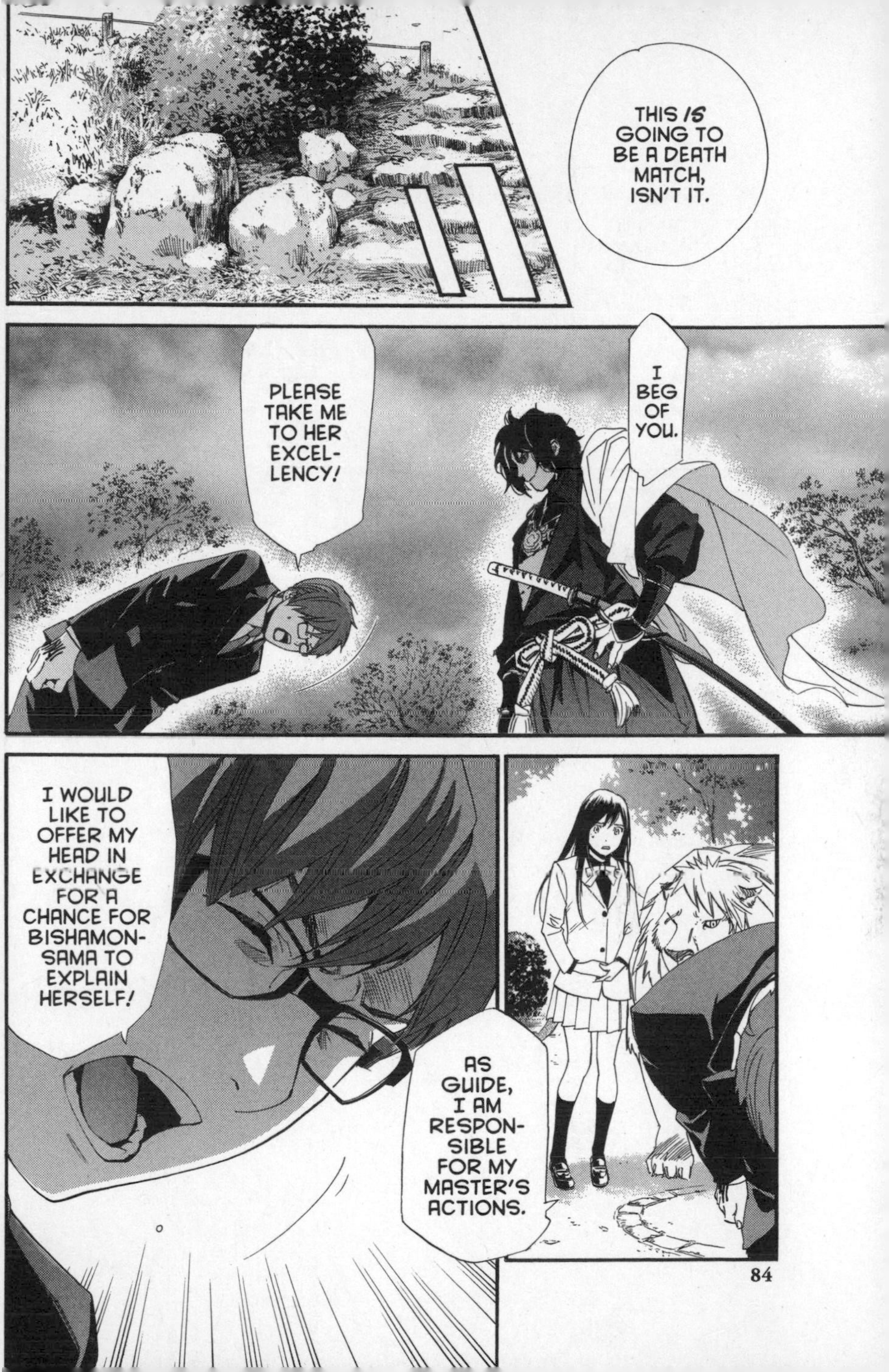
THIS *IS* GOING TO BE A DEATH MATCH, ISN'T IT.
I BEG OF YOU.
PLEASE TAKE ME TO HER EXCELLENCY!
AS GUIDE, I AM RESPONSIBLE FOR MY MASTER'S ACTIONS.
I WOULD LIKE TO OFFER MY HEAD IN EXCHANGE FOR A CHANCE FOR BISHAMON-SAMA TO EXPLAIN HERSELF!

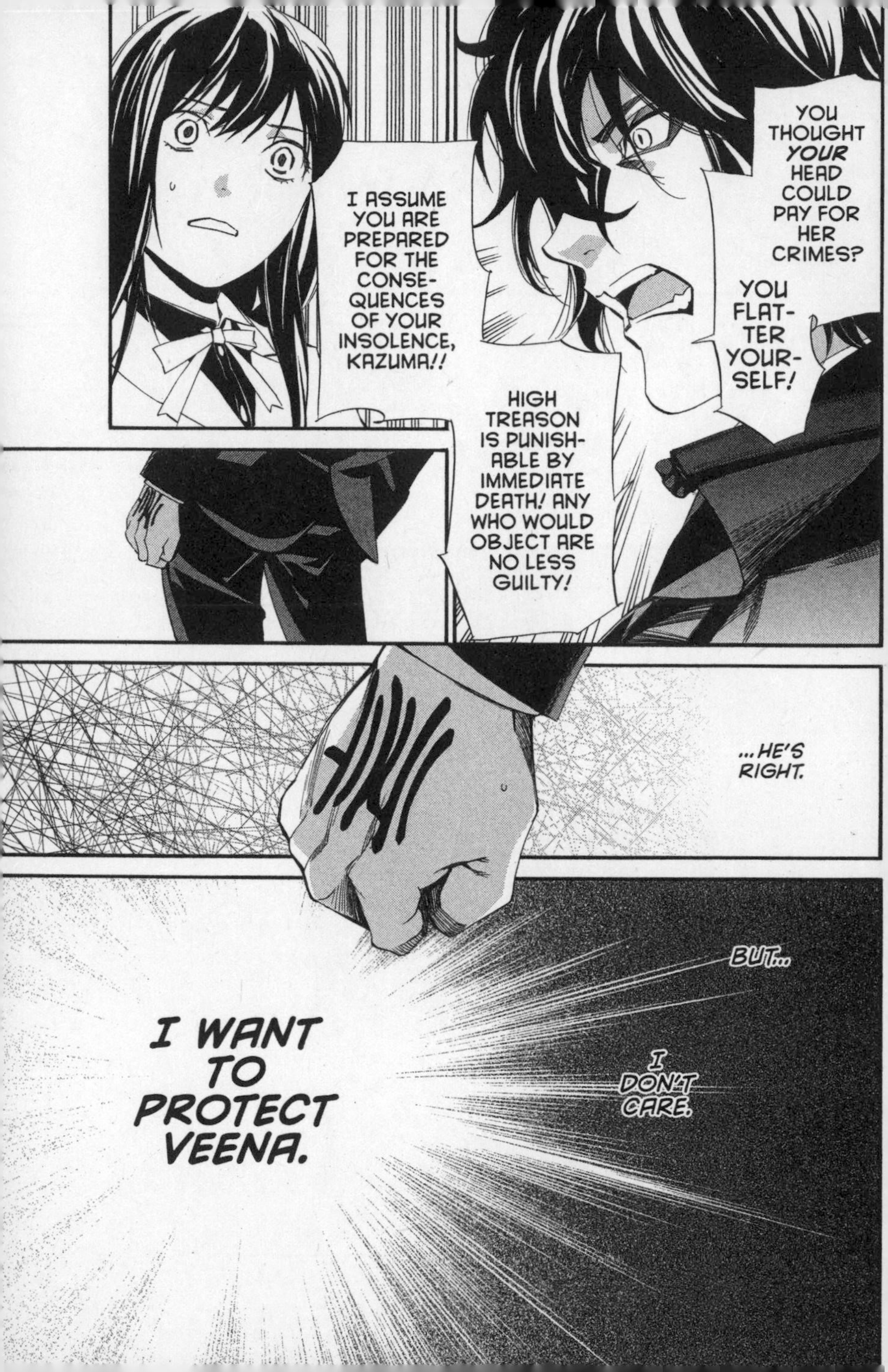
YOU THOUGHT *YOUR* HEAD COULD PAY FOR HER CRIMES?
YOU FLATTER YOURSELF!
I ASSUME YOU ARE PREPARED FOR THE CONSEQUENCES OF YOUR INSOLENCE, KAZUMA!!
HIGH TREASON IS PUNISHABLE BY IMMEDIATE DEATH! ANY WHO WOULD OBJECT ARE NO LESS GUILTY!
...HE'S RIGHT.
BUT...
I DON'T CARE.
I WANT TO PROTECT VEENA.

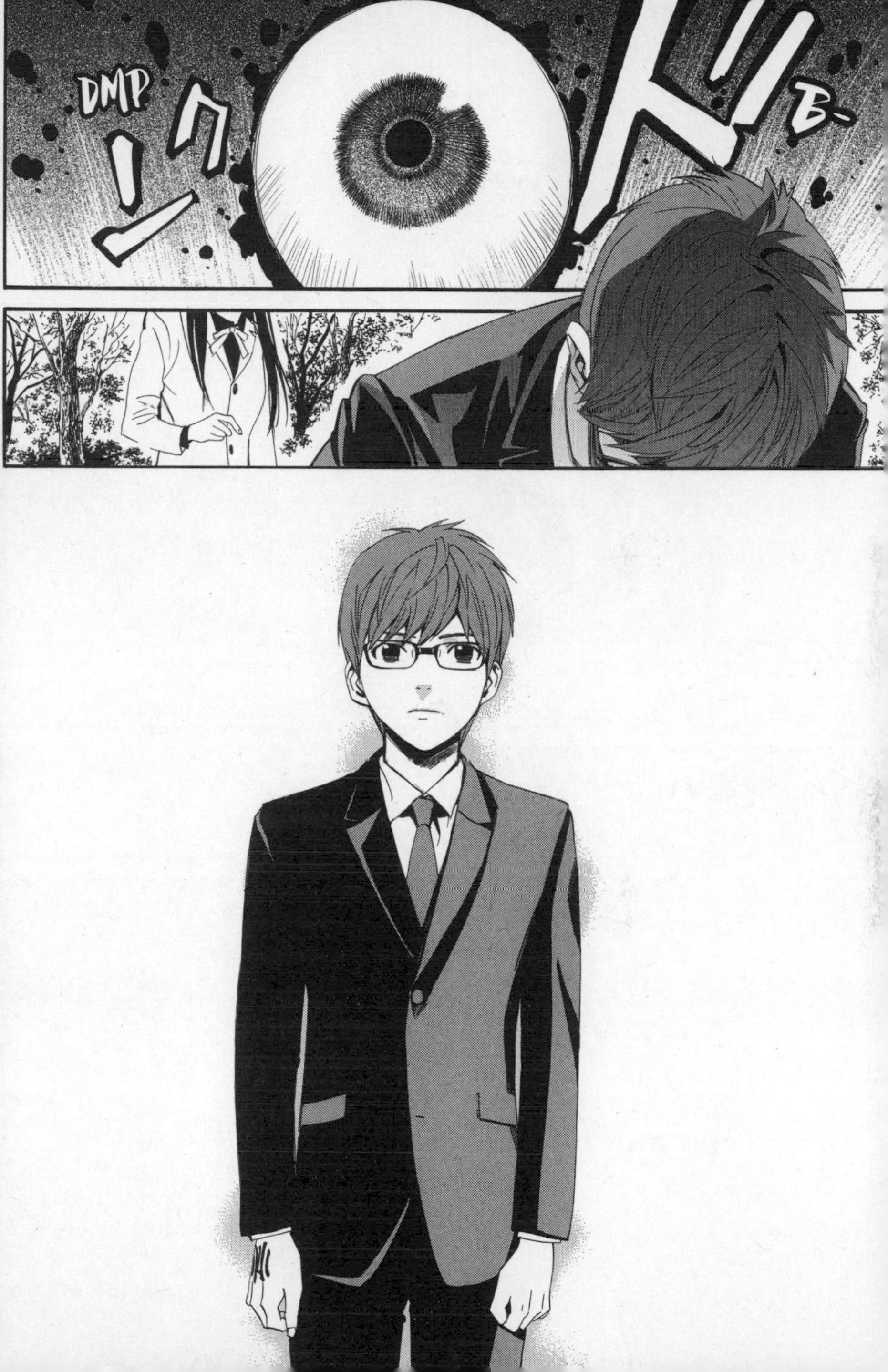
B-
DMP

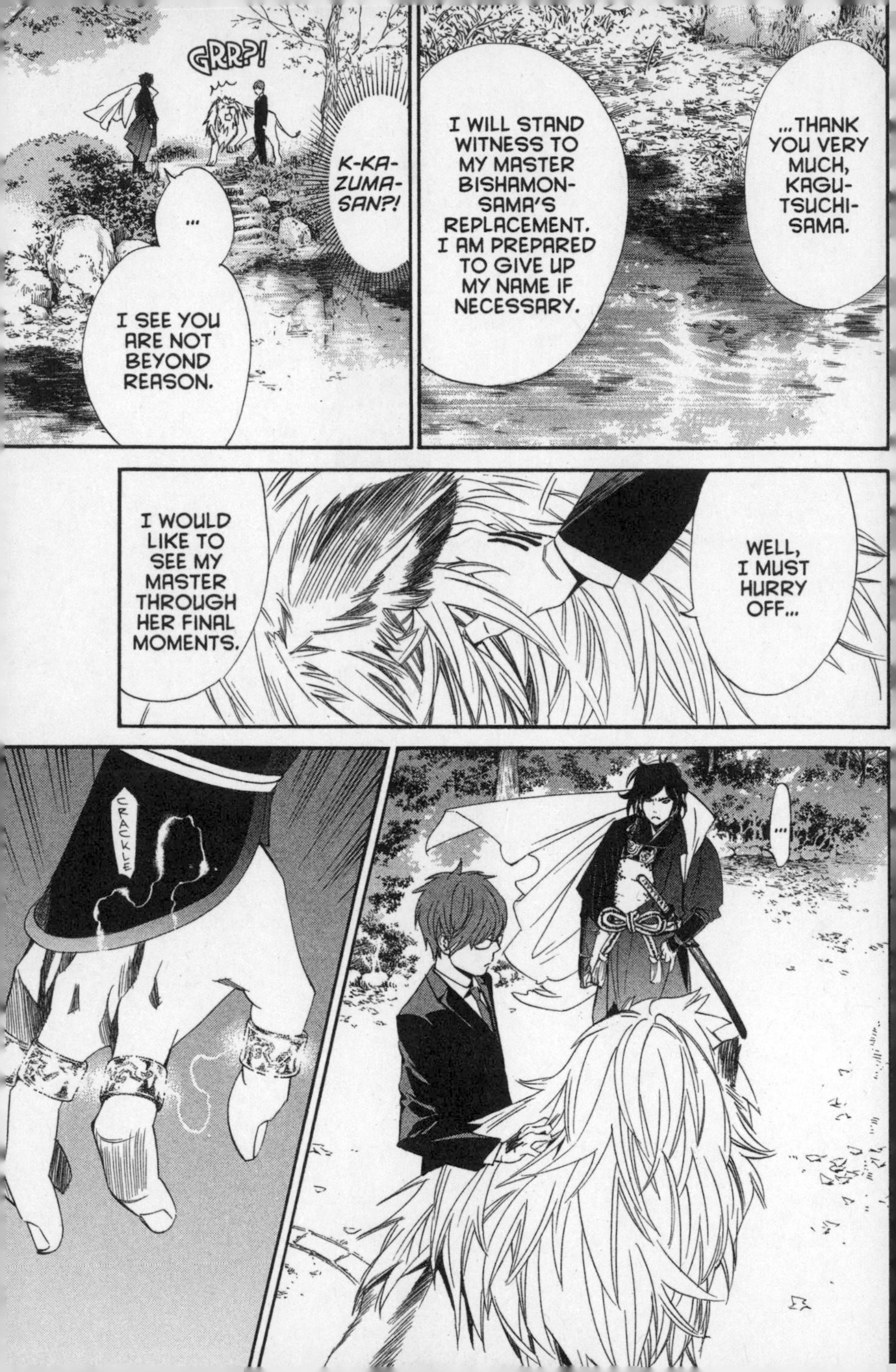
...THANK YOU VERY MUCH, KAGU-TSUCHI-SAMA.
I WILL STAND WITNESS TO MY MASTER BISHAMON-SAMA'S REPLACEMENT. I AM PREPARED TO GIVE UP MY NAME IF NECESSARY.
GRR?!
K-KAZUMA-SAN?!
...
I SEE YOU ARE NOT BEYOND REASON.
WELL, I MUST HURRY OFF...
I WOULD LIKE TO SEE MY MASTER THROUGH HER FINAL MOMENTS.
...
CRACKLE

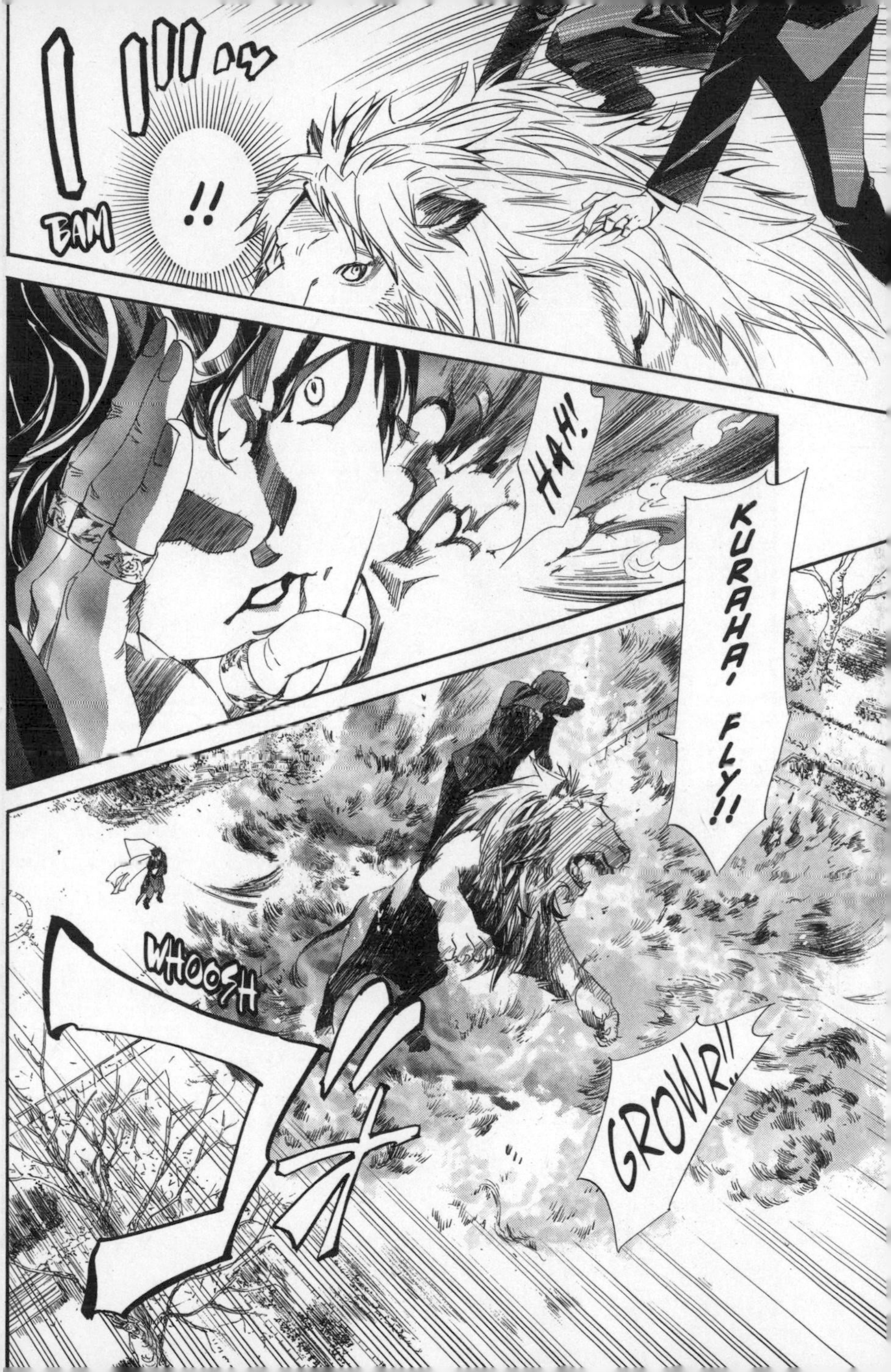
!!
BAM
HAH!
KURAHA, FLY!!
GROWR!!
WHOOSH

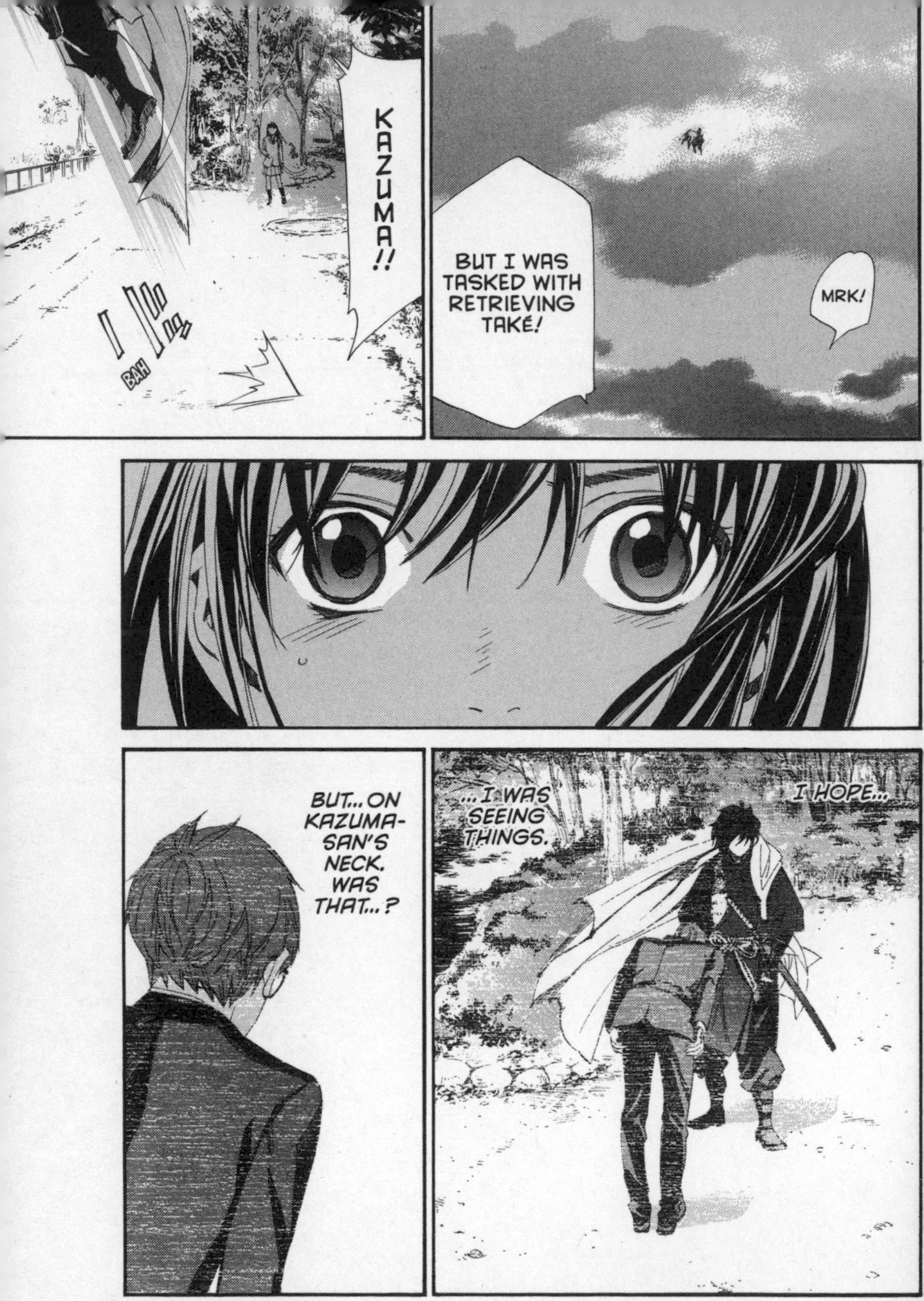
MRK!
BUT I WAS TASKED WITH RETRIEVING TAKÉ!
KAZUMA!!
BAH
I HOPE...
...I WAS SEEING THINGS.
BUT...ON KAZUMA-SAN'S NECK. WAS THAT...?

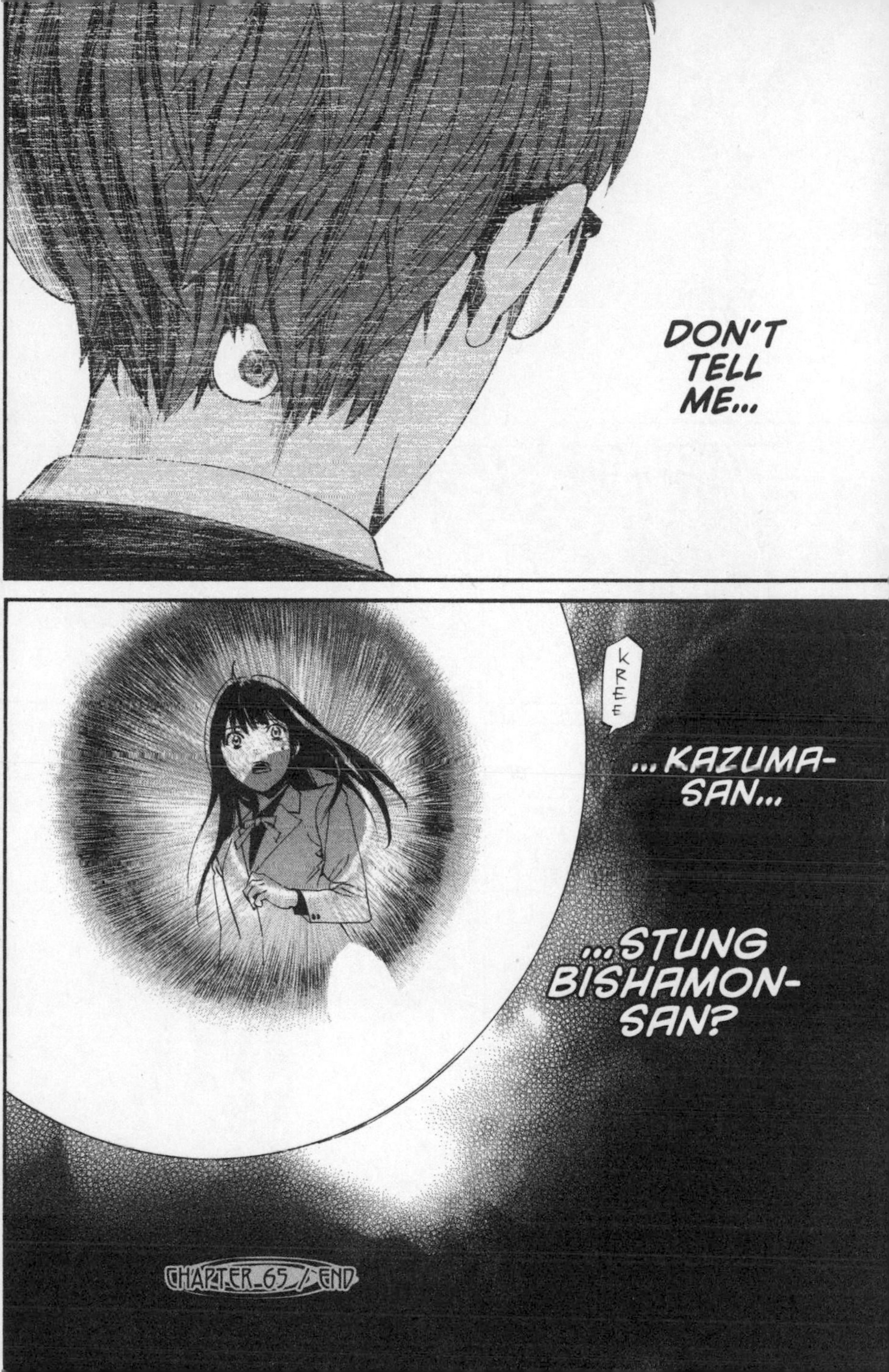
DON'T TELL ME...
KREE
...KAZUMA-SAN...
...STUNG BISHAMON-SAN?
CHAPTER_65 / END

野

兔

神

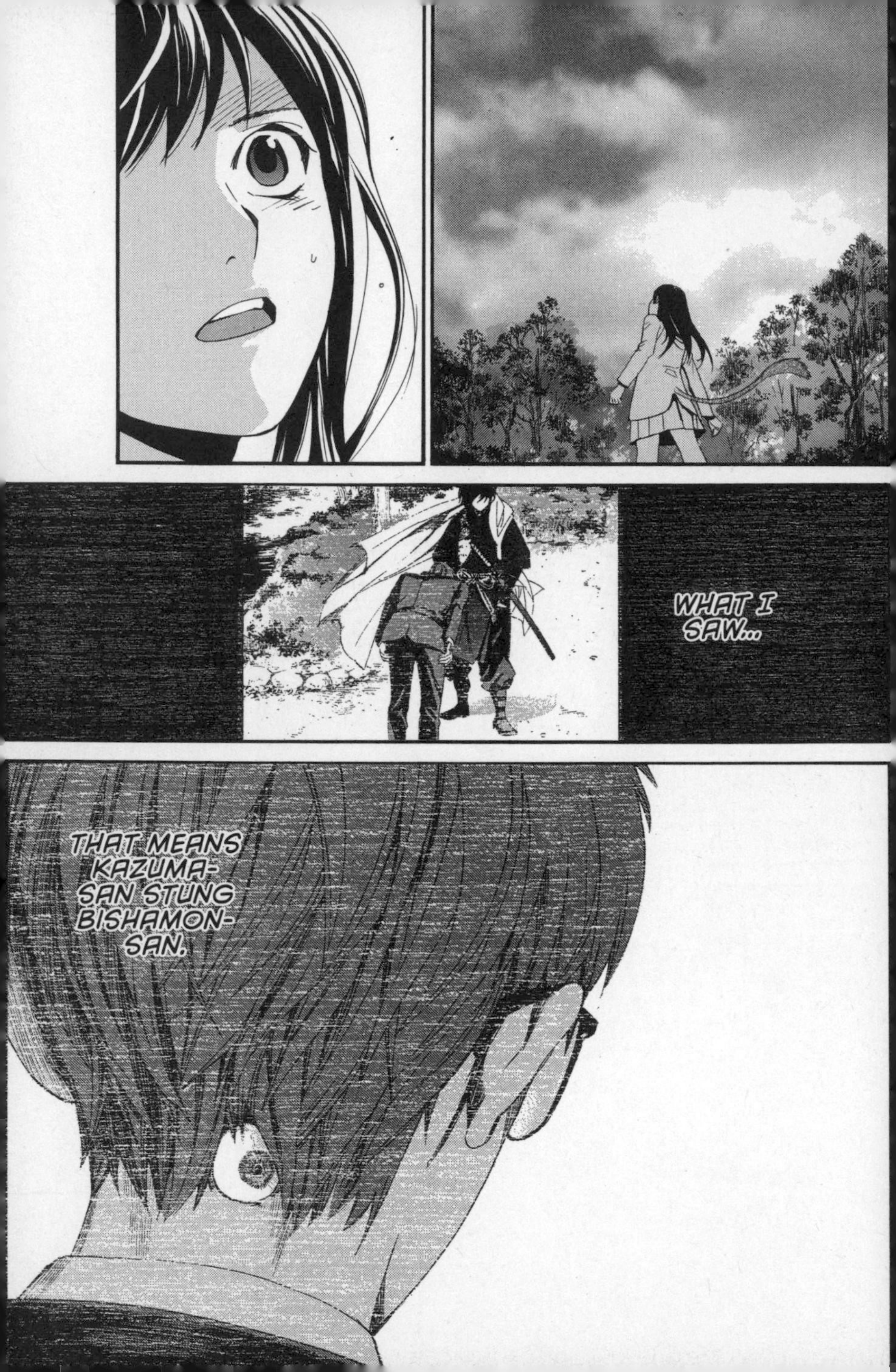
WHAT I SAW...
THAT MEANS KAZUMA-SAN STUNG BISHAMON-SAN.

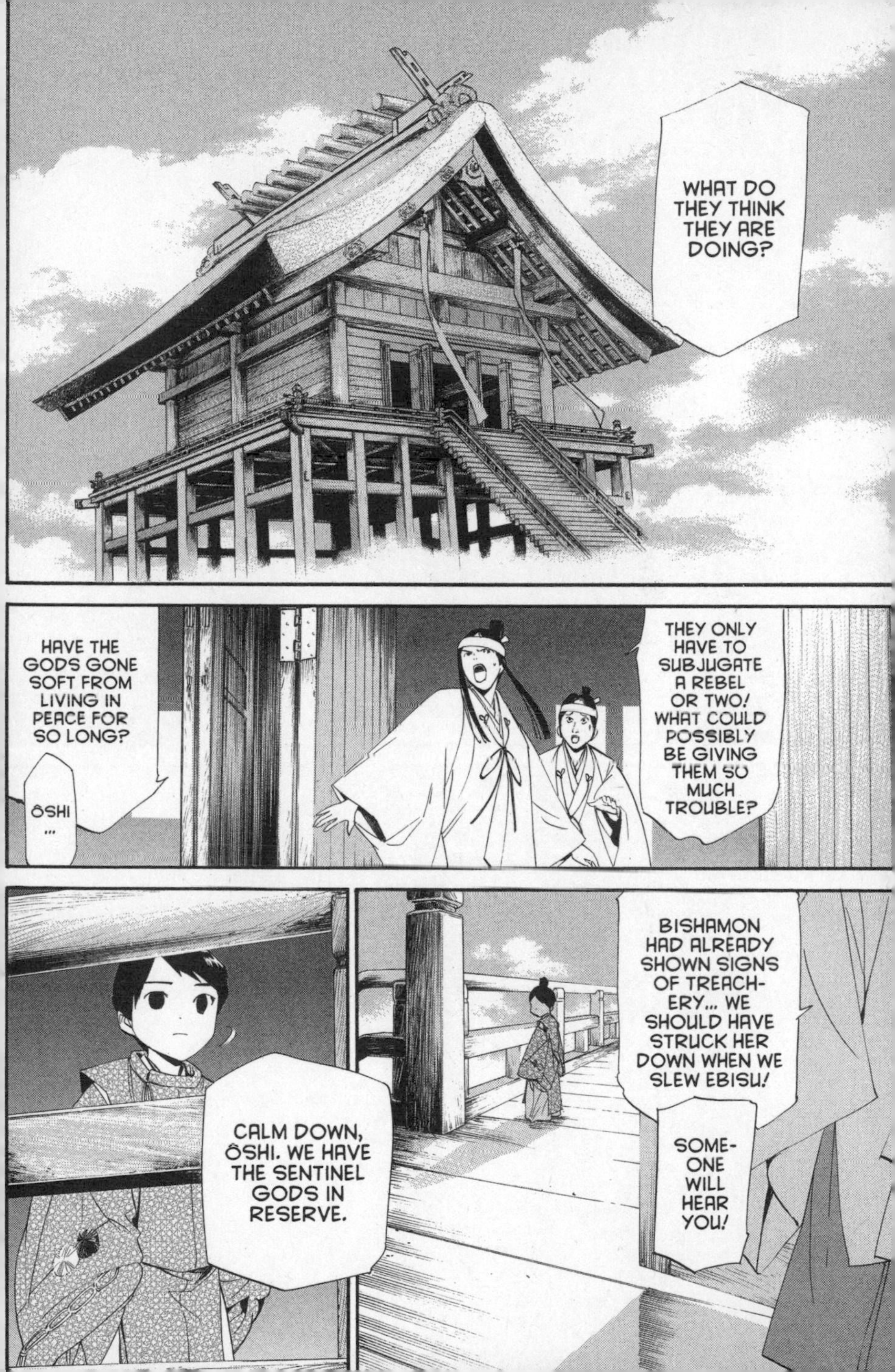
WHAT DO THEY THINK THEY ARE DOING?
THEY ONLY HAVE TO SUBJUGATE A REBEL OR TWO! WHAT COULD POSSIBLY BE GIVING THEM SO MUCH TROUBLE?
HAVE THE GODS GONE SOFT FROM LIVING IN PEACE FOR SO LONG?
ÔSHI ...
BISHAMON HAD ALREADY SHOWN SIGNS OF TREACH-ERY... WE SHOULD HAVE STRUCK HER DOWN WHEN WE SLEW EBISU!
SOME-ONE WILL HEAR YOU!
CALM DOWN, ÔSHI. WE HAVE THE SENTINEL GODS IN RESERVE.

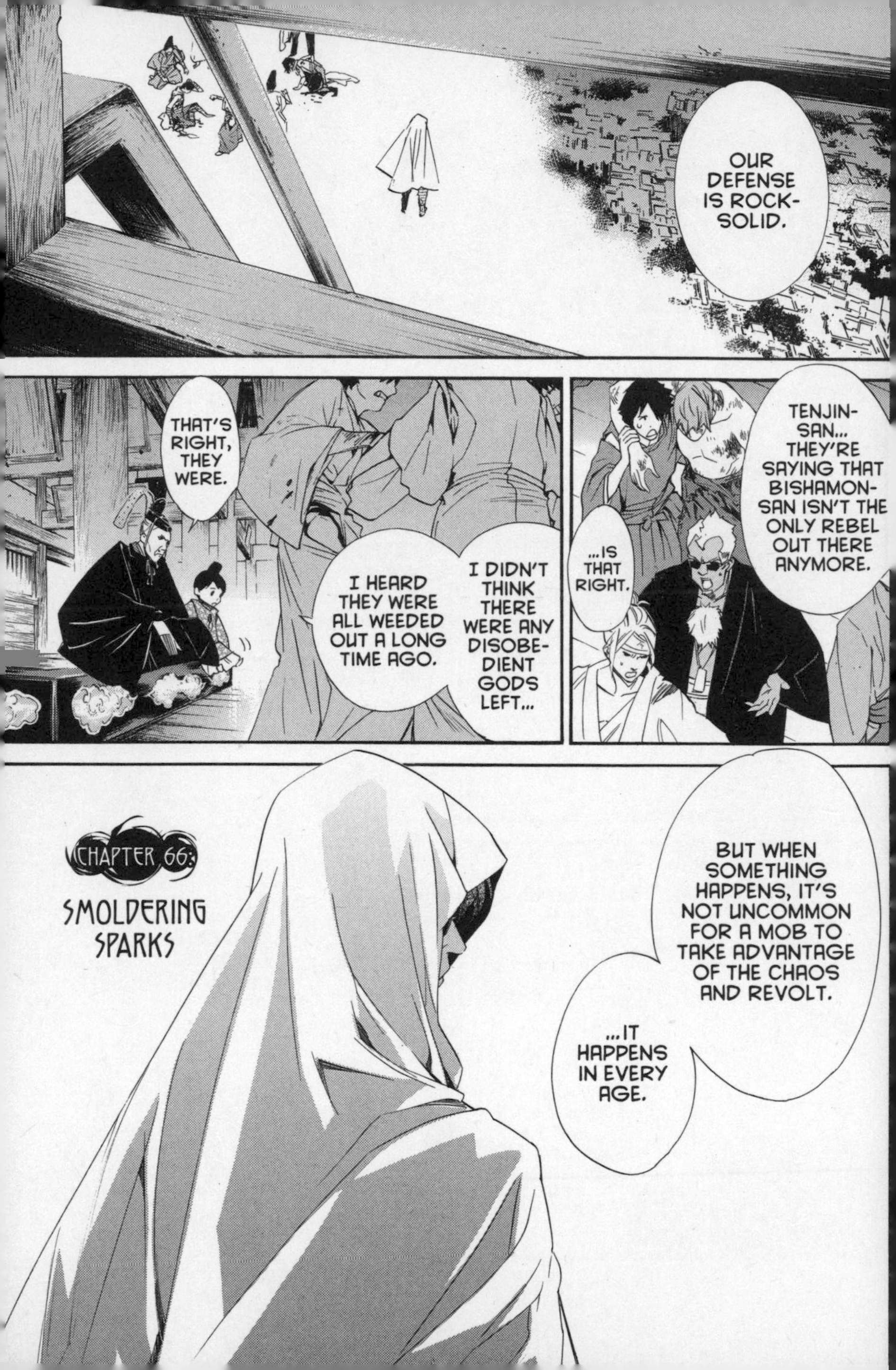
OUR DEFENSE IS ROCK-SOLID.
TENJIN-SAN... THEY'RE SAYING THAT BISHAMON-SAN ISN'T THE ONLY REBEL OUT THERE ANYMORE.
...IS THAT RIGHT.
I DIDN'T THINK THERE WERE ANY DISOBEDIENT GODS LEFT...
I HEARD THEY WERE ALL WEEDED OUT A LONG TIME AGO.
THAT'S RIGHT, THEY WERE.
BUT WHEN SOMETHING HAPPENS, IT'S NOT UNCOMMON FOR A MOB TO TAKE ADVANTAGE OF THE CHAOS AND REVOLT.
...IT HAPPENS IN EVERY AGE.
CHAPTER 66:
SMOLDERING SPARKS

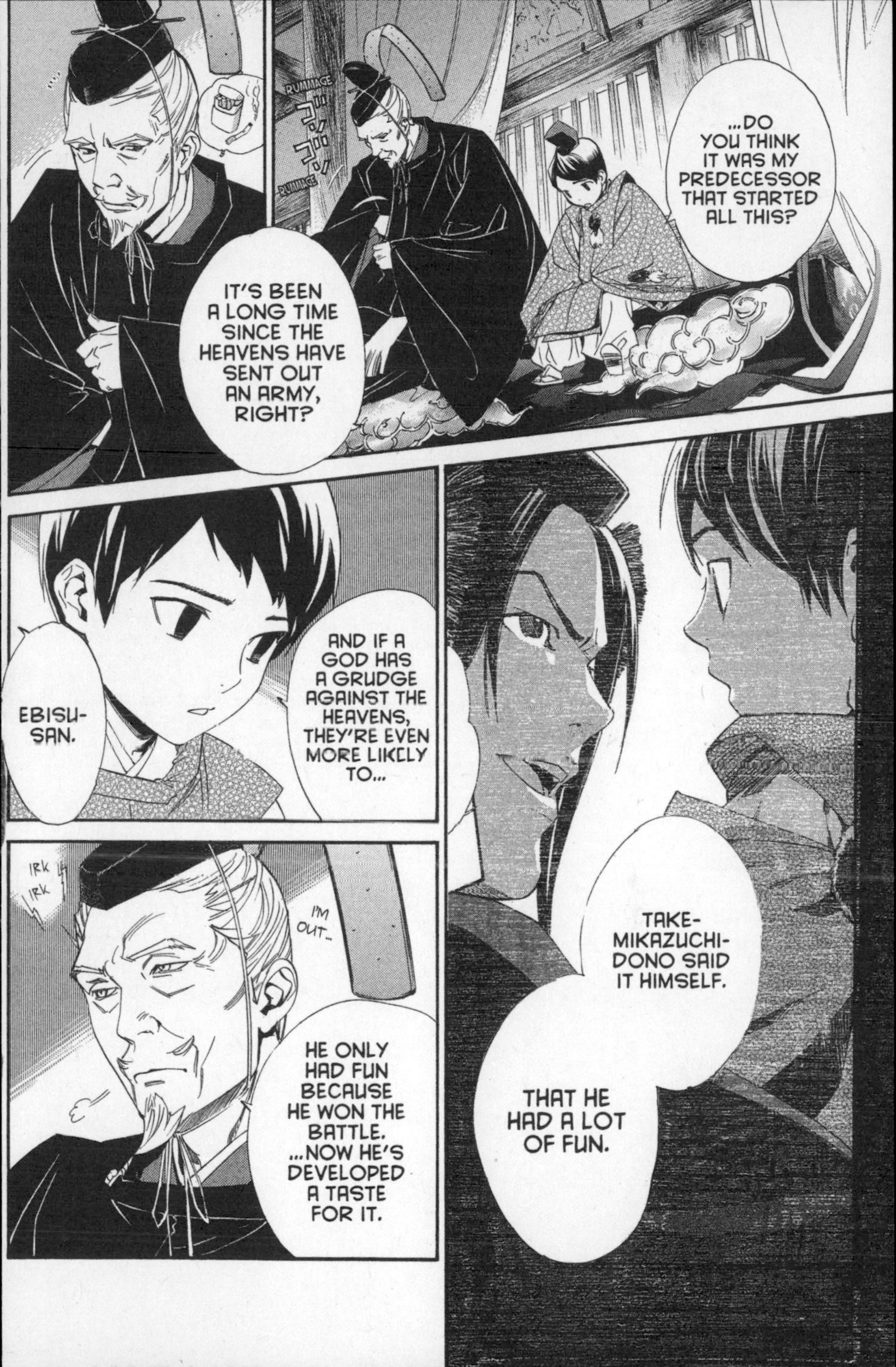
...DO YOU THINK IT WAS MY PREDECESSOR THAT STARTED ALL THIS?
RUMMAGE
RUMMAGE
IT'S BEEN A LONG TIME SINCE THE HEAVENS HAVE SENT OUT AN ARMY, RIGHT?
...
TAKE-MIKAZUCHI-DONO SAID IT HIMSELF.
THAT HE HAD A LOT OF FUN.
AND IF A GOD HAS A GRUDGE AGAINST THE HEAVENS, THEY'RE EVEN MORE LIKELY TO...
EBISU-SAN.
I'M OUT...
IRK IRK
HE ONLY HAD FUN BECAUSE HE WON THE BATTLE. ...NOW HE'S DEVELOPED A TASTE FOR IT.

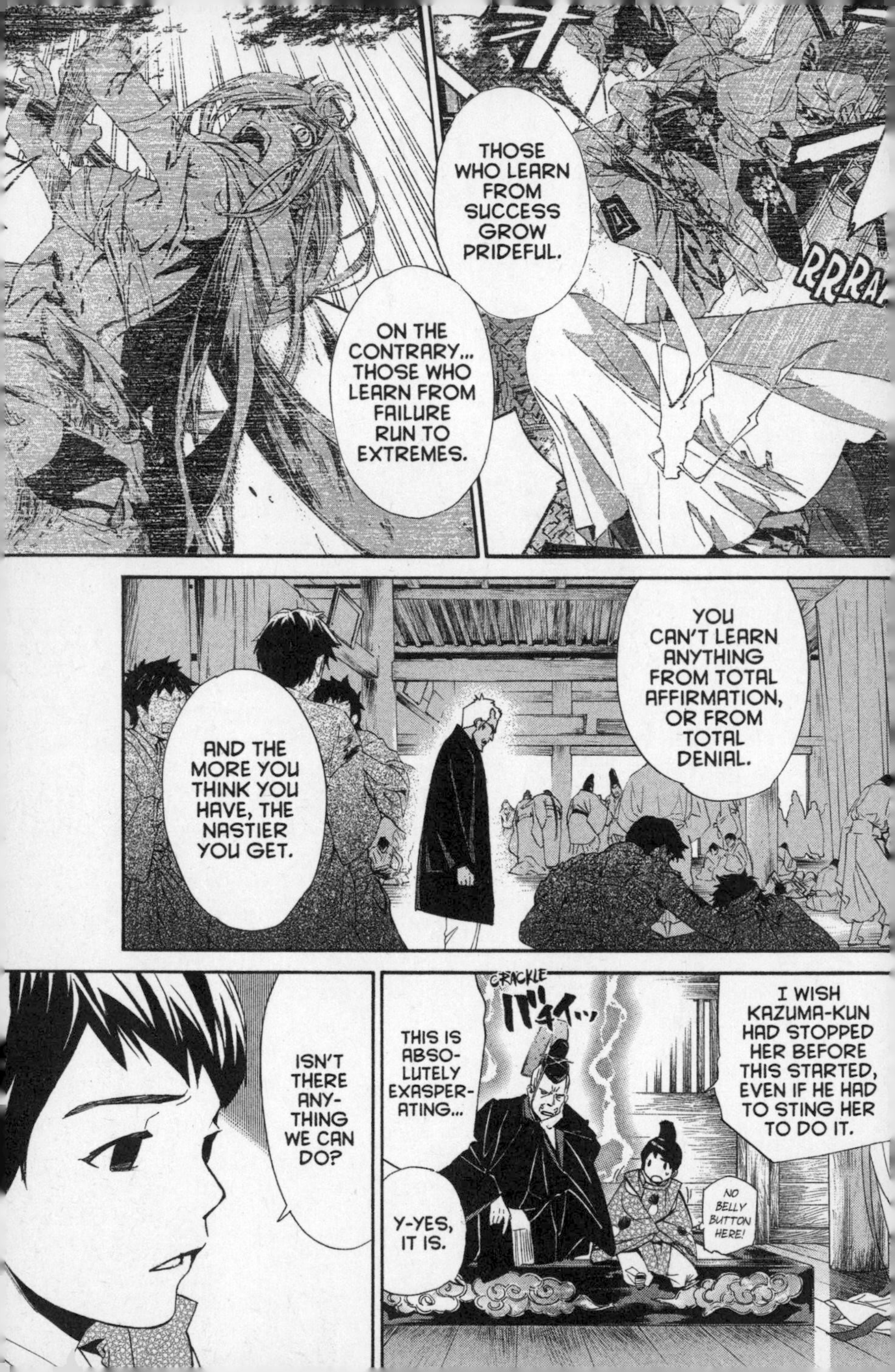
RRRA…
THOSE WHO LEARN FROM SUCCESS GROW PRIDEFUL.
ON THE CONTRARY… THOSE WHO LEARN FROM FAILURE RUN TO EXTREMES.
YOU CAN'T LEARN ANYTHING FROM TOTAL AFFIRMATION, OR FROM TOTAL DENIAL.
AND THE MORE YOU THINK YOU HAVE, THE NASTIER YOU GET.
I WISH KAZUMA-KUN HAD STOPPED HER BEFORE THIS STARTED, EVEN IF HE HAD TO STING HER TO DO IT.
CRACKLE
バチイッ
THIS IS ABSOLUTELY EXASPERATING…
NO BELLY BUTTON HERE!
Y-YES, IT IS.
ISN'T THERE ANYTHING WE CAN DO?

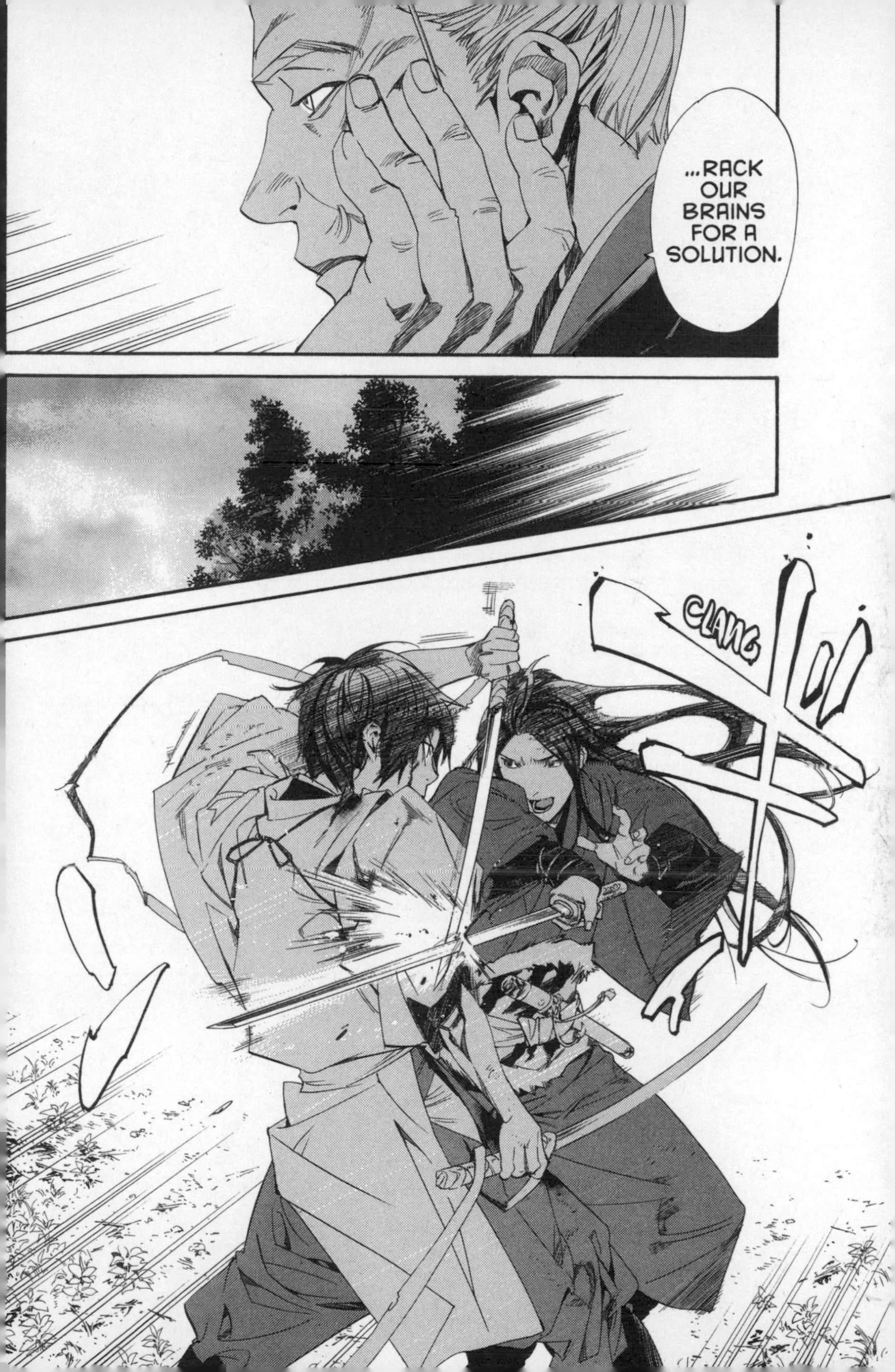
...RACK OUR BRAINS FOR A SOLUTION.
CLANG

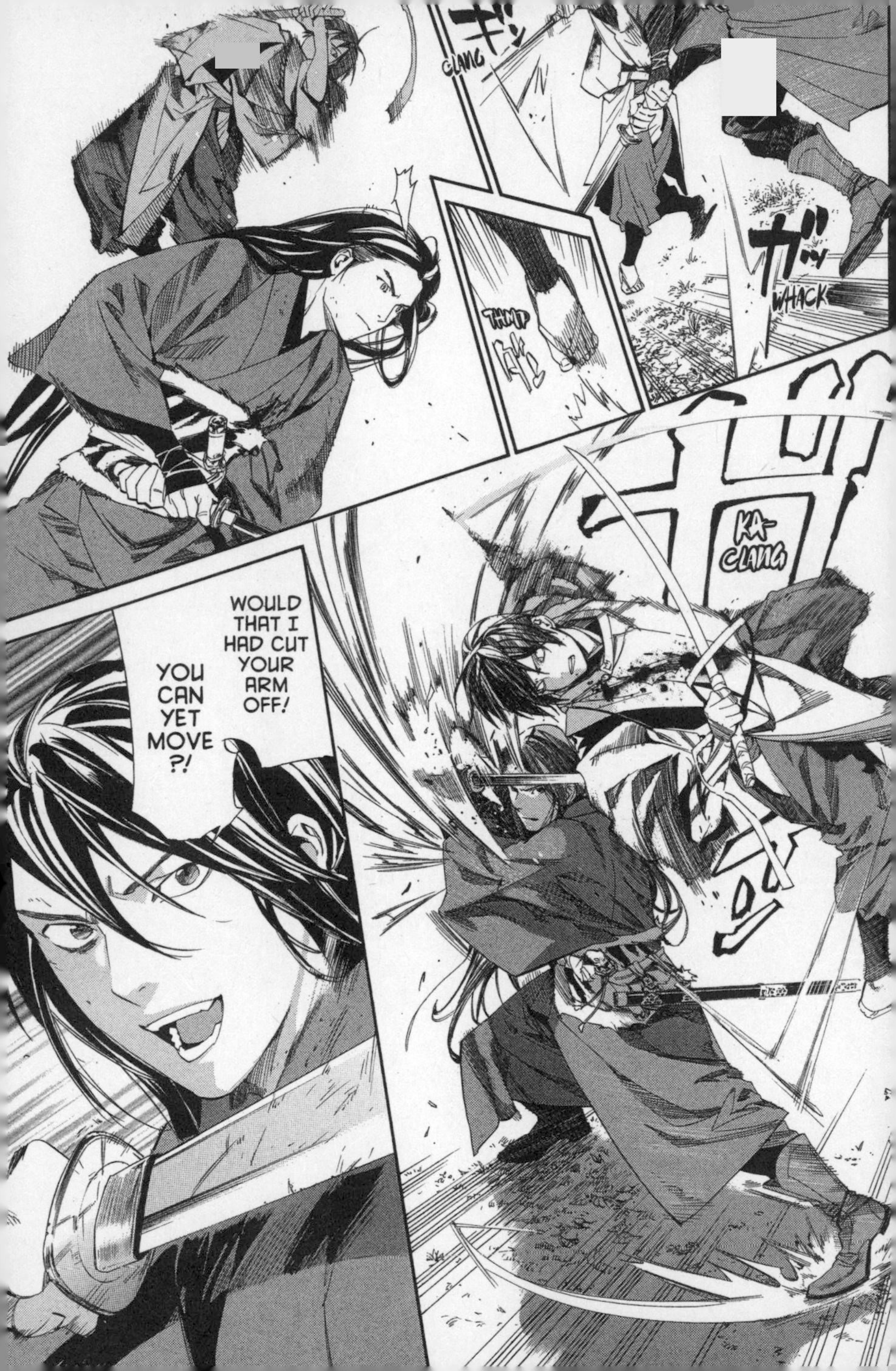
CLANG
WHACK
THUMP
KA-CLANG
WOULD THAT I HAD CUT YOUR ARM OFF!
YOU CAN YET MOVE?!

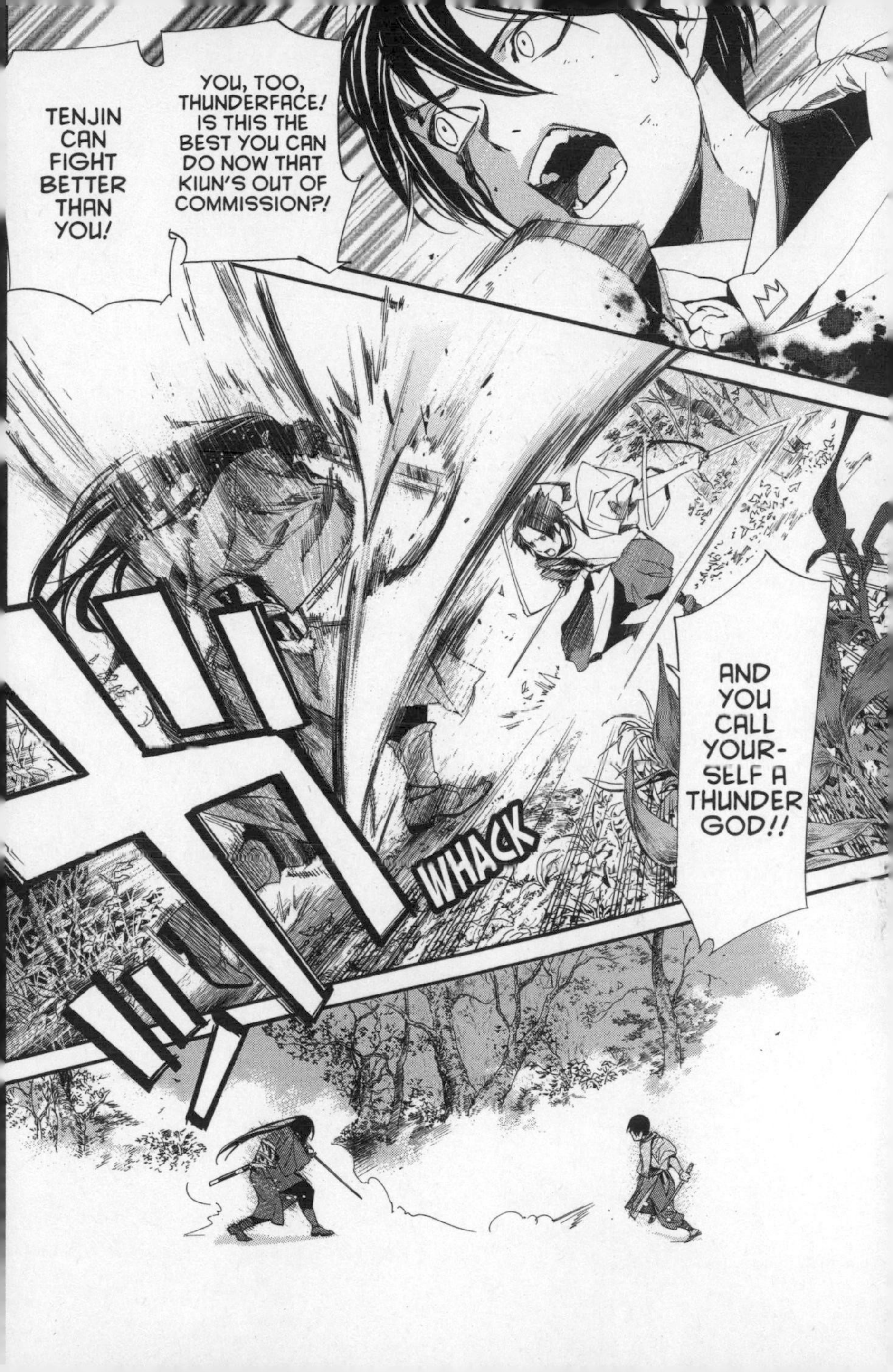
YOU, TOO, THUNDERFACE! IS THIS THE BEST YOU CAN DO NOW THAT KIUN'S OUT OF COMMISSION?!
TENJIN CAN FIGHT BETTER THAN YOU!
AND YOU CALL YOURSELF A THUNDER GOD!!
WHACK

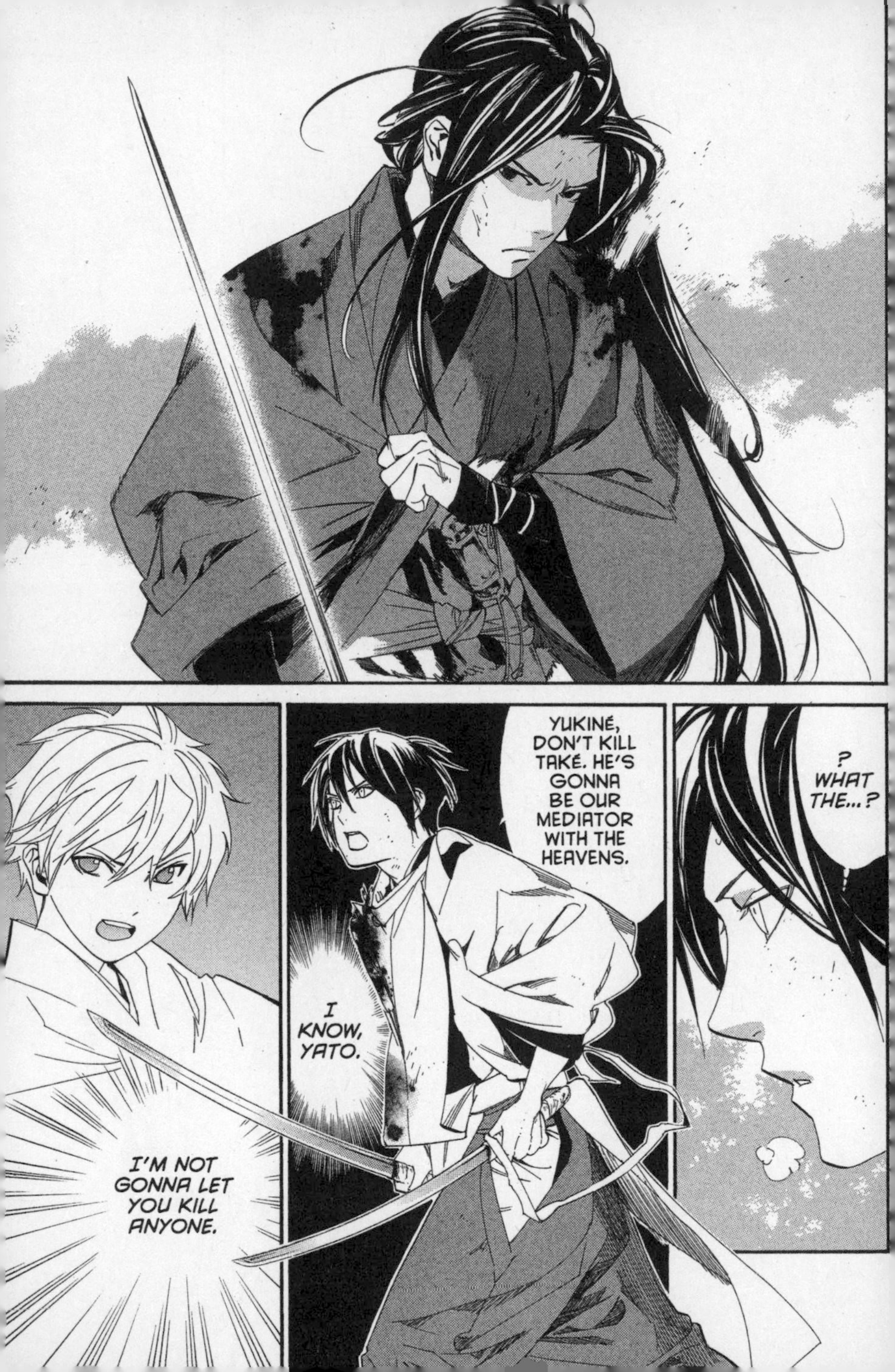
? WHAT THE...?
YUKINÉ, DON'T KILL TAKÉ. HE'S GONNA BE OUR MEDIATOR WITH THE HEAVENS.
I KNOW, YATO.
I'M NOT GONNA LET YOU KILL ANYONE.

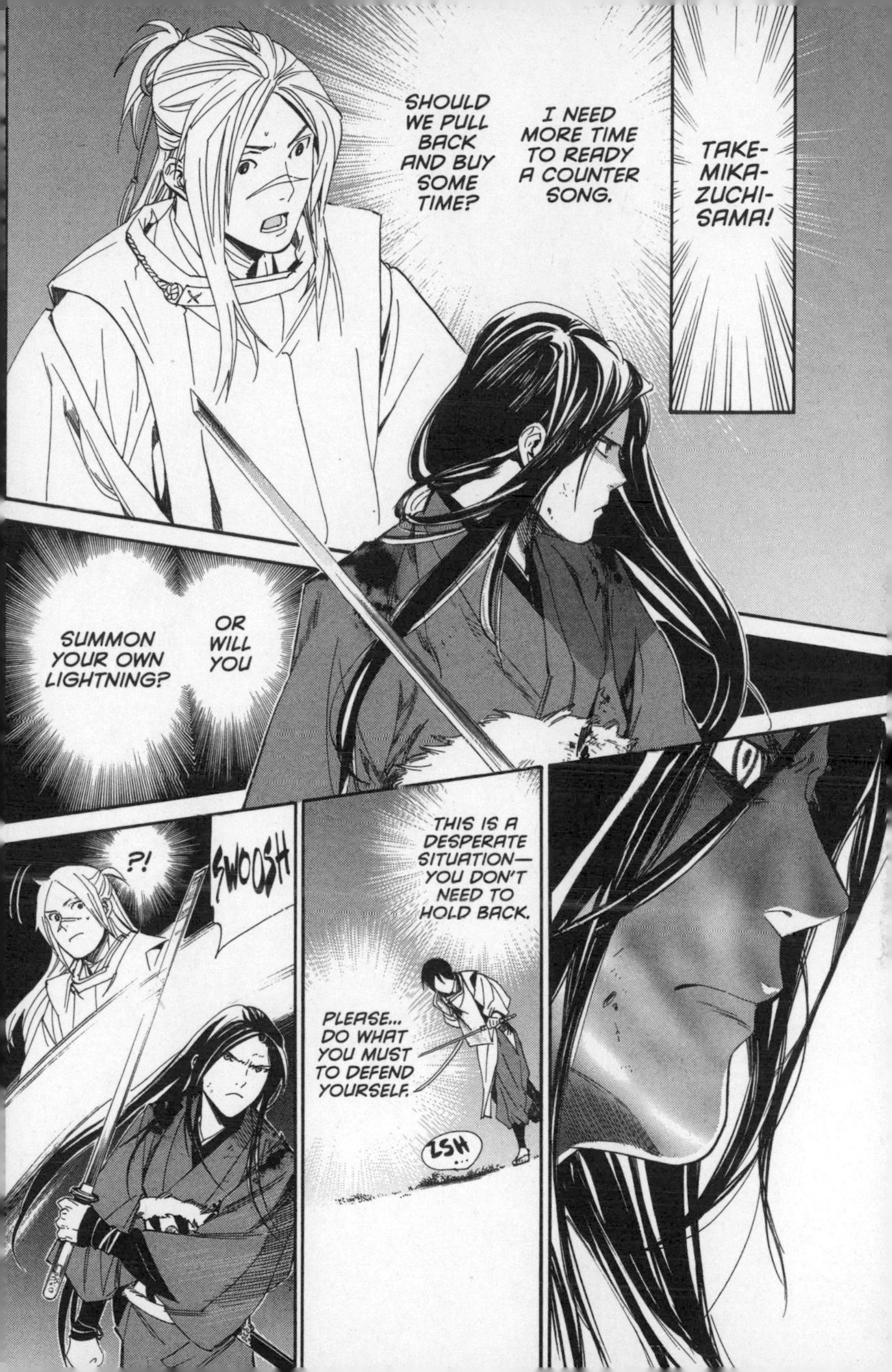
TAKE-MIKA-ZUCHI-SAMA!
I NEED MORE TIME TO READY A COUNTER SONG.
SHOULD WE PULL BACK AND BUY SOME TIME?
OR WILL YOU
SUMMON YOUR OWN LIGHTNING?
THIS IS A DESPERATE SITUATION—YOU DON'T NEED TO HOLD BACK.
PLEASE... DO WHAT YOU MUST TO DEFEND YOURSELF.
ZSH...
SWOOSH
?!

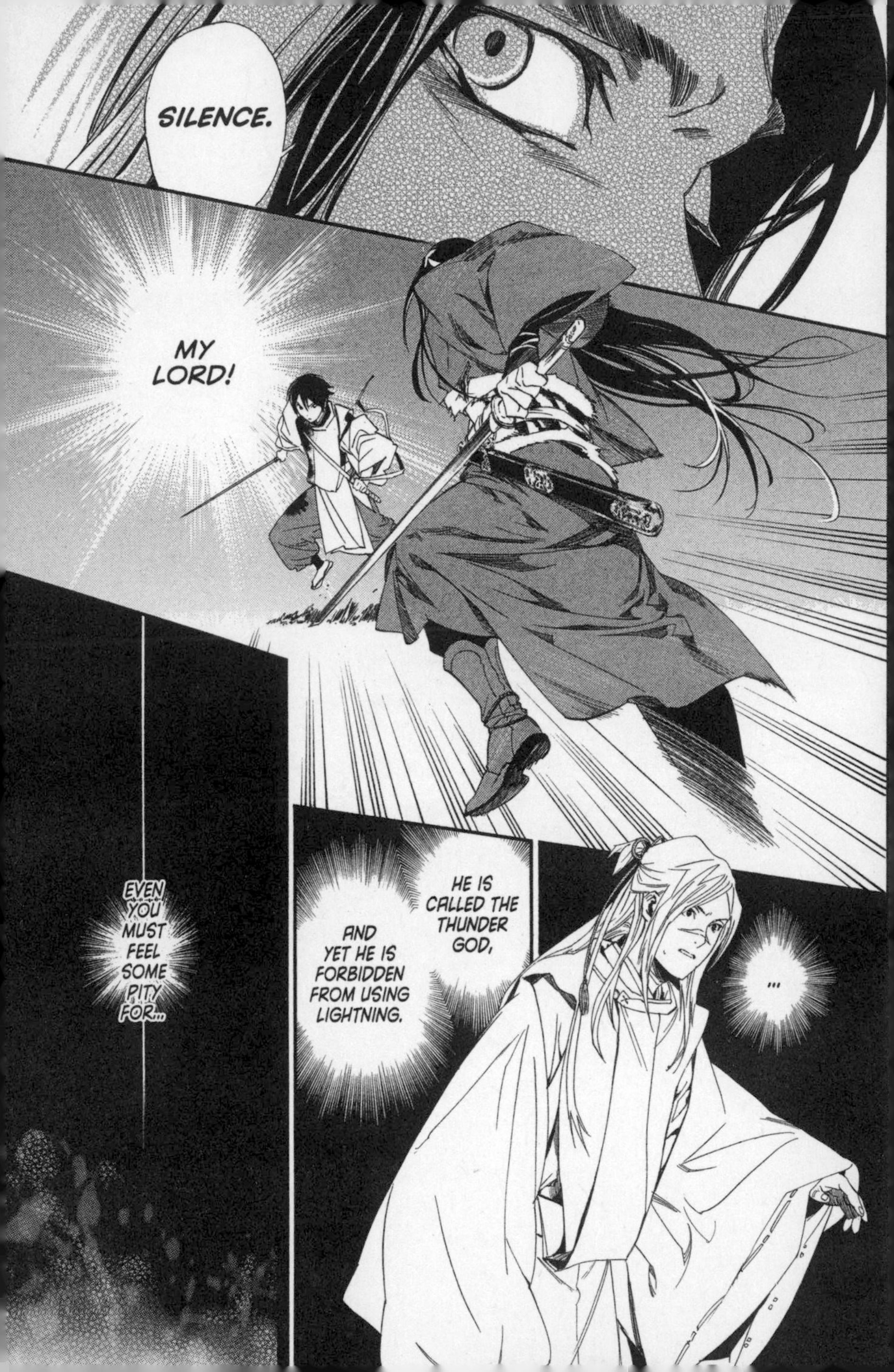
SILENCE.
MY LORD!
...
HE IS CALLED THE THUNDER GOD,
AND YET HE IS FORBIDDEN FROM USING LIGHTNING.
EVEN YOU MUST FEEL SOME PITY FOR...

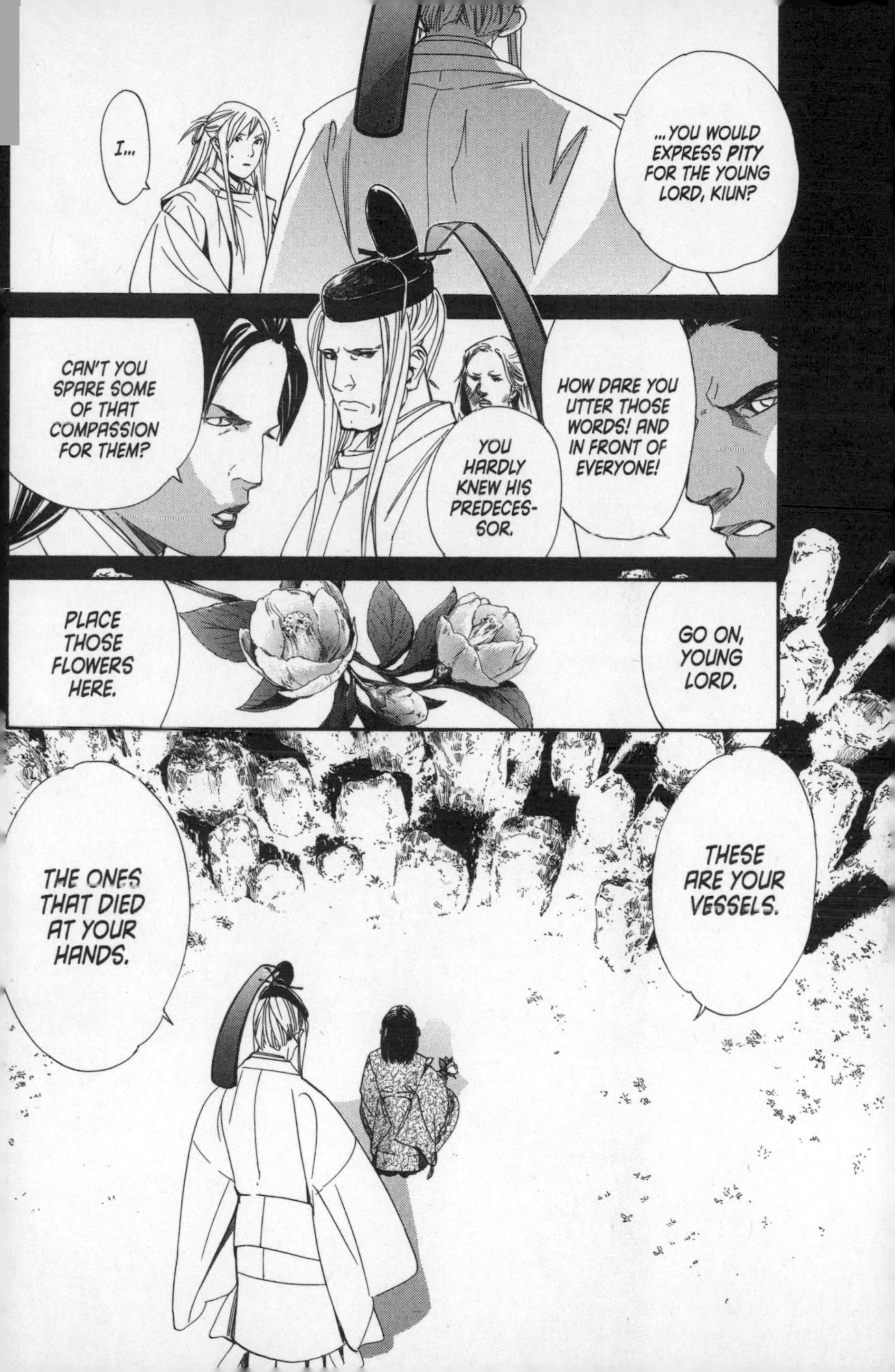
...YOU WOULD EXPRESS PITY FOR THE YOUNG LORD, KIUN?
I...
HOW DARE YOU UTTER THOSE WORDS! AND IN FRONT OF EVERYONE!
YOU HARDLY KNEW HIS PREDECES-SOR.
CAN'T YOU SPARE SOME OF THAT COMPASSION FOR THEM?
GO ON, YOUNG LORD.
PLACE THOSE FLOWERS HERE.
THESE ARE YOUR VESSELS.
THE ONES THAT DIED AT YOUR HANDS.

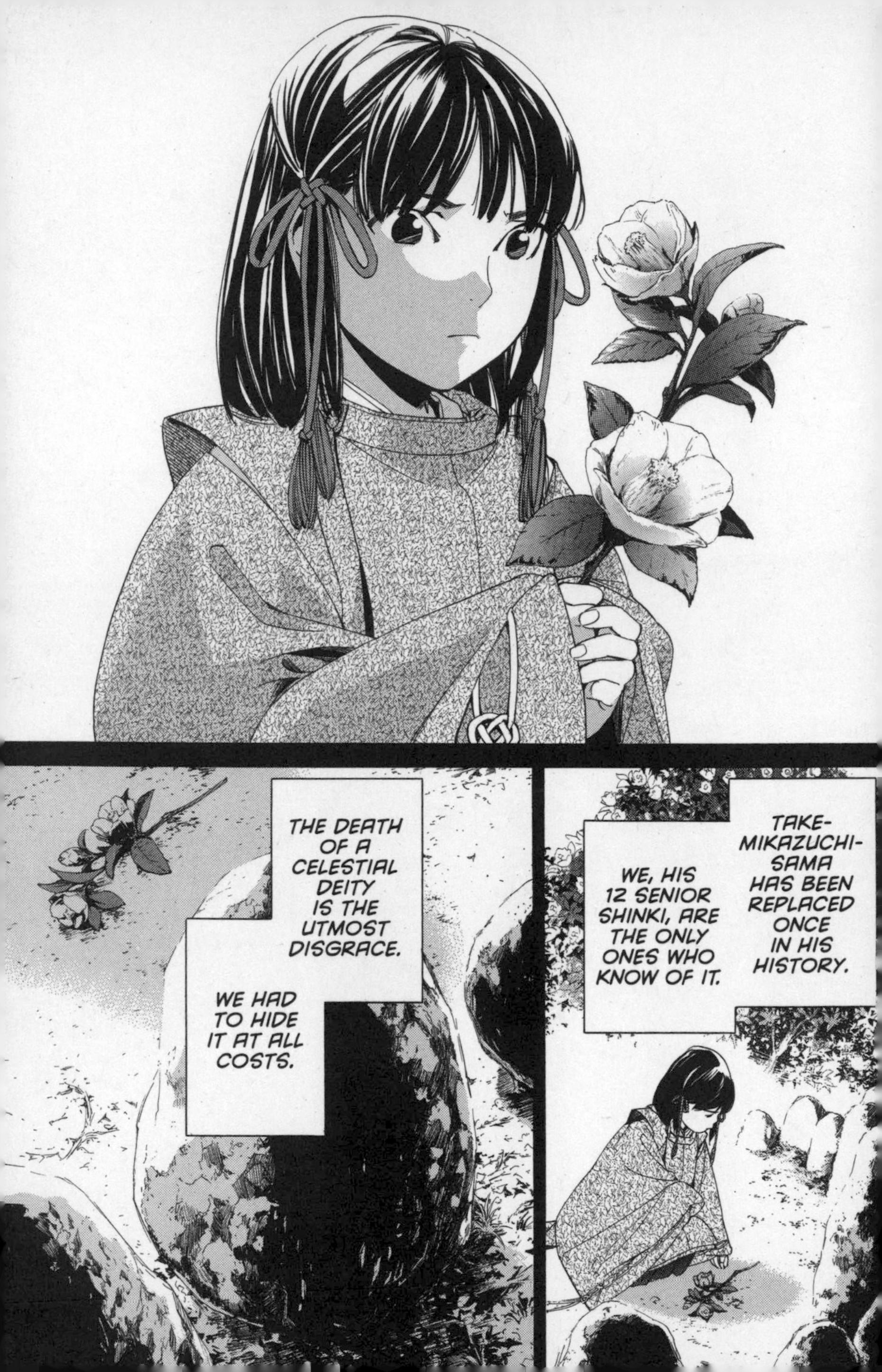
TAKE-MIKAZUCHI-SAMA HAS BEEN REPLACED ONCE IN HIS HISTORY.
WE, HIS 12 SENIOR SHINKI, ARE THE ONLY ONES WHO KNOW OF IT.
THE DEATH OF A CELESTIAL DEITY IS THE UTMOST DISGRACE.
WE HAD TO HIDE IT AT ALL COSTS.

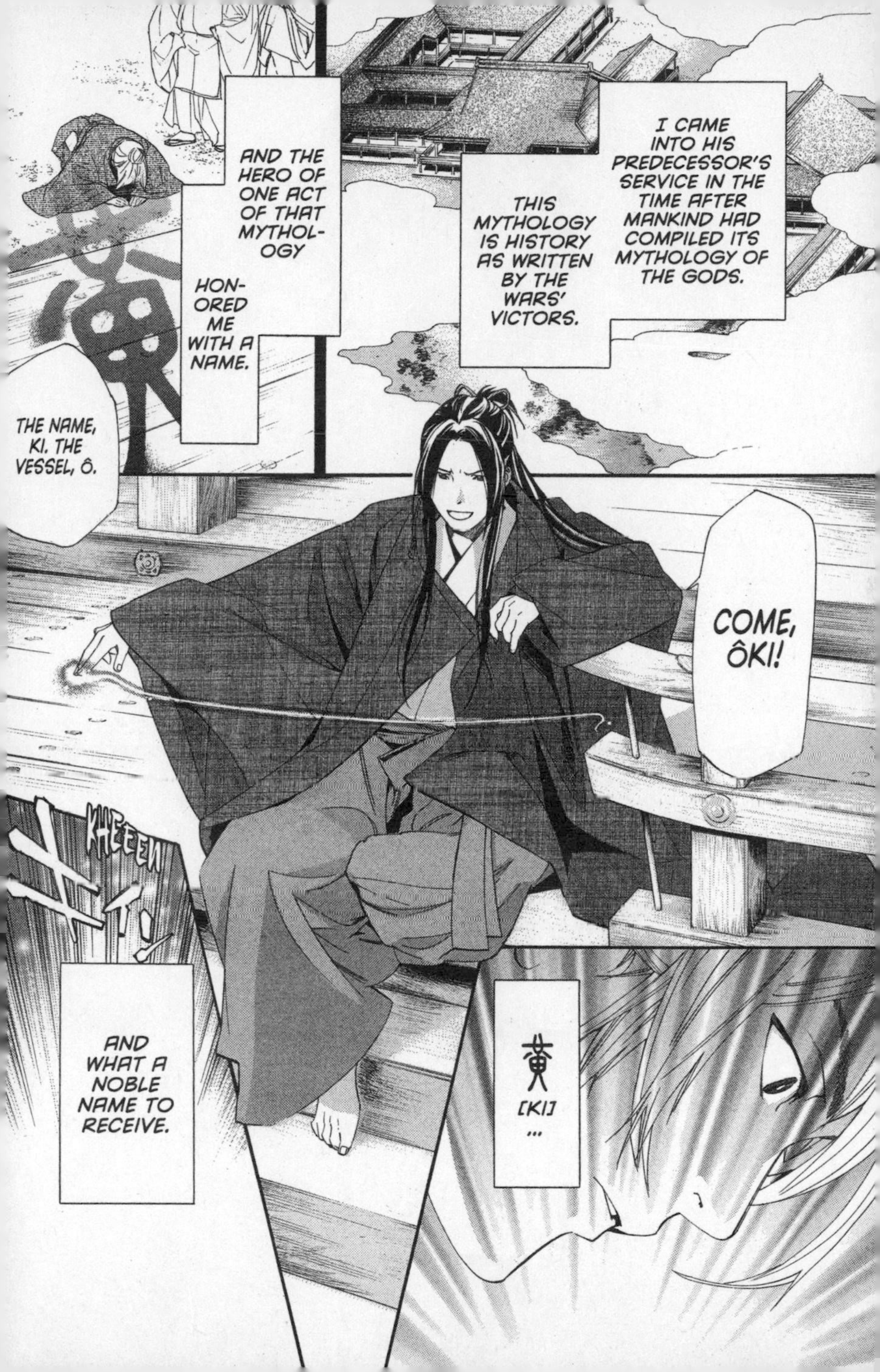
I CAME INTO HIS PREDECESSOR'S SERVICE IN THE TIME AFTER MANKIND HAD COMPILED ITS MYTHOLOGY OF THE GODS.
THIS MYTHOLOGY IS HISTORY AS WRITTEN BY THE WARS' VICTORS.
AND THE HERO OF ONE ACT OF THAT MYTHOL-OGY
HON-ORED ME WITH A NAME.
THE NAME, KI. THE VESSEL, Ô.
COME, ÔKI!
KHEEEEN
黄 [KI] ...
AND WHAT A NOBLE NAME TO RECEIVE.

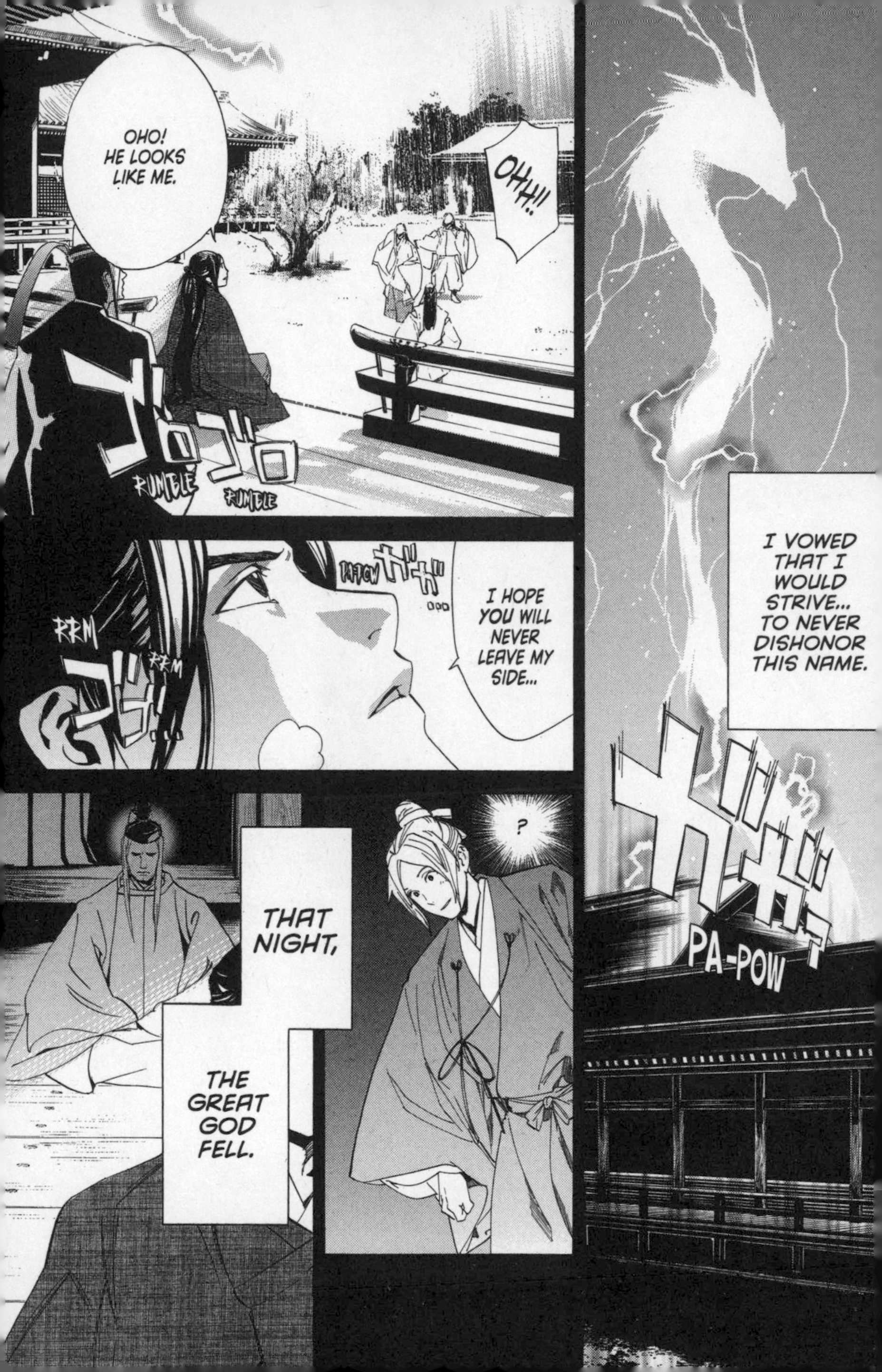
I VOWED THAT I WOULD STRIVE... TO NEVER DISHONOR THIS NAME.
PA-POW
OHH!!
OHO! HE LOOKS LIKE ME.
RUMBLE
RUMBLE
PA-POW
I HOPE YOU WILL NEVER LEAVE MY SIDE...
RRM
RRM
?
THAT NIGHT,
THE GREAT GOD FELL.

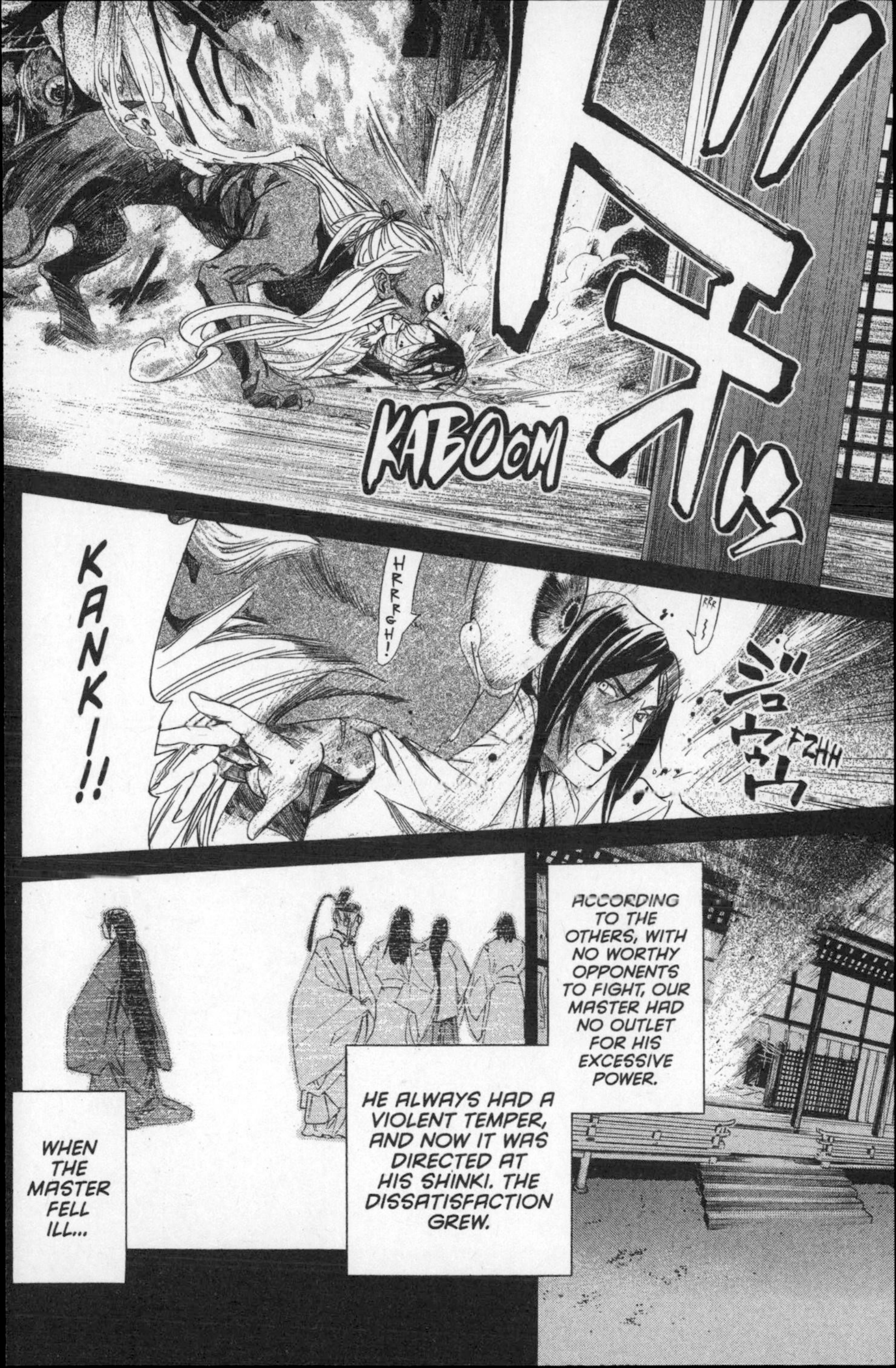
KABOOM
RRR
FZHH
HRRRGH!
KANKI!!
ACCORDING TO THE OTHERS, WITH NO WORTHY OPPONENTS TO FIGHT, OUR MASTER HAD NO OUTLET FOR HIS EXCESSIVE POWER.
HE ALWAYS HAD A VIOLENT TEMPER, AND NOW IT WAS DIRECTED AT HIS SHINKI. THE DISSATISFACTION GREW.
WHEN THE MASTER FELL ILL...

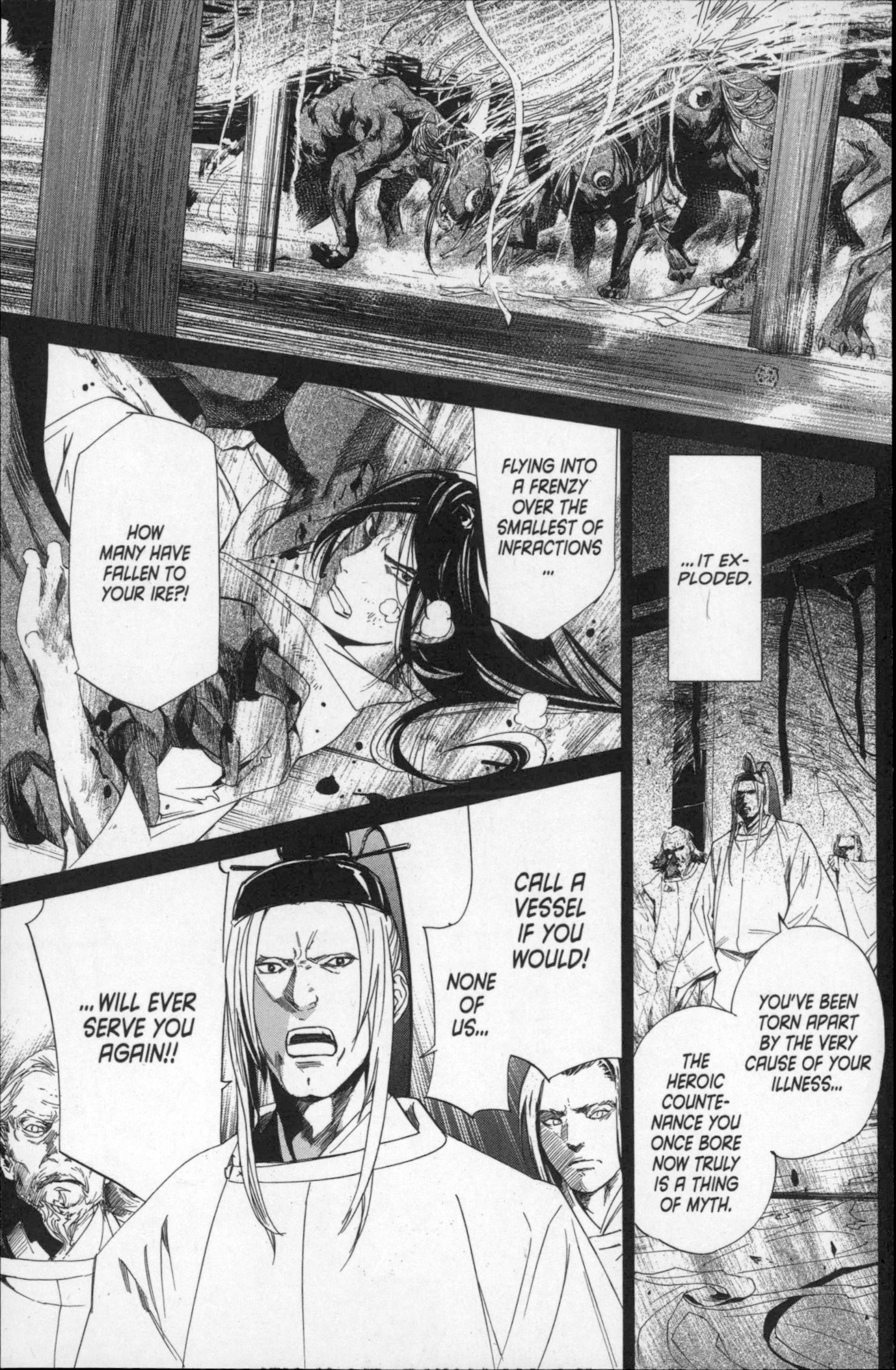
...IT EXPLODED.
YOU'VE BEEN TORN APART BY THE VERY CAUSE OF YOUR ILLNESS...
THE HEROIC COUNTENANCE YOU ONCE BORE NOW TRULY IS A THING OF MYTH.
FLYING INTO A FRENZY OVER THE SMALLEST OF INFRACTIONS...
HOW MANY HAVE FALLEN TO YOUR IRE?!
CALL A VESSEL IF YOU WOULD!
NONE OF US...
...WILL EVER SERVE YOU AGAIN!!

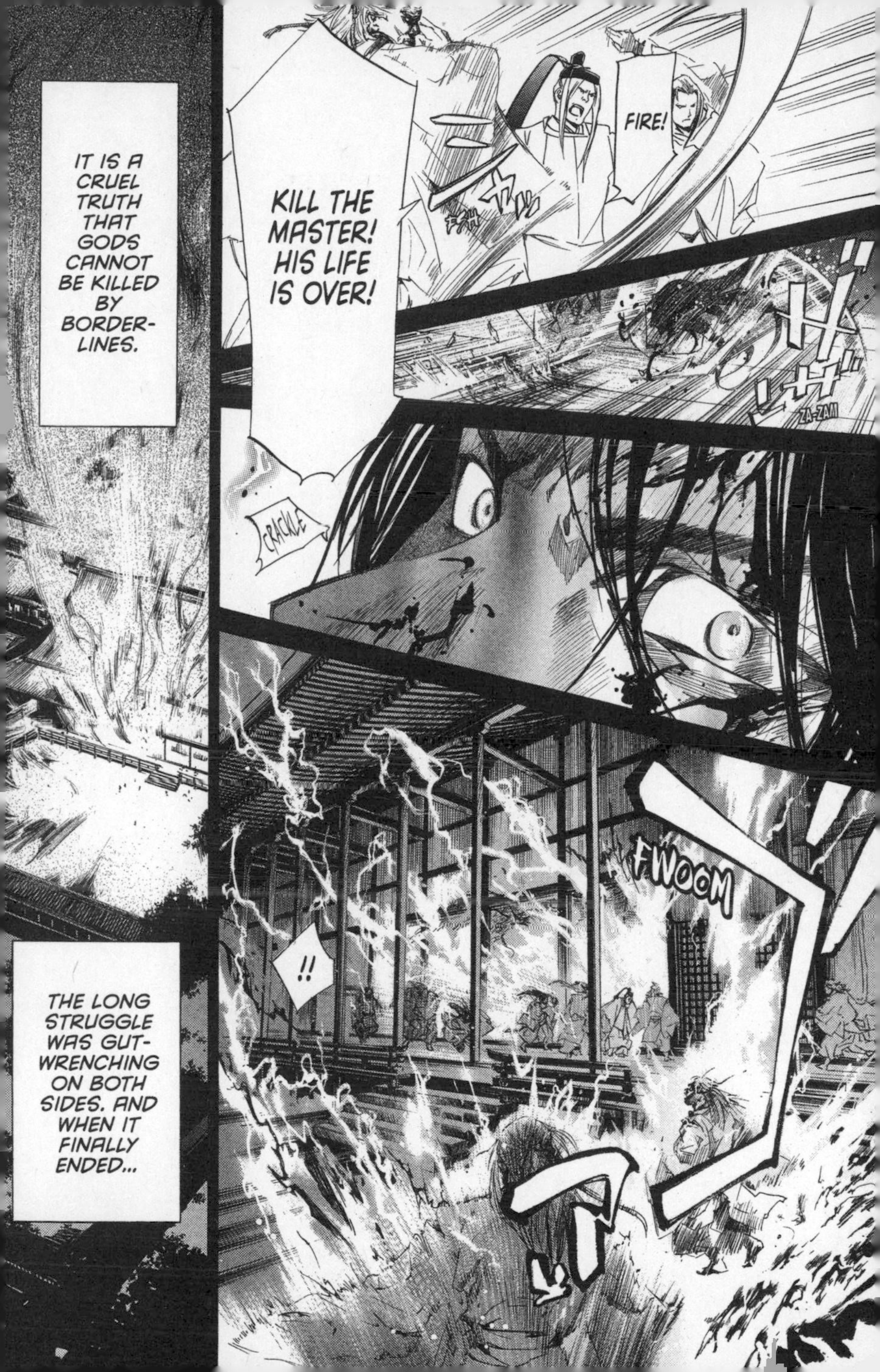
FIRE!
KILL THE MASTER! HIS LIFE IS OVER!
ZA-ZAM
IT IS A CRUEL TRUTH THAT GODS CANNOT BE KILLED BY BORDER-LINES.
CRACKLE
FWOOM
!!
THE LONG STRUGGLE WAS GUT-WRENCHING ON BOTH SIDES. AND WHEN IT FINALLY ENDED...

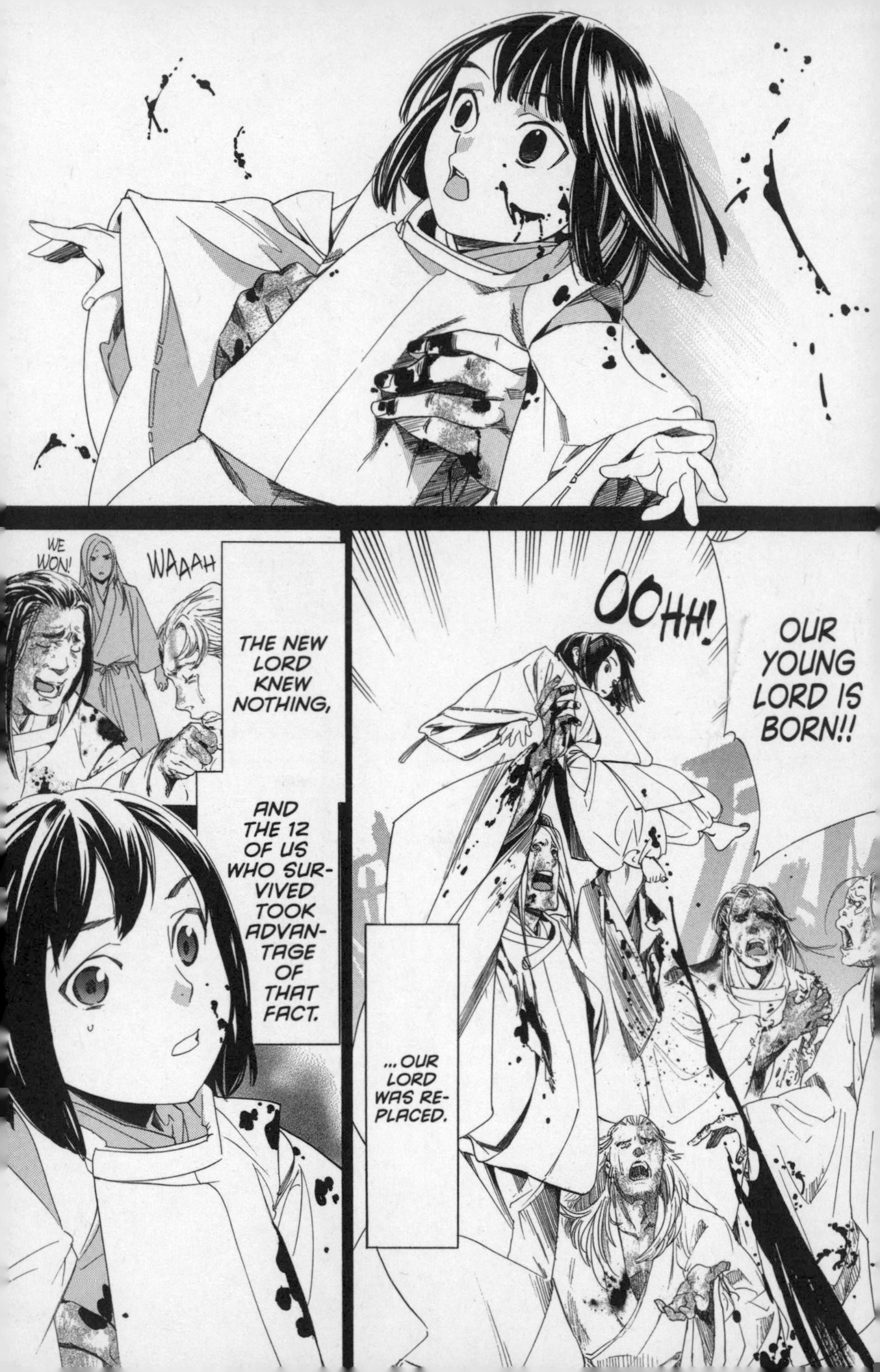
OUR YOUNG LORD IS BORN!!
OOHH!
...OUR LORD WAS REPLACED.
THE NEW LORD KNEW NOTHING,
WAAAH
WE WON!
AND THE 12 OF US WHO SUR-VIVED TOOK ADVAN-TAGE OF THAT FACT.

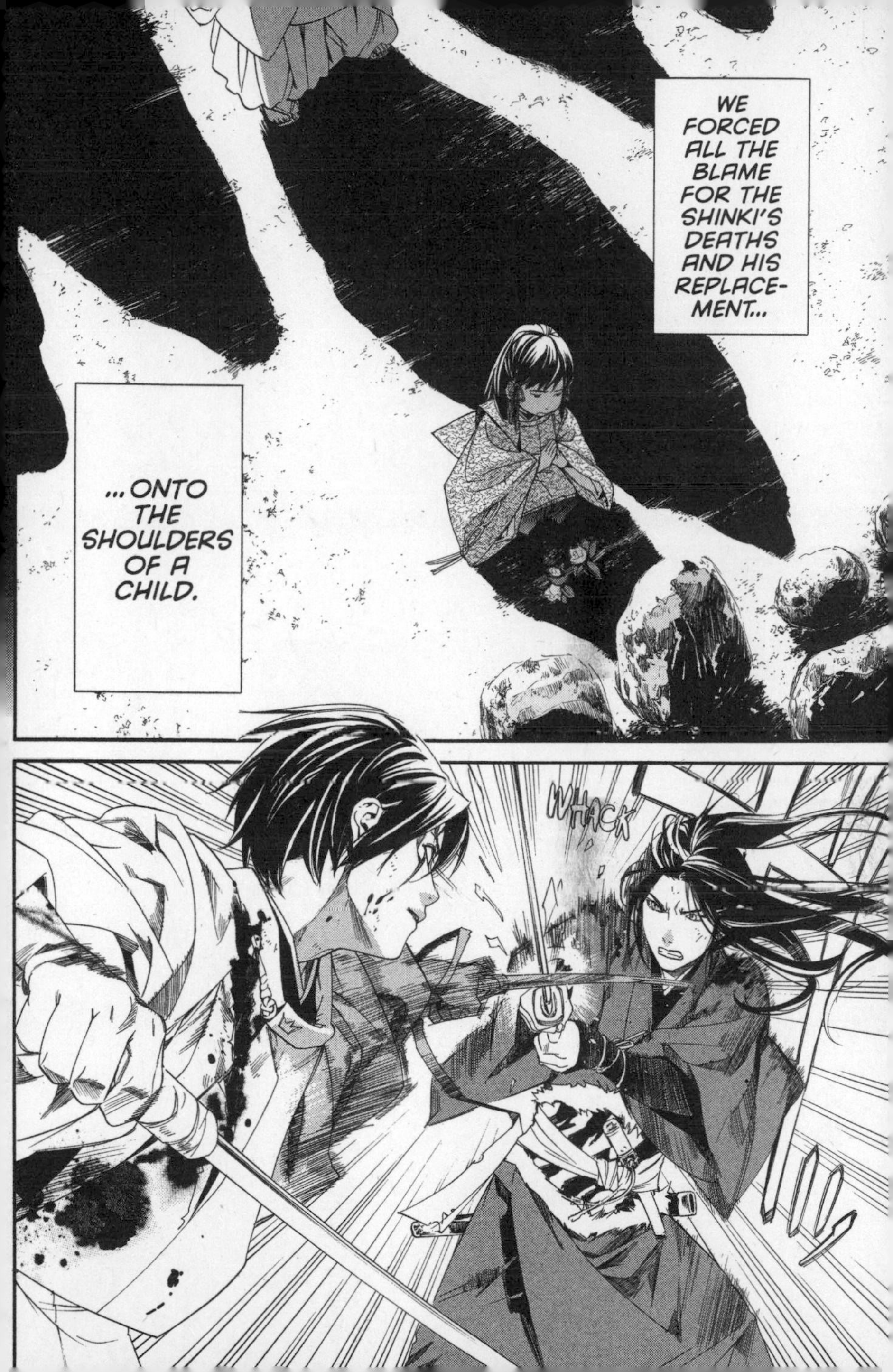
WE FORCED ALL THE BLAME FOR THE SHINKI'S DEATHS AND HIS REPLACEMENT...
...ONTO THE SHOULDERS OF A CHILD.
WHACK

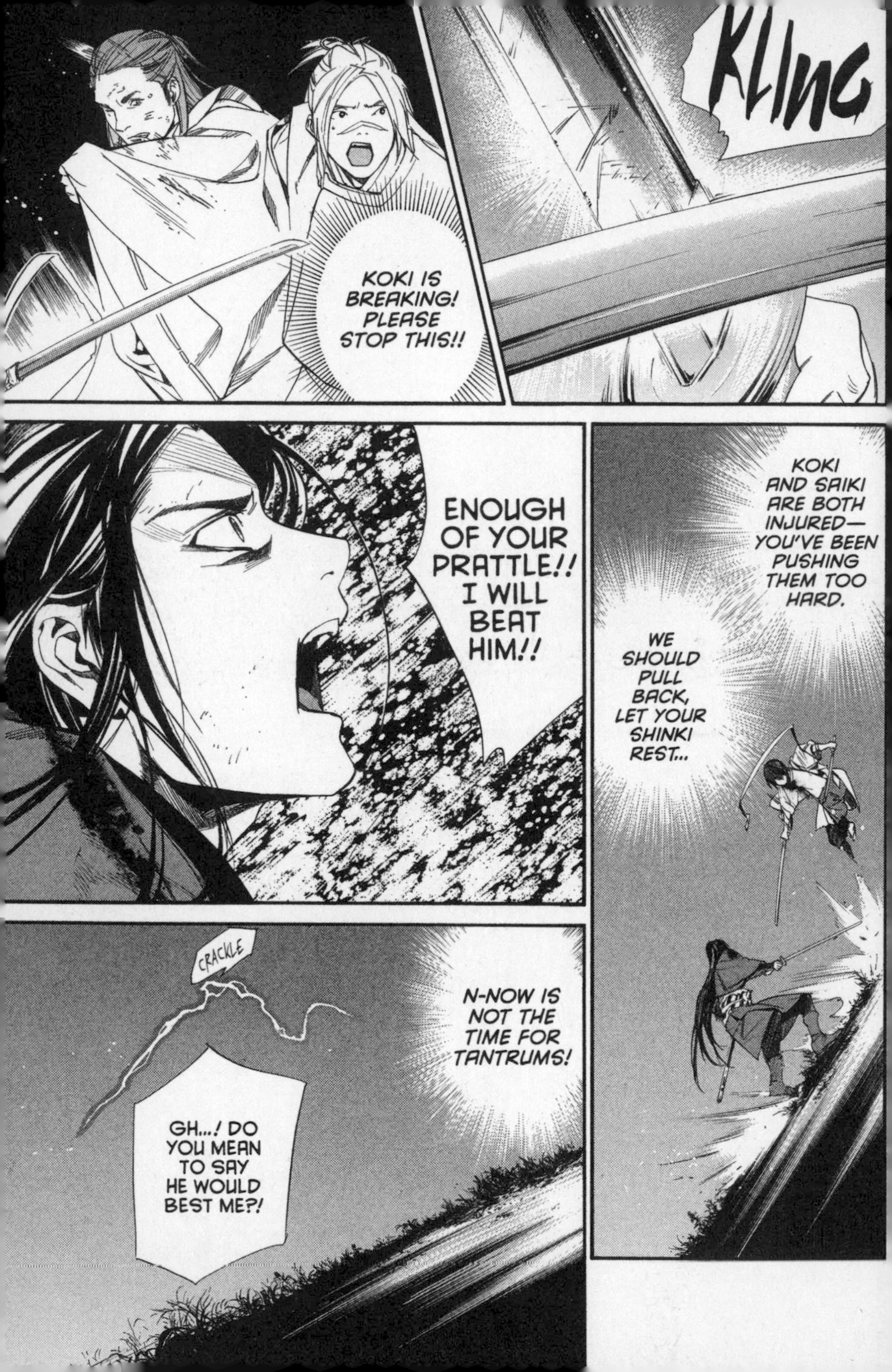

KLING
KOKI IS BREAKING! PLEASE STOP THIS!!
KOKI AND SAIKI ARE BOTH INJURED—YOU'VE BEEN PUSHING THEM TOO HARD.
WE SHOULD PULL BACK, LET YOUR SHINKI REST...
ENOUGH OF YOUR PRATTLE!! I WILL BEAT HIM!!
N-NOW IS NOT THE TIME FOR TANTRUMS!
CRACKLE
GH...! DO YOU MEAN TO SAY HE WOULD BEST ME?!

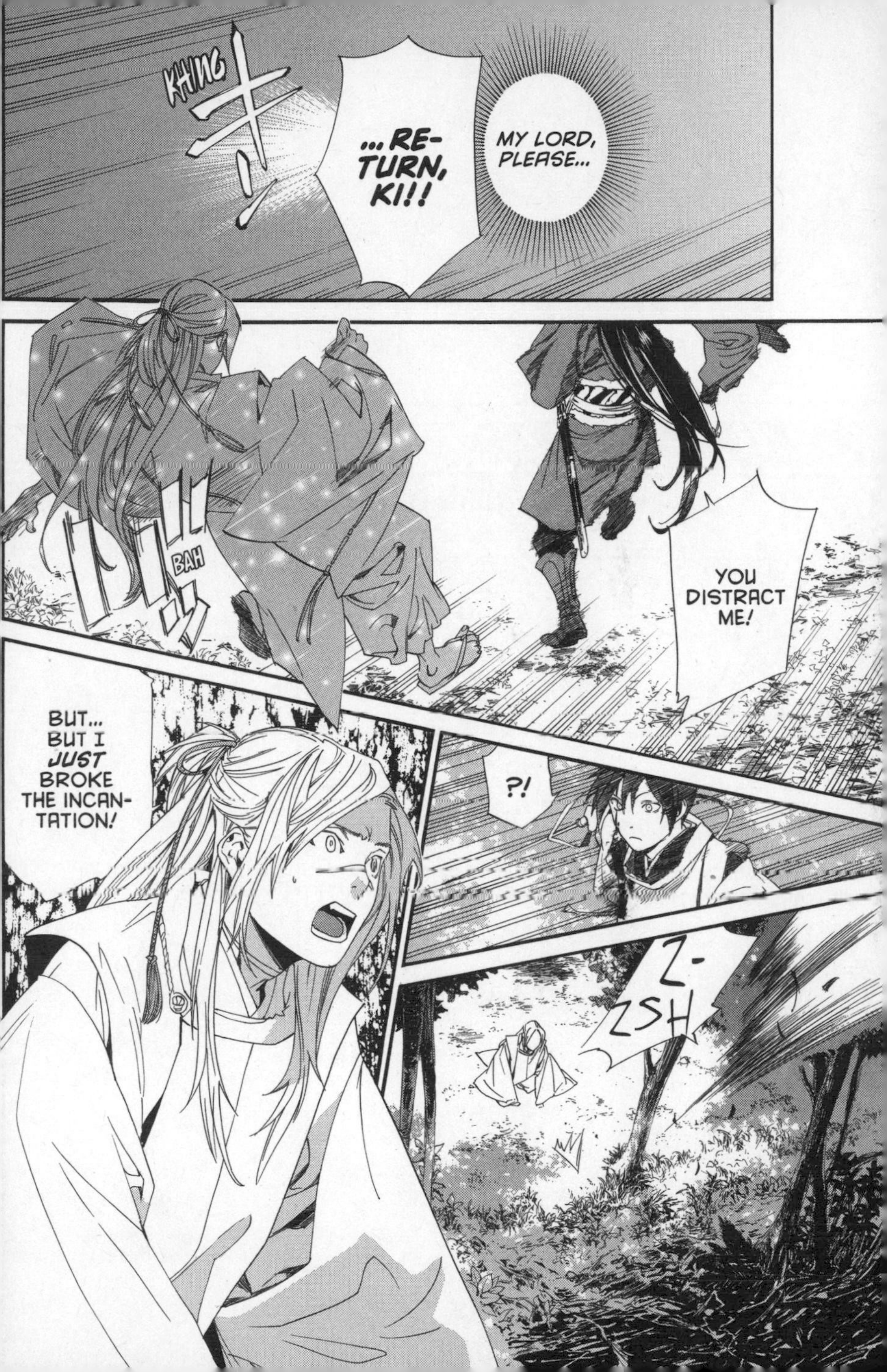
MY LORD, PLEASE...
...RE-TURN, KI!!
KHING
YOU DISTRACT ME!
BAH
?!
Z-ZSH
BUT... BUT I *JUST* BROKE THE INCANTATION!

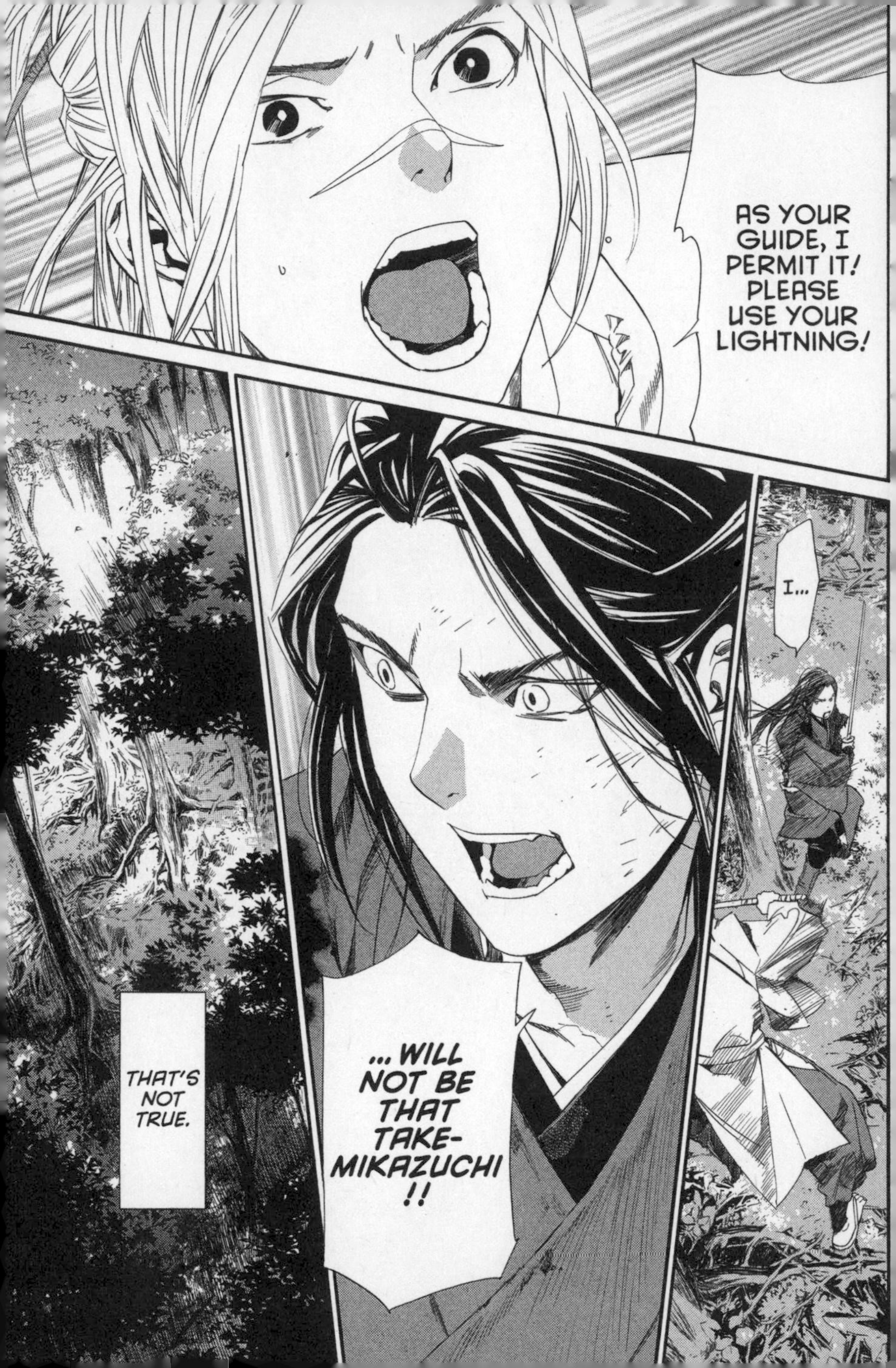
AS YOUR GUIDE, I PERMIT IT! PLEASE USE YOUR LIGHTNING!
I...
...WILL NOT BE THAT TAKE-MIKAZUCHI !!
THAT'S NOT TRUE.

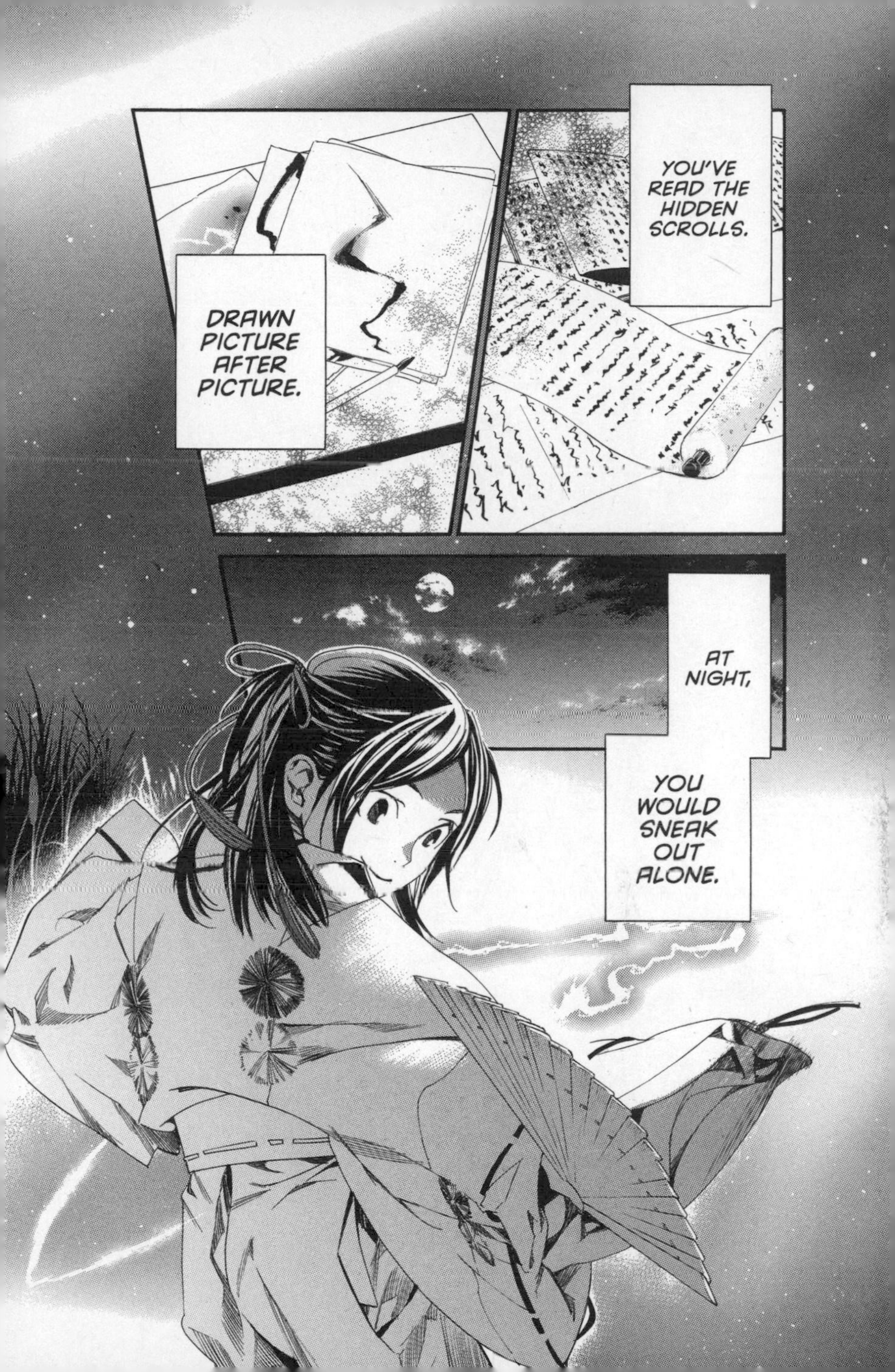
YOU'VE READ THE HIDDEN SCROLLS.
DRAWN PICTURE AFTER PICTURE.
AT NIGHT,
YOU WOULD SNEAK OUT ALONE.

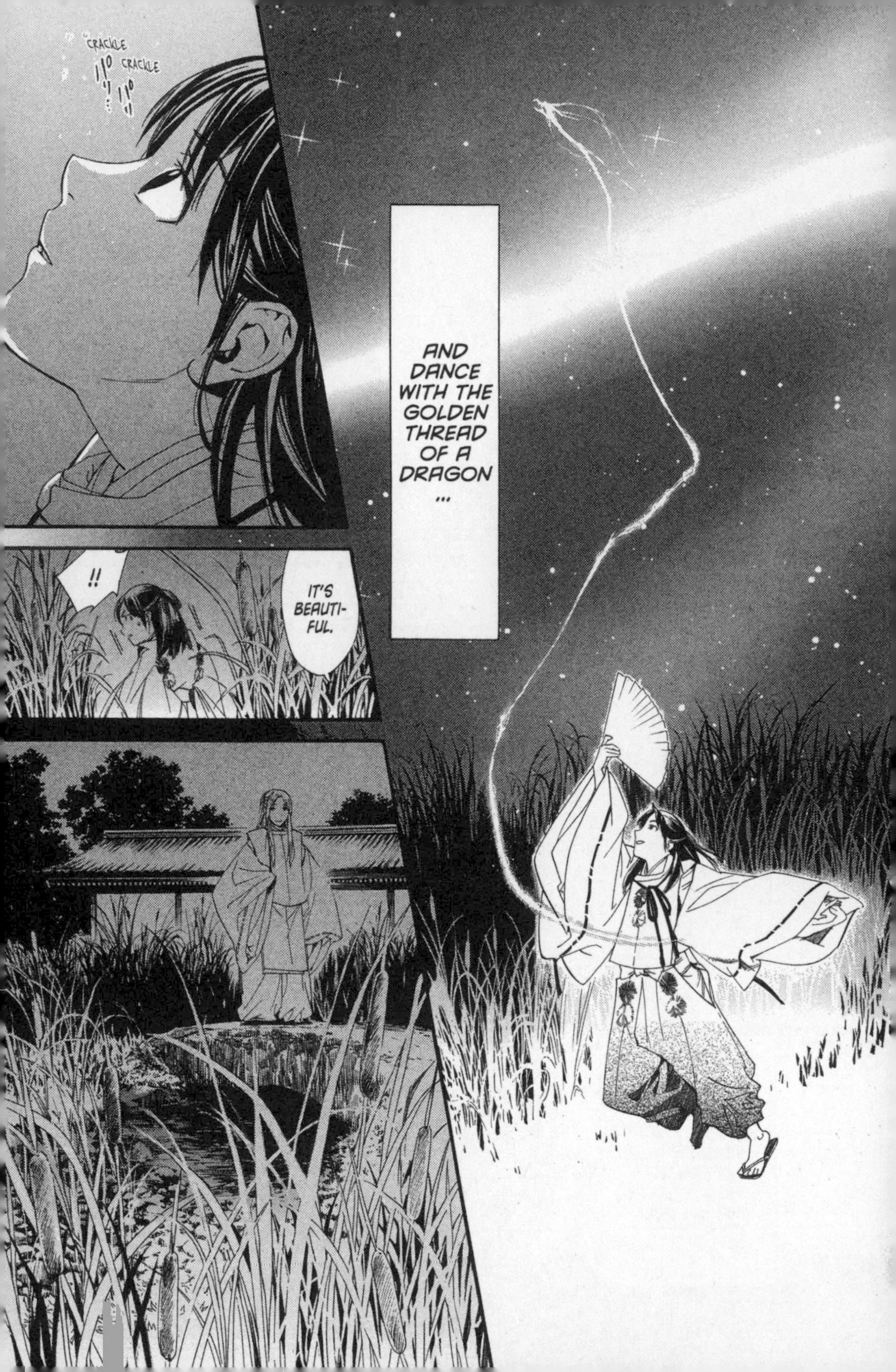
AND DANCE WITH THE GOLDEN THREAD OF A DRAGON ...
CRACKLE CRACKLE
IT'S BEAUTI-FUL.
!!

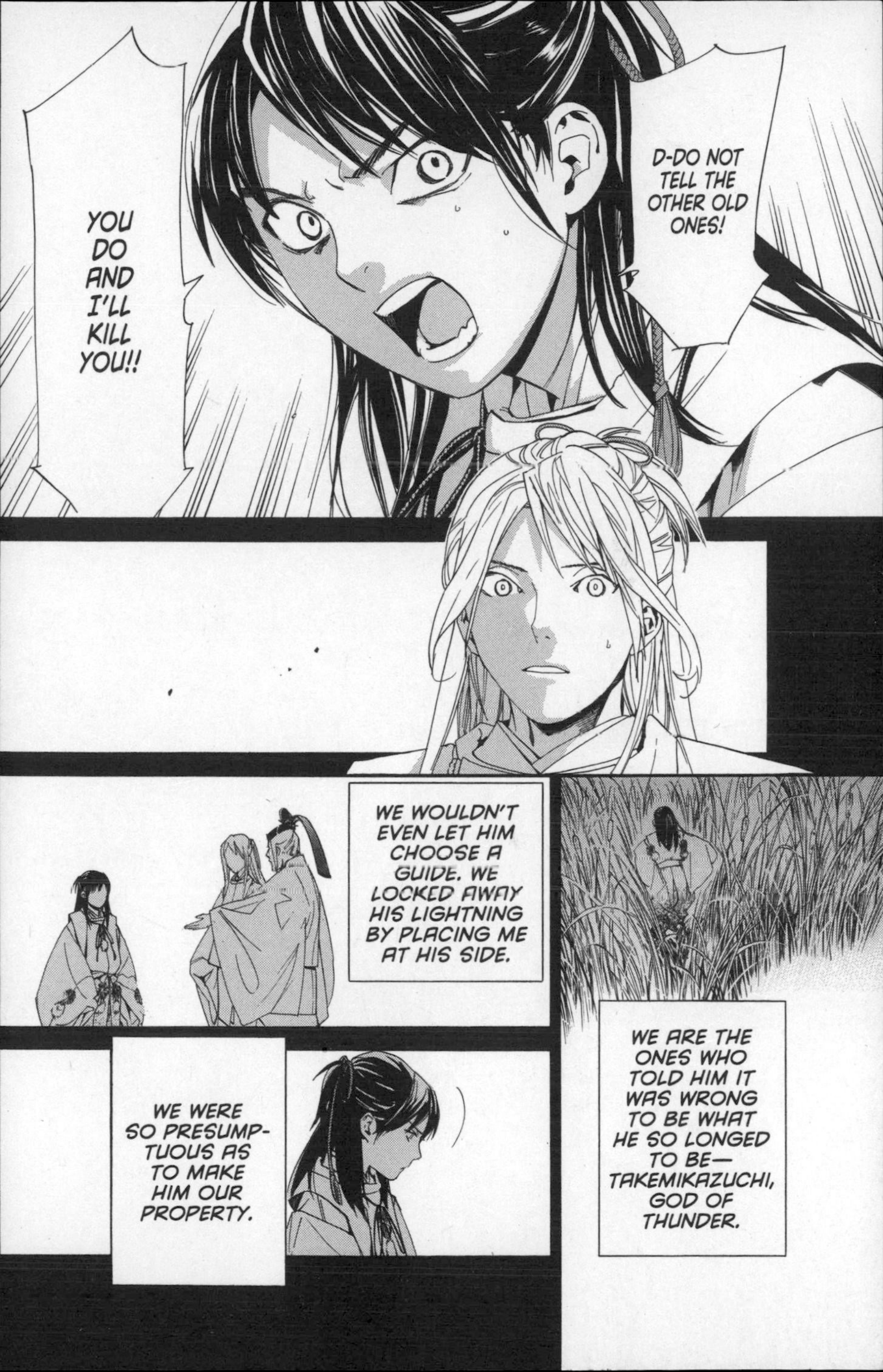
D-DO NOT TELL THE OTHER OLD ONES!
YOU DO AND I'LL KILL YOU!!
WE ARE THE ONES WHO TOLD HIM IT WAS WRONG TO BE WHAT HE SO LONGED TO BE—TAKEMIKAZUCHI, GOD OF THUNDER.
WE WOULDN'T EVEN LET HIM CHOOSE A GUIDE. WE LOCKED AWAY HIS LIGHTNING BY PLACING ME AT HIS SIDE.
WE WERE SO PRESUMPTUOUS AS TO MAKE HIM OUR PROPERTY.

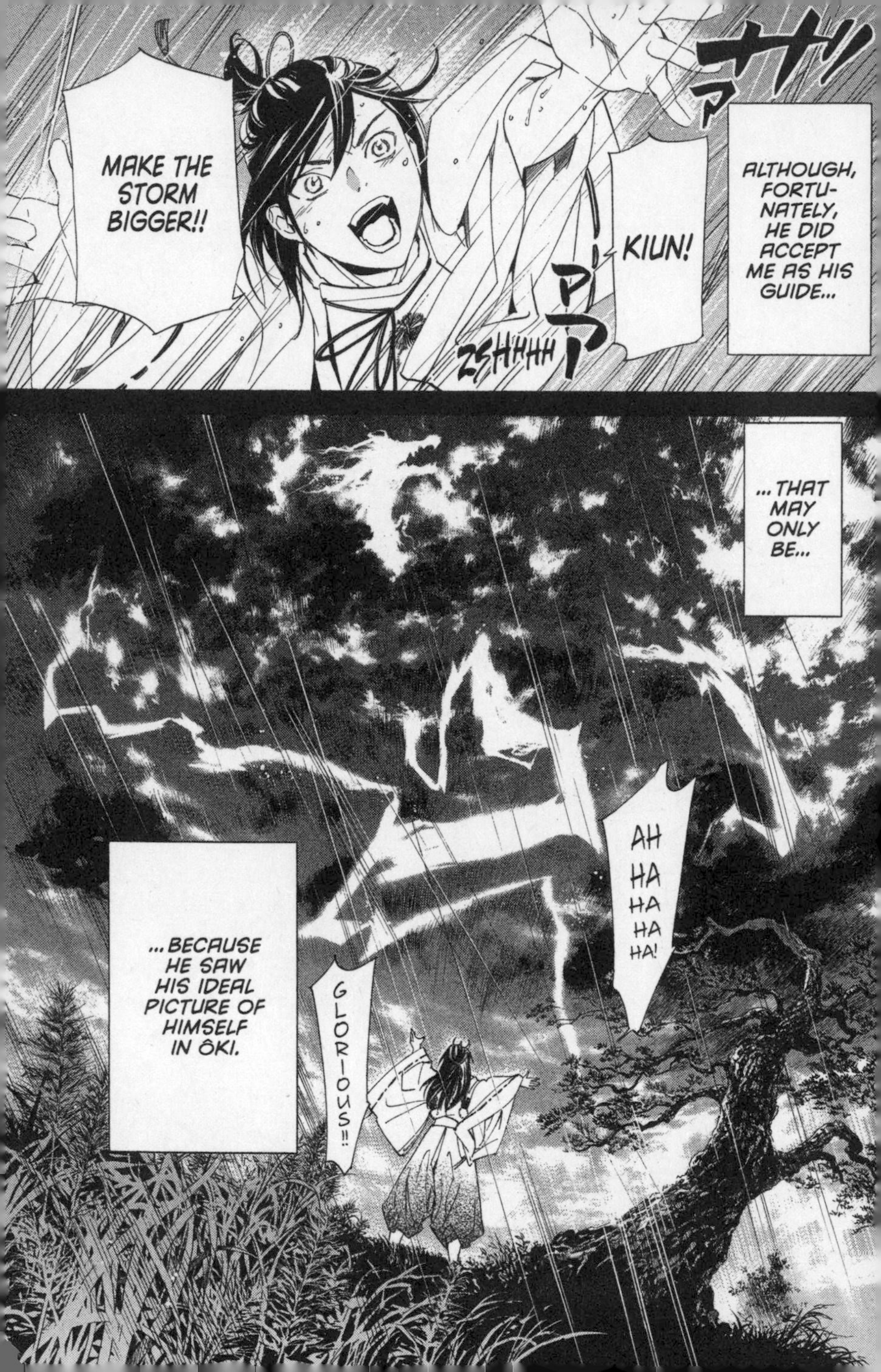
ALTHOUGH, FORTUNATELY, HE DID ACCEPT ME AS HIS GUIDE...
KIUN!
ZSHHHH
MAKE THE STORM BIGGER!!
...THAT MAY ONLY BE...
AH HA HA HA HA!
GLORIOUS!!
...BECAUSE HE SAW HIS IDEAL PICTURE OF HIMSELF IN ÔKI.

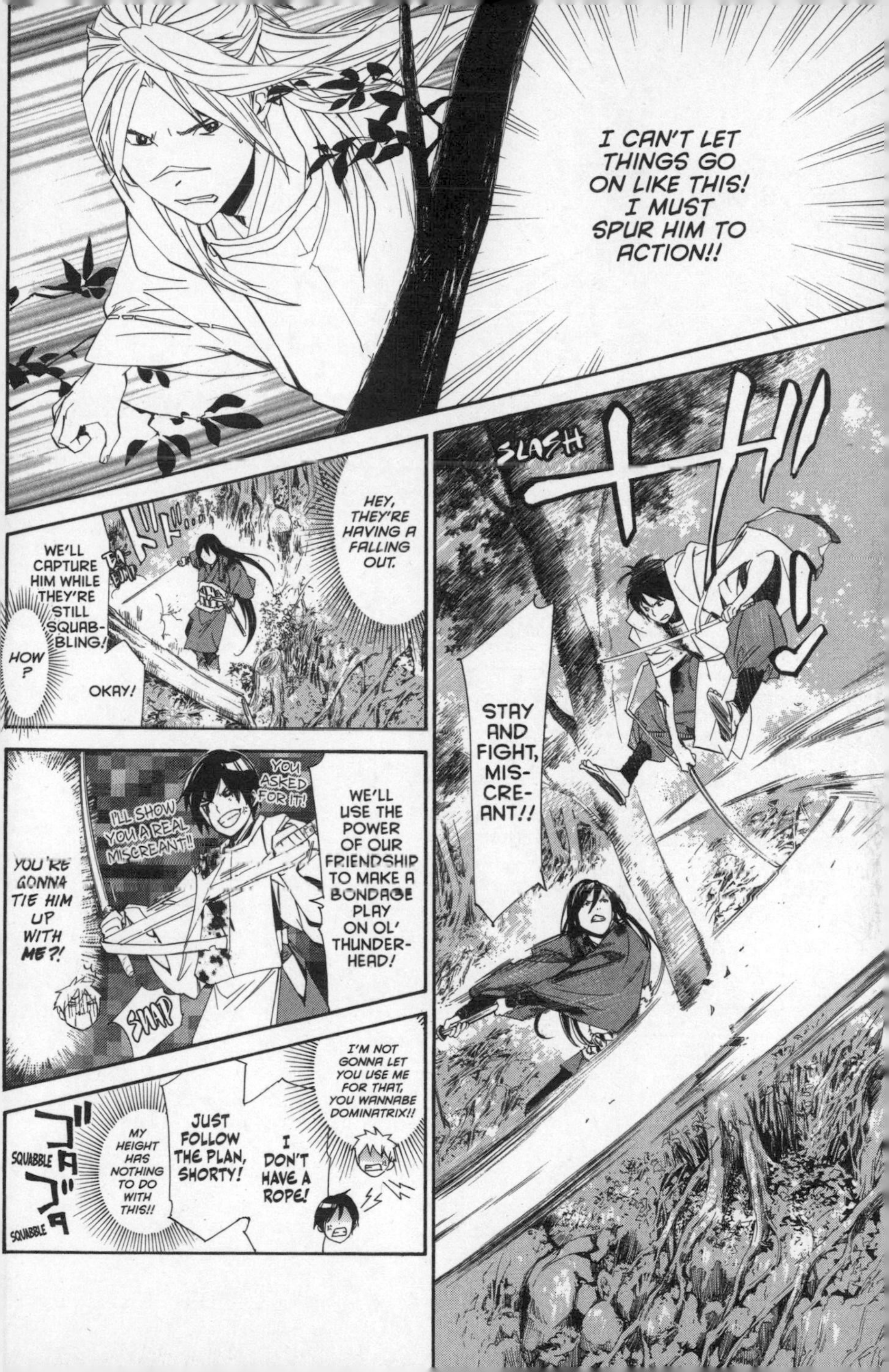

I CAN'T LET THINGS GO ON LIKE THIS! I MUST SPUR HIM TO ACTION!!
SLASH
STAY AND FIGHT, MIS-CRE-ANT!!
HEY, THEY'RE HAVING A FALLING OUT.
WE'LL CAPTURE HIM WHILE THEY'RE STILL SQUAB-BLING!
HOW?
OKAY!
WE'LL USE THE POWER OF OUR FRIENDSHIP TO MAKE A BONDAGE PLAY ON OL' THUNDER-HEAD!
YOU ASKED FOR IT!
I'LL SHOW YOU A REAL MISCREANT!!
YOU'RE GONNA TIE HIM UP WITH ME?!
SNAP
I'M NOT GONNA LET YOU USE ME FOR THAT, YOU WANNABE DOMINATRIX!!
I DON'T HAVE A ROPE!
JUST FOLLOW THE PLAN, SHORTY!
MY HEIGHT HAS NOTHING TO DO WITH THIS!!
SQUABBLE
SQUABBLE

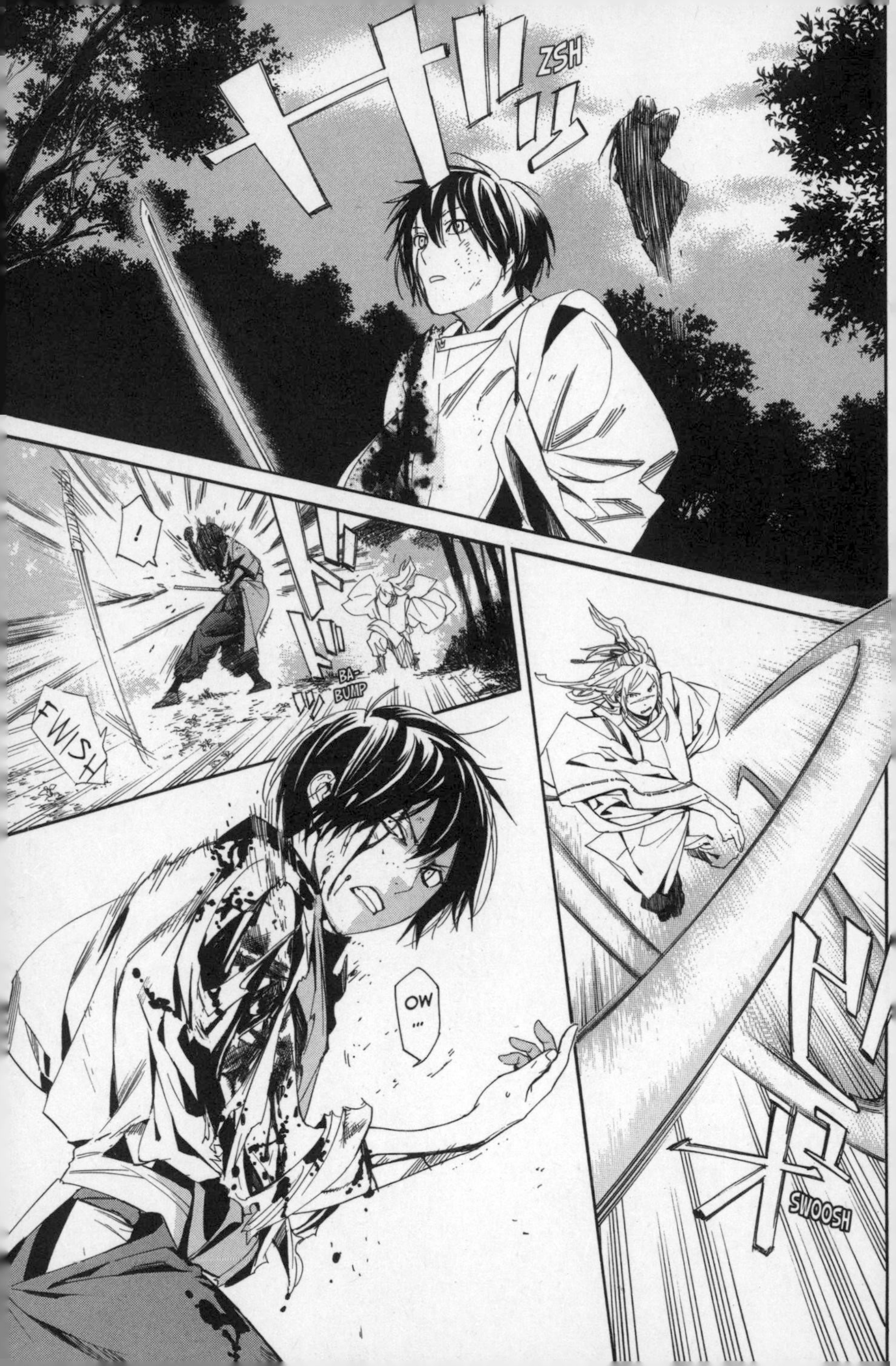
ZSH
!
BA-BUMP
FWISH
SWOOSH
OW
...

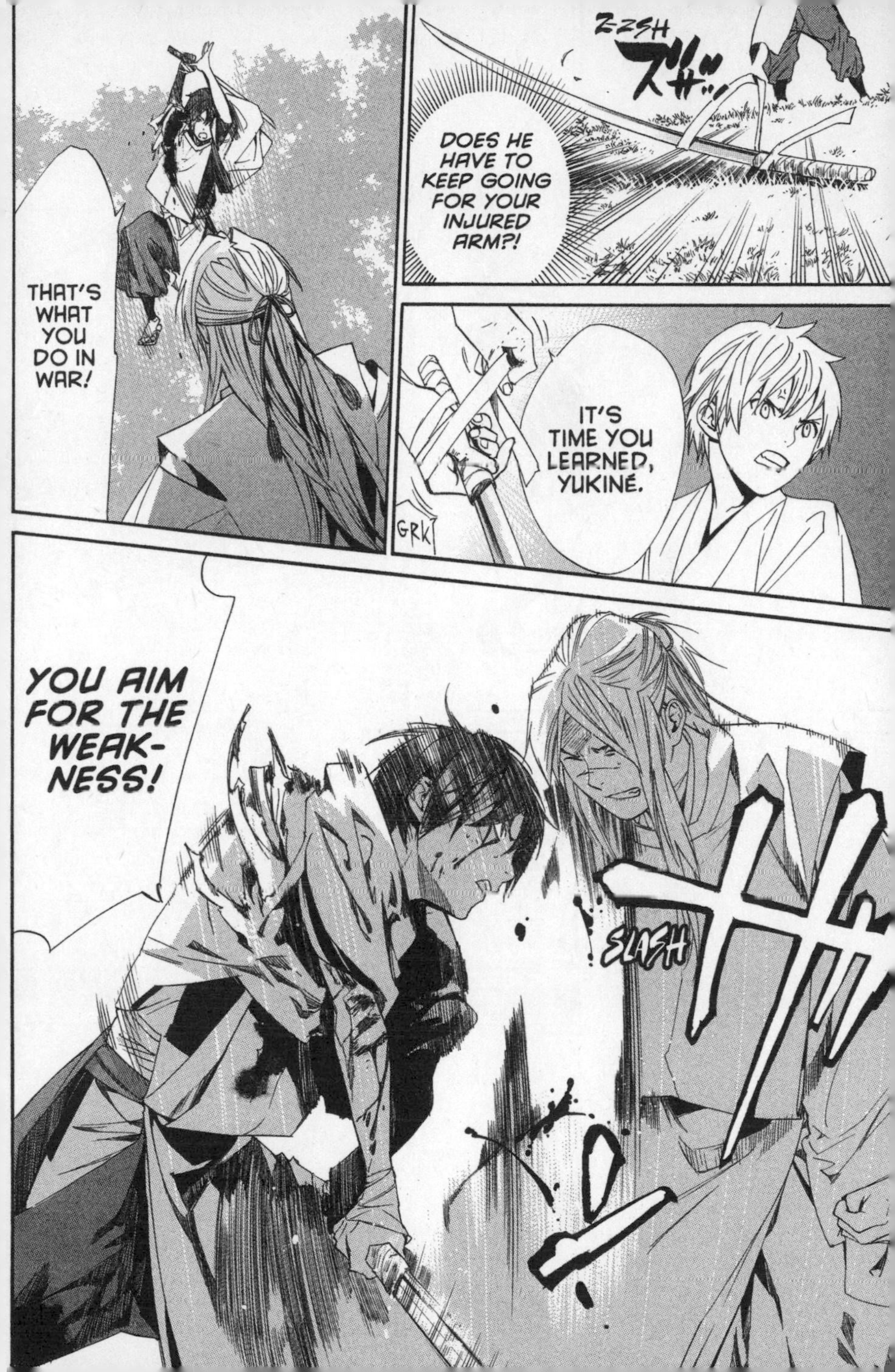
Z-ZSH
DOES HE HAVE TO KEEP GOING FOR YOUR INJURED ARM?!
IT'S TIME YOU LEARNED, YUKINÉ.
GRK
THAT'S WHAT YOU DO IN WAR!
YOU AIM FOR THE WEAK-NESS!
SLASH

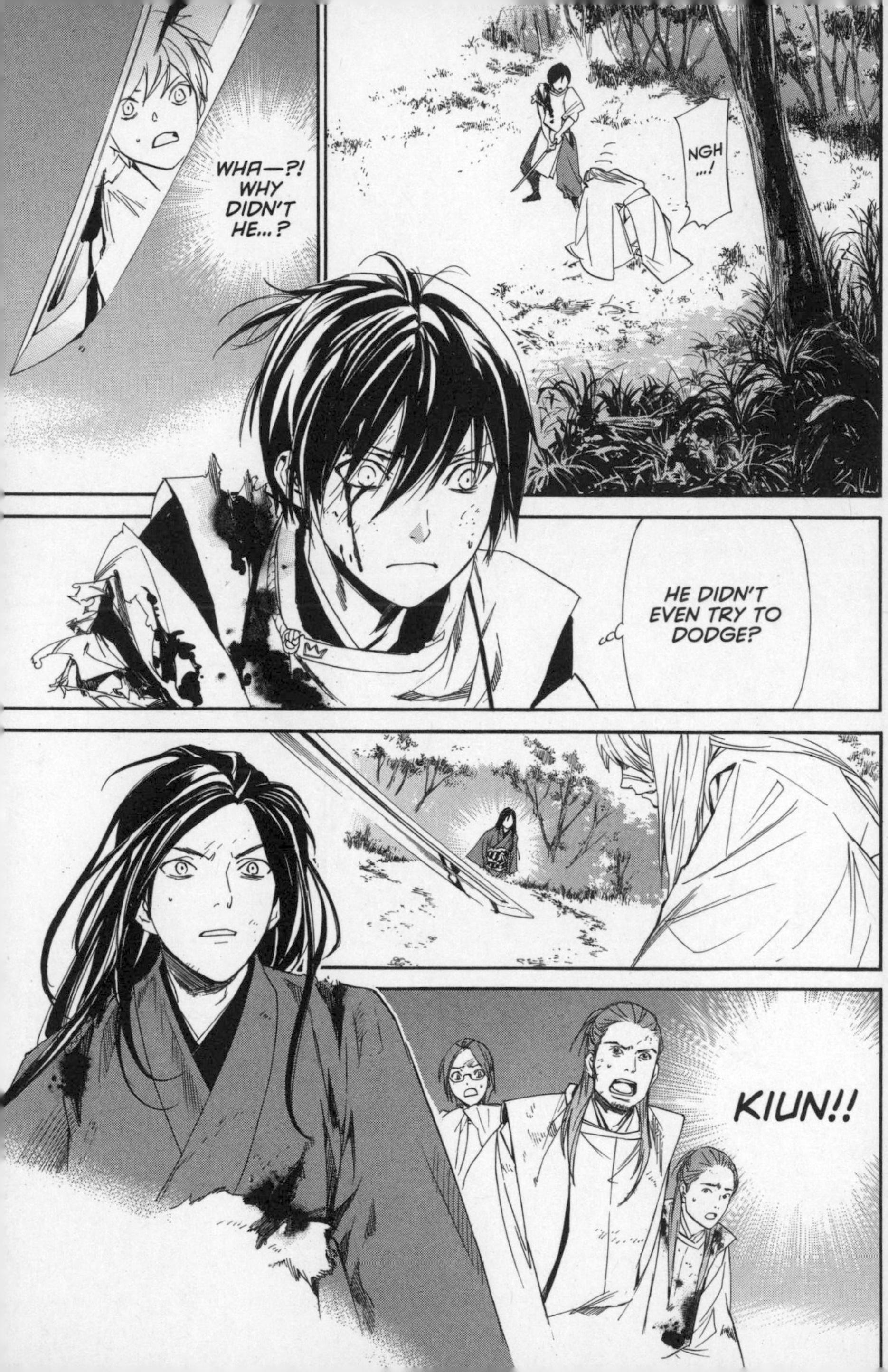
NGH ...!
WHA—?! WHY DIDN'T HE...?
HE DIDN'T EVEN TRY TO DODGE?
KIUN!!

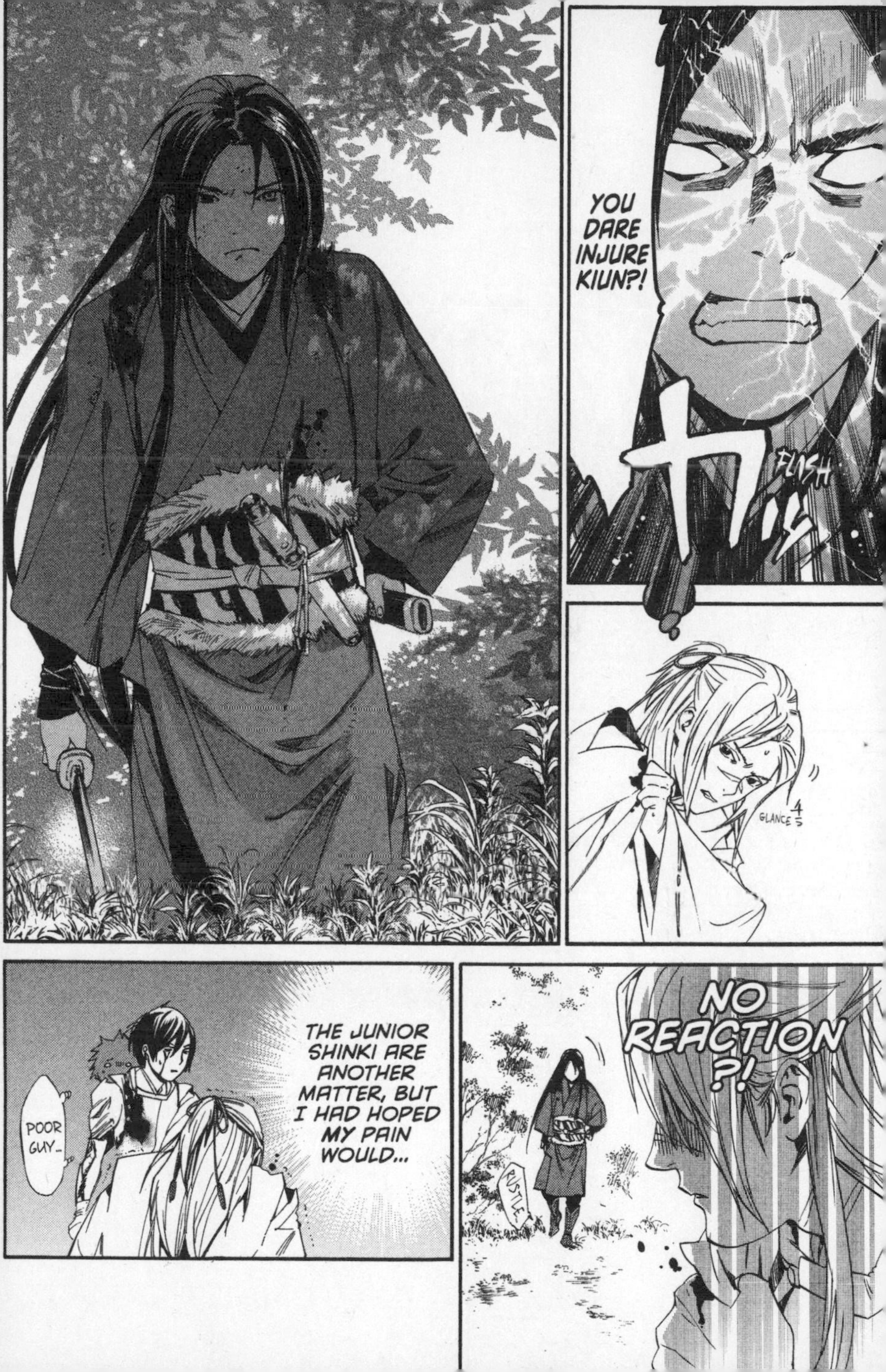
YOU DARE INJURE KIUN?!
FLASH
GLANCE
NO REACTION?!
RUSTLE
THE JUNIOR SHINKI ARE ANOTHER MATTER, BUT I HAD HOPED MY PAIN WOULD...
POOR GUY...

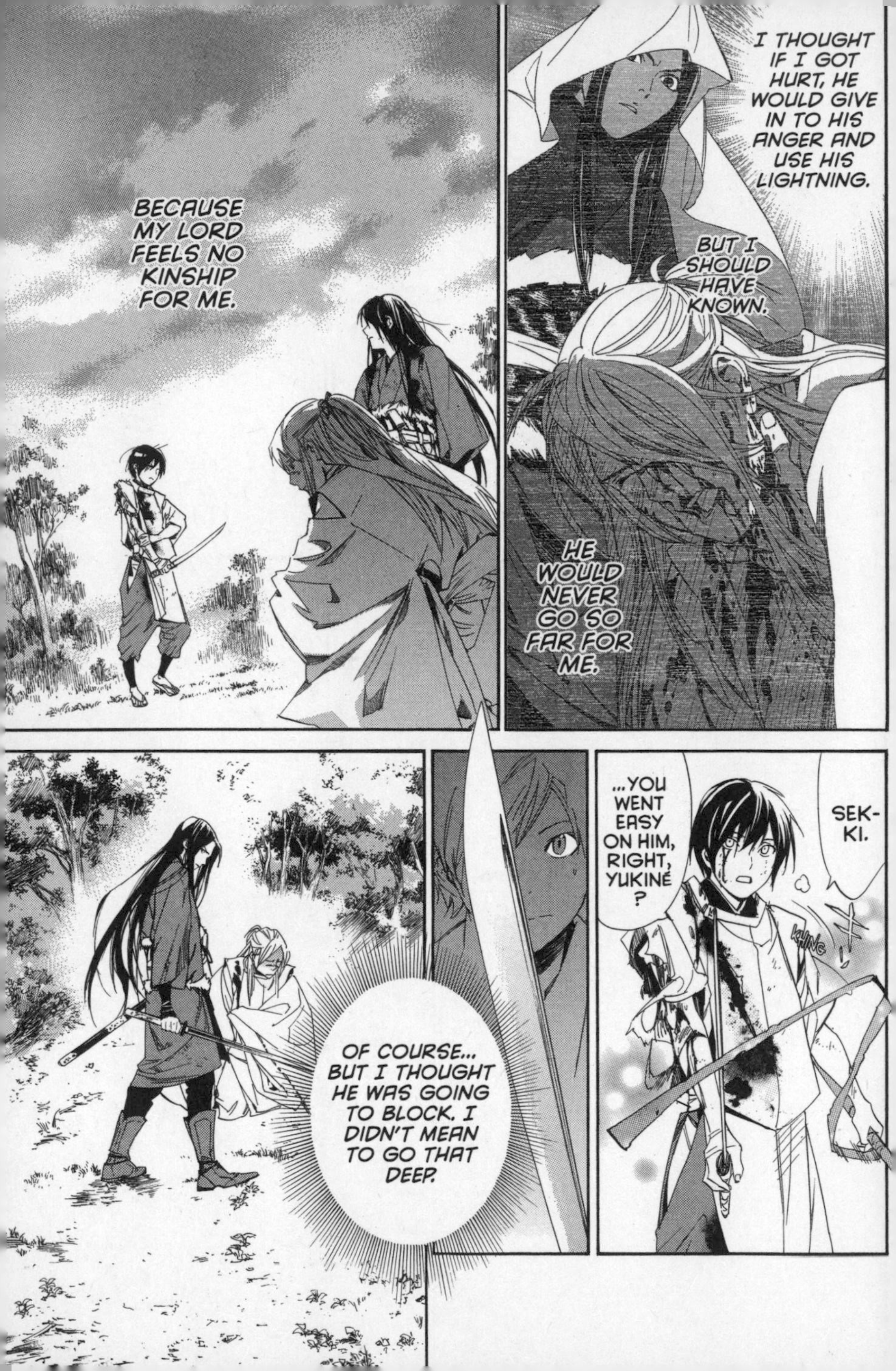
I THOUGHT IF I GOT HURT, HE WOULD GIVE IN TO HIS ANGER AND USE HIS LIGHTNING.
BUT I SHOULD HAVE KNOWN.
HE WOULD NEVER GO SO FAR FOR ME.
BECAUSE MY LORD FEELS NO KINSHIP FOR ME.
SEK-KI.
...YOU WENT EASY ON HIM, RIGHT, YUKINE?
KHING
OF COURSE... BUT I THOUGHT HE WAS GOING TO BLOCK. I DIDN'T MEAN TO GO THAT DEEP.

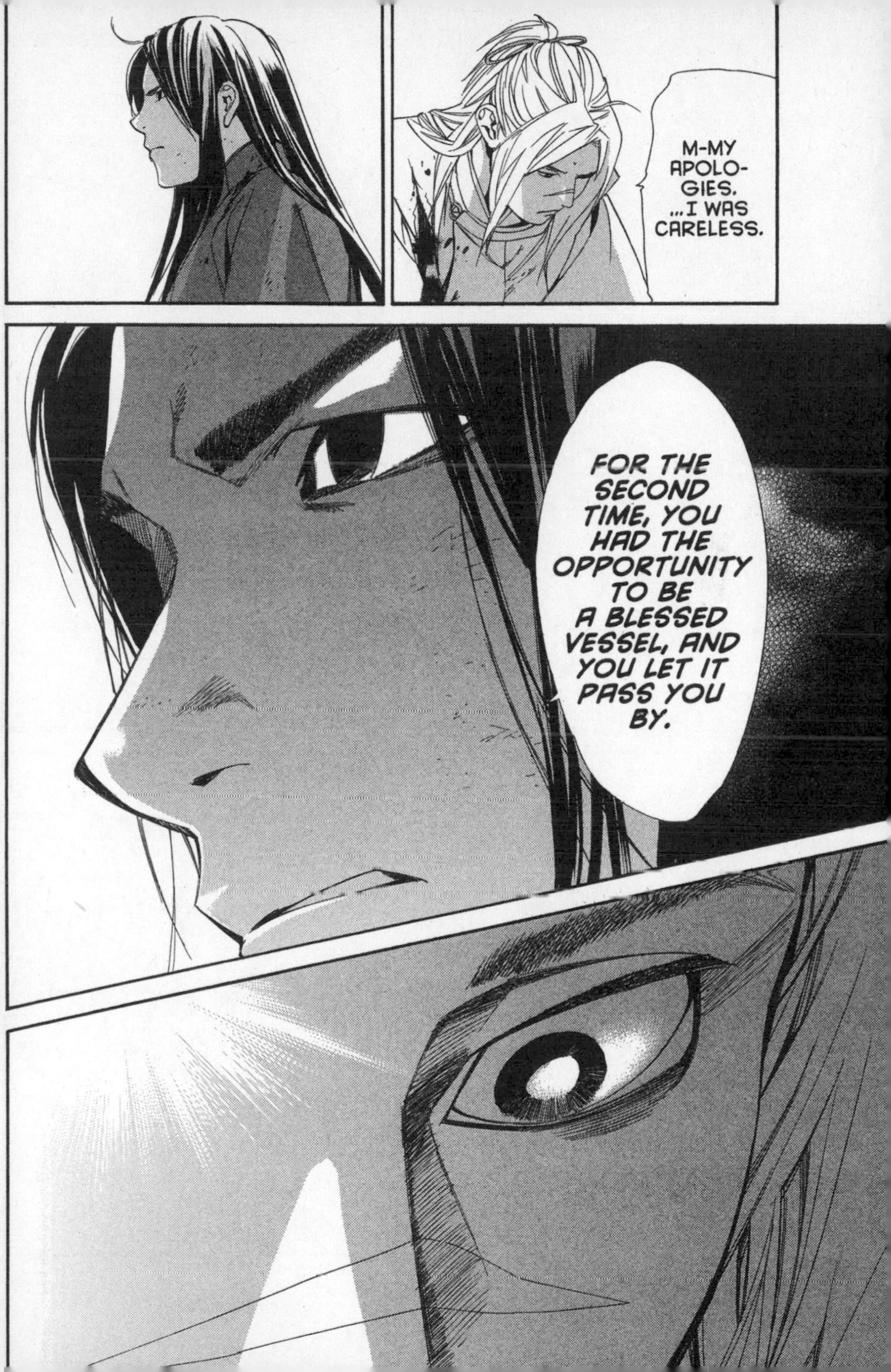
M-MY APOLOGIES. ...I WAS CARELESS.
FOR THE SECOND TIME, YOU HAD THE OPPORTUNITY TO BE A BLESSED VESSEL, AND YOU LET IT PASS YOU BY.

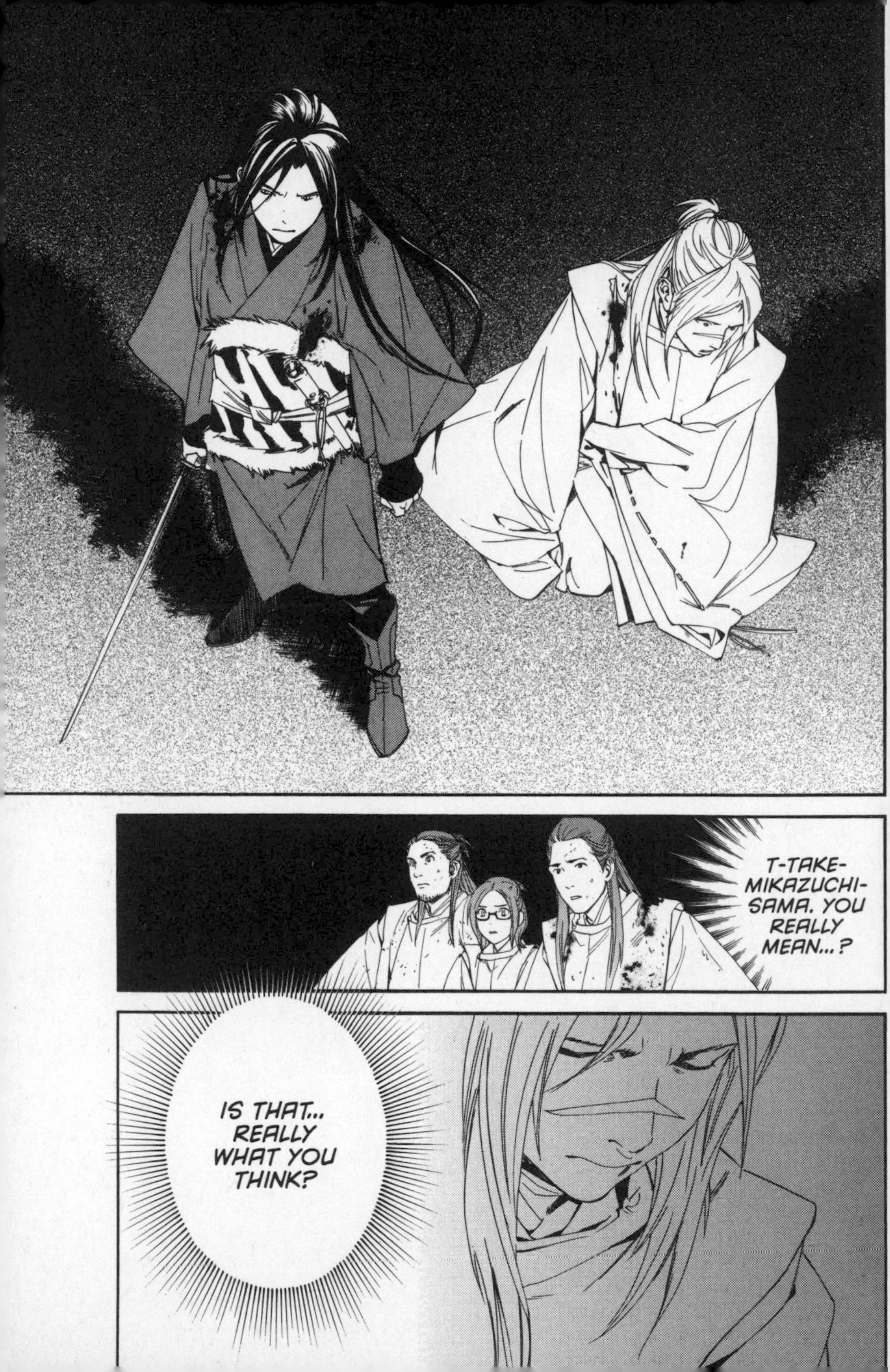
T-TAKE-MIKAZUCHI-SAMA. YOU REALLY MEAN...?
IS THAT... REALLY WHAT YOU THINK?

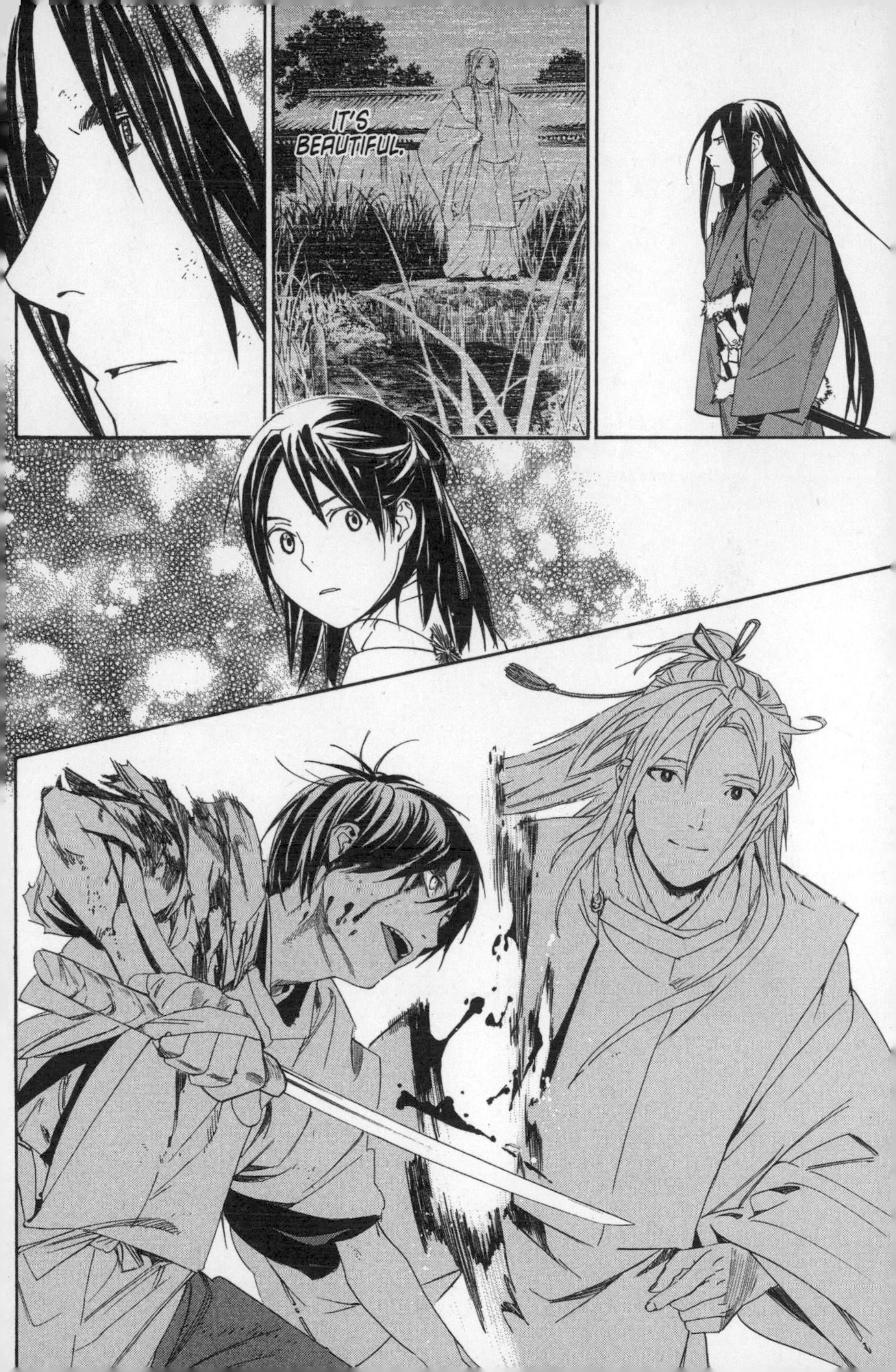
IT'S BEAUTIFUL.

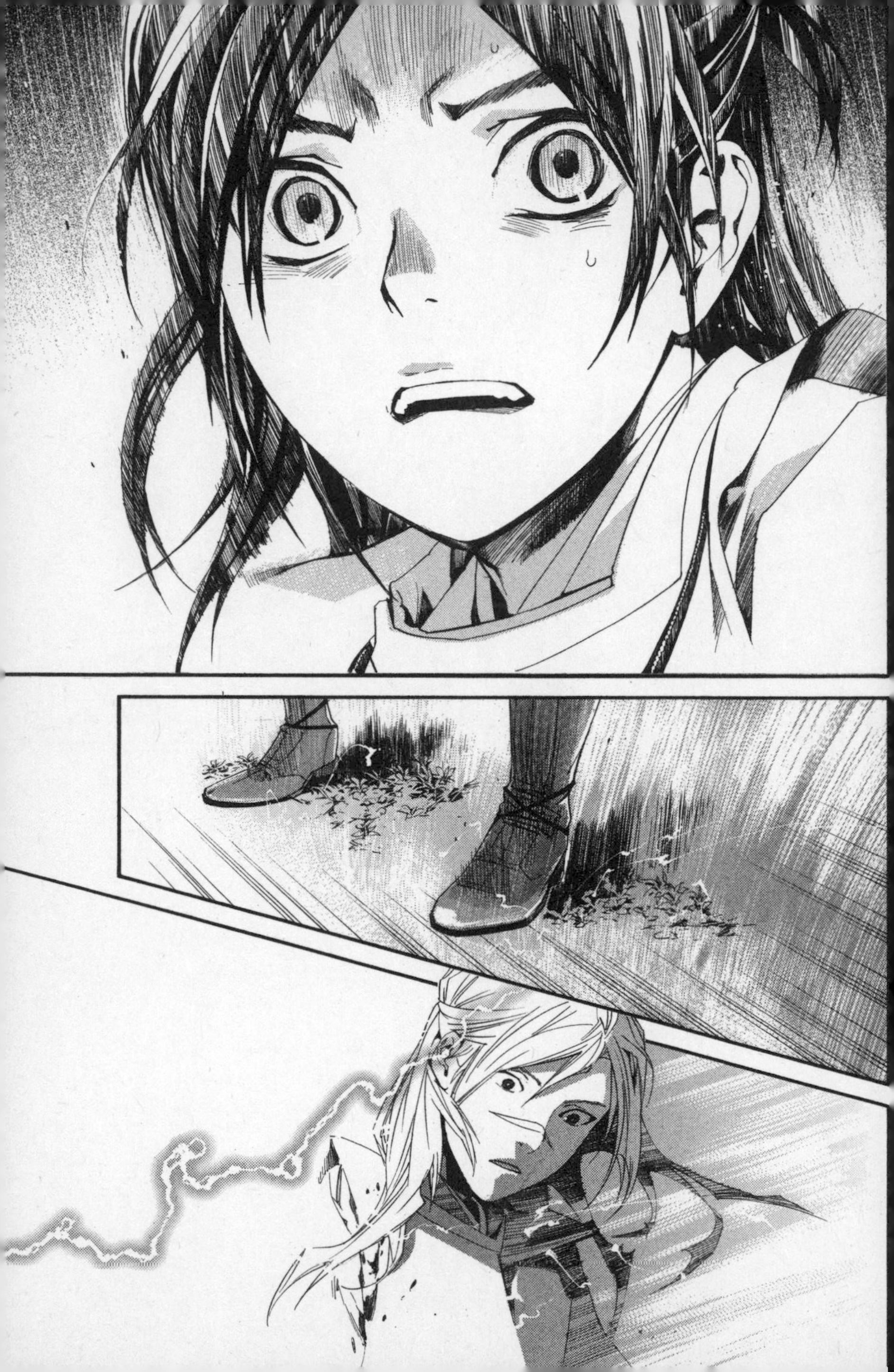

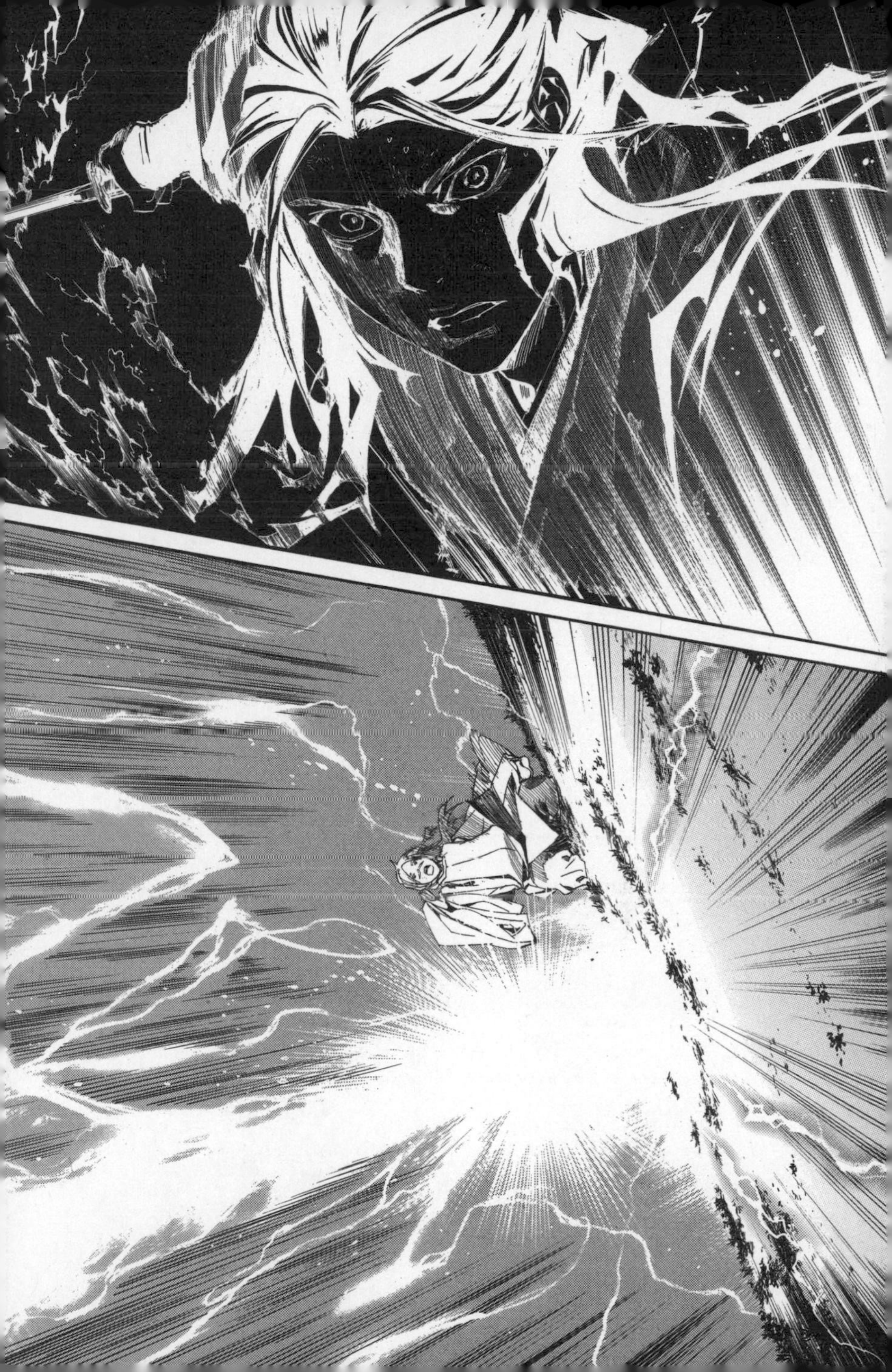

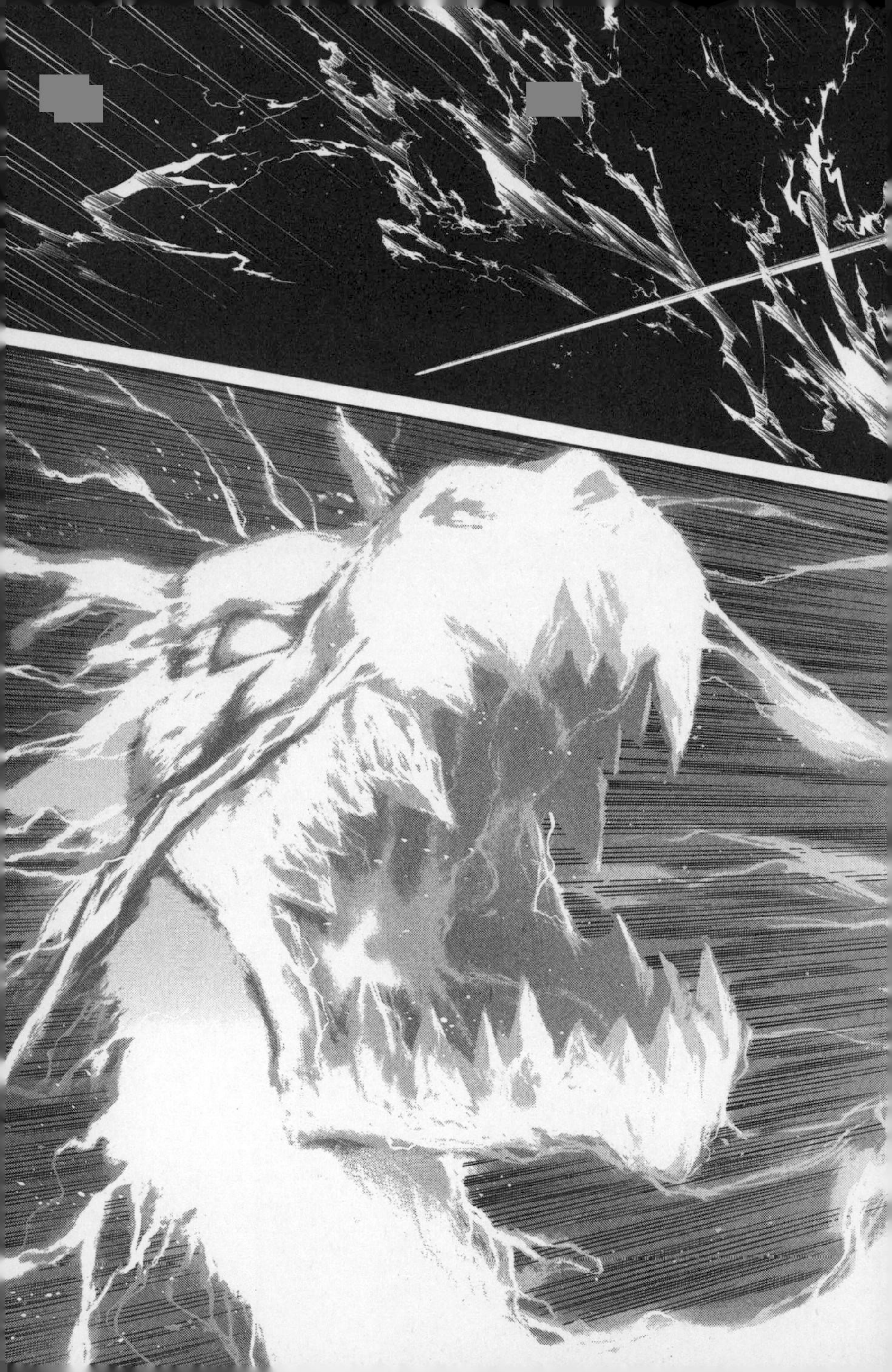

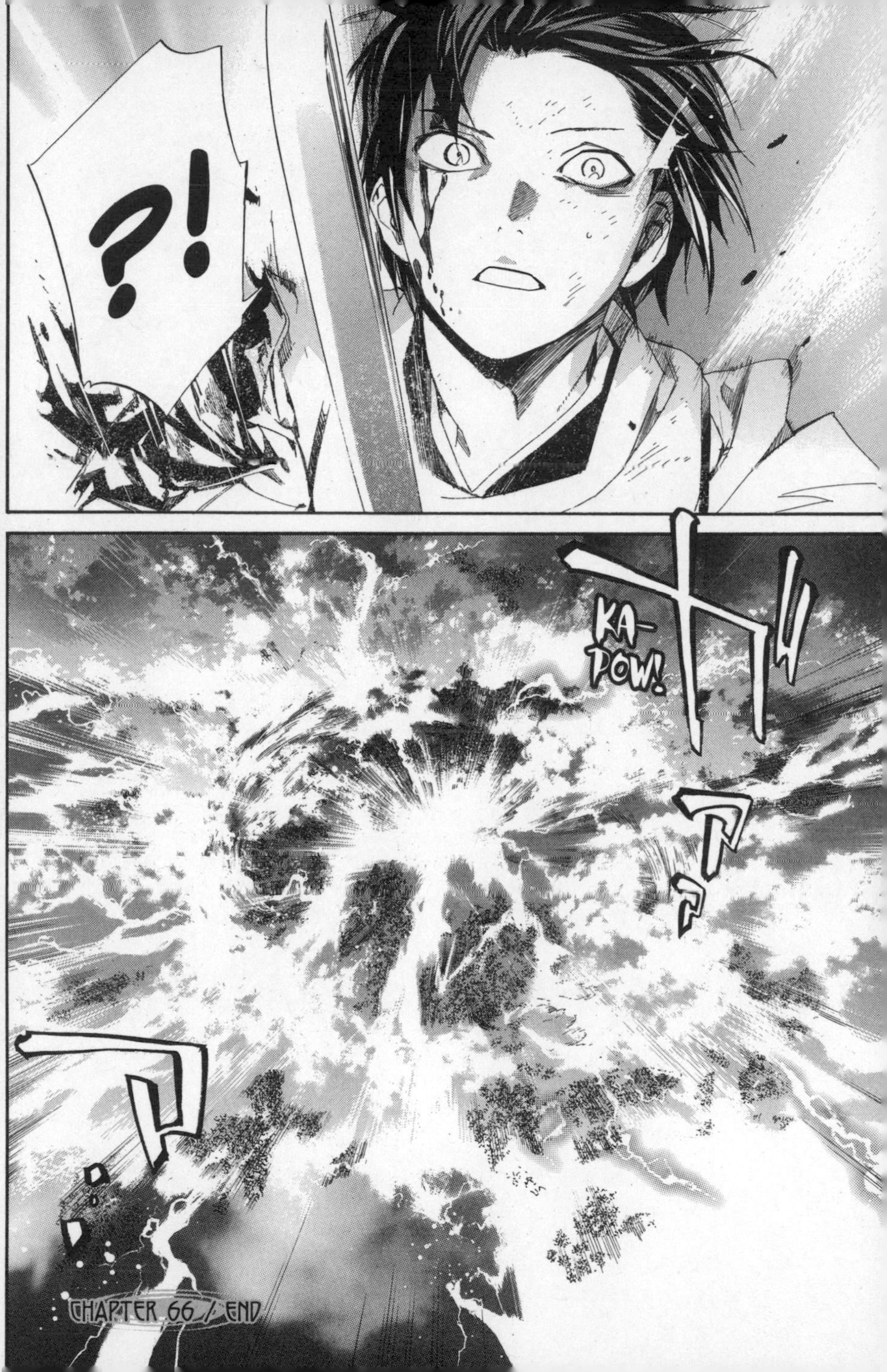
?!
KA-POW!
CHAPTER 66 / END

野

豈

神

[illegible]

[illegible]

師

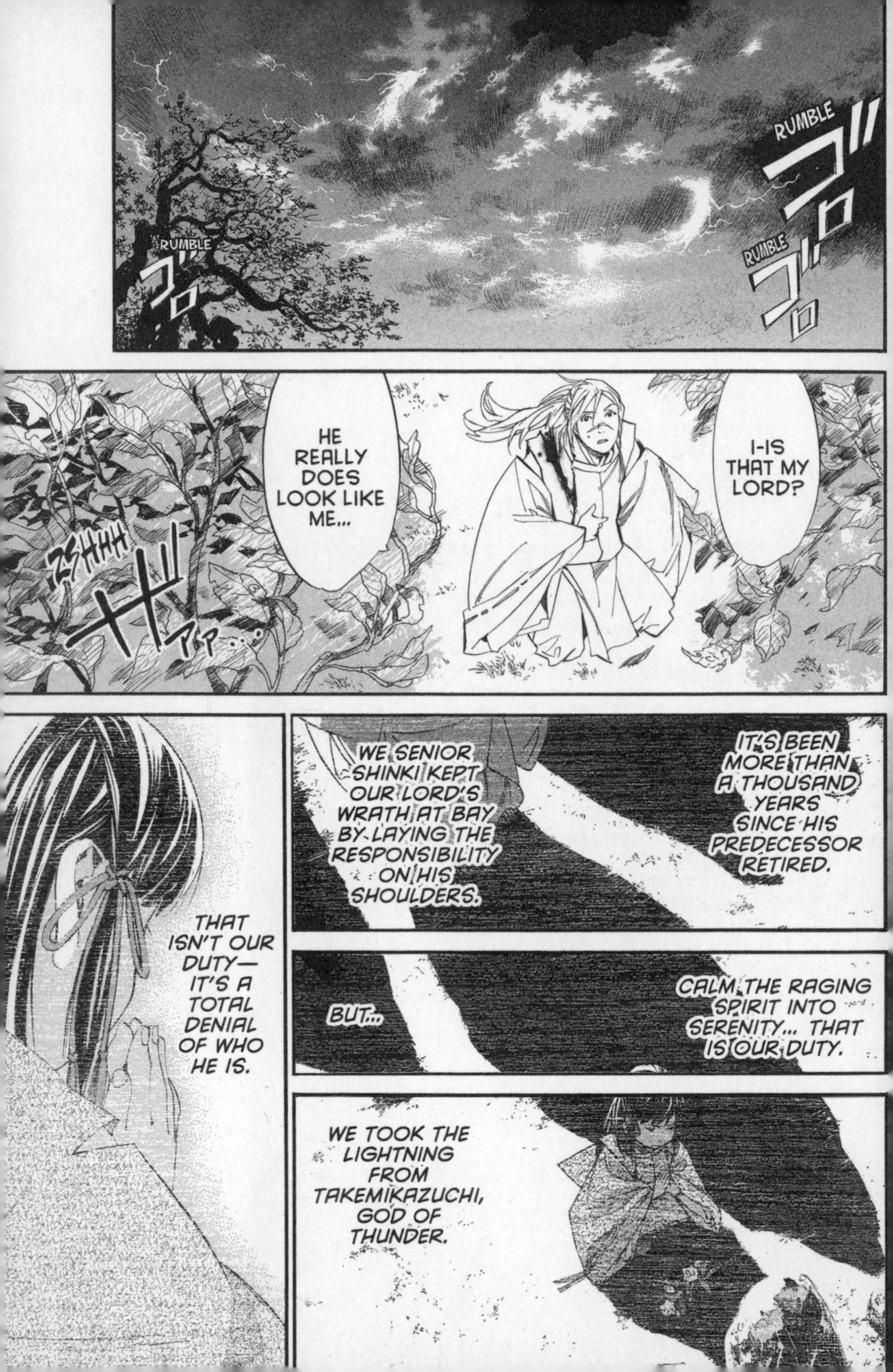
RUMBLE
RUMBLE
RUMBLE
I-IS THAT MY LORD?
HE REALLY DOES LOOK LIKE ME...
ZSHHH
IT'S BEEN MORE THAN A THOUSAND YEARS SINCE HIS PREDECESSOR RETIRED.
WE SENIOR SHINKI KEPT OUR LORD'S WRATH AT BAY BY LAYING THE RESPONSIBILITY ON HIS SHOULDERS.
CALM THE RAGING SPIRIT INTO SERENITY... THAT IS OUR DUTY.
BUT...
WE TOOK THE LIGHTNING FROM TAKEMIKAZUCHI, GOD OF THUNDER.
THAT ISN'T OUR DUTY— IT'S A TOTAL DENIAL OF WHO HE IS.

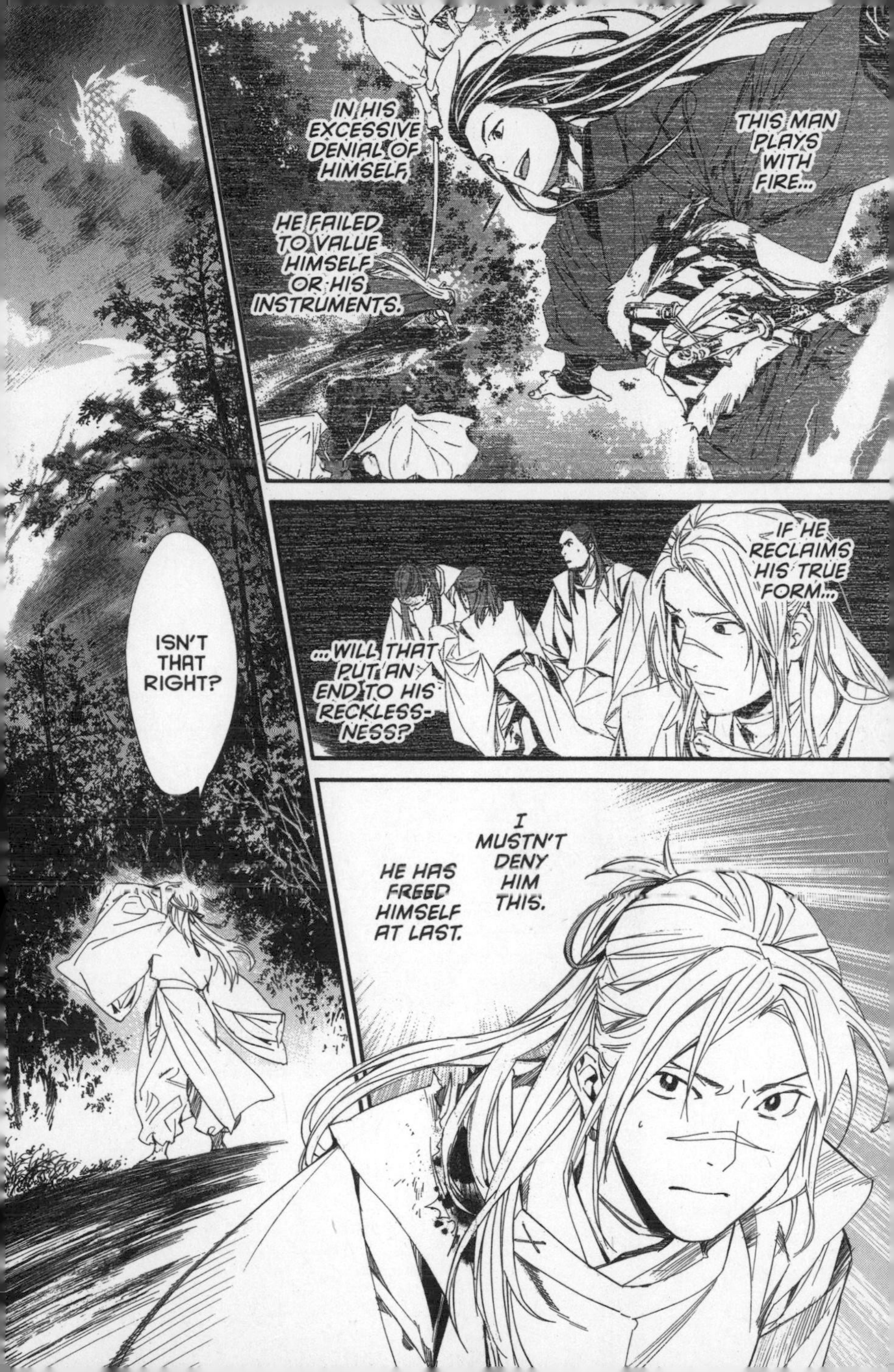
THIS MAN PLAYS WITH FIRE...
IN HIS EXCESSIVE DENIAL OF HIMSELF,
HE FAILED TO VALUE HIMSELF OR HIS INSTRUMENTS.
IF HE RECLAIMS HIS TRUE FORM...
...WILL THAT PUT AN END TO HIS RECKLESS-NESS?
I MUSTN'T DENY HIM THIS.
HE HAS FREED HIMSELF AT LAST.
ISN'T THAT RIGHT?

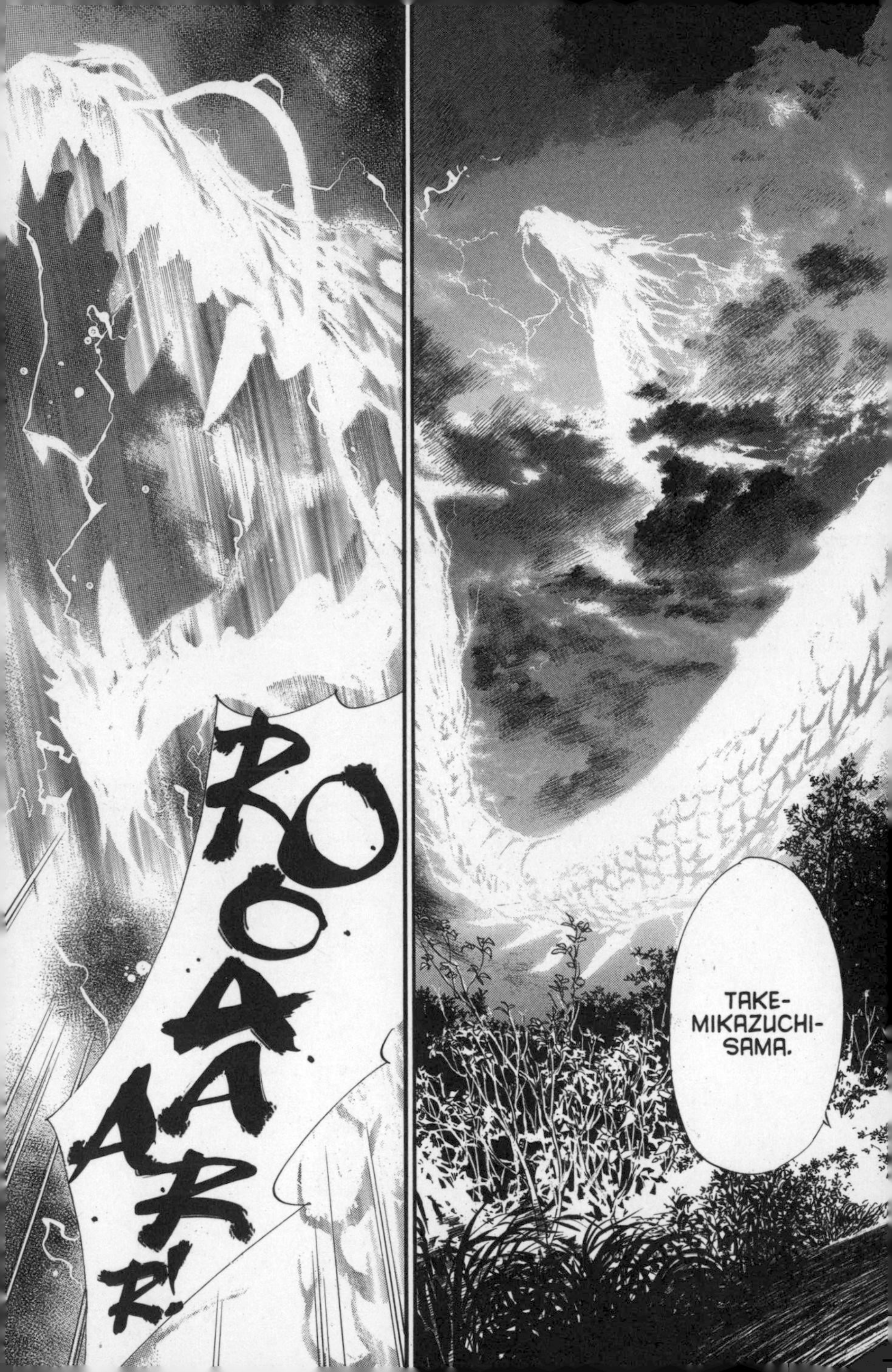
TAKE-MIKAZUCHI-SAMA.
ROOAAARR!

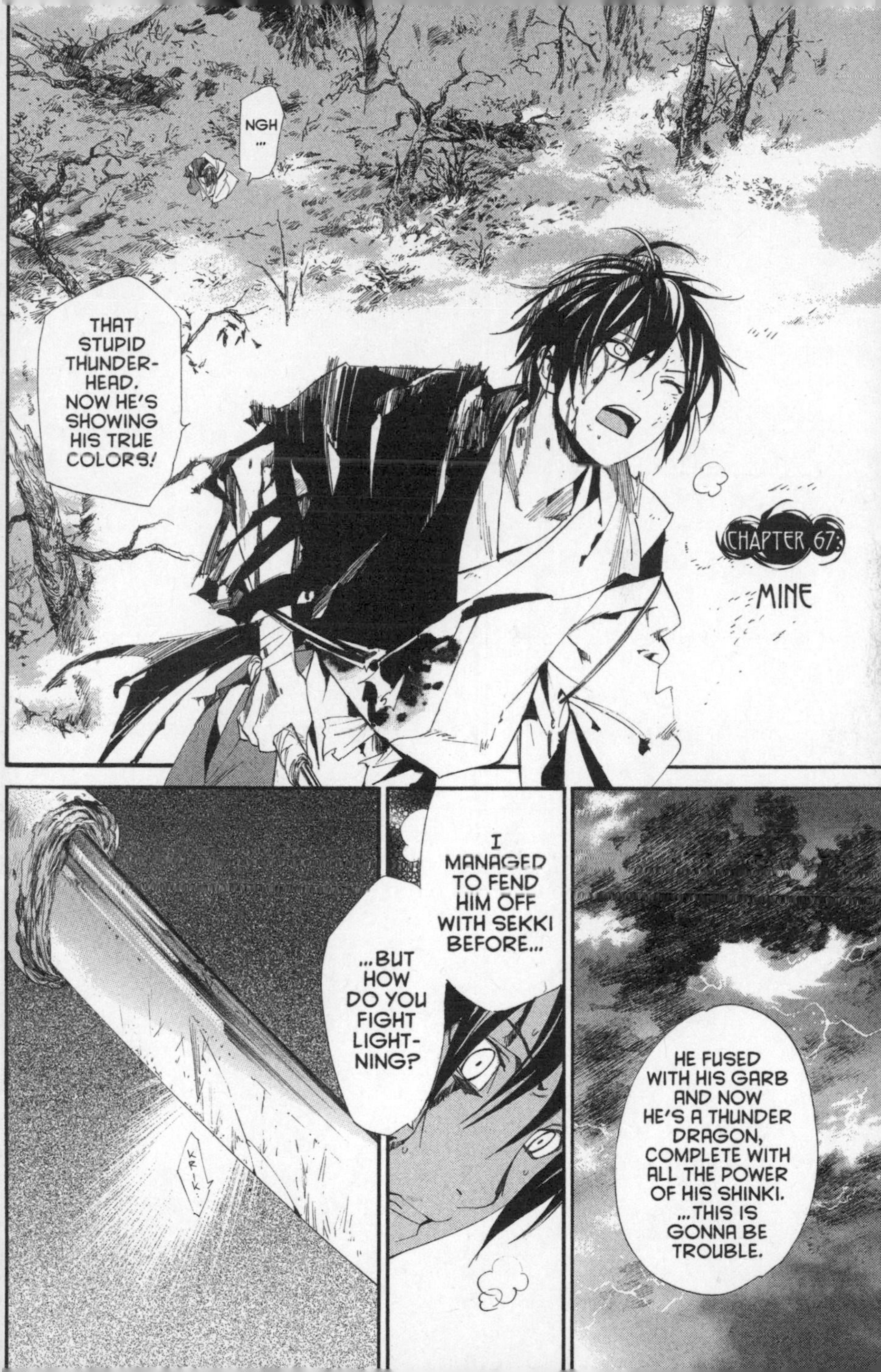
NGH...
THAT STUPID THUNDER-HEAD. NOW HE'S SHOWING HIS TRUE COLORS!
CHAPTER 67:
MINE
HE FUSED WITH HIS GARB AND NOW HE'S A THUNDER DRAGON, COMPLETE WITH ALL THE POWER OF HIS SHINKI. ...THIS IS GONNA BE TROUBLE.
I MANAGED TO FEND HIM OFF WITH SEKKI BEFORE...
...BUT HOW DO YOU FIGHT LIGHT-NING?
KRIK

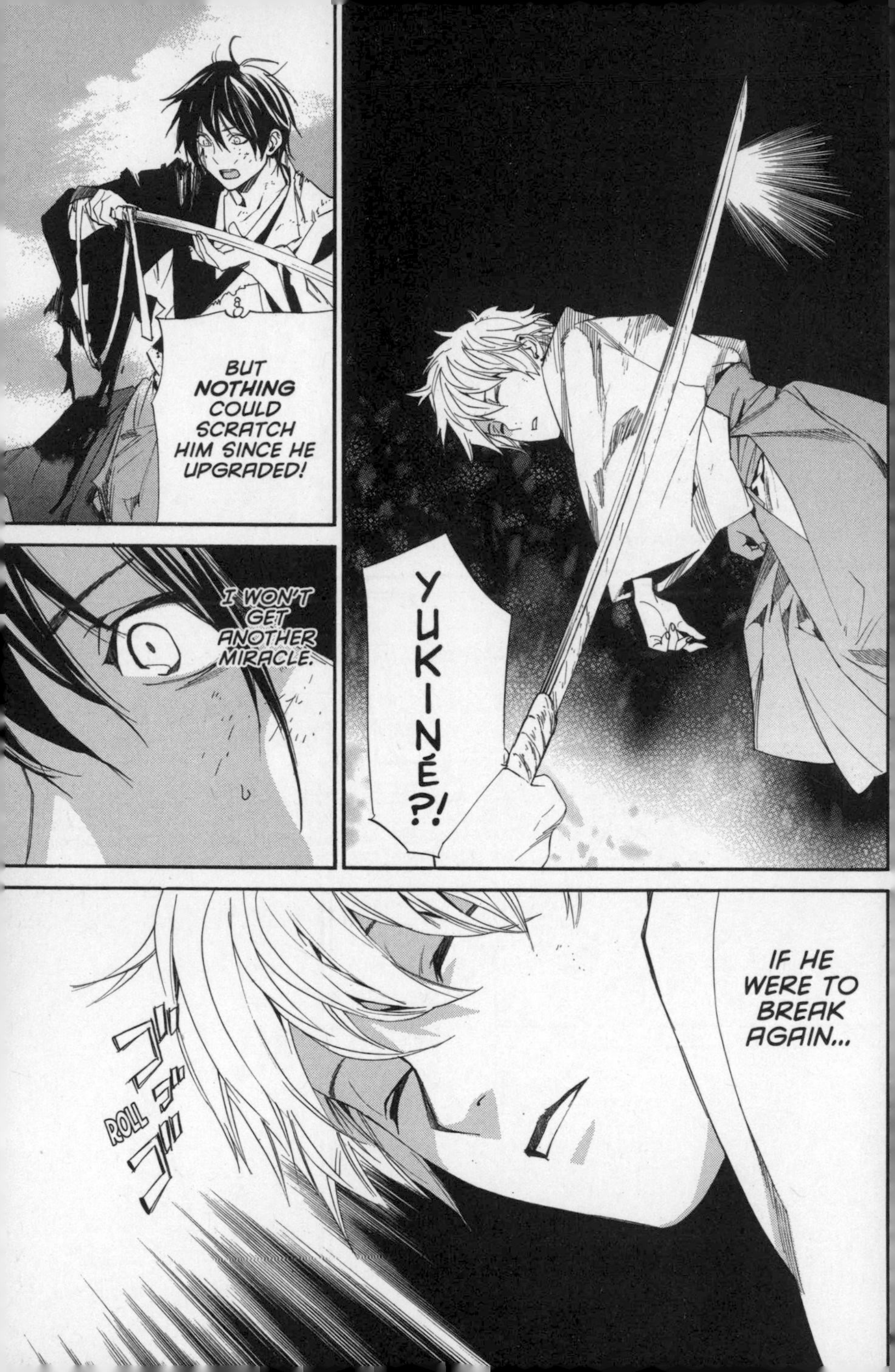
YUKINÉ?!
BUT NOTHING COULD SCRATCH HIM SINCE HE UPGRADED!
I WON'T GET ANOTHER MIRACLE.
IF HE WERE TO BREAK AGAIN...
ROLL

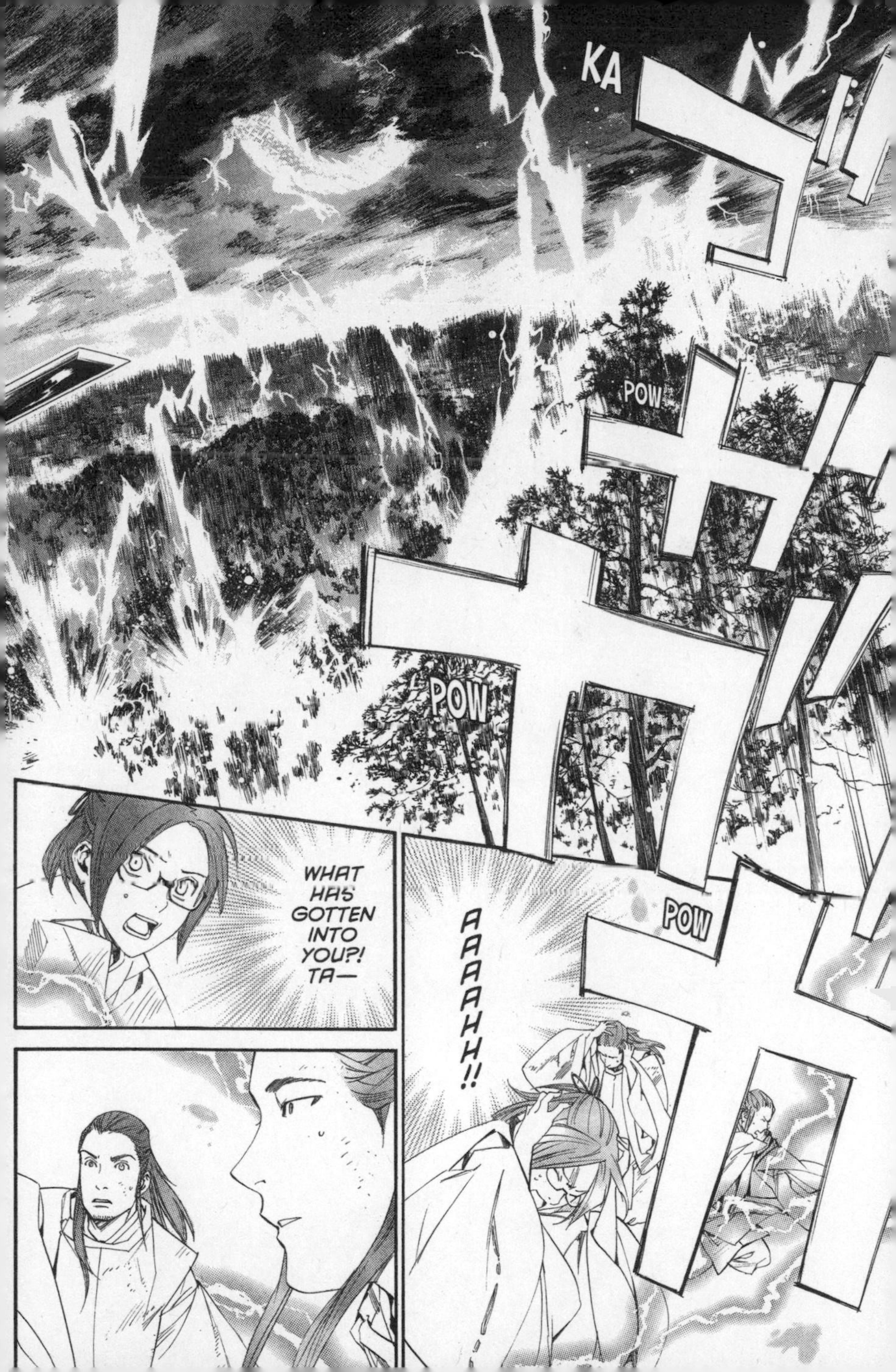
KA
POW
POW
POW
AAAAAHH!!
WHAT HAS GOTTEN INTO YOU?! TA—

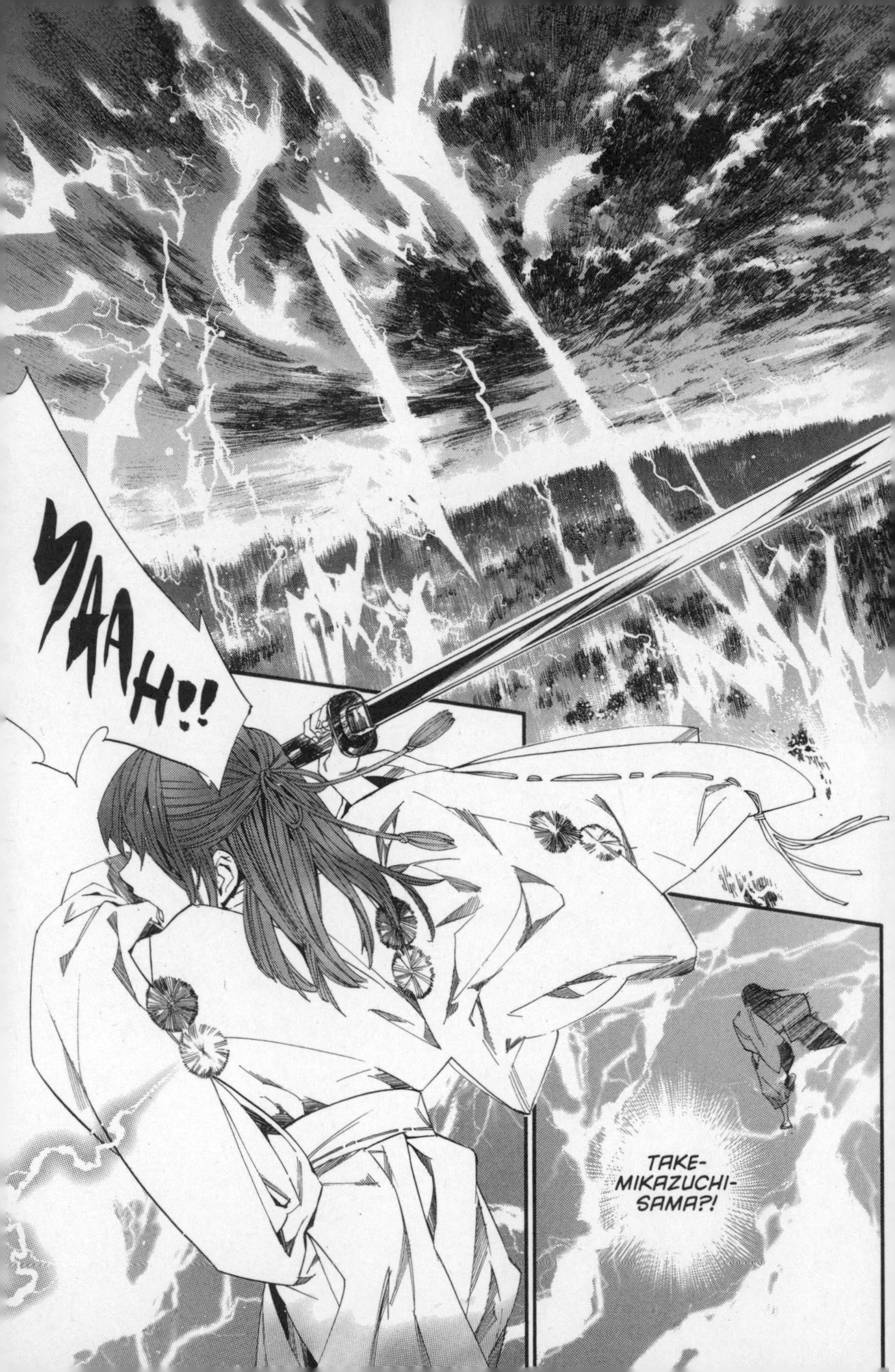
SHAAH!!
TAKE-MIKAZUCHI-SAMA?!

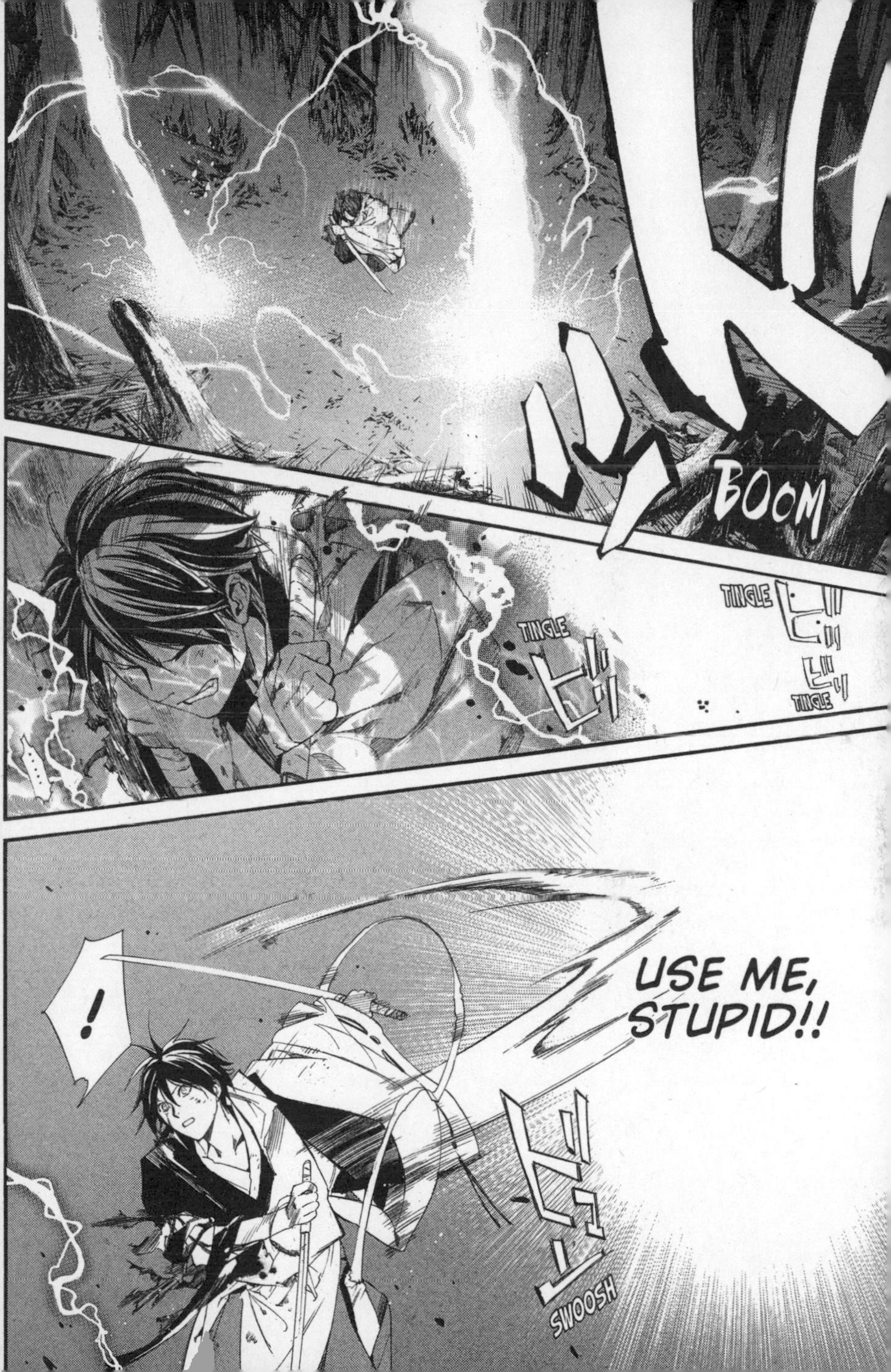
BOOM
TINGLE
TINGLE
TINGLE
...
USE ME, STUPID!!
SWOOSH
!

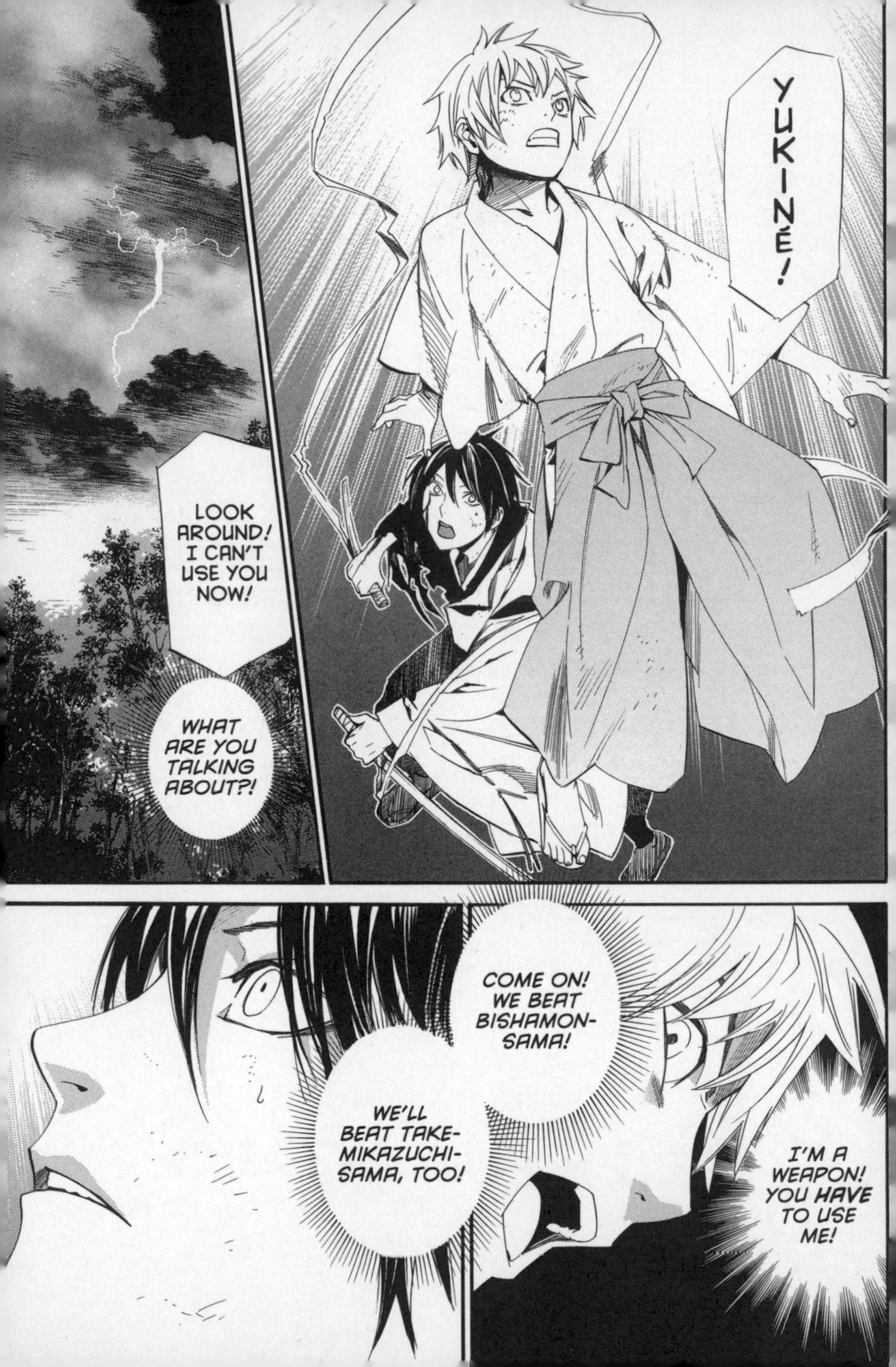

YUKINÉ!
LOOK AROUND! I CAN'T USE YOU NOW!
WHAT ARE YOU TALKING ABOUT?!
COME ON! WE BEAT BISHAMON-SAMA!
WE'LL BEAT TAKE-MIKAZUCHI-SAMA, TOO!
I'M A WEAPON! YOU HAVE TO USE ME!

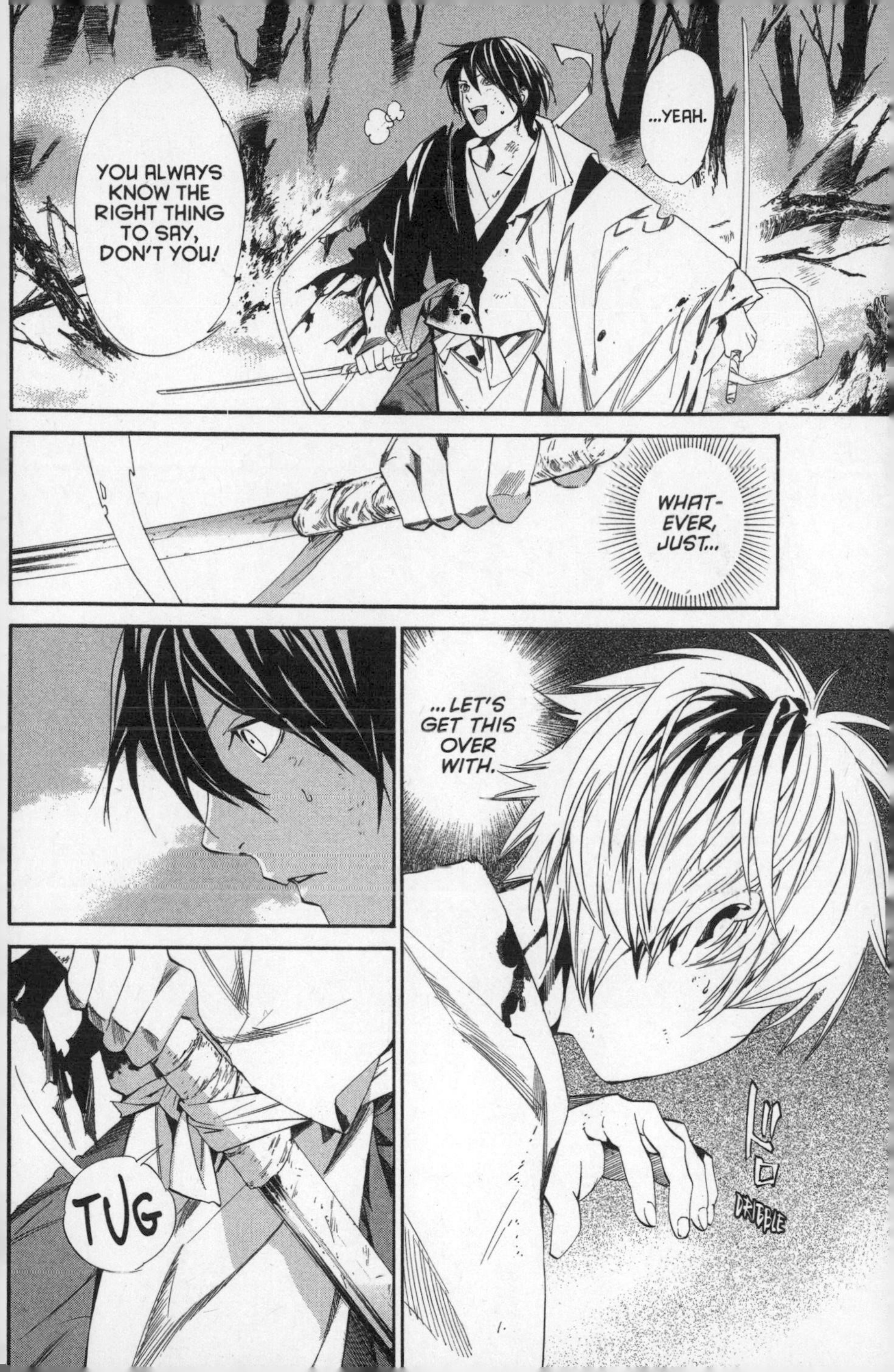
...YEAH.
YOU ALWAYS KNOW THE RIGHT THING TO SAY, DON'T YOU!
WHAT-EVER, JUST...
...LET'S GET THIS OVER WITH.
DRIBBLE
TUG

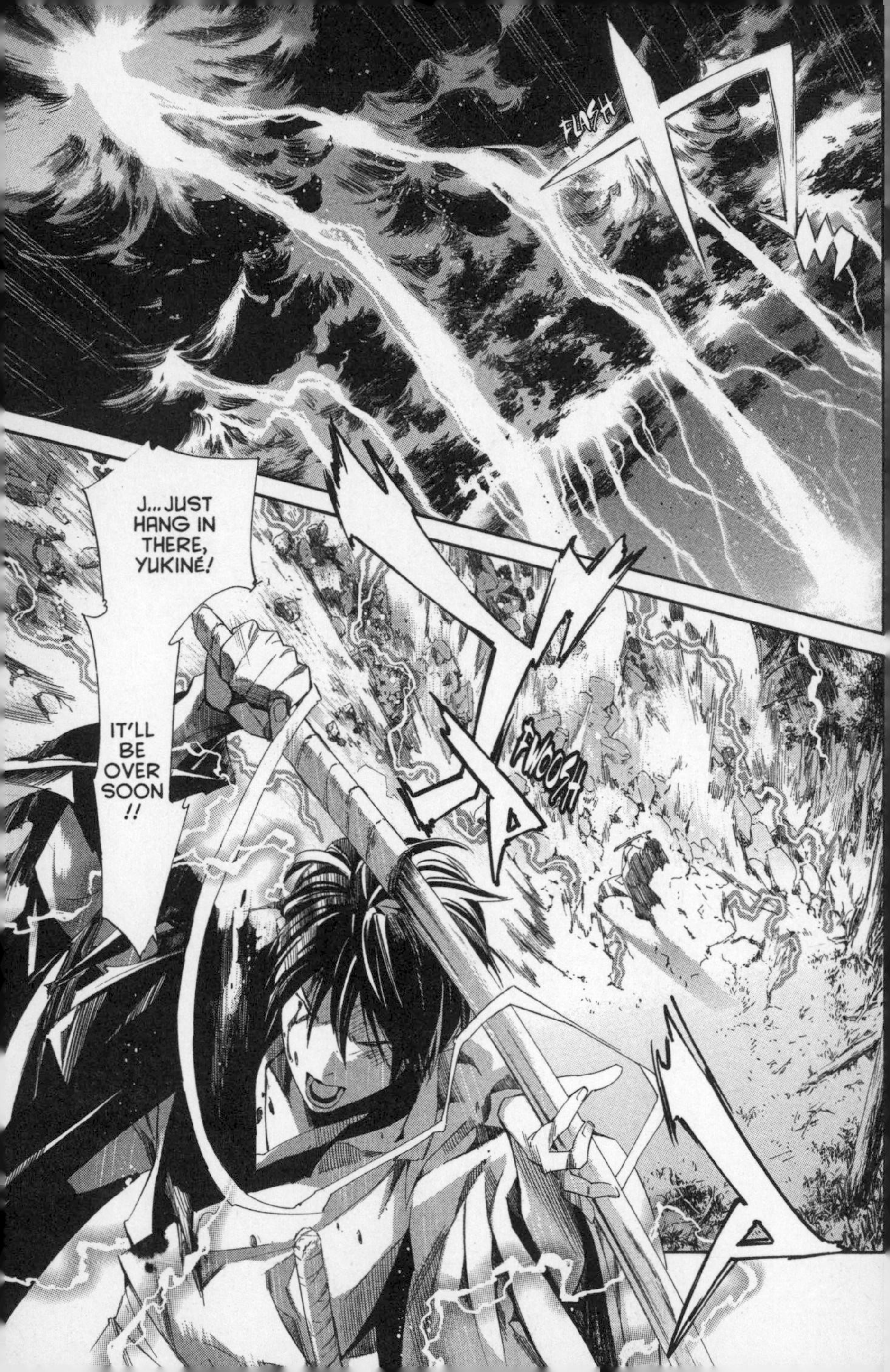
FLASH
J...JUST HANG IN THERE, YUKINÉ!
IT'LL BE OVER SOON !!
FWOOSH

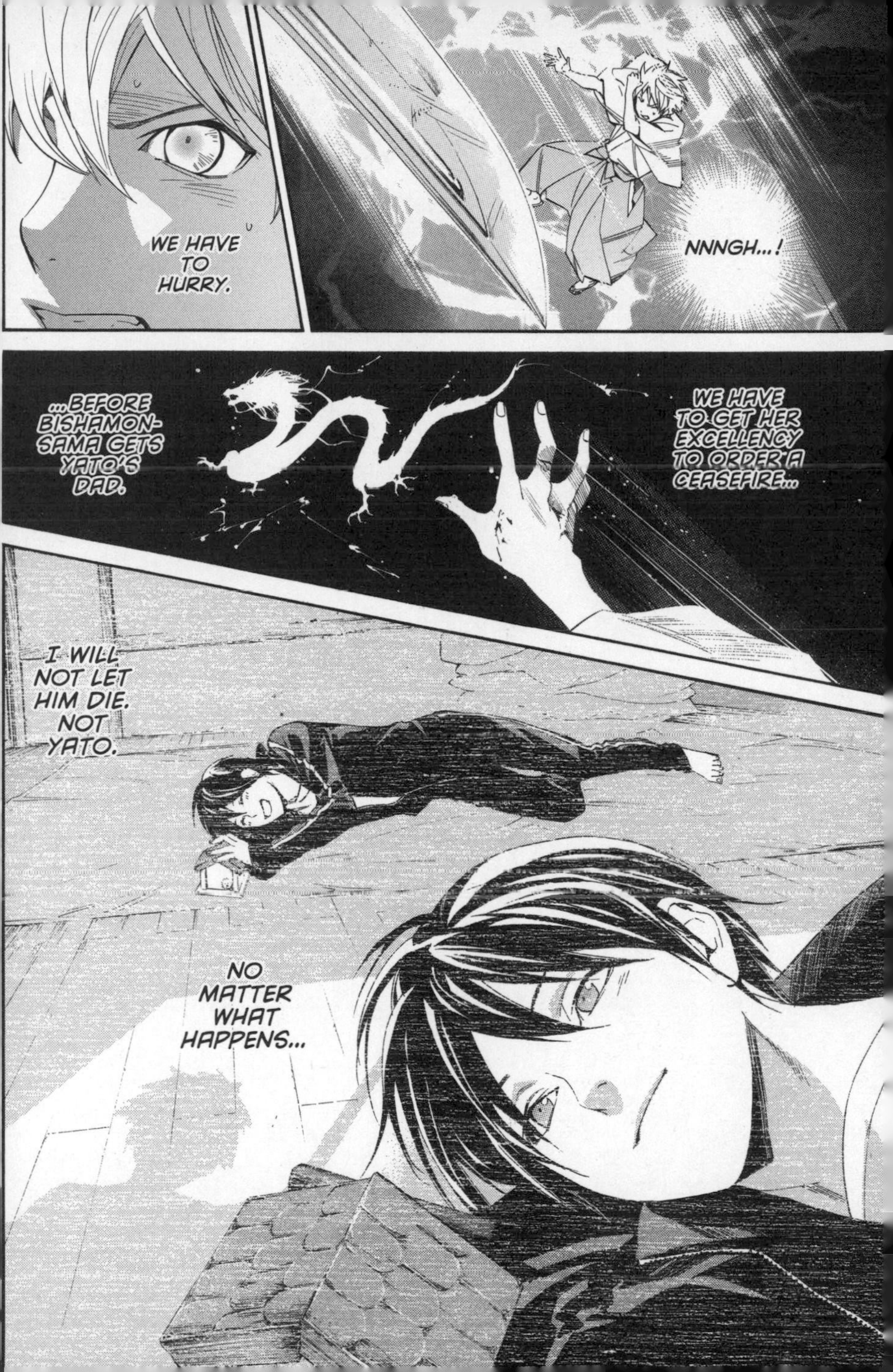
NNNGH...!
WE HAVE TO HURRY.
WE HAVE TO GET HER EXCELLENCY TO ORDER A CEASEFIRE...
...BEFORE BISHAMON-SAMA GETS YATO'S DAD.
I WILL NOT LET HIM DIE. NOT YATO.
NO MATTER WHAT HAPPENS...

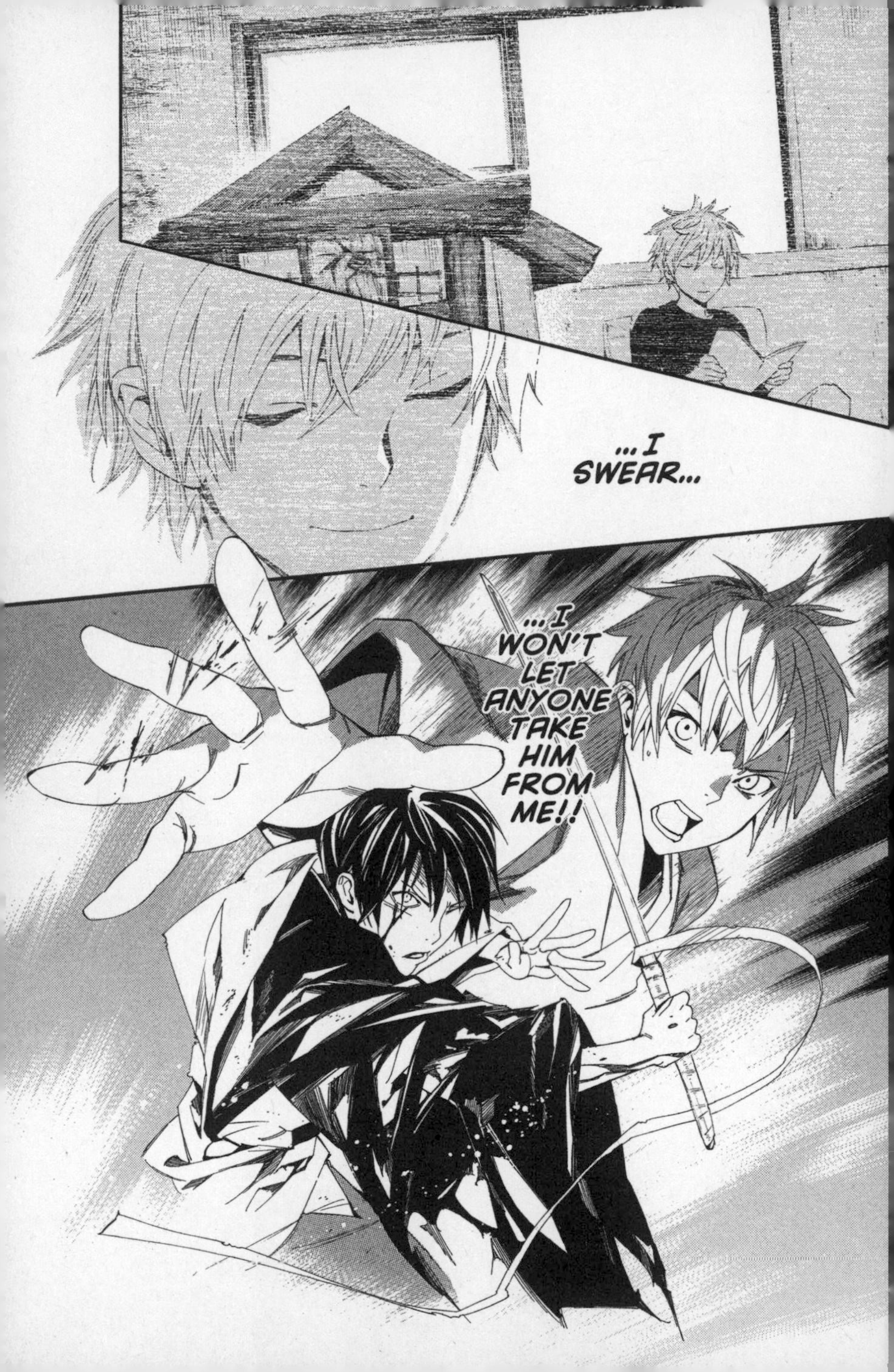
...I SWEAR...
...I WON'T LET ANYONE TAKE HIM FROM ME!!

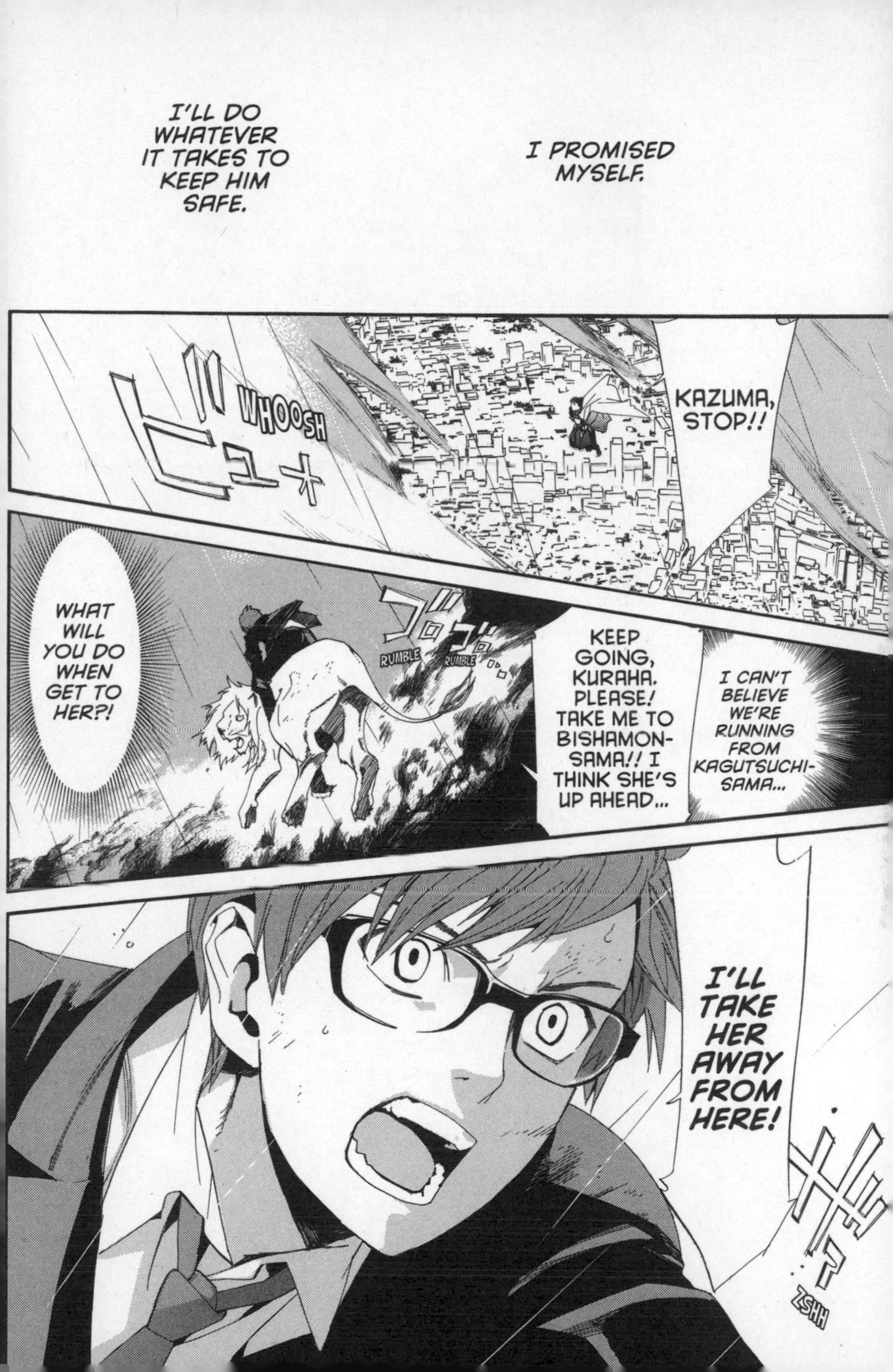
I PROMISED MYSELF.
I'LL DO WHATEVER IT TAKES TO KEEP HIM SAFE.
KAZUMA, STOP!!
WHOOSH
I CAN'T BELIEVE WE'RE RUNNING FROM KAGUTSUCHI-SAMA...
KEEP GOING, KURAHA. PLEASE! TAKE ME TO BISHAMON-SAMA!! I THINK SHE'S UP AHEAD...
RUMBLE RUMBLE
WHAT WILL YOU DO WHEN GET TO HER?!
I'LL TAKE HER AWAY FROM HERE!
ZSHH

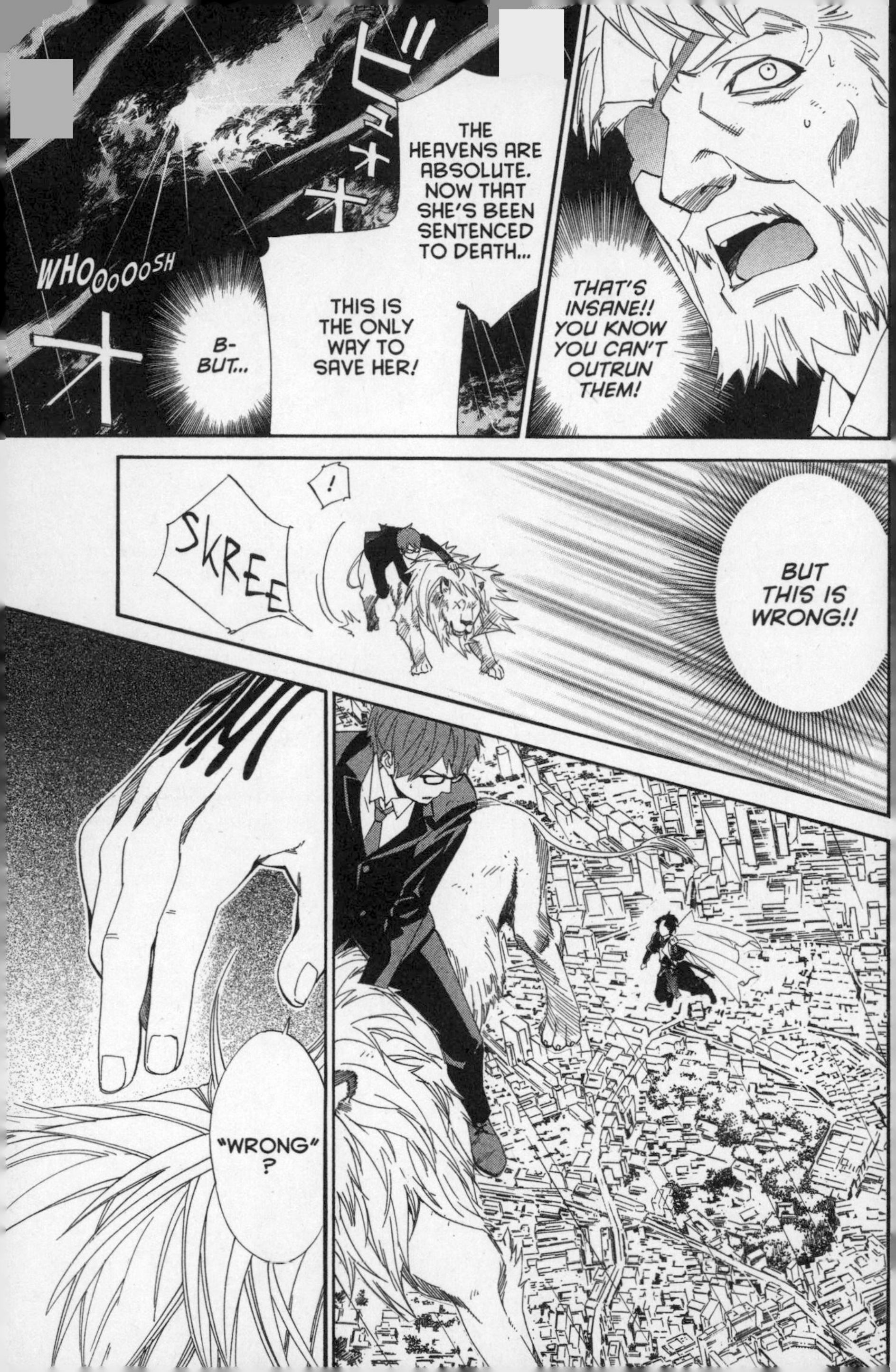
THAT'S INSANE!! YOU KNOW YOU CAN'T OUTRUN THEM!
THE HEAVENS ARE ABSOLUTE. NOW THAT SHE'S BEEN SENTENCED TO DEATH...
THIS IS THE ONLY WAY TO SAVE HER!
WHOOOOOSH
B-BUT...
BUT THIS IS WRONG!!
!
SKREE
"WRONG"?

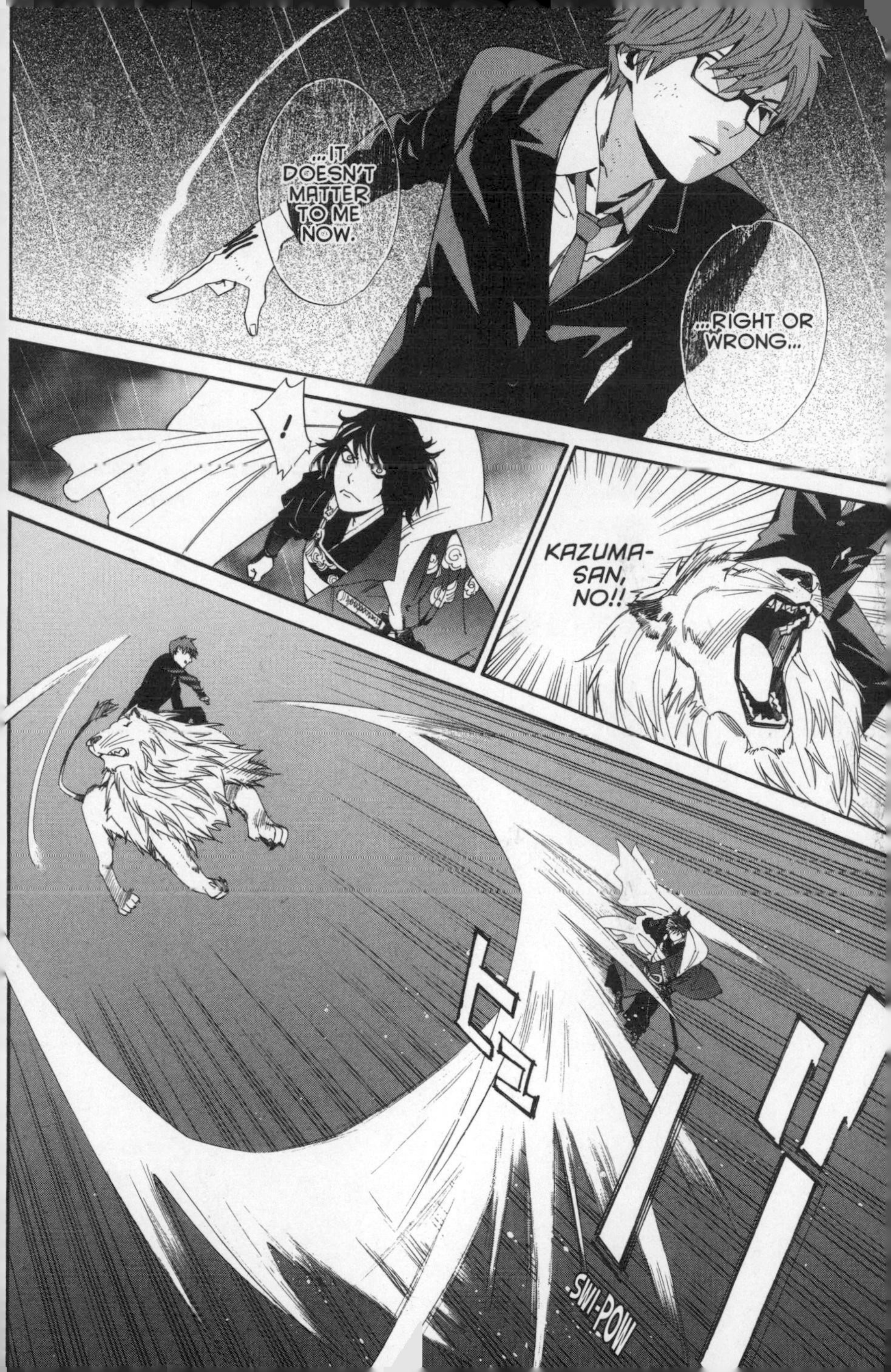
...RIGHT OR WRONG...
...IT DOESN'T MATTER TO ME NOW.
KAZUMA-SAN, NO!!
!
SWI-POW

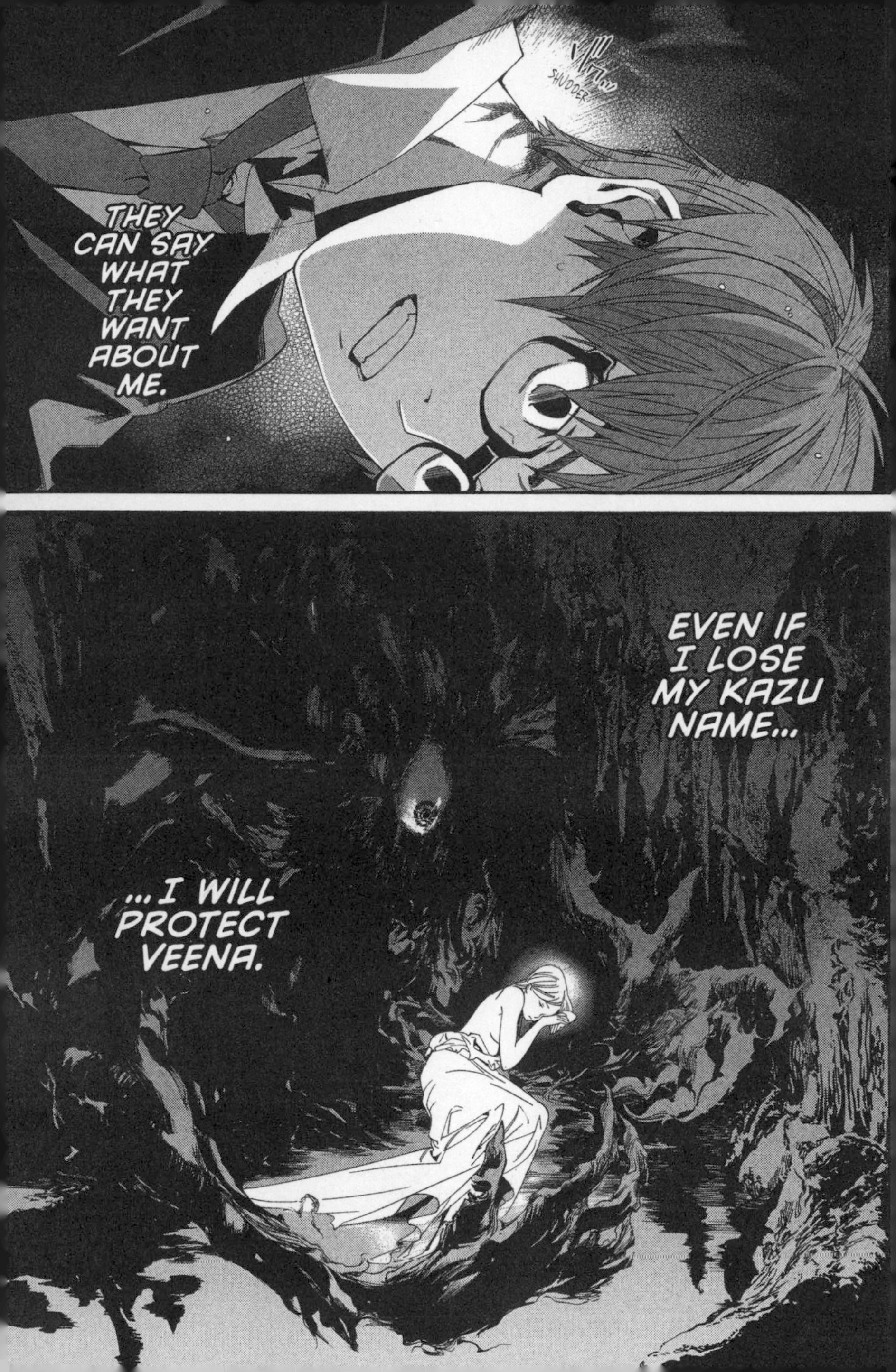
SHUDDER
THEY CAN SAY WHAT THEY WANT ABOUT ME.
EVEN IF I LOSE MY KAZU NAME...
...I WILL PROTECT VEENA.

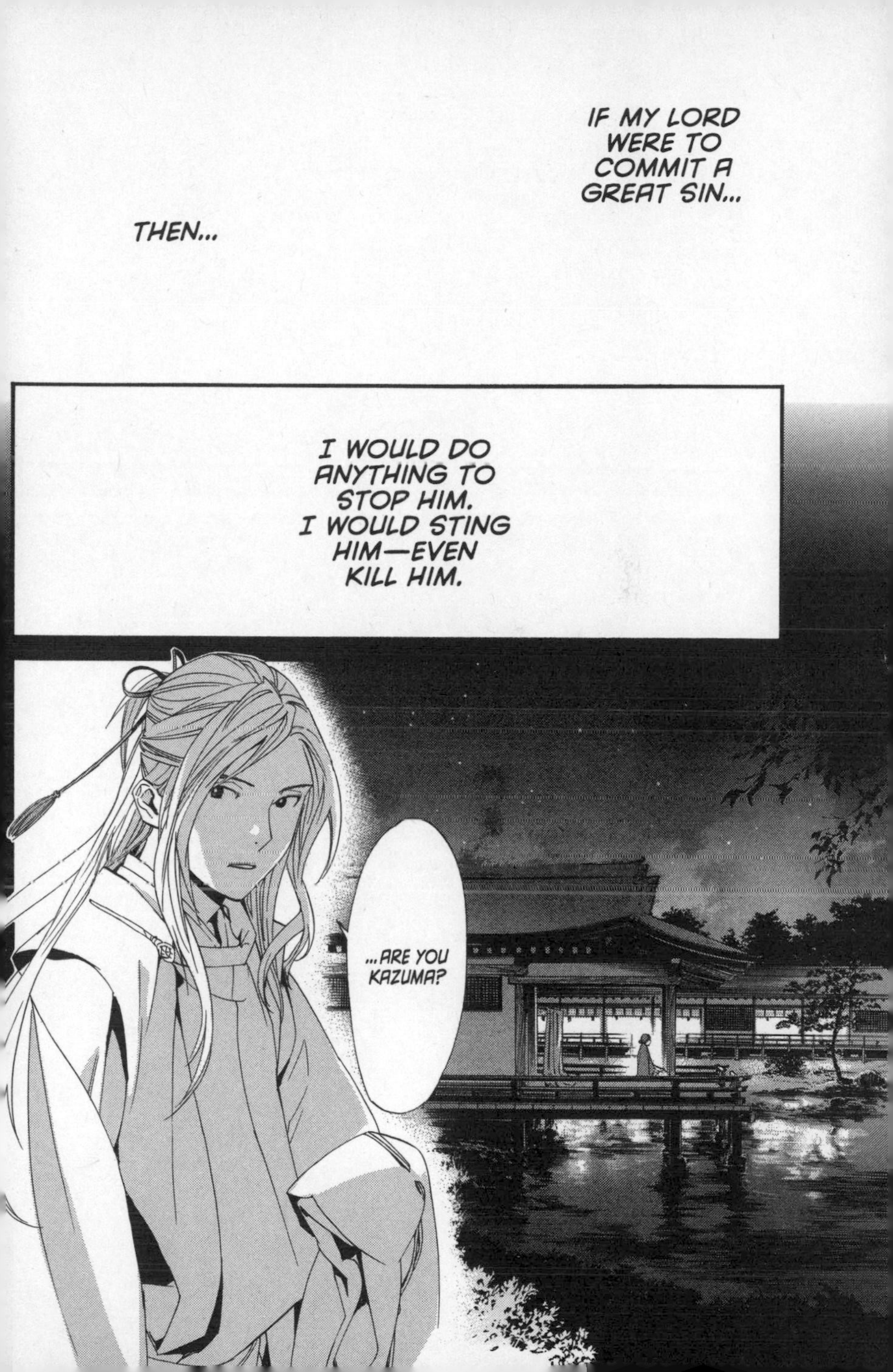
IF MY LORD WERE TO COMMIT A GREAT SIN...
THEN...
I WOULD DO ANYTHING TO STOP HIM. I WOULD STING HIM—EVEN KILL HIM.
...ARE YOU KAZUMA?

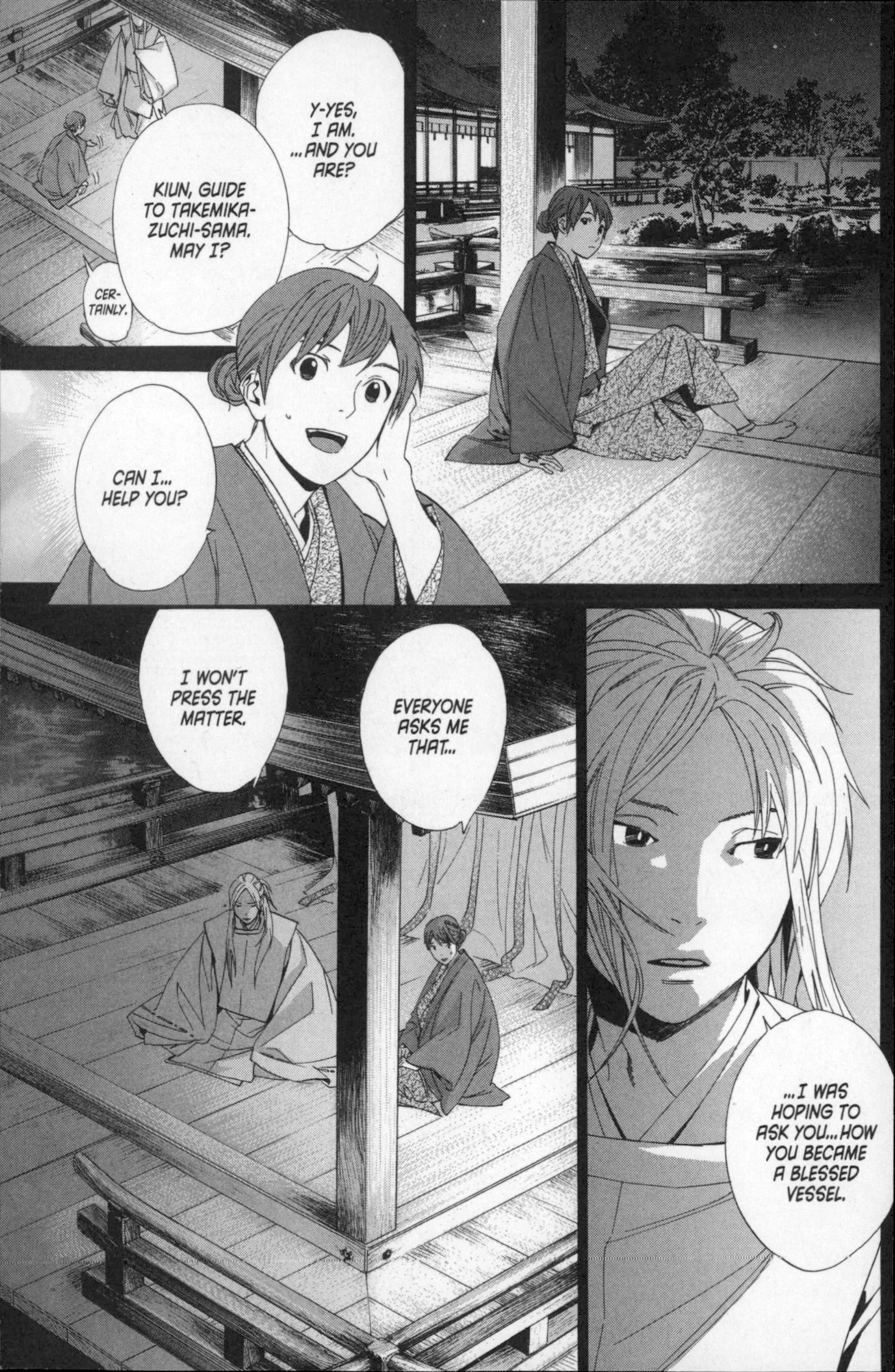
Y-YES, I AM. ...AND YOU ARE?
KIUN, GUIDE TO TAKEMIKA-ZUCHI-SAMA. MAY I?
CER-TAINLY.
CAN I... HELP YOU?
...I WAS HOPING TO ASK YOU...HOW YOU BECAME A BLESSED VESSEL.
EVERYONE ASKS ME THAT...
I WON'T PRESS THE MATTER.

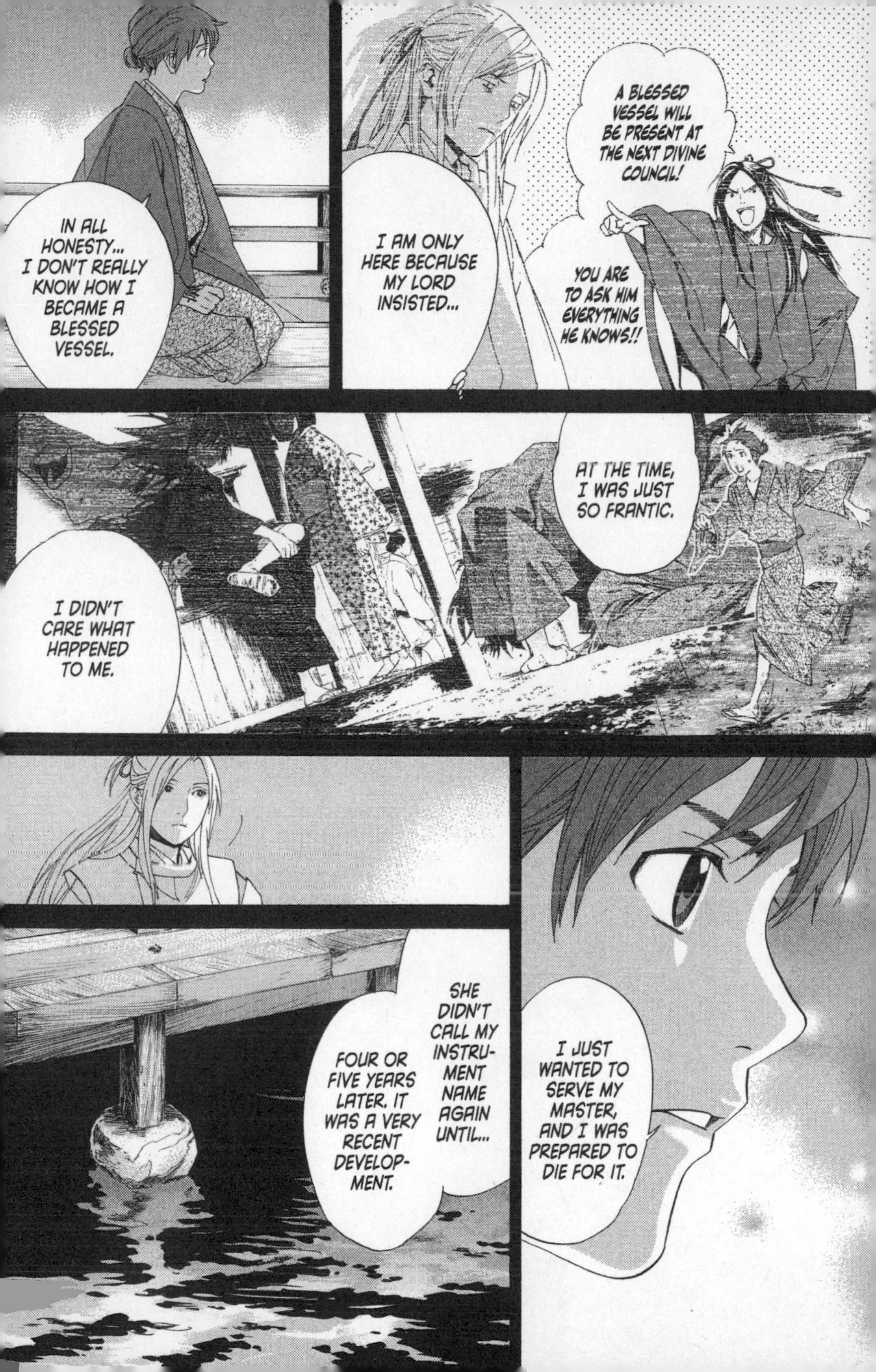
A BLESSED VESSEL WILL BE PRESENT AT THE NEXT DIVINE COUNCIL!
YOU ARE TO ASK HIM EVERYTHING HE KNOWS!!
I AM ONLY HERE BECAUSE MY LORD INSISTED...
IN ALL HONESTY... I DON'T REALLY KNOW HOW I BECAME A BLESSED VESSEL.
AT THE TIME, I WAS JUST SO FRANTIC.
I DIDN'T CARE WHAT HAPPENED TO ME.
I JUST WANTED TO SERVE MY MASTER, AND I WAS PREPARED TO DIE FOR IT.
SHE DIDN'T CALL MY INSTRU-MENT NAME AGAIN UNTIL...
FOUR OR FIVE YEARS LATER. IT WAS A VERY RECENT DEVELOP-MENT.

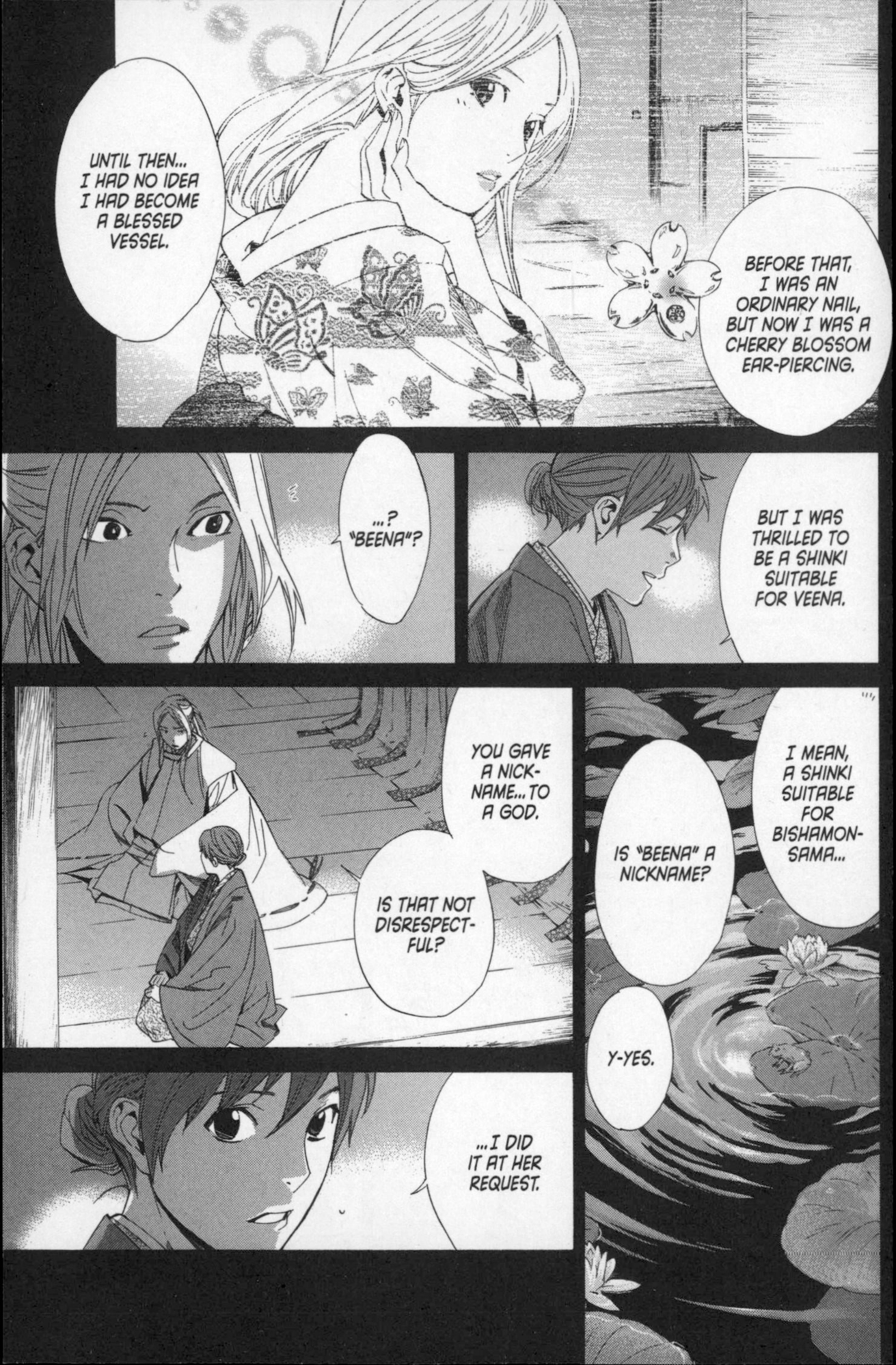
UNTIL THEN... I HAD NO IDEA I HAD BECOME A BLESSED VESSEL.
BEFORE THAT, I WAS AN ORDINARY NAIL, BUT NOW I WAS A CHERRY BLOSSOM EAR-PIERCING.
BUT I WAS THRILLED TO BE A SHINKI SUITABLE FOR VEENA.
...? "BEENA"?
I MEAN, A SHINKI SUITABLE FOR BISHAMON-SAMA...
IS "BEENA" A NICKNAME?
Y-YES.
YOU GAVE A NICK-NAME... TO A GOD.
IS THAT NOT DISRESPECT-FUL?
...I DID IT AT HER REQUEST.

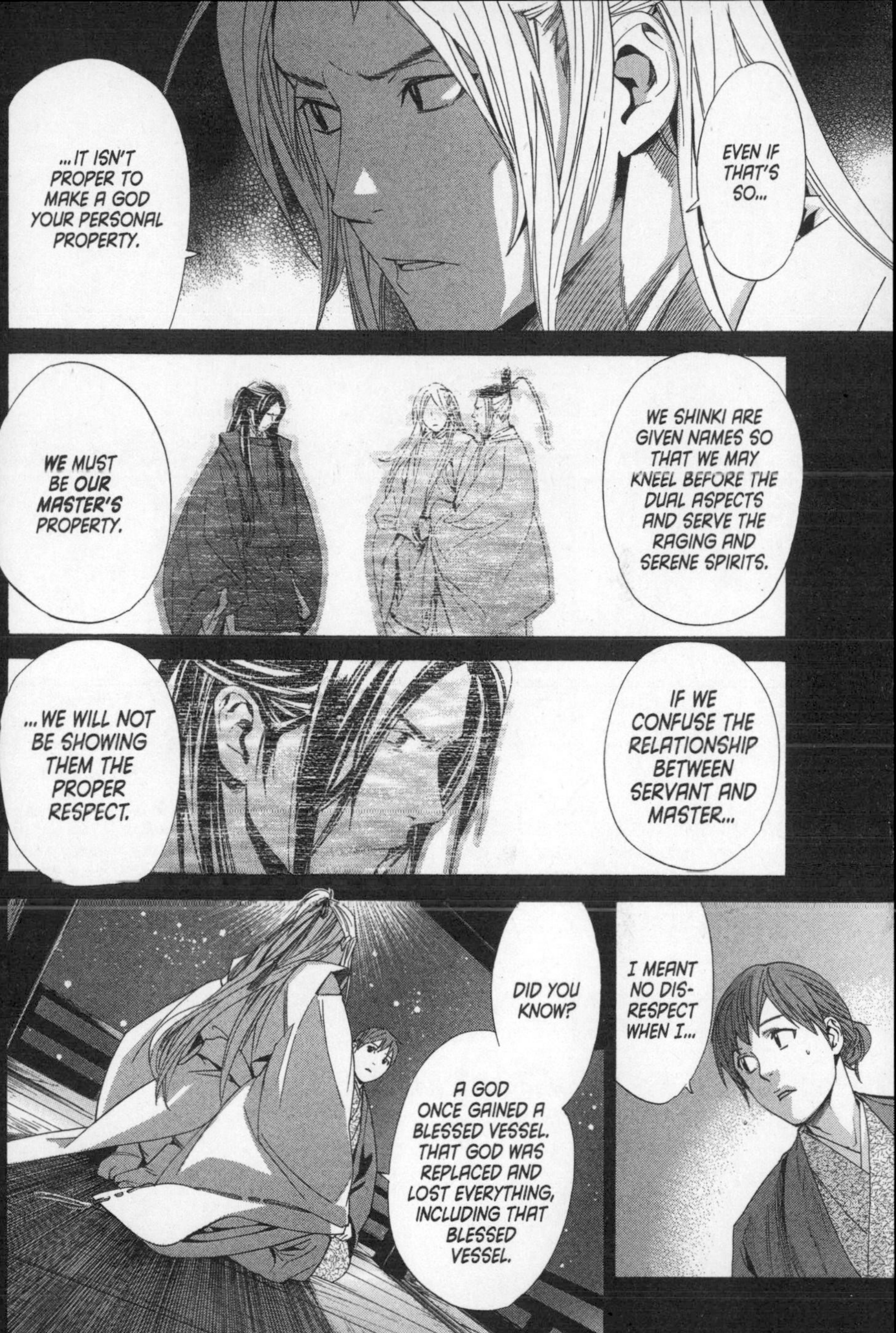
EVEN IF THAT'S SO...
...IT ISN'T PROPER TO MAKE A GOD YOUR PERSONAL PROPERTY.
WE SHINKI ARE GIVEN NAMES SO THAT WE MAY KNEEL BEFORE THE DUAL ASPECTS AND SERVE THE RAGING AND SERENE SPIRITS.
WE MUST BE OUR MASTER'S PROPERTY.
IF WE CONFUSE THE RELATIONSHIP BETWEEN SERVANT AND MASTER...
...WE WILL NOT BE SHOWING THEM THE PROPER RESPECT.
I MEANT NO DIS-RESPECT WHEN I...
DID YOU KNOW?
A GOD ONCE GAINED A BLESSED VESSEL. THAT GOD WAS REPLACED AND LOST EVERYTHING, INCLUDING THAT BLESSED VESSEL.

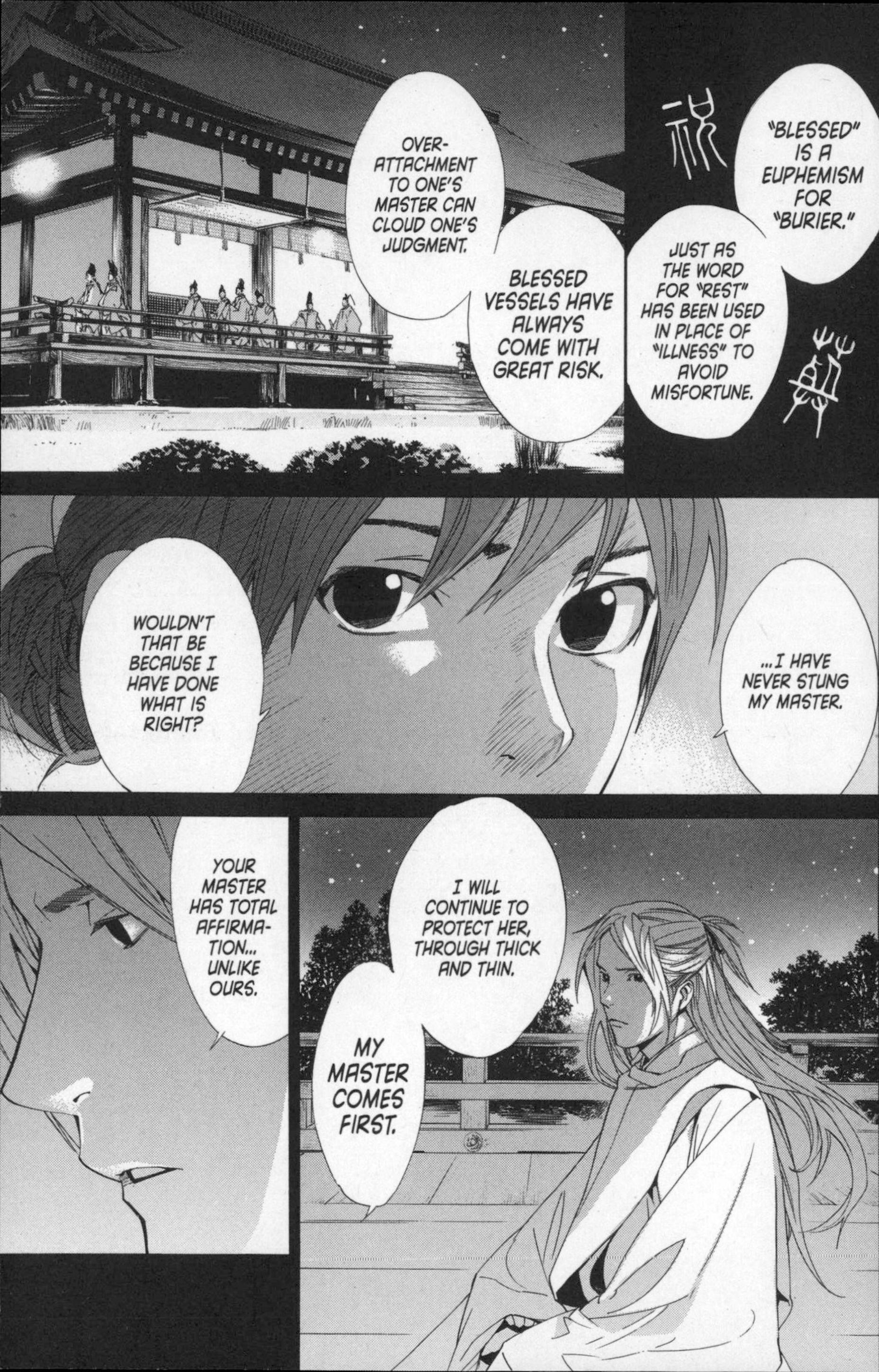
"BLESSED" IS A EUPHEMISM FOR "BURIER."
JUST AS THE WORD FOR "REST" HAS BEEN USED IN PLACE OF "ILLNESS" TO AVOID MISFORTUNE.
BLESSED VESSELS HAVE ALWAYS COME WITH GREAT RISK.
OVER-ATTACHMENT TO ONE'S MASTER CAN CLOUD ONE'S JUDGMENT.
...I HAVE NEVER STUNG MY MASTER.
WOULDN'T THAT BE BECAUSE I HAVE DONE WHAT IS RIGHT?
I WILL CONTINUE TO PROTECT HER, THROUGH THICK AND THIN.
MY MASTER COMES FIRST.
YOUR MASTER HAS TOTAL AFFIRMATION... UNLIKE OURS.

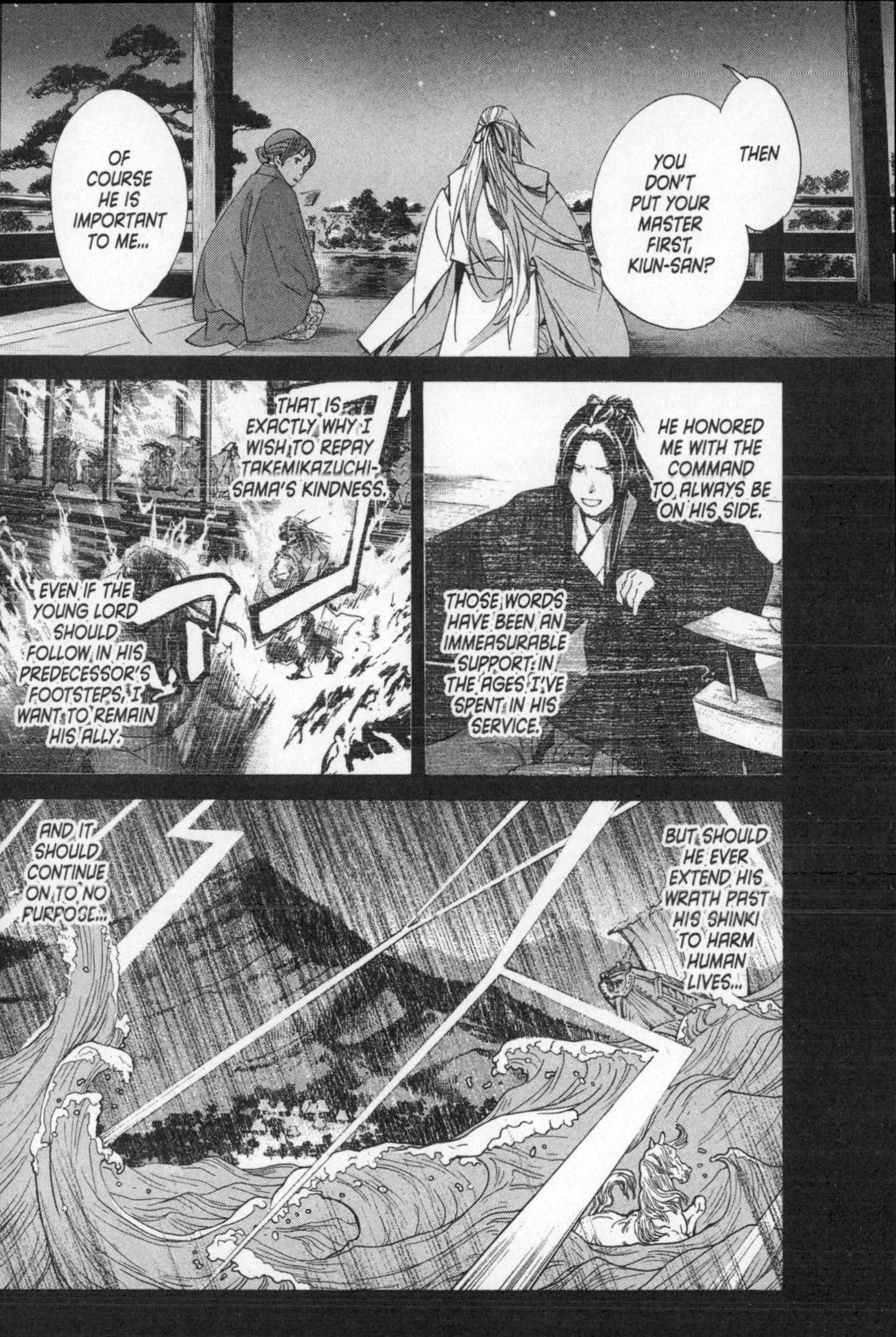
THEN
YOU DON'T PUT YOUR MASTER FIRST, KIUN-SAN?
OF COURSE HE IS IMPORTANT TO ME...
HE HONORED ME WITH THE COMMAND TO ALWAYS BE ON HIS SIDE.
THOSE WORDS HAVE BEEN AN IMMEASURABLE SUPPORT IN THE AGES I'VE SPENT IN HIS SERVICE.
THAT IS EXACTLY WHY I WISH TO REPAY TAKEMIKAZUCHI-SAMA'S KINDNESS.
EVEN IF THE YOUNG LORD SHOULD FOLLOW IN HIS PREDECESSOR'S FOOTSTEPS, I WANT TO REMAIN HIS ALLY.
BUT SHOULD HE EVER EXTEND HIS WRATH PAST HIS SHINKI TO HARM HUMAN LIVES...
AND IT SHOULD CONTINUE ON TO NO PURPOSE...

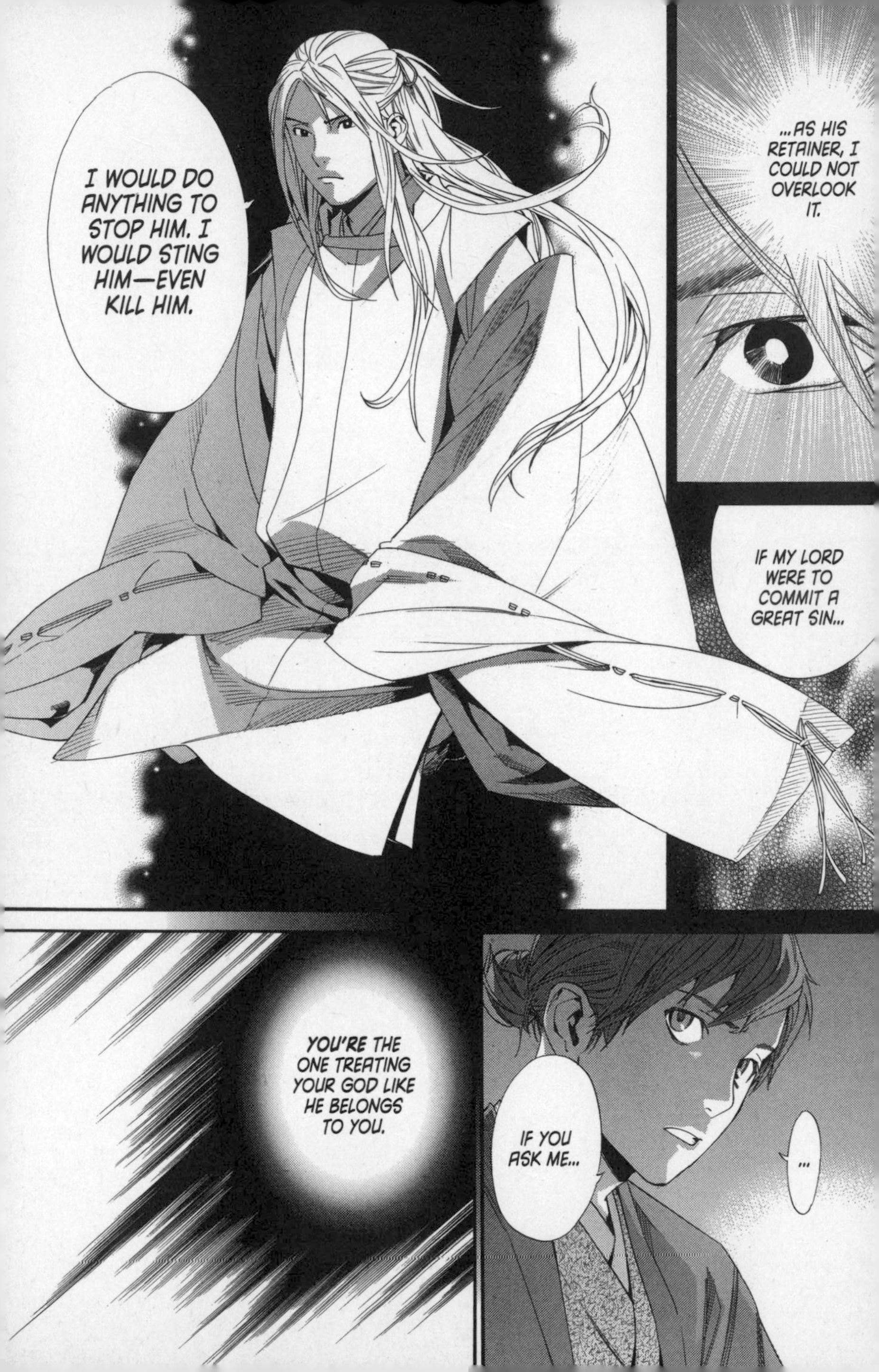
...AS HIS RETAINER, I COULD NOT OVERLOOK IT.
IF MY LORD WERE TO COMMIT A GREAT SIN...
I WOULD DO ANYTHING TO STOP HIM. I WOULD STING HIM—EVEN KILL HIM.
...
IF YOU ASK ME...
YOU'RE THE ONE TREATING YOUR GOD LIKE HE BELONGS TO YOU.

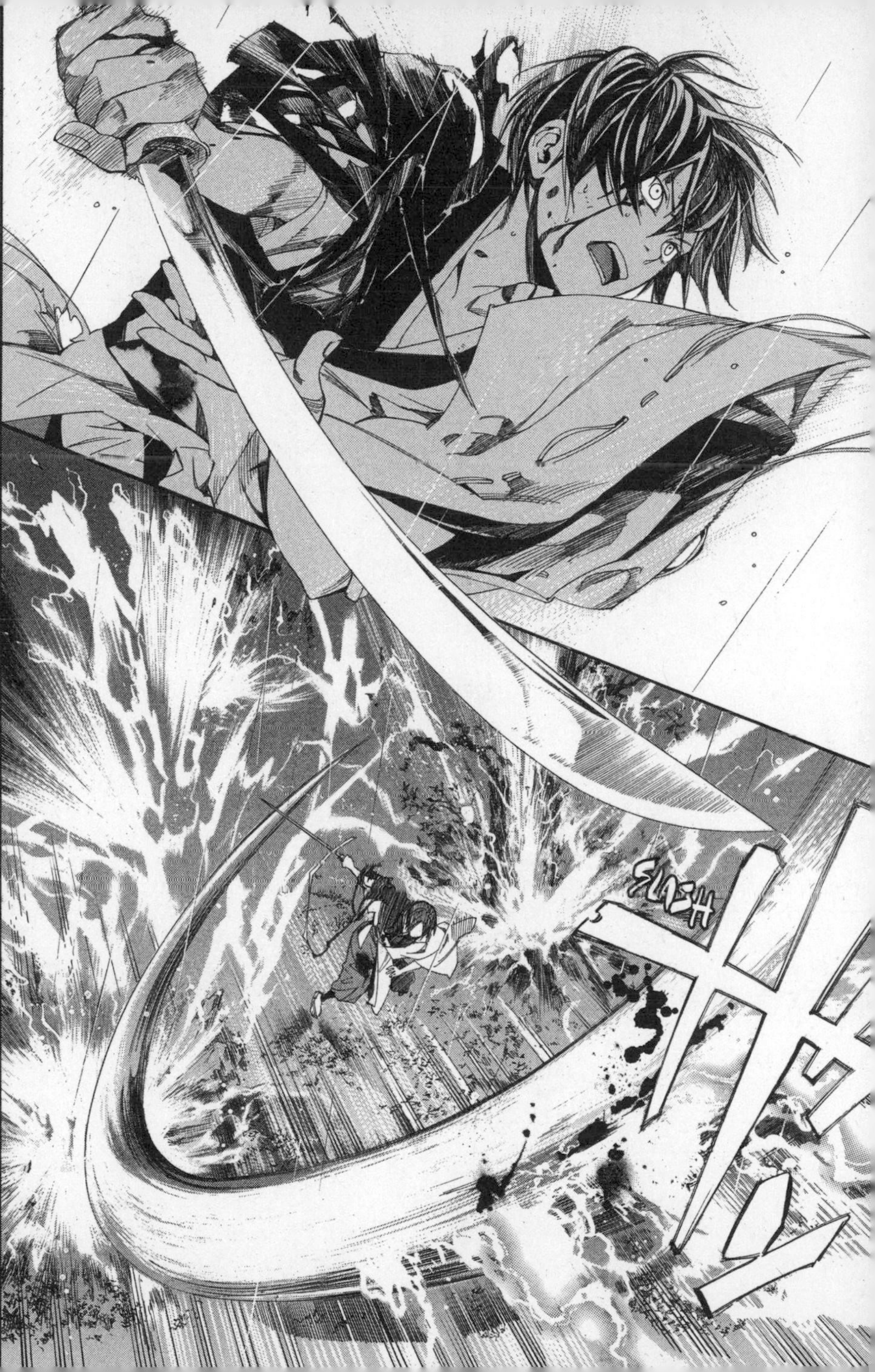
SLASH

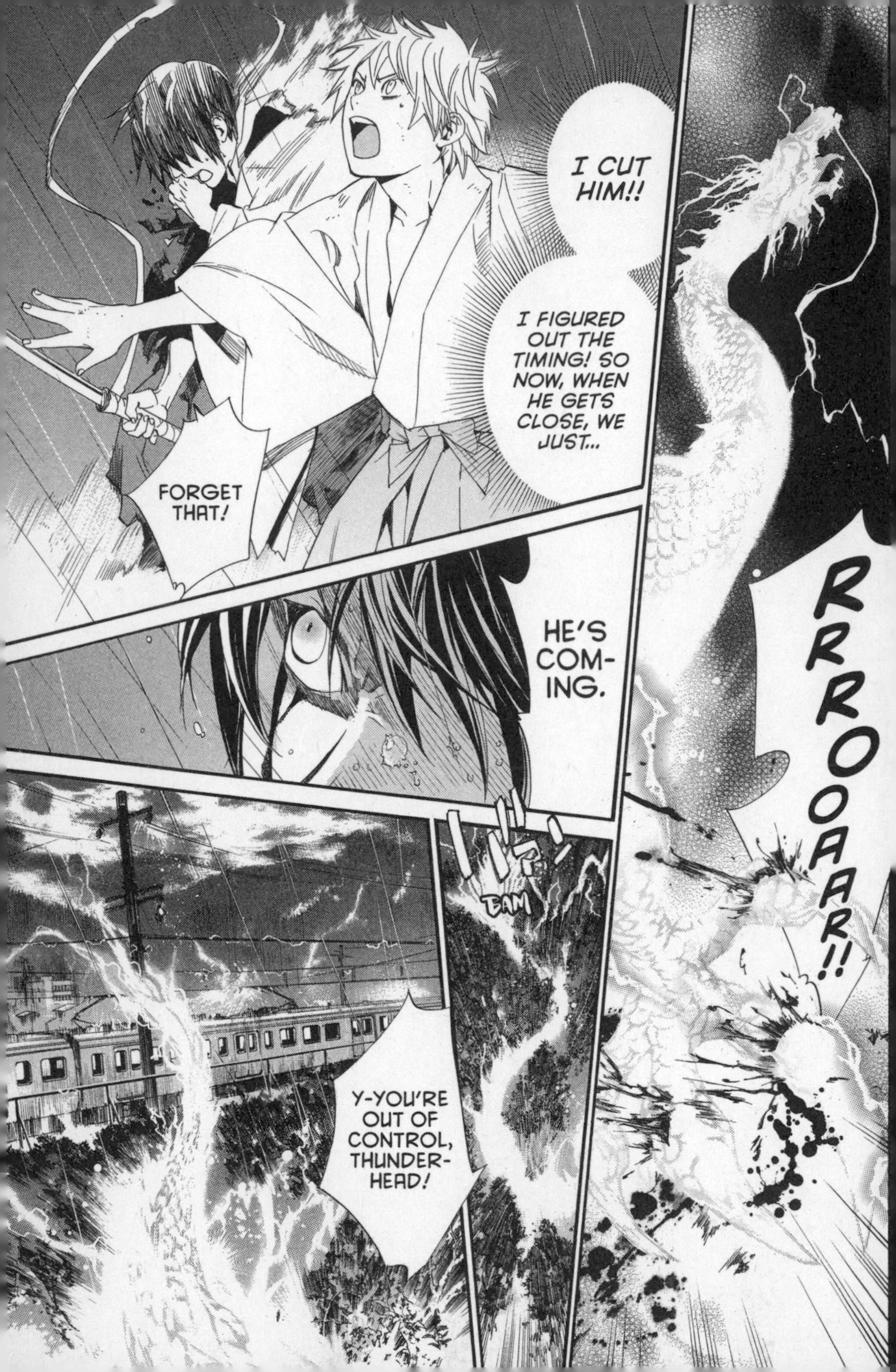
RRROOAAR!!
I CUT HIM!!
I FIGURED OUT THE TIMING! SO NOW, WHEN HE GETS CLOSE, WE JUST...
FORGET THAT!
HE'S COMING.
BAM
Y-YOU'RE OUT OF CONTROL, THUNDERHEAD!

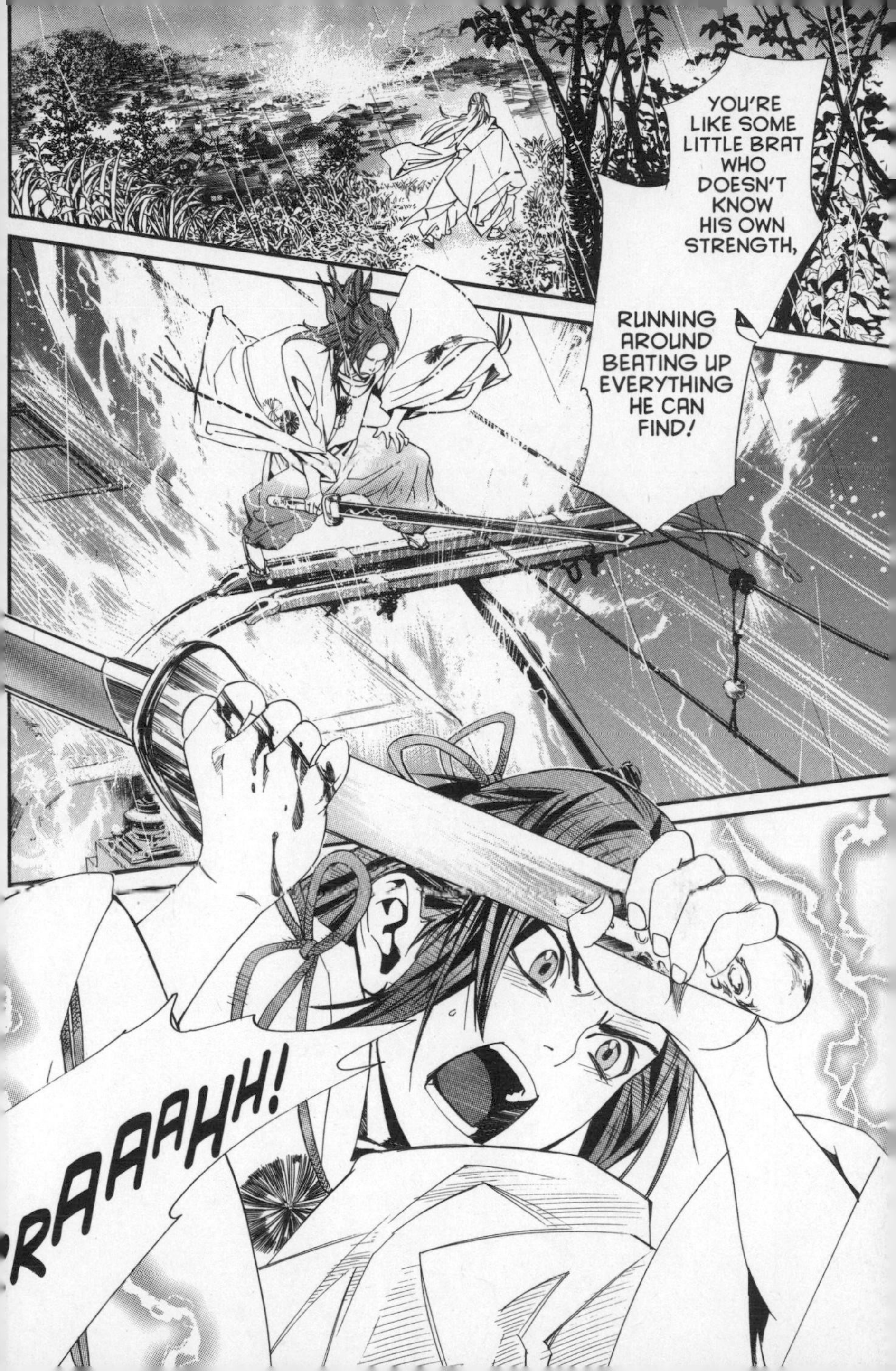
YOU'RE LIKE SOME LITTLE BRAT WHO DOESN'T KNOW HIS OWN STRENGTH,
RUNNING AROUND BEATING UP EVERYTHING HE CAN FIND!
RAAAHH!

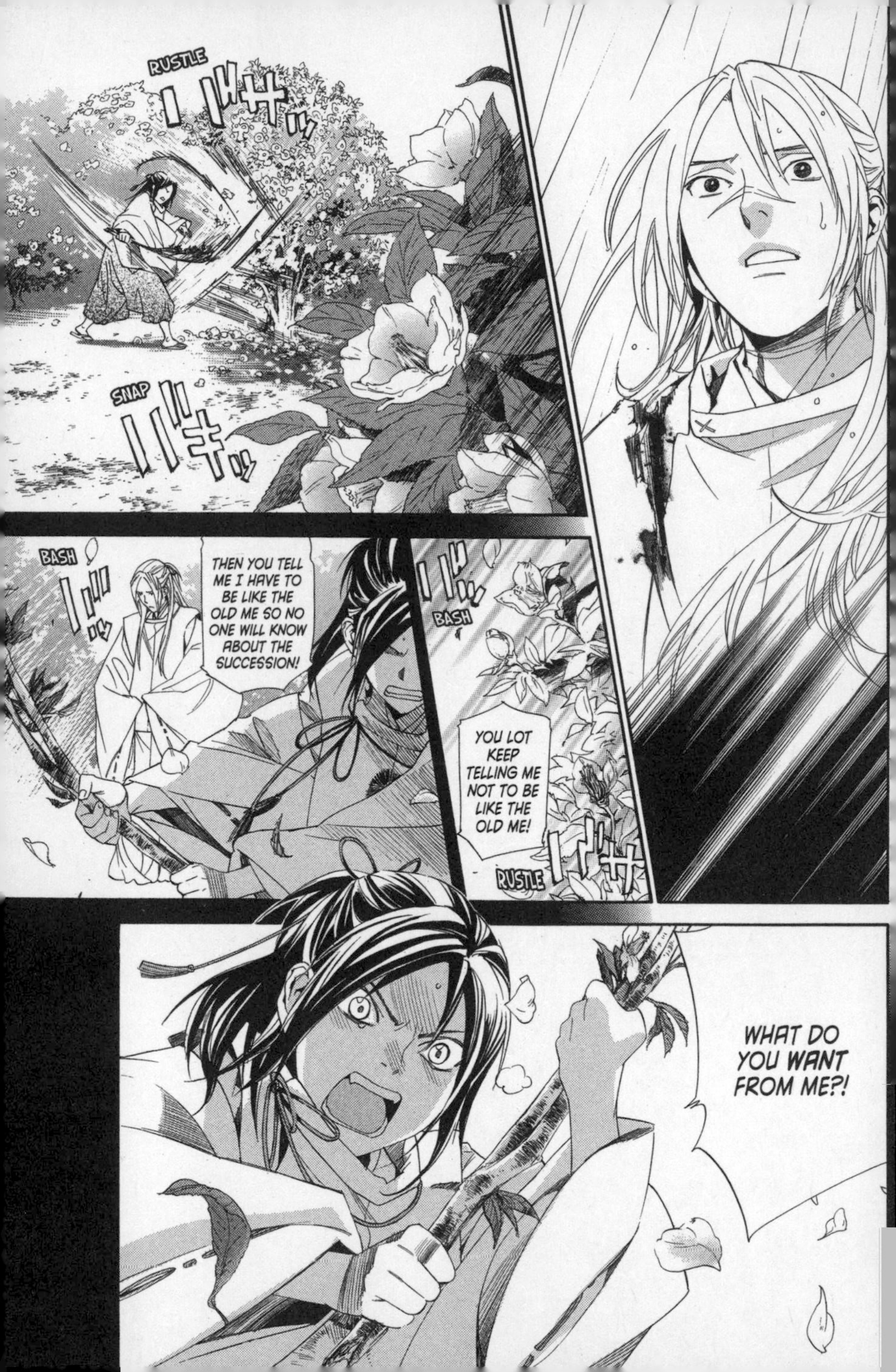
RUSTLE
SNAP
BASH
YOU LOT KEEP TELLING ME NOT TO BE LIKE THE OLD ME!
RUSTLE
BASH
THEN YOU TELL ME I HAVE TO BE LIKE THE OLD ME SO NO ONE WILL KNOW ABOUT THE SUCCESSION!
WHAT DO YOU WANT FROM ME?!

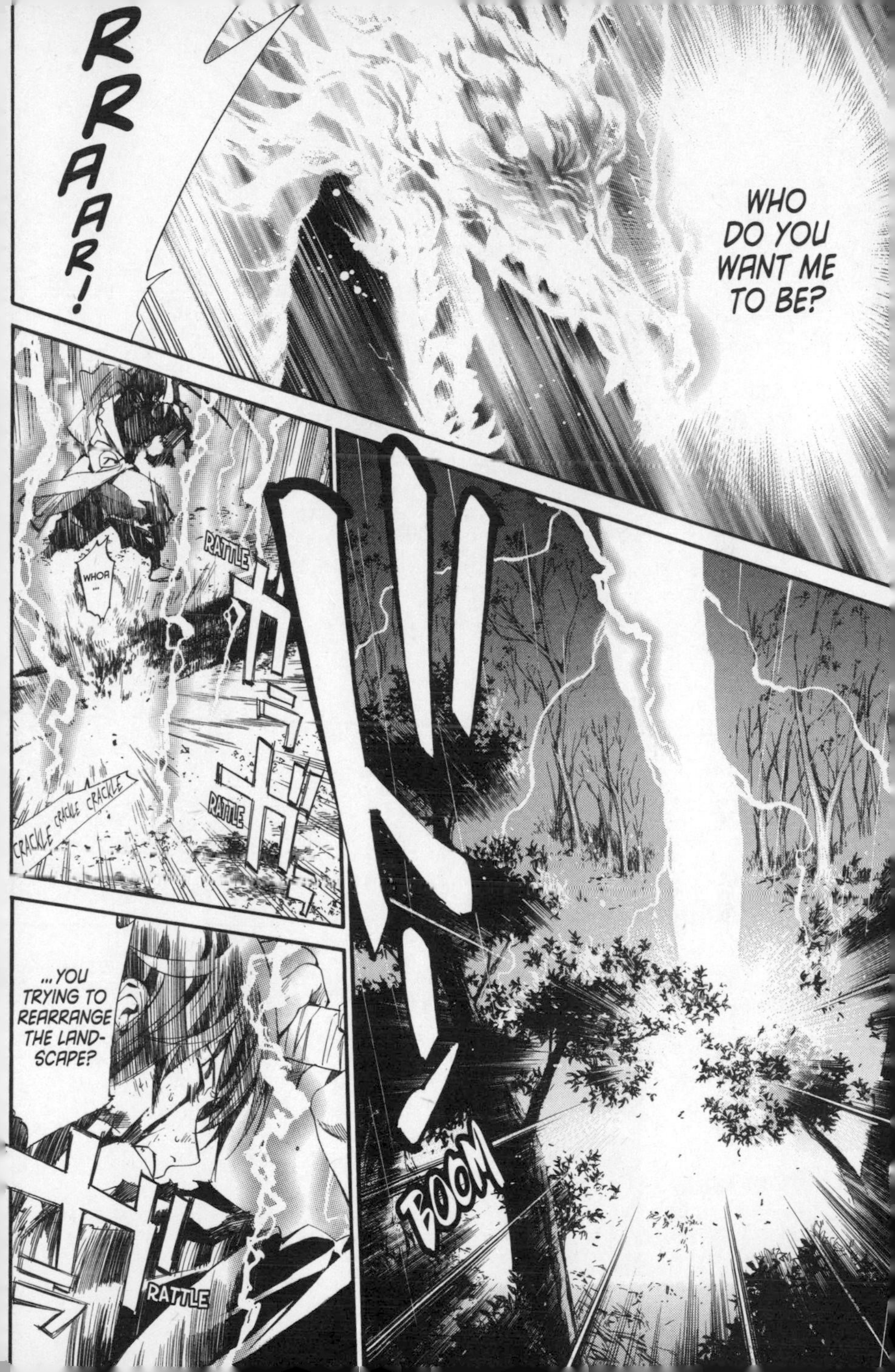
WHO DO YOU WANT ME TO BE?
RRAAR!
BOOM
RATTLE
WHOA...
RATTLE
CRACKLE CRACKLE CRACKLE
...YOU TRYING TO REARRANGE THE LAND-SCAPE?
RATTLE

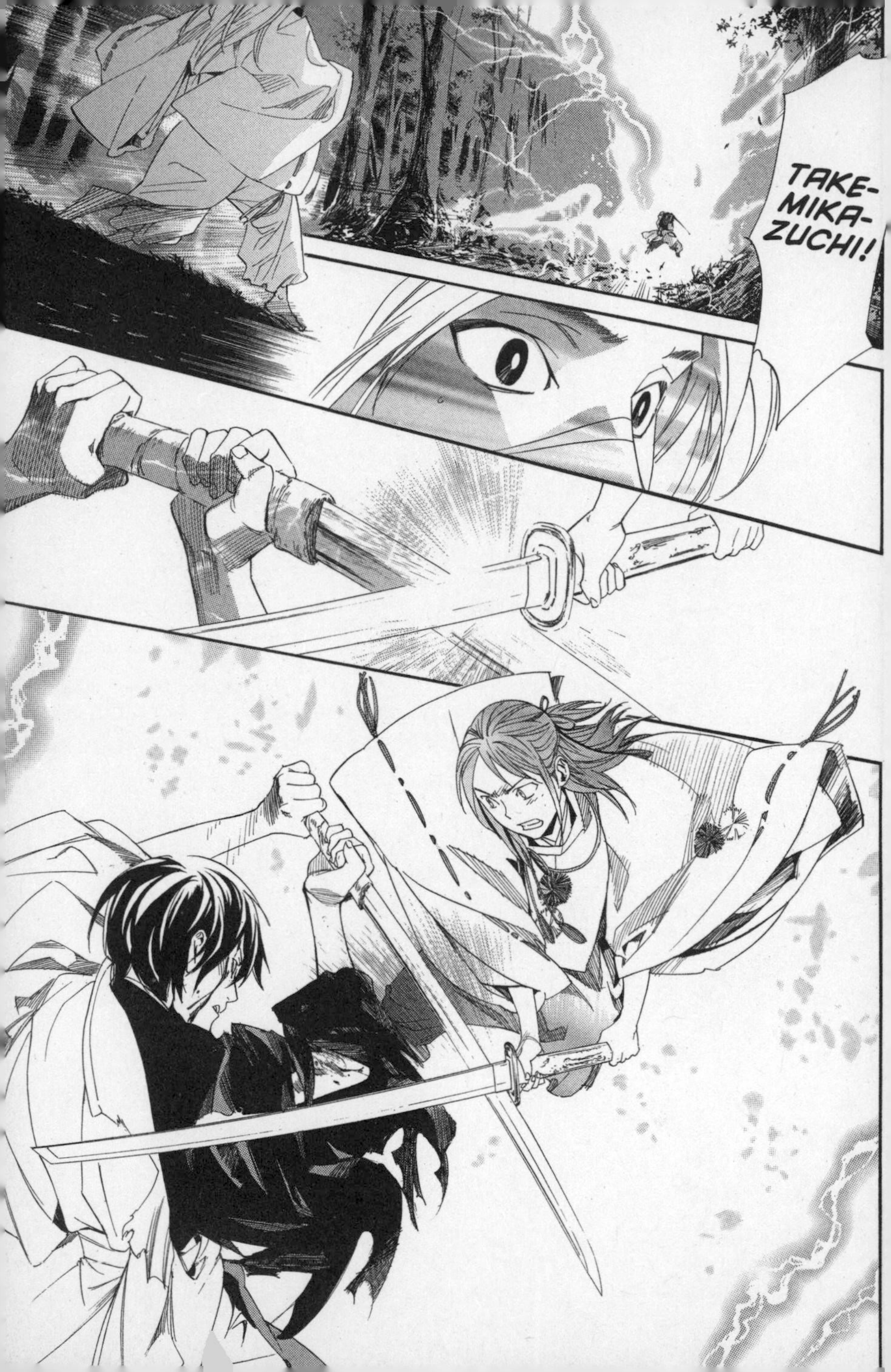
TAKE-MIKA-ZUCHI!

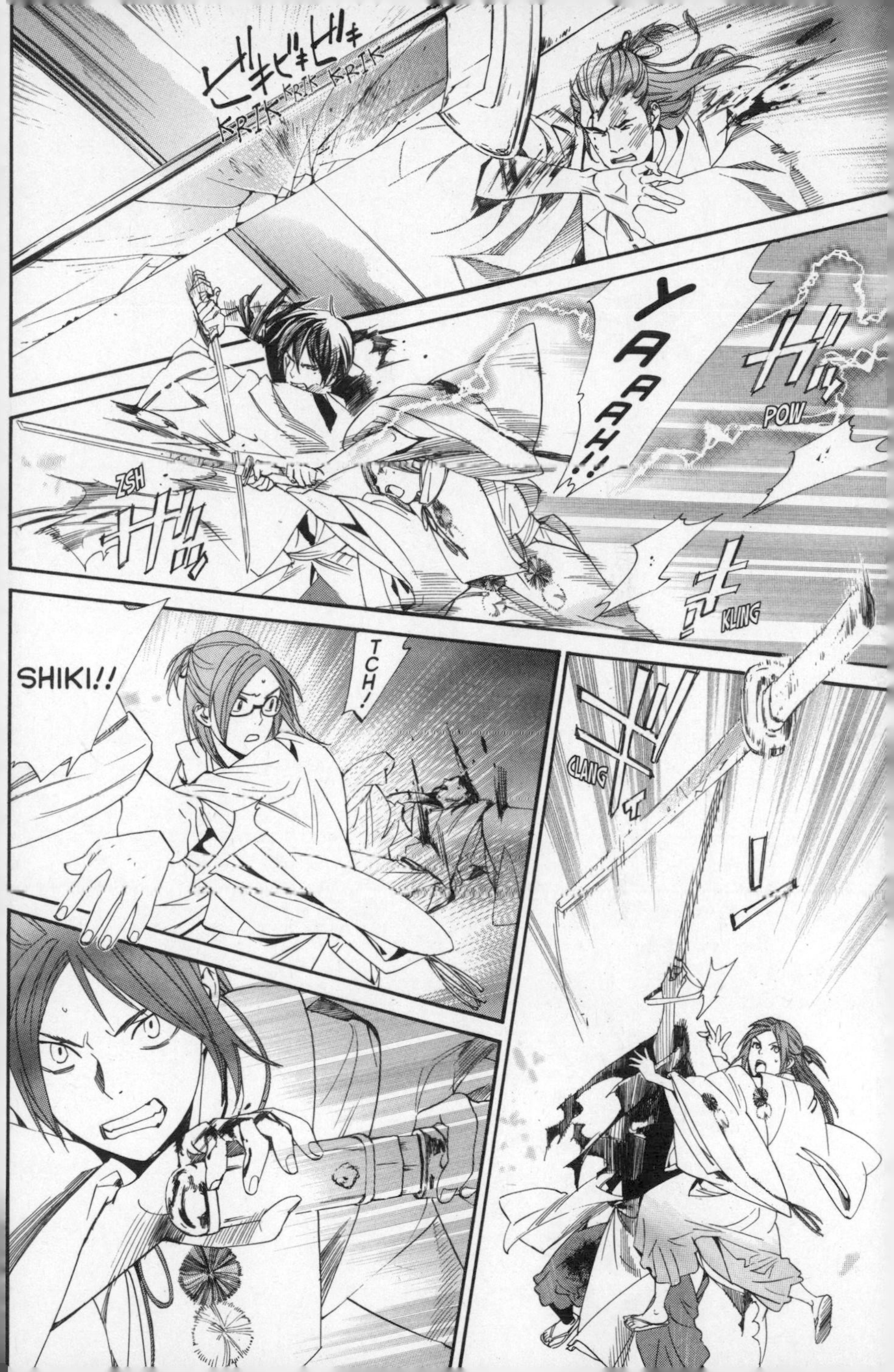
KRIK KRIK KRIK
POW
YAAAH!!
KLING
ZSH
CLANG
TCH!
SHIKI!!

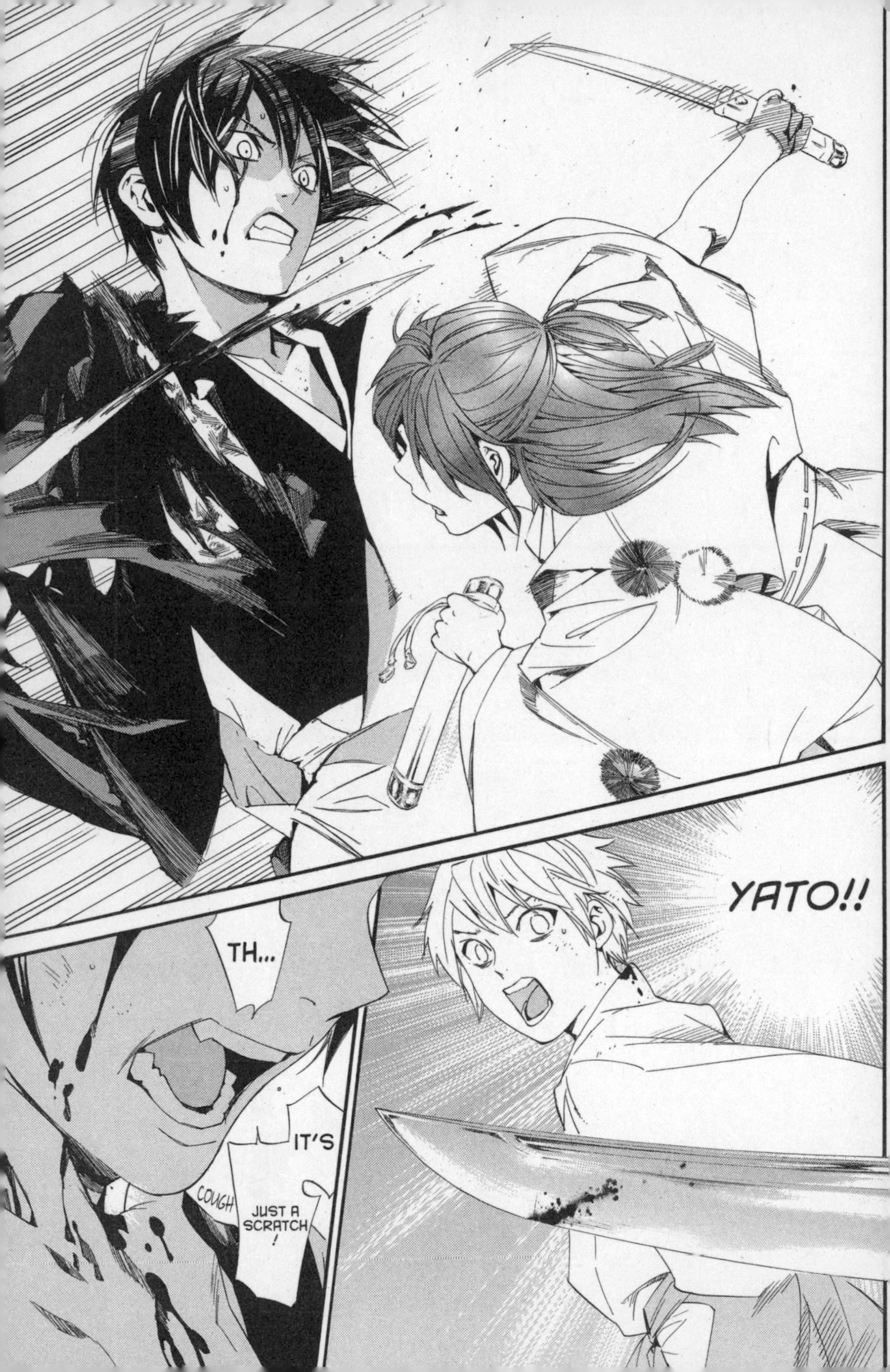
YATO!!
TH...
IT'S
COUGH
JUST A SCRATCH!

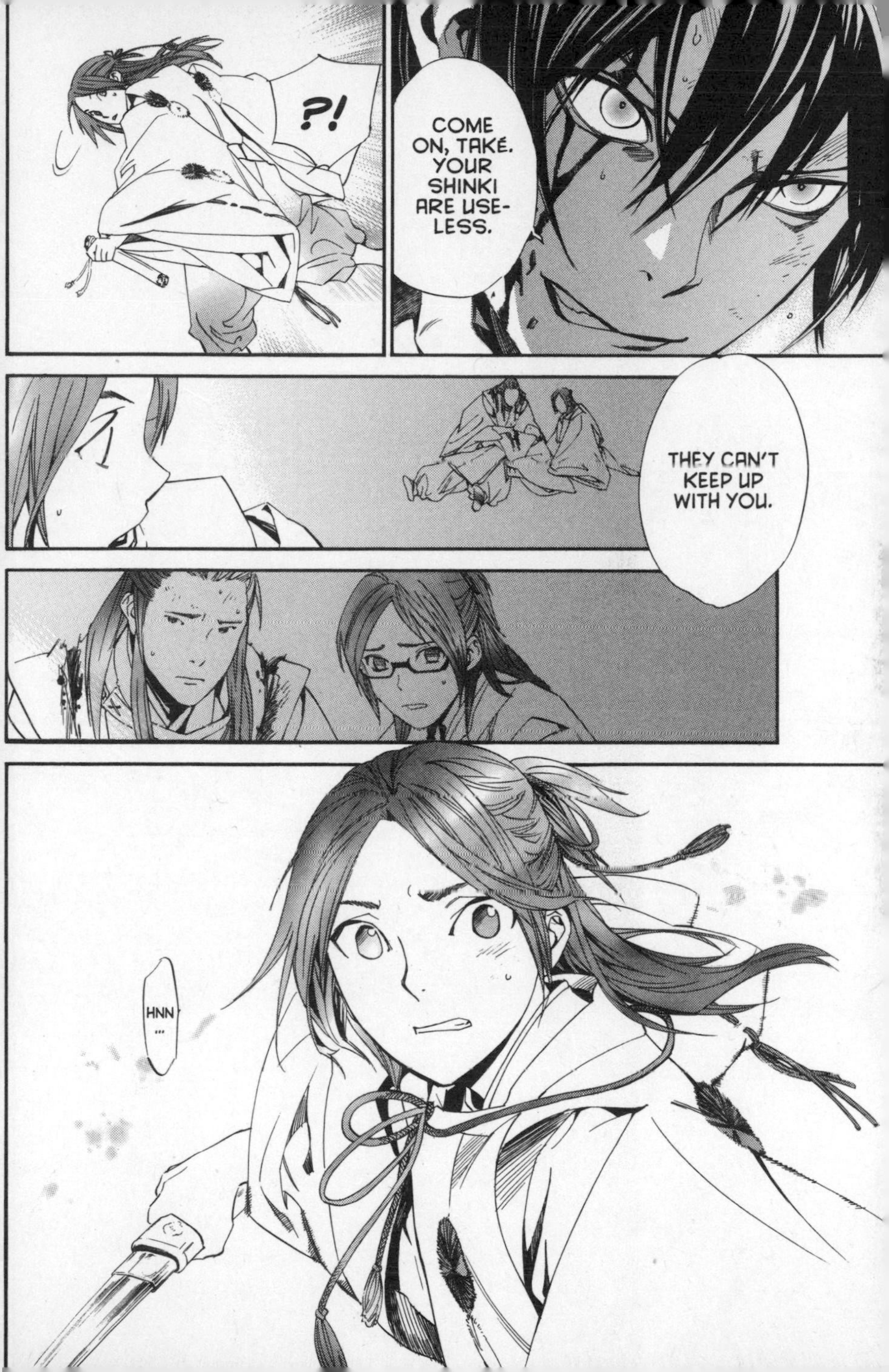
COME ON, TAKÉ. YOUR SHINKI ARE USE-LESS.
?!
THEY CAN'T KEEP UP WITH YOU.
HNN ...

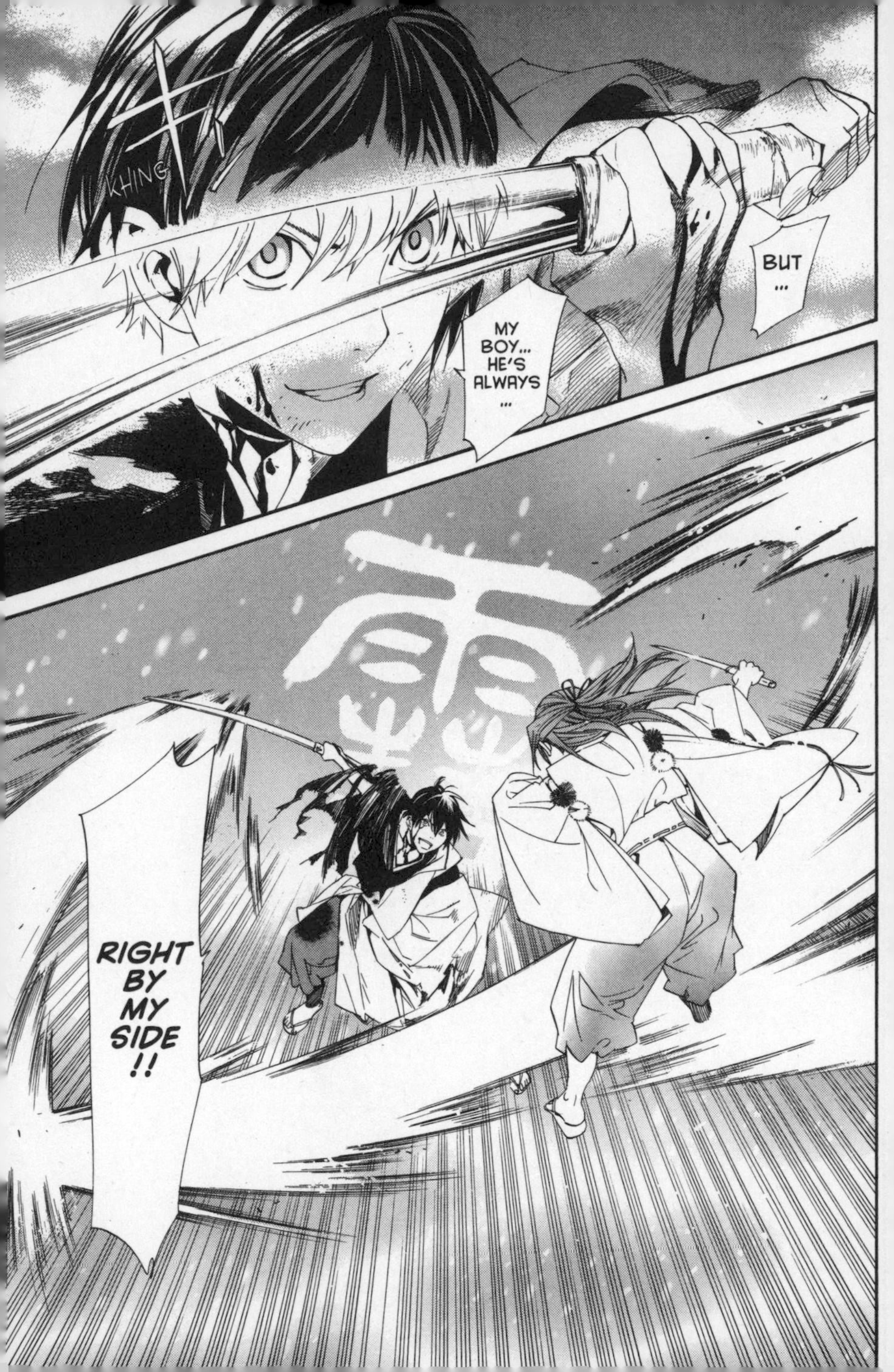
KHING
BUT ...
MY BOY... HE'S ALWAYS ...
RIGHT BY MY SIDE !!

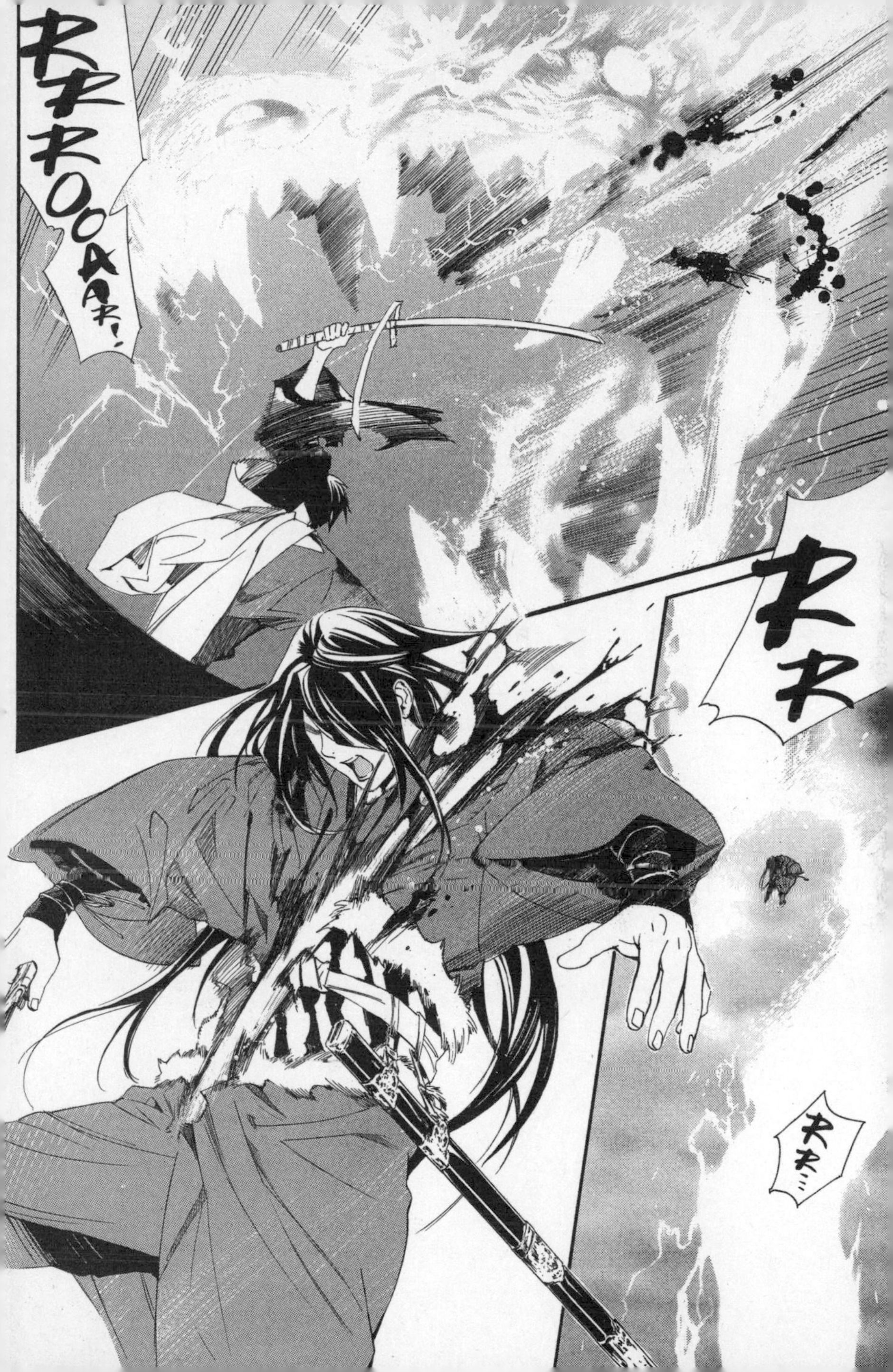

RRR
RRROOOAAR!
RR...

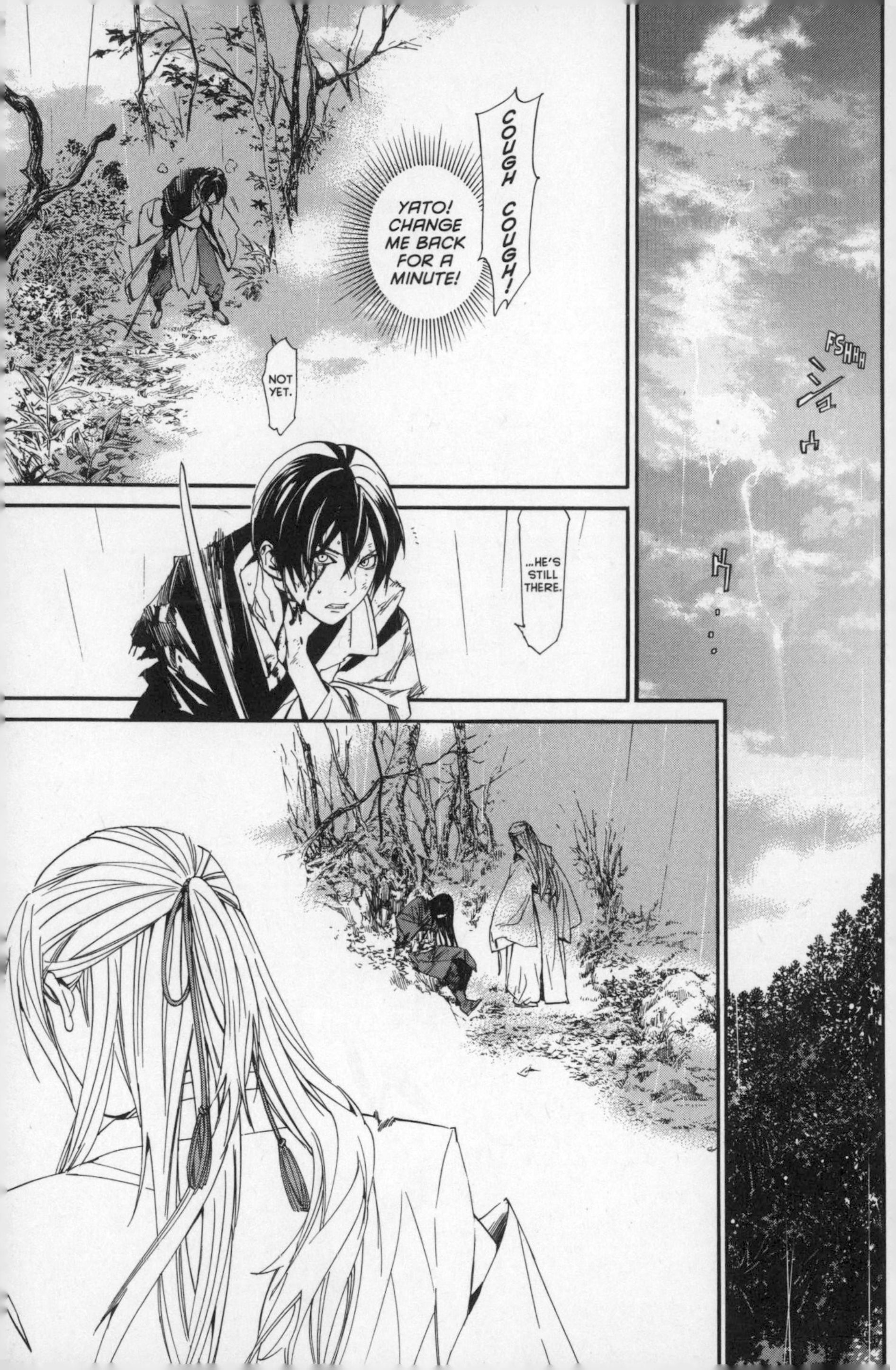
FSHHH
COUGH COUGH!
YATO! CHANGE ME BACK FOR A MINUTE!
NOT YET.
...HE'S STILL THERE.

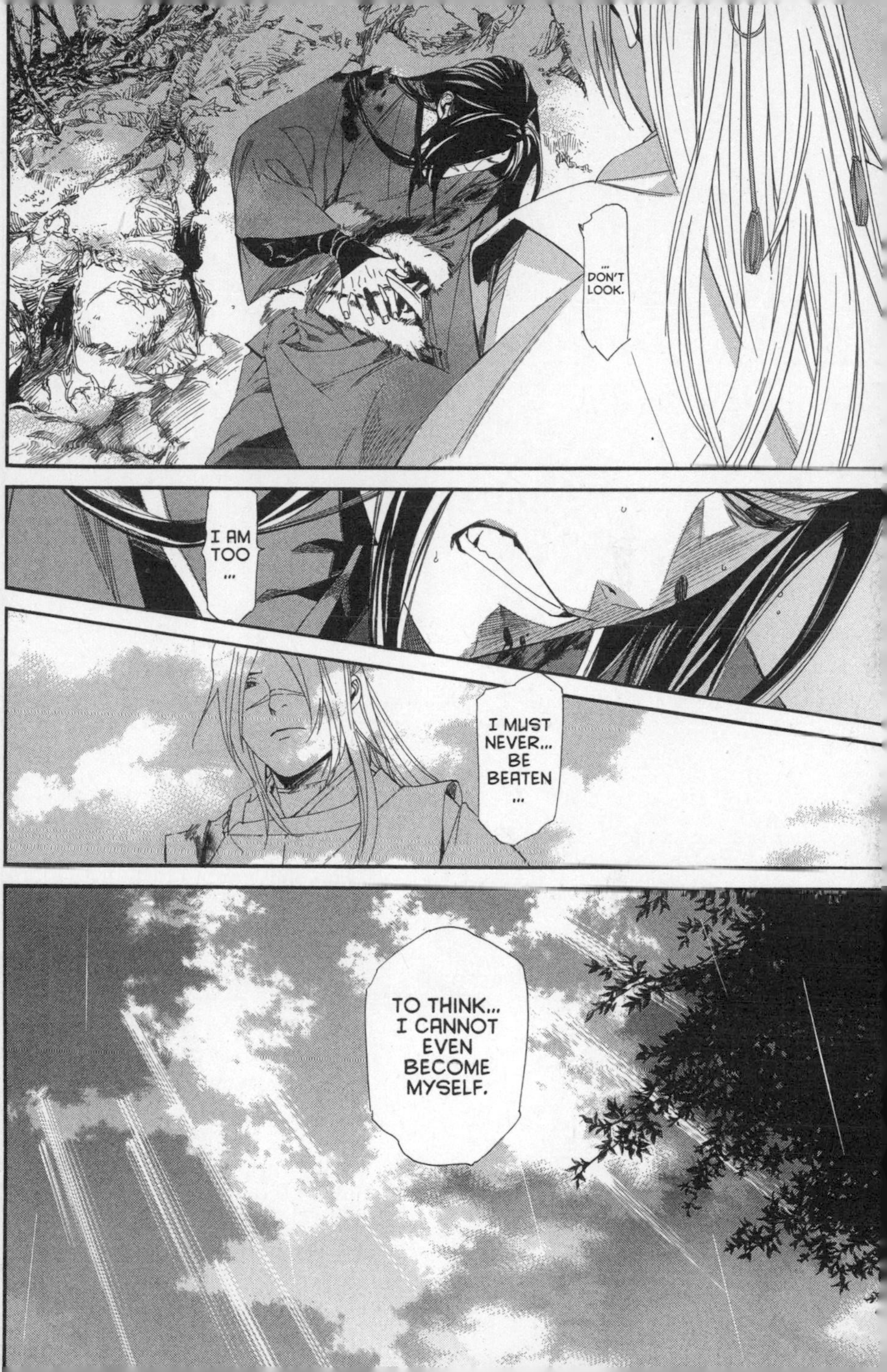
... DON'T LOOK.
I AM TOO ...
I MUST NEVER... BE BEATEN ...
TO THINK... I CANNOT EVEN BECOME MYSELF.

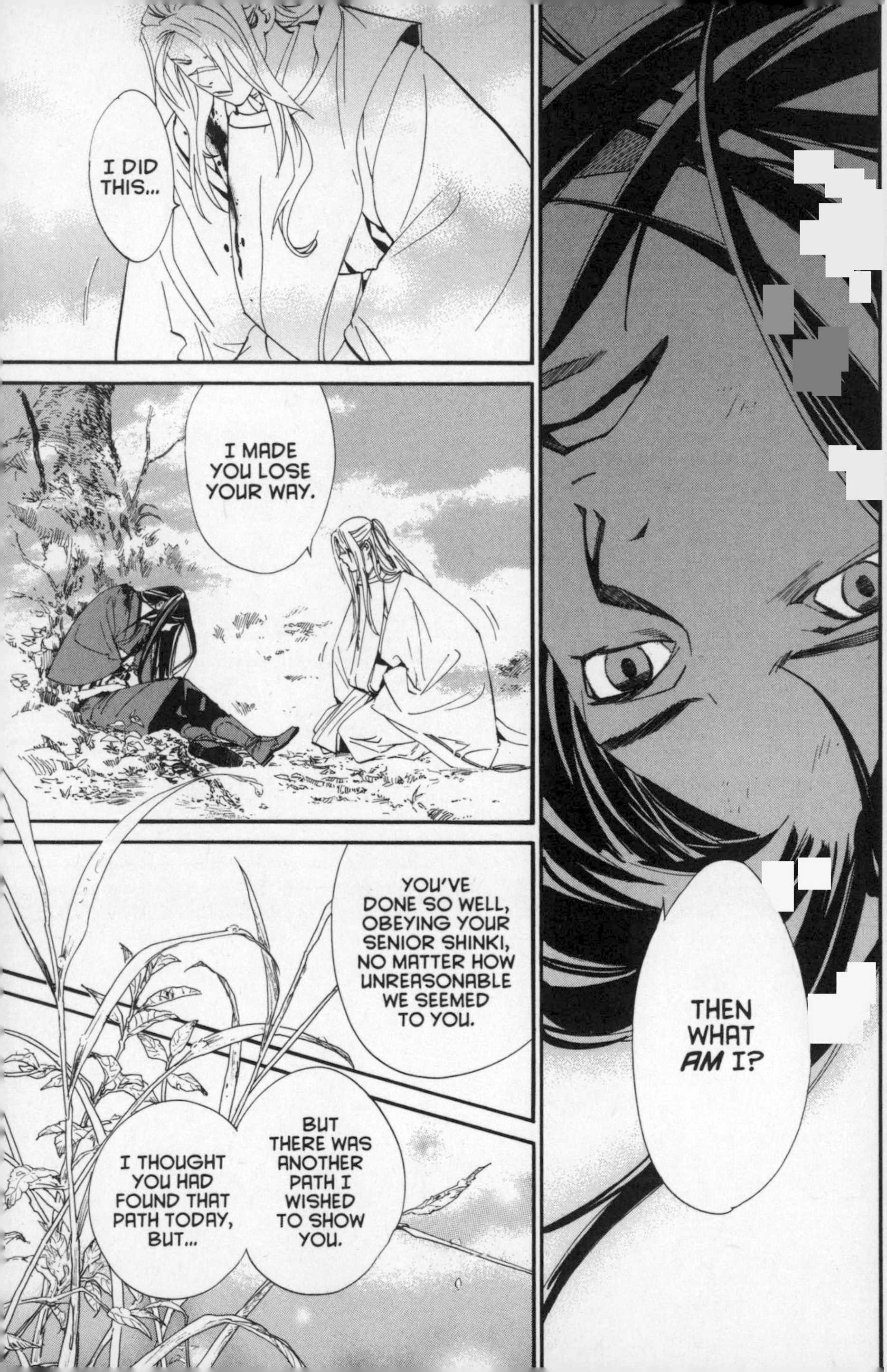
THEN WHAT *AM* I?
I DID THIS...
I MADE YOU LOSE YOUR WAY.
YOU'VE DONE SO WELL, OBEYING YOUR SENIOR SHINKI, NO MATTER HOW UNREASONABLE WE SEEMED TO YOU.
BUT THERE WAS ANOTHER PATH I WISHED TO SHOW YOU.
I THOUGHT YOU HAD FOUND THAT PATH TODAY, BUT...

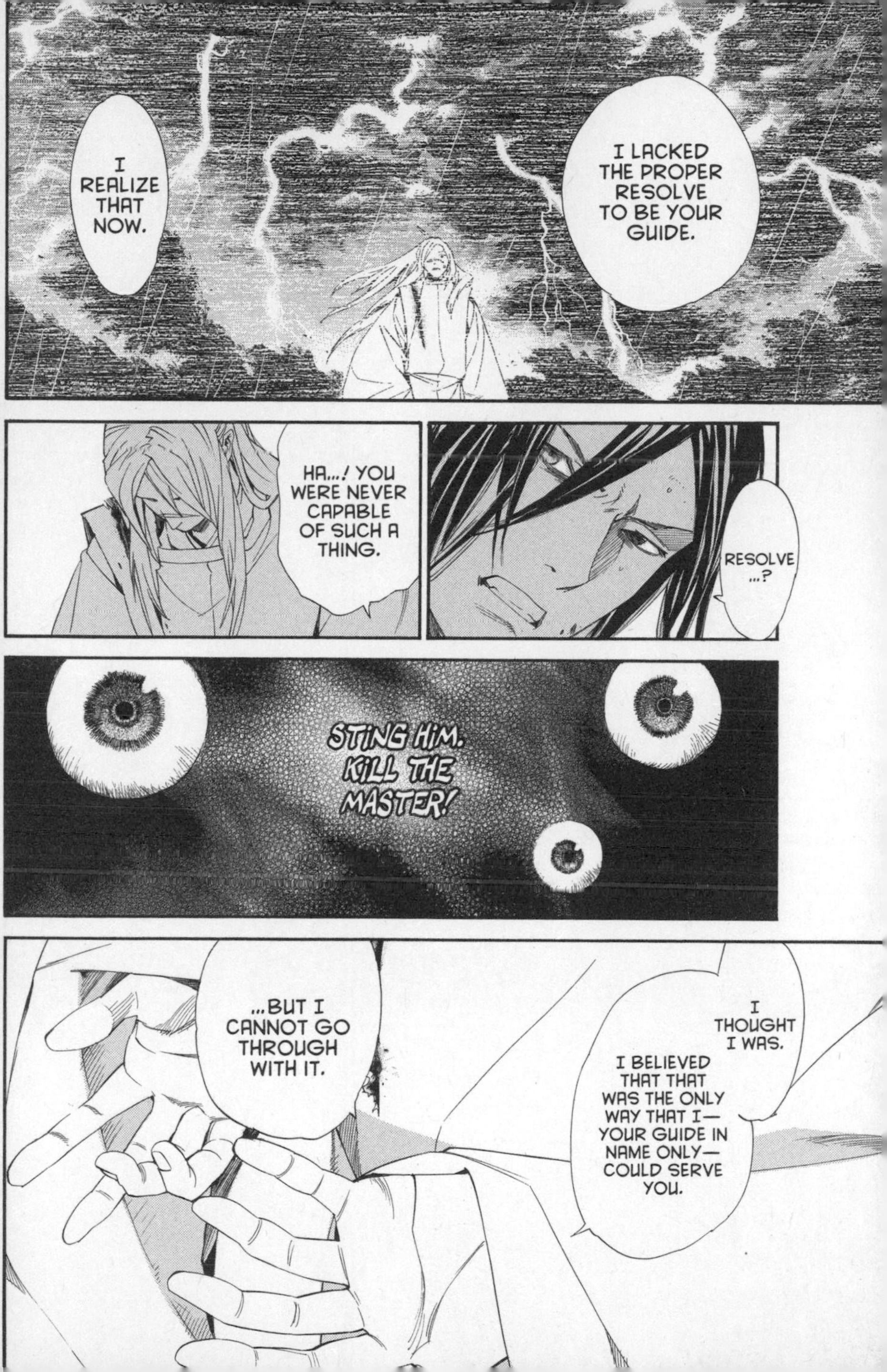
I LACKED THE PROPER RESOLVE TO BE YOUR GUIDE.
I REALIZE THAT NOW.
RESOLVE ...?
HA...! YOU WERE NEVER CAPABLE OF SUCH A THING.
STING HIM. KILL THE MASTER!
I THOUGHT I WAS.
I BELIEVED THAT THAT WAS THE ONLY WAY THAT I— YOUR GUIDE IN NAME ONLY— COULD SERVE YOU.
...BUT I CANNOT GO THROUGH WITH IT.

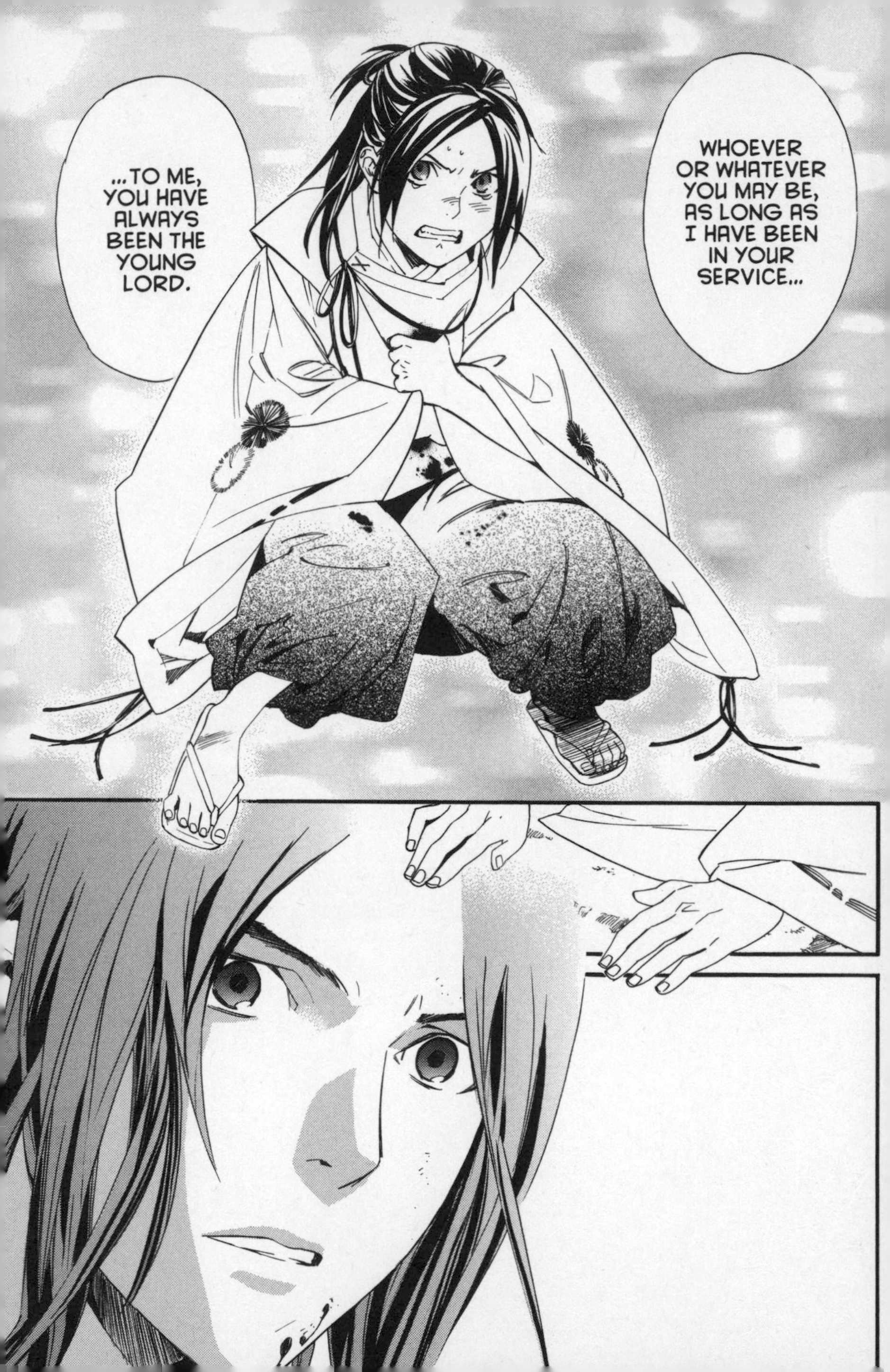
WHOEVER OR WHATEVER YOU MAY BE, AS LONG AS I HAVE BEEN IN YOUR SERVICE...
...TO ME, YOU HAVE ALWAYS BEEN THE YOUNG LORD.

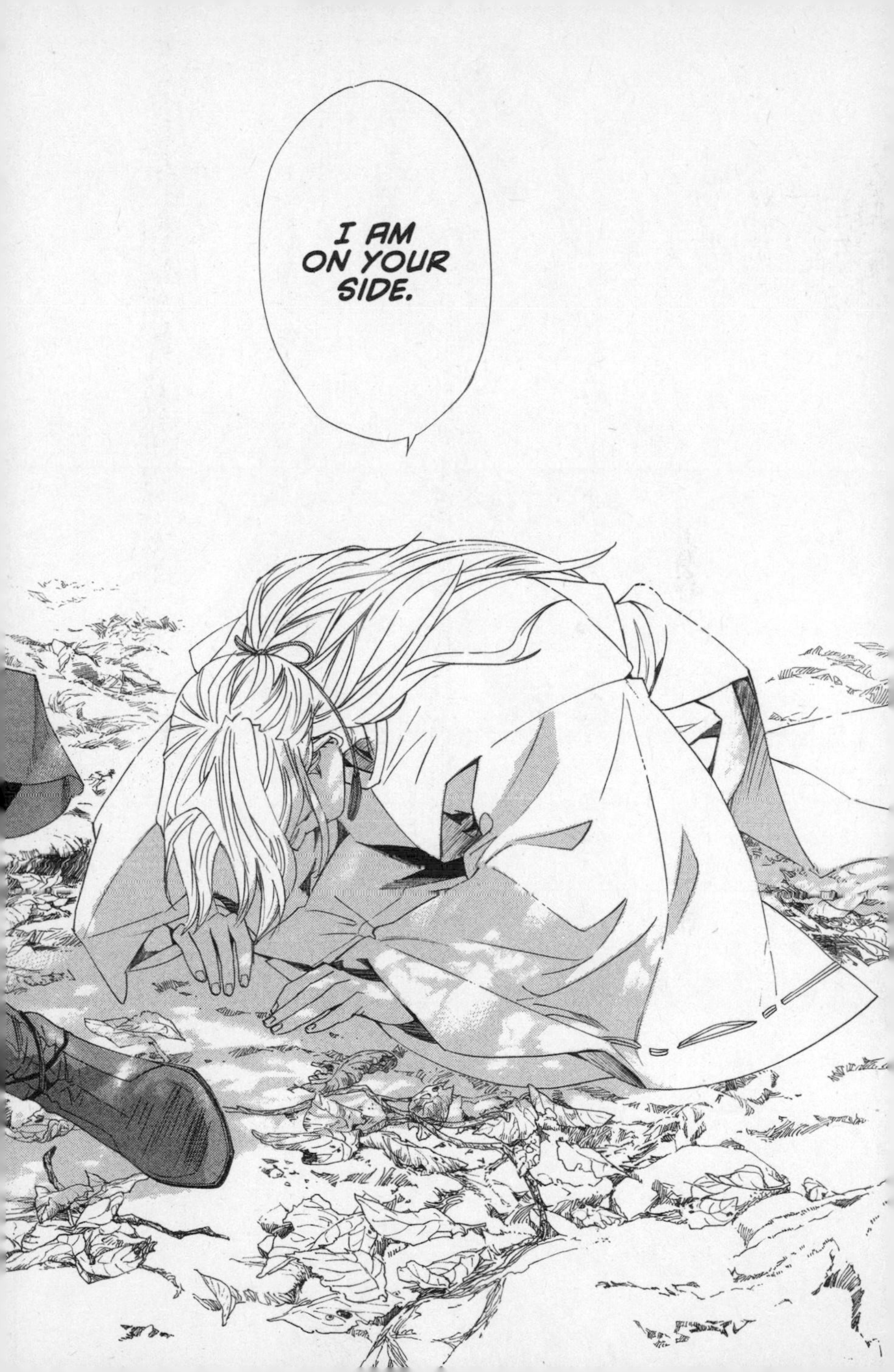
I AM ON YOUR SIDE.

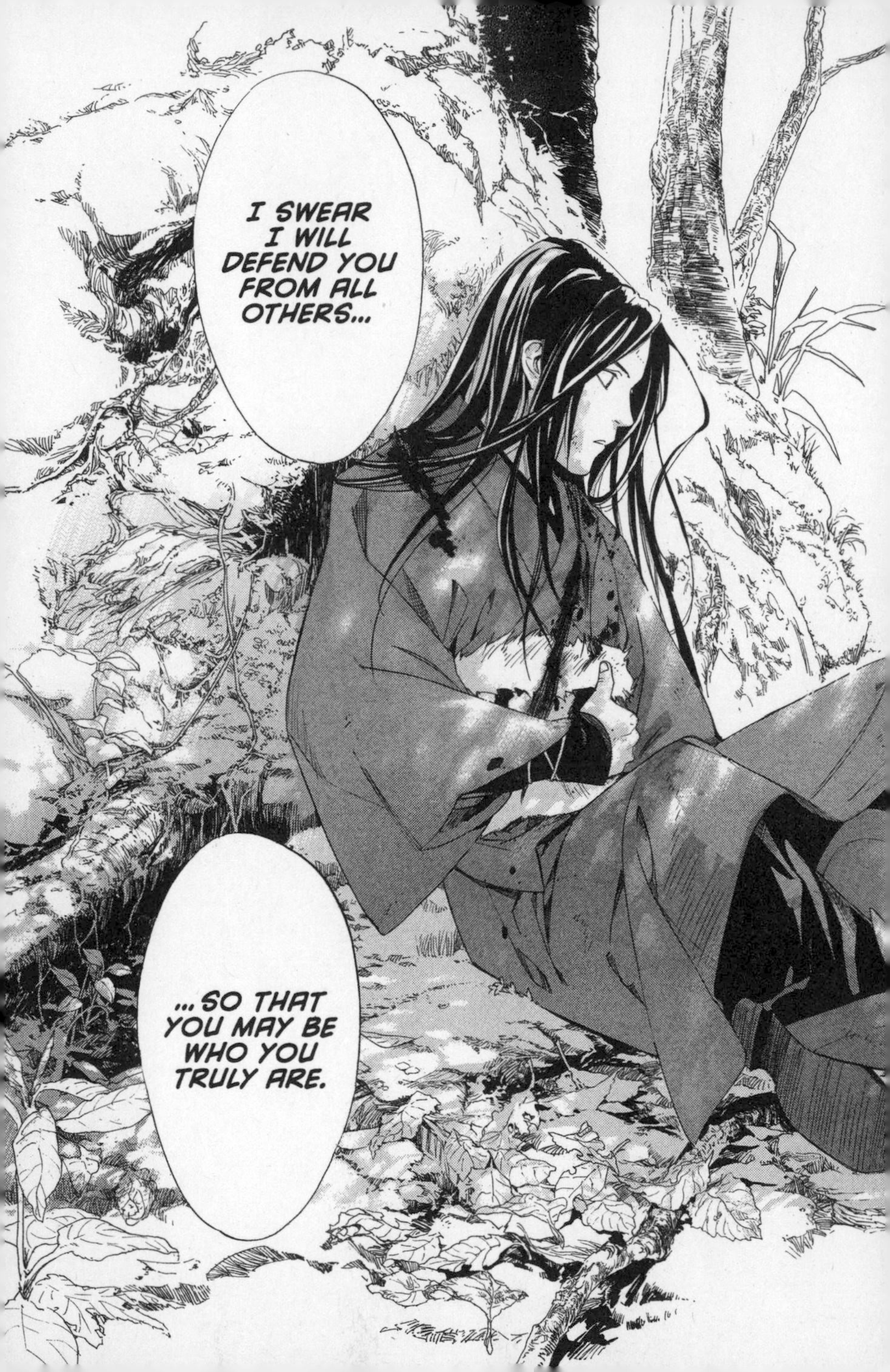
I SWEAR I WILL DEFEND YOU FROM ALL OTHERS...
...SO THAT YOU MAY BE WHO YOU TRULY ARE.

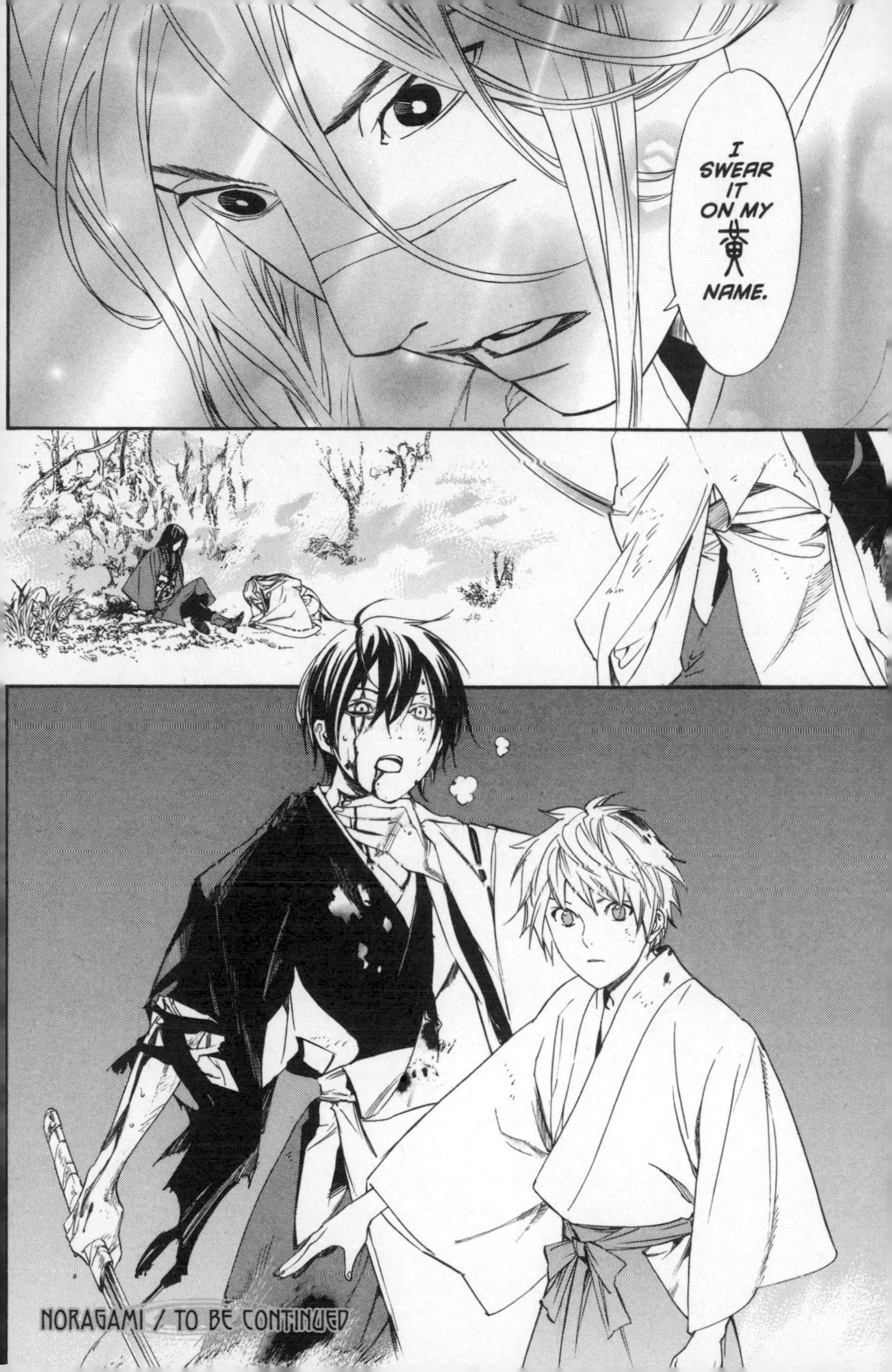
I SWEAR IT ON MY NAME.
NORAGAMI / TO BE CONTINUED

野

覺

禪

ATROCIOUS MANGA

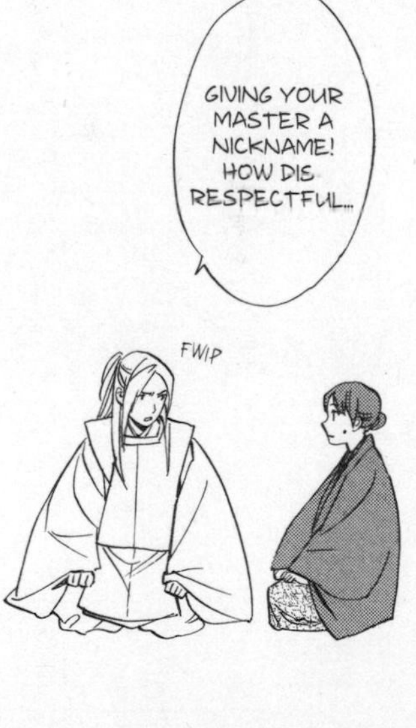
GIVING YOUR MASTER A NICKNAME! HOW DIS RESPECTFUL...
FWIP

NO MERCY FROM KIUN

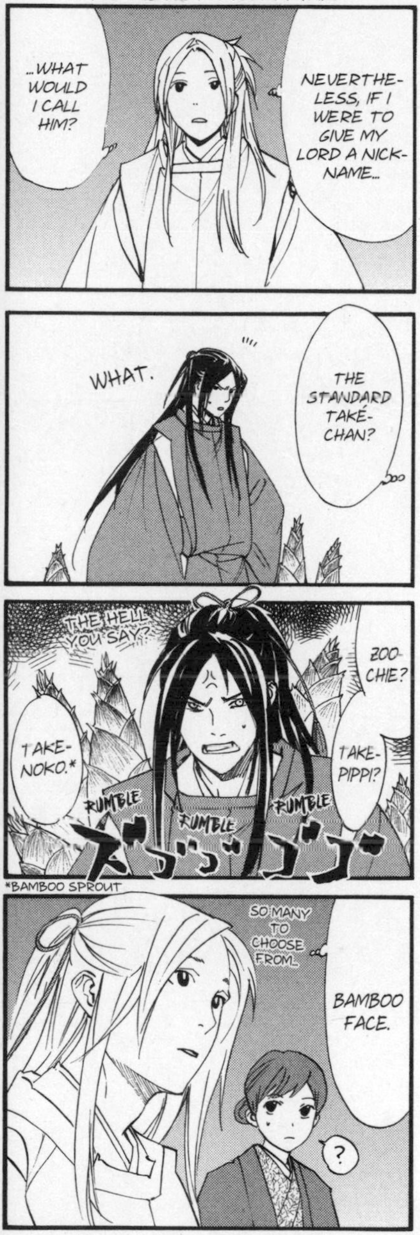
NEVERTHE-LESS, IF I WERE TO GIVE MY LORD A NICK-NAME...
...WHAT WOULD I CALL HIM?
THE STANDARD TAKÉ-CHAN?
WHAT.
ZOO-CHIE?
TAKE-PIPPI?
THE HELL YOU SAY?!
TAKE-NOKO.*
RUMBLE
RUMBLE
RUMBLE
SO MANY TO CHOOSE FROM...
BAMBOO FACE.
?

*BAMBOO SPROUT

NO MERCY FROM KIUN

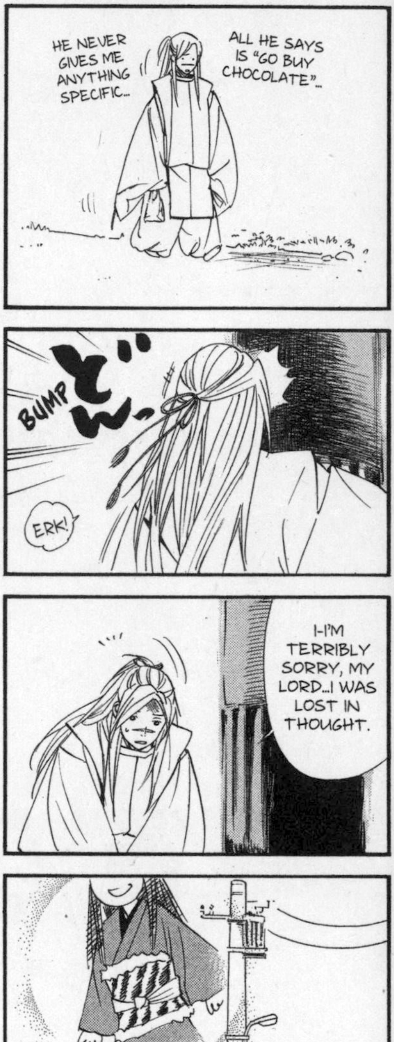
ALL HE SAYS IS "GO BUY CHOCOLATE"...
HE NEVER GIVES ME ANYTHING SPECIFIC...
BUMP
どん
ERK!
I-I'M TERRIBLY SORRY, MY LORD...I WAS LOST IN THOUGHT.

MR. PHONE POLE

NO MERCY FROM KIUN

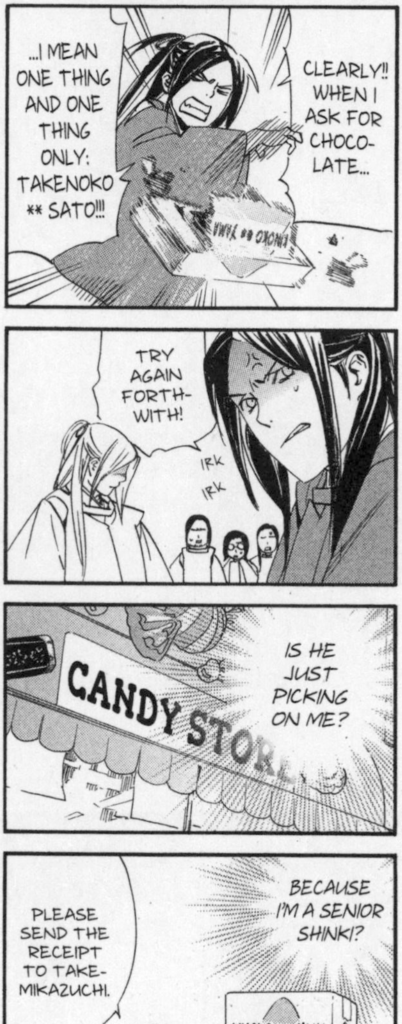
CLEARLY!! WHEN I ASK FOR CHOCO-LATE...
...I MEAN ONE THING AND ONE THING ONLY: TAKENOKO ** SATO!!!
TRY AGAIN FORTH-WITH!
IRK
IRK
CANDY STORE
IS HE JUST PICKING ON ME?
BECAUSE I'M A SENIOR SHINKI?
PLEASE SEND THE RECEIPT TO TAKE-MIKAZUCHI.
KINOKO •• YAMA
•• YAMA
KINOKO •• YAMA
•• YAMA
KINOKO •• YAMA

THE CANDY WAS ALL ENJOYED BY HIS STAFF.

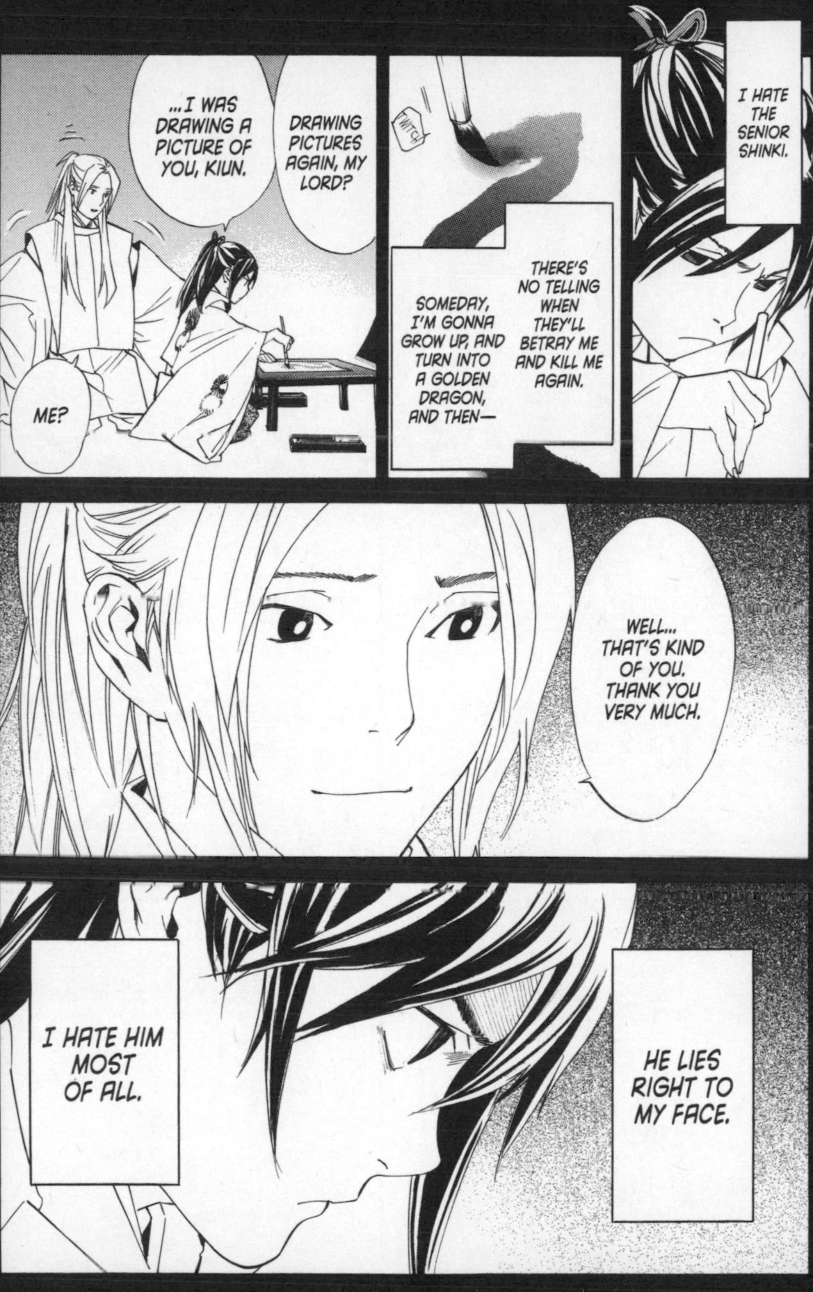
I HATE THE SENIOR SHINKI.
TWITCH
THERE'S NO TELLING WHEN THEY'LL BETRAY ME AND KILL ME AGAIN.
SOMEDAY, I'M GONNA GROW UP, AND TURN INTO A GOLDEN DRAGON, AND THEN—
DRAWING PICTURES AGAIN, MY LORD?
...I WAS DRAWING A PICTURE OF YOU, KIUN.
ME?
WELL... THAT'S KIND OF YOU. THANK YOU VERY MUCH.
HE LIES RIGHT TO MY FACE.
I HATE HIM MOST OF ALL.

NO MERCY FROM KIUN

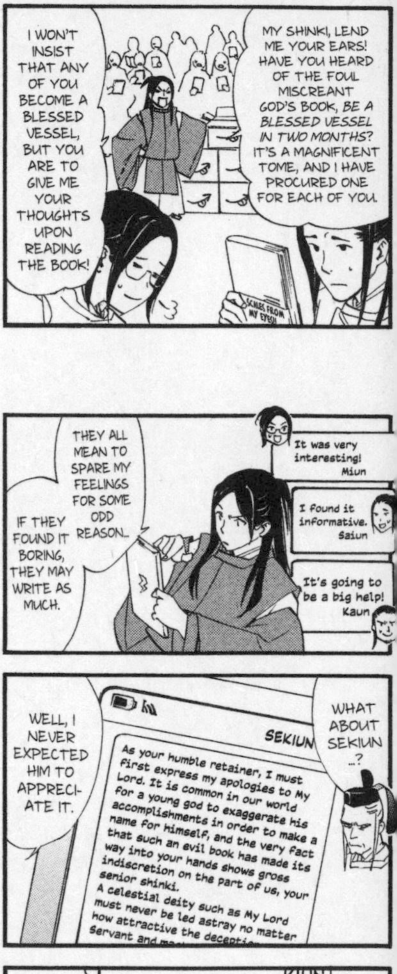
MY SHINKI, LEND ME YOUR EARS! HAVE YOU HEARD OF THE FOUL MISCREANT GOD'S BOOK, *BE A BLESSED VESSEL IN TWO MONTHS*? IT'S A MAGNIFICENT TOME, AND I HAVE PROCURED ONE FOR EACH OF YOU.
I WON'T INSIST THAT ANY OF YOU BECOME A BLESSED VESSEL, BUT YOU ARE TO GIVE ME YOUR THOUGHTS UPON READING THE BOOK!
It was very interesting! Miun
I found it informative. Saiun
It's going to be a big help! Kaun
THEY ALL MEAN TO SPARE MY FEELINGS FOR SOME ODD REASON...
IF THEY FOUND IT BORING, THEY MAY WRITE AS MUCH.
WHAT ABOUT SEKIUN...?
SEKIUN
As your humble retainer, I must first express my apologies to My Lord. It is common in our world for a young god to exaggerate his accomplishments in order to make a name for himself, and the very fact that such an evil book has made its way into your hands shows gross indiscretion on the part of us, your senior shinki.
A celestial deity such as My Lord must never be led astray no matter how attractive the deception
WELL, I NEVER EXPECTED HIM TO APPRECIATE IT.
KIUN...
KIUN
I sold mine.
THE SCOUNDREL! THAT WAS A GIFT FROM HIS MASTER!!

NO MALICE FROM TAKÉ

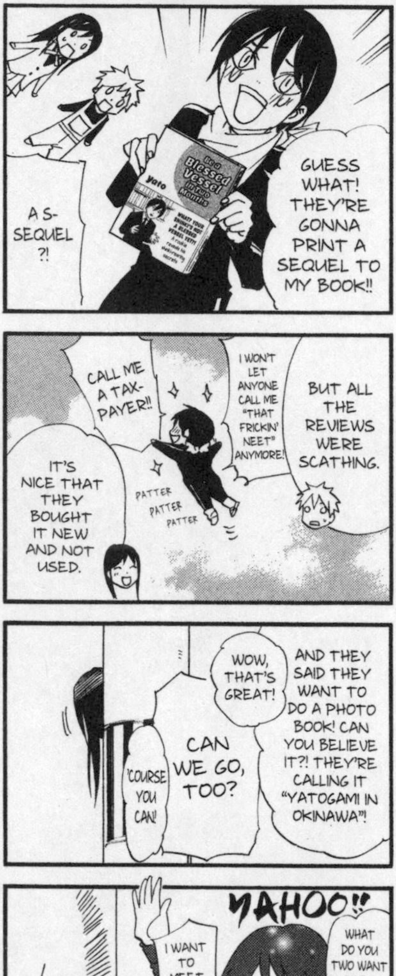
GUESS WHAT! THEY'RE GONNA PRINT A SEQUEL TO MY BOOK!!
Be a Blessed Vessel in Two Months
Yato
A S-SEQUEL?!
BUT ALL THE REVIEWS WERE SCATHING.
I WON'T LET ANYONE CALL ME "THAT FRICKIN' NEET" ANYMORE!
CALL ME A TAX-PAYER!!
PATTER PATTER PATTER
IT'S NICE THAT THEY BOUGHT IT NEW AND NOT USED.
AND THEY SAID THEY WANT TO DO A PHOTO BOOK! CAN YOU BELIEVE IT?! THEY'RE CALLING IT "YATOGAMI IN OKINAWA"!
WOW, THAT'S GREAT!
CAN WE GO, TOO?
'COURSE YOU CAN!
MAHOO!!
WHAT DO YOU TWO WANT TO DO THERE?
I WANT TO MEET A SHISA GUARDIAN!!
I CAN'T WAIT TO SEE IT...
FOUL MISCREANT!
I WANT TO MEET THEIR RIBS!
...

THANK YOU TO EVERYONE WHO READ THIS FAR!

TRANSLATION NOTES

Japanese is a tricky language for most Westerners, and translation is often more art than science. For your edification and reading pleasure, here are notes on some of the places where we could have gone in a different direction in our translation of the work, or where a Japanese cultural reference is used.

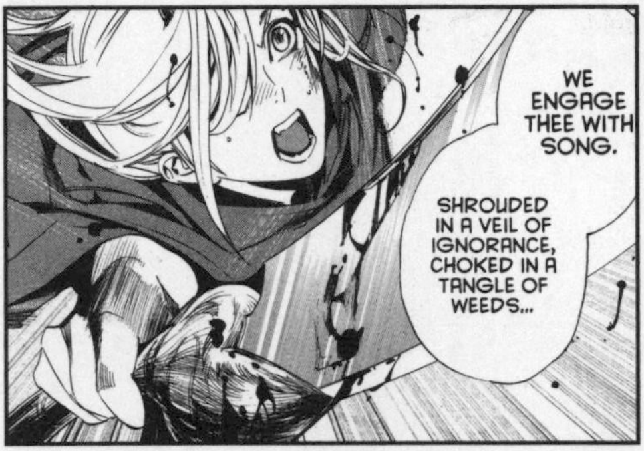
WE ENGAGE THEE WITH SONG.
SHROUDED IN A VEIL OF IGNORANCE, CHOKED IN A TANGLE OF WEEDS...

Engage thee with song, page 29

The translators hope that the English version of this song covers the double meanings that are important to this spell, but there are a few specifics we felt were worth noting. The "tangle of weeds" mentioned is actually a specific lichen known commonly as "old man's beard." Shinatsuhiko and Sakuya specifically use the Chinese name of the plant, pronounced in Japanese as *jora*, which literally means "woman ivy." With different *kanji*, it can mean roughly "feminine robe" (hence the "veil" in the translation), and the word *jora* can also refer to sitting cross-legged, furthering the imagery of entanglement.

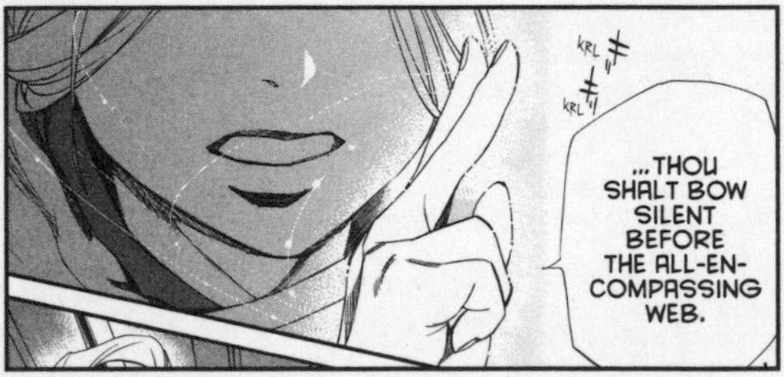
KRL
KRL
...THOU SHALT BOW SILENT BEFORE THE ALL-EN-COMPASSING WEB.

The "all-encompassing web" is an *ichimô*, which, with the *kanji* provided in the original Japanese version of the song, means "single net," referring to the net with which they are about to capture Bishamon. The word can also mean "single hope," "single hair" (the reader can see a fine thread dancing around near Shinatsuhiko's fingers), or "view of everything."

Lightning warding incantation, page 60

This is another poem that has been around for centuries. It can be found in the *Shin Kokin Wakashū*, or "New Collection of Poems Ancient and Modern," although in this case the word "modern" refers to around the 13th century. Like the firefighting incantation, the author of this poem is unknown, and it is unclear whether it was always used to ward off lightning, or if Kazuma or someone before him adapted it into a lightning ward.

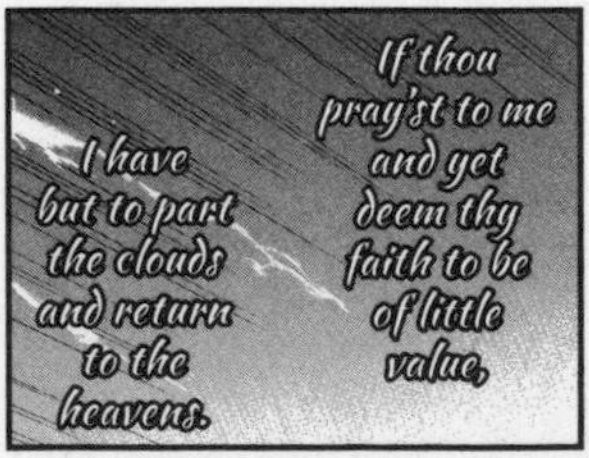
If thou pray'st to me and yet deem thy faith to be of little value,
I have but to part the clouds and return to the heavens.

Aya, page 79

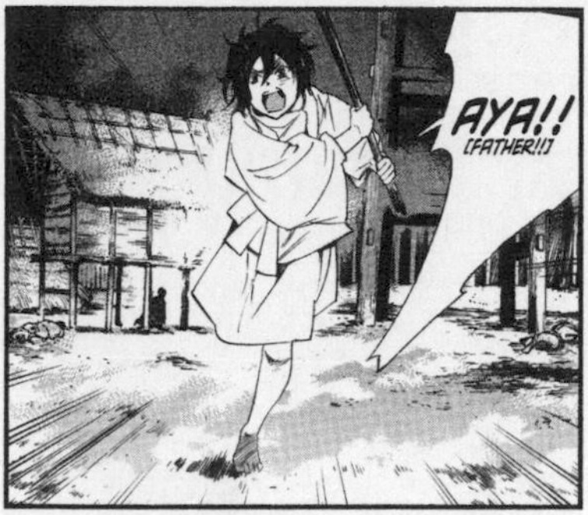
AYA!!
[FATHER!!]

Nana's use of the word *aya* to mean "father" tells the reader that she speaks the Tsugaru dialect, which is famous across Japan for being so different from standard Japanese as to be nearly incomprehensible to non-locals. Perhaps more importantly, it tells us that she lived in the Tsugaru area, which is on the northern tip of Japan's main island. This puts her in the same region as the Emishi.

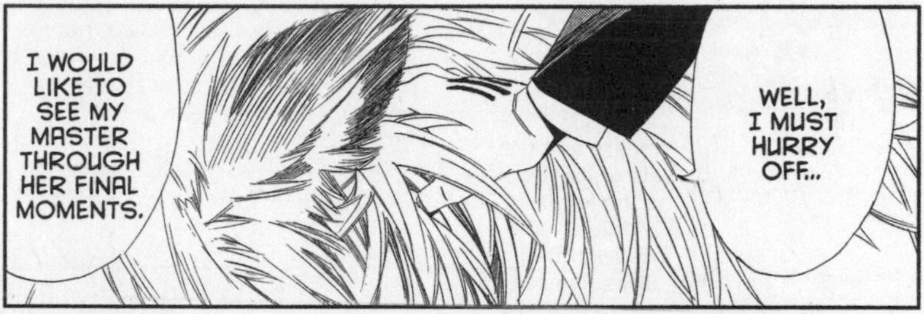
WELL, I MUST HURRY OFF...
I WOULD LIKE TO SEE MY MASTER THROUGH HER FINAL MOMENTS.

I would like to see my master through her final moments, page 87

More literally, Kazuma says he must hurry off so as to "take death water to [his] master." This comes from a practice in Japan of giving water to the dying or recently deceased to relieve their final thirst, but the phrase refers to not only alleviating thirst, but caring for someone in their dying moments.

Sentinel gods, page 94

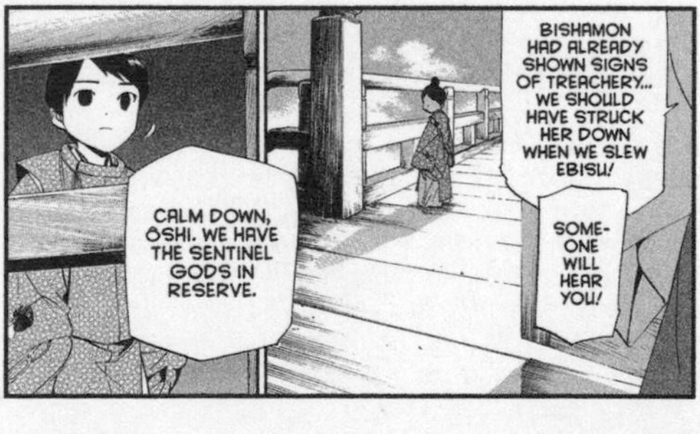
BISHAMON HAD ALREADY SHOWN SIGNS OF TREACHERY... WE SHOULD HAVE STRUCK HER DOWN WHEN WE SLEW EBISU!
SOME-ONE WILL HEAR YOU!
CALM DOWN, ŌSHI. WE HAVE THE SENTINEL GODS IN RESERVE.

The sentinel gods, or *sae no kami*, are deities whose job it is to stand guard over people, villages, etc. to prevent (*sae*) natural disasters, plagues, and so forth. The character for *sae* is used in words such as *jôsa* (fortress), and gives an impression of immovable strength.

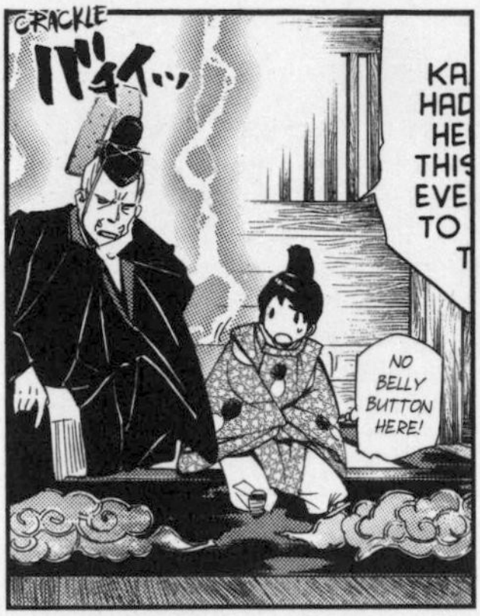
CRACKLE
バチイッ
NO BELLY BUTTON HERE!

No belly button here, page 97

According to Japanese tradition, thunder gods have a fondness for belly buttons, so children have been warned for centuries to keep their navels safe during thunderstorms. When Tenjin, who is himself a thunder god, starts to get irritable enough to cause alarm, good little Ebisu makes efforts to ensure that his button remains firmly on his belly.

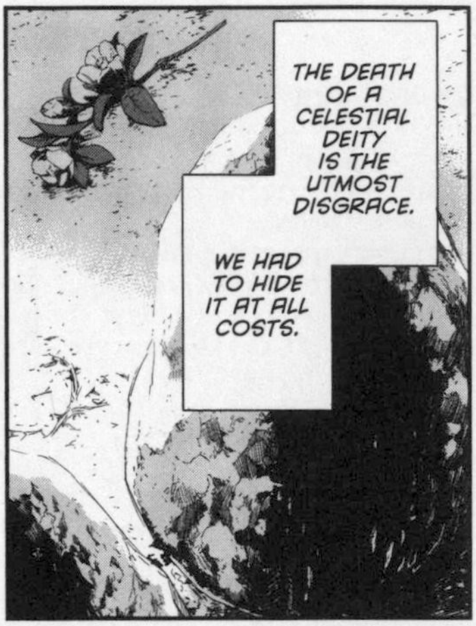
THE DEATH OF A CELESTIAL DEITY IS THE UTMOST DISGRACE.
WE HAD TO HIDE IT AT ALL COSTS.

Celestial deity, page 105

In the divine hierarchy, the myriad gods of the *yaoyorozu no kami* are actually at the lowest of three levels of deities. The next level above them is the *kunitsu-kami*, the terrestrial or earthly deities, and the highest level is the *amatsu-kami*—the celestial or heavenly deities. These are the deities who were born to and live in Takama-ga-hara.

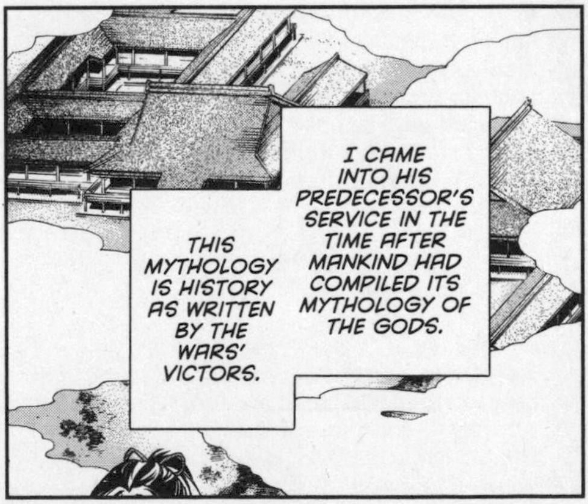
I CAME INTO HIS PREDECESSOR'S SERVICE IN THE TIME AFTER MANKIND HAD COMPILED ITS MYTHOLOGY OF THE GODS.
THIS MYTHOLOGY IS HISTORY AS WRITTEN BY THE WARS' VICTORS.

Man's compiled history of the gods, page 106

The reader may be interested to know that the specific compilations Kiun refers to are the *Kojiki* and the *Nihon Shoki*, both of which tell the history of Japan from its mythological beginnings and were finished in the eighth century.

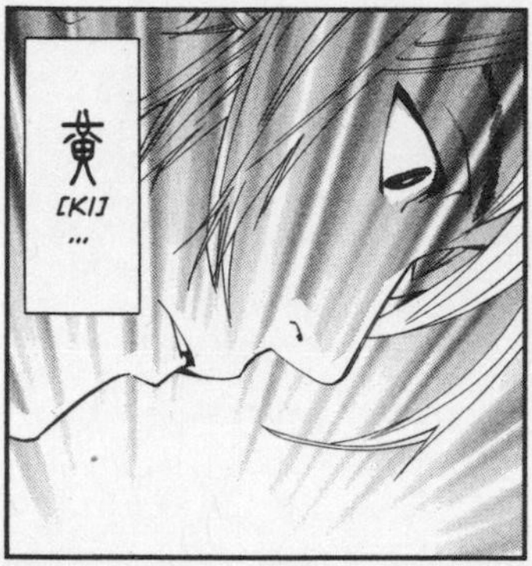
黄
[KI]
...

The noble name *ki*, page 106

The symbol for *ki* simply means "yellow," but it has great symbolic meaning as well. For one, yellow is the color of the earth, and so represents all land. It is the color of gold, and so represents light and all that glitters. Finally, the character (黄) can be used interchangeably with another one (皇), which means "emperor." A very noble name indeed.

Beena, page 155

Because the V sound doesn't exist in Japanese, Kiun struggles to pronounce Kazuma's pet name for Bishamon. Instead, he uses the next closest thing, which is the B sound. The nickname most likely derives from her Sanskrit name, Vaiśravaṇa.

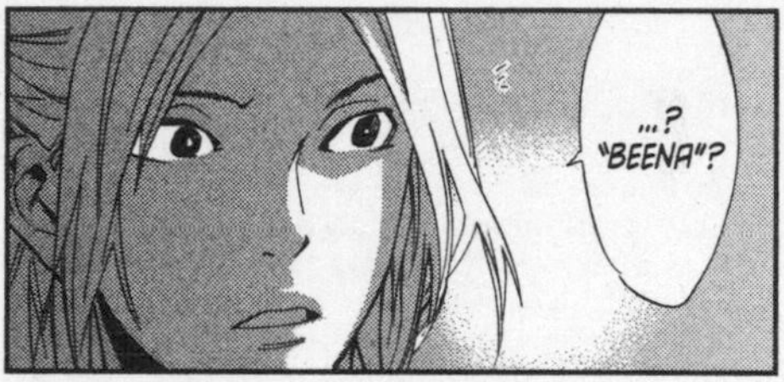
...? "BEENA"?

Euphemisms, page 157

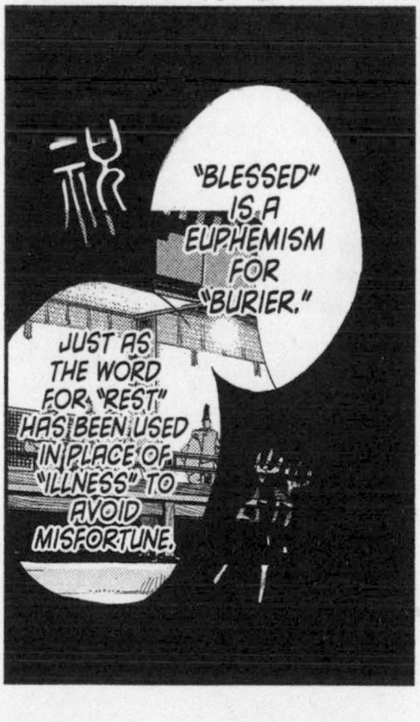
"BLESSED" IS A EUPHEMISM FOR "BURIER."
JUST AS THE WORD FOR "REST" HAS BEEN USED IN PLACE OF "ILLNESS" TO AVOID MISFORTUNE,

Longtime readers may remember that the word "blight," referring to the infections brought upon gods by ayakashi and badly-behaved shinki, comes from the word *yasumi*, which literally means "rest." The word was also used by Shinto priestesses at the Ise Shrine to discuss illnesses, as the word for illness (*yamai*) was ominous. Other words, such as for blood and death, were similarly replaced with happier words. It may be worth noting that when Kiun related the tale of Takemikazuchi's predecessor, he was not afraid to say that he "fell ill" and did not use the euphemism (which, granted, would not have been much of a euphemism in the English translation).

In the case of "blessed" and "burier," the words are actually very much the same, with only a minor change in pronunciation, but different *kanji* characters are used to write them, indicating that, even in writing, they wanted to avoid the appearance of evil.

Okinawan delights, page 183

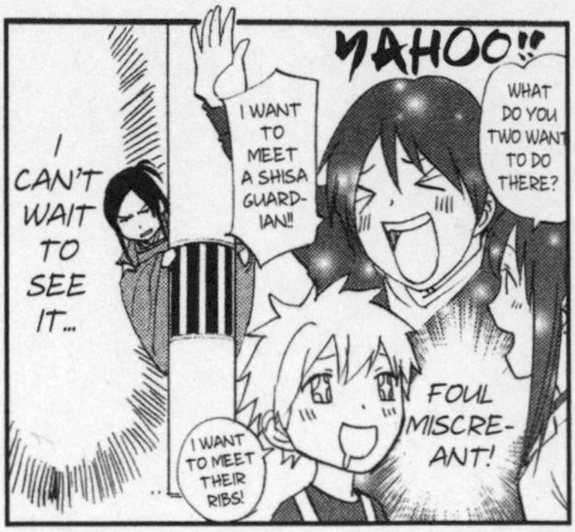

YAHOO!!
WHAT DO YOU TWO WANT TO DO THERE?
I WANT TO MEET A SHISA GUARDIAN!!
I CAN'T WAIT TO SEE IT...
FOUL MISCREANT!
I WANT TO MEET THEIR RIBS!

Okinawa is quite a distance from the main islands of Japan, so getting to visit can be a special treat. Yato is excited to see the Shisa, an Okinawan guardian deity represented by a lion dog that can be seen in statues all over the prefecture. Of course, Yato doesn't specify whether he sees the Shisa as an adorable mascot character like Capyper, or if he wants to ask the Shisa for tips on marketability. The ribs Yukiné is interested in are probably a traditional Okinawan dish called *rafute*, which is pork ribs stewed in soy sauce and brown sugar.

Takenoko vs. Kinoko, page 191

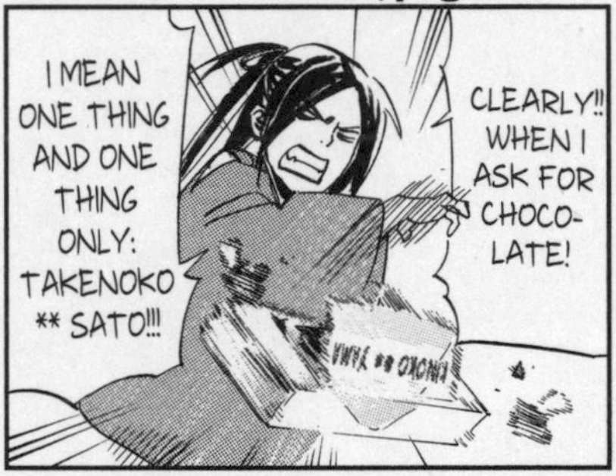

CLEARLY!! WHEN I ASK FOR CHOCOLATE!
I MEAN ONE THING AND ONE THING ONLY: TAKENOKO ** SATO!!!

This is a reference to two popular snack foods in Japan, Kinoko no Yama (mushroom mountain) and Takenoko no Sato (village of the bamboo shoots). Kinoko no Yama are little mushroom-shaped cookies, with the stem made out of a breadstick and a cap dipped in chocolate to resemble a mushroom. Takenoko no Sato uses the same concept to make bamboo shoot cookies, but with a slightly different type of breadstick and a different ratio of chocolate to cookie. They are marketed in the United States as Chocorooms and Chococones. As may be apparent, everyone has their own preference, and it may also be apparent why Takemikazuchi and Kiun chose respective favorites. But both snacks are made by the same company, so whichever side of the debate you're on, Meiji wins.

野

首

師